HASIDISM

THE MOVEMENT AND ITS MASTERS

By the Same Author

The Will and Testament of the Biala Rabbi

A Guide to Hasidism

The Slave Who Saved the City

The Jewish Literary Treasures of England and America

A Guide to Life

The Legacy of Polish Jewry

The World of Hasidism

Treasures of Judaica

Hasidism and the State of Israel

The Hasidic Story Book

HASIDISM

THE MOVEMENT AND ITS MASTERS

BY HARRY M. RABINOWICZ

JASON ARONSON INC.
NORTHVALE, NEW JERSEY
LONDON

10 9 8 7 6 5 4 3 2

Library of Congress Cataloging-in-Publication Data

Rabinowicz, Harry M., 1919–
Hasidism: the movement and its masters.

Rev. ed. of: The world of Hasidism. 1970.
Bibliography: p.
Includes index.
1. Hasidism–History. I. Rabinowicz, Harry M.,
1919– World of Hasidism. II. Title.
BM198.R274 1988 296.8′33 87-37427
ISBN 0-87668-998-5

Manufactured in the United States of America. Jason Aronson Inc. offers books and cassettes. For information and catalog write to Jason Aronson Inc., 230 Livingston Street, Northvale, NJ 07647.

In cherished remembrance of my dear sister,
Rachel Anne Rabinowicz

"She openeth her mouth with wisdom;
And the law of lovingkindness is on her tongue."

Proverbs 31:26

Contents

Preface

In the mid-eighteenth century, Eastern Europe gave birth to the greatest revivalist movement in Jewish history. This was Hasidism, the cataclysmic force that wiped away the narrow intellectualism that had estranged the Jewish masses from their heritage. Hasidism was not a new form of Judaism but a renewal of Judaism. It focused upon sublimely simple principles – the joy of living, love of God and man, service to God and man, sincerity and dedication. From the hasidic perspective, the man in the marketplace could draw as near to his Father in Heaven as could the scholar in his study. Mystically, almost miraculously, Hasidism brought joy, comfort, and courage to these suffering stepchildren of humanity. It offered a form of otherworldly ecstasy to the ordinary Jew, to the untutored and destitute as well as to the learned and privileged. In emphasizing deeds of lovingkindness carried out with joyful intensity, Hasidism kindled the latent spirituality and creativity of the Jewish masses, and they responded with passion. Emotion was translated into prayer, into song, into action. Hasidism is more than a collection of ideas and noble purposes. It is a way of life, a civilization, a culture with a message that transcends the barriers of time and place.

Like drowning men, the Jews of Eastern Europe clutched at this rejuvenated Judaism. From the Ukraine, the movement spread across the border to Poland, Hungary, and Rumania. As the flames of Jewish life were extinguished in Nazi Europe, sparks flew even farther and the fires began to burn with new brilliance in Israel and the United States. Great men arose, *tzaddikim,* who by precept and by practice led the people in the paths of the Torah, helped them to live full and satisfying lives on earth, and helped them to reach for a world beyond this world. During the past two centuries, hasidic Jewry has produced more outstanding leaders than in any other period since the Talmudic era.

Hasidic philosophy has added a new dimension to daily life, and some 3,000 works of hasidic literature have enriched the minds of men. The *hasidim* lived in a world of their own. They were known by the dress they wore, by the way they spoke, and by the melodies they hummed. This new breed of leaders emerged to guide the community with wisdom and inspiration. The power of the rebbe was far-reaching. The hasidic firmament was a complex universe composed of many planets, each set in its appointed place, each revolving around its own orbit, each contributing to the radiance that illuminated the Jewish world.

The six years between 1939 and 1945 saw the catastrophic climax of a millennium of East European culture as Nazi-occupied Eastern Europe became the graveyard of six million Jews. As the Holocaust raged, the lights of Hasidism were dimmed. The Jewish quarters of Warsaw, Lodz, and Lublin, once citadels of piety and learning, became piles of rubble, physical symbols of the almost total annihilation of their Jewish communities.

But Hasidism refused to die. Out of the ashes it rose again. Today, the United States and Israel are home to many great dynasties. Pietists proudly proclaim their identity as *hasidim* of Lubavitch, Satmar, Ger, Belz, and Vishnitz. Hasidic courts flourish in New York, Jerusalem, Tel Aviv, and Bnei Berak, and new hasidic *yeshivot* are constantly being established.

From his headquarters in New York, the rebbe of Lubavitch directs his spiritual empire and expands the already far-reaching, manifold activities of the movement. He exercises control over hundreds of educational institutions, and his disciples carry the message of Hasidism to the campuses of universities throughout the Western world.

In recent years the movement, which had flashed with such meteoric speed and dazzling brilliance across the Jewish firmament, has drawn the attention of theologians, philosophers, and historians. Many writings have appeared, ranging from analytical studies to folkloric interpretations. Yet there are few books in English or Hebrew that give a concise account of Hasidism as a whole, and specifically its history during the last century. In this respect, this book breaks new ground. Originally published in 1970 under the title *The World of Hasidism,* this work has been extensively revised and updated. I offer it as an introduction to Hasidism, as a tribute to my own parents, and to the memory of the two million *hasidim* who perished in the Nazi Holocaust.

I want to express my deep and warm gratitude to my wife for her unstinting help and constant encouragement. I am particularly indebted to Mr. Arthur Kurzweil, editor at Jason Aronson Inc., for the deep and sustained interest he has taken in the work throughout its preparation.

London
June 1988

HASIDISM

THE MOVEMENT AND ITS MASTERS

Chapter 1

"Here Dwelleth the Lord"

The history of the Jews in Poland can be traced continuously, period by period, over a thousand years. Jews had begun to settle there before Christianity had found general acceptance in Eastern Europe, and so closely did the Jews associate themselves with their new homeland that its name was etymólogically interpreted in Hebrew either as *Polin* ("Here shall ye dwell"), or *Polaniah* ("Here dwelleth the Lord").

Poland stretched from Smolensk beyond the Dnieper in the east, to almost the Oder in the west, from the Duchy of Courland on the Baltic in the north, to the Dniester in the south. From all directions–from the south and from the east, from the land of the *Khazars* (Crimea), but mostly from Western Europe–Jewish emigrants flowed in ceaseless streams toward Poland and Lithuania. Many factors were responsible for these mass migrations: the First Crusade of 1096, which had brought death and desolation to the ancient communities that flourished on the Rhine and the Moselle; the Black Death (1248–1351), for which the Jews were the inevitable scapegoats; the expulsion from France in 1394; the terror of the fanatical fourteenth-century Flagellants; vexatious discriminatory legislation and repeated massacres. The hysterical cry: "Kill a Jew and save a soul!" echoed on throughout a blood-stained Europe.

Just as centuries later Turkey was to play host to the Spanish and Portuguese exiles, so Poland welcomed these fugitives from Germany. The Mongol invasions of 1237 devastated large areas, and Boleslaw the Pious, Prince of Great Poland (1247–1279), was among the many East European rulers who received the newcomers with warmth. Under the Magdeburg Law they were even granted special privileges. Indeed, some of these East European rulers were centuries ahead of their time in tolerance and ecumenism. "The Russians may pray according to their usage, the Poles according to theirs," declared Grand Duke Gedymin (1316–1341) of Lithuania, "and we Lithuanians shall worship according to our own custom. For have we not all one God?"[1]

A Mutually Advantageous Relationship

Nowhere in Europe was the mystique of "blue blood" more cherished than in Poland. This "vanity of birth," wrote Daniel Defoe, "is carried (in Poland) to a monstrous extravagance." In Poland the aristocracy, which formed about 8 percent of the population, paid virtually no taxes and enjoyed many financial dispensations. They were, for instance, exempt from the payment of import and export duties. The peasants, on the other hand, were enslaved and subject to feudal jurisdiction, which until 1768 included, among other severe punitive measures, a master's right to inflict the death penalty. The serf either tended his lord's land or paid dues in the form of produce. Peasants rarely owned land. They were serfs, and their personal freedom was severely restricted by their lord's supervision. They could not marry, move away, or enter another trade without the lord's permission. They could be sentenced without redress to severe corporal punishment or to long prison terms.

Poland needed middle-class administrators to develop its industry and commerce, and the nobility needed financiers. The Jewish immigrants were well equipped to play these diverse roles. With practical measures, Poland made her new and much-needed citizens feel at home. As early as 1264, Prince Boleslaw the Pious of Great Poland and Kalish granted Jews inviolability of person and property. These rights were enforced by almost all the Polish kings and became part of the country's Common Law. Jews were free to travel wherever they wished. They were exempted from the jurisdiction of the Common Courts and were empowered to settle among themselves disputes in which both the plaintiff and the defendant were Jews. A "Jews' judge" (*judex Judaeorum*) was to adjudicate Jews "in the neighborhood of the synagogue or in some other places chosen by the Jews." A Christian taking a Jew to court had to have both Jewish and Christian witnesses. Penalties for vandalism of Jewish cemeteries or synagogues were specified. King Casimir IV (1447–1492) confirmed these privileges. The Jews in Poland had the legal status of free men "attached to the Treasury" and dependent upon the King. The Jews in Poland were not barred from carrying arms. Rabbi Solomon Luria maintained that the Jews with privileges (or residence rights) were equal to the knights, and that the king had no right to take away their property. It is no wonder that Rabbi Moses Isserles (1532–1572) lauded in lyrical terms the hospitality of the newfound homeland: "Had not the Lord appointed this land as a refuge, the fate of Israel would indeed have been unbearable. By the grace of God, both the King and the nobles are favorably disposed toward us. In this country there is no fierce hatred as there is in Germany."[2]

By 1570 some 300,000 Jews had settled in Poland, residing in 160 localities and forming the second largest Jewish community in the world (the largest being in Turkey). At a time when Polish sovereignty extended from the Baltic to the Black Sea, the Jews were quick to recognize the country's economic potential. At a time when Jews in other lands were restricted mainly to the occupations of moneylending and petty trading, Poland's Jews were able to participate in all branches of industrial endeavor. They imported from the East and exported to the West. They were silversmiths, tailors, printers, bakers, metal workers, and innkeepers. They managed estates, collected tolls and customs, and even distilled liquor. One-third of the Jewish population became artisans of diverse kinds. Jewish guilds were established in more than fifty places. They dealt with many types of merchandise: honey, grain, timber, cattle, horses, fish, and textiles. The statute of Wislica (1347), even exempted Jews from the obligation of military service.

Allied to these opportunities was an almost unparalleled degree of religious freedom, and Polish Jewry became the most elaborately organized Jewish community in Europe.

Jewish Self-Government

On August 13, 1551, Sigismund II Augustus, the last ruler of the Jagiellonian dynasty, who reigned from 1548 to 1572, laid the foundation for Jewish autonomy. Not since the days of the Patriarchs and the Exilarchs of Palestine and Babylon had Diaspora Jews been able to enjoy so full a measure of self-government. Each community had its own *kehillah* (town council) that regulated every phase of life from the cradle to the grave: from the assessment and collection of taxes to the supervision of schools; from the maintenance of cemeteries to the selection of a *shtadlan* (intercessor), who mediated between the Jews and the king or nobles.

Above the local *kehillah* rose a complex structure of supervisory organizations. The *kehillot* were responsible to district councils (*gelilot*). The *gelilot* in turn were subject to the provincial councils (*medinot*), and, finally, the *medinot* were under the jurisdiction of the supreme governing body, "The Council of the Four Lands." This *Vaad Arba Aratzot* (or Congressus Judaicus) embraced Little Poland (including Krakow and Lublin), Greater Poland (Congress Poland), Volhynia (Ostrog and Kremenetz), Red Russia (Eastern Galicia) and, for a while, Lithuania (Brest and Grodno). In 1623 a separate body was formed, called "The Council of the Principal Communities of the Province of Lithuania."

Functioning on a parliamentary level, the Council acted as the state's agent for Jewish taxation. It dealt with questions of industry and commerce, regulated the elections of the *kehillot,* and approved the school curricula. "The representatives of the Council of the Four Lands," remarked historian Nathan Hannover, "remind one of the *Sanhedrin,* which in ancient days assembled in the Chamber of Hewn Stones (*lishkat hagazit*) in the Temple."[3] Backed by the power and the resources of the state, the rabbinate was almost as powerful as it had been in the days of Hillel and Shammai.

The Pinkasim *as Historical Documents*

The Minute Books (*Pinkasim*) of the Councils of Lithuania and of the Four Lands, edited and published by Simon Dubnow and Israel Halpern respectively, shed much light on the diversity of rabbinic activities in sixteenth and seventeenth-century Poland.[4] These records show that while they dealt knowledgeably with political and financial matters, the rabbis concentrated their energies primarily upon maintaining high moral and ethical standards within their communities.

A wide assortment of far-reaching edicts were issued by the rabbinate. Overly lavish celebrations and extravagances in dress were effectively curbed through a series of what amounted to sumptuary laws. "One is permitted to wear only two rings on a weekday, four on the Sabbath and six on festivals." Fraudulent business dealings, with Jew or Gentile, were severely punished. One who declared bankruptcy was subject to stringent penalties: he was imprisoned for twelve months and was barred from appointment to any religious office. "If he already holds such office, he is to be deposed, and he shall not be called up to the Reading of the Law for a whole year or until he repays all his notes to his creditors."[5] The rabbinate even assumed responsibility for the contents of printed books by requiring that all works first receive rabbinic approval (*haskamah*) in order to be published.

A Golden Age of Torah Scholarship

This elaborate "state within a state" was the ideal setting for intensive Torah education. *Torah iz di beste sechorah* (Torah is the best merchandise) runs the old Yiddish adage that was the credo of the Polish Jew. The sixteenth century was the golden age of Polish Jewry, no less splendid than the golden age (900–1200) of Spanish Jewry, or the talmudic period in Babylon.

Nathan Hannover records, with justifiable pride:

> In no country was the study of the Torah so widespread among the Jews as in the kingdom of Poland. Every Jewish community maintained a *yeshivah,* paying its principal a large salary to enable him to conduct the institution without financial worry and to devote himself entirely to the pursuit of learning. . . . The (poor) boys obtained their food either from the charity fund or from the public kitchen. . . . A community of fifty families would support no fewer than thirty of these young men and boys, one family supplying board for one college student and his two pupils, the former sitting at the family table like one of the sons. . . . There was scarcely a Jewish house in the whole kingdom of Poland where the Torah was not studied, and where either the head of the

family, or his son, or his son-in-law, or the *yeshivah* student boarding with him, was not an expert in Jewish learning.[6]

This Torah-centered life paid rich dividends. Polish Jewry brought forth a galaxy of savants, who charted new approaches to the fathomless "sea of the Talmud" and to the elucidation of the Codes. The *Haggahot* ("Glosses") of Rabbi Moses Isserles to Rabbi Joseph Karo's *Shulhan Arukh* ("Prepared Table") became textbooks for Ashkenazi Jewry. Scholars from Italy, Germany, and the Holy Land sought guidance from Isserles and deferred to his judgments. Other great leaders in Torah study included Rabbi Solomon Luria (known as the *Maharshal*) and Meir ben Gedaliah (the *Maharam*).

Rabbi Jacob Pollak, founder of the great *yeshivah* in Krakow in the late 15th century, became known as the father of talmudic studies in Poland. Talmudic learning spread from his *yeshivah* throughout Poland and to Jewish centers in other parts of Europe. During the following two centuries, the fame of Poland's rabbis and *yeshivot* attracted many scholars, including the youngest son of Manasseh ben Israel (1604–1657), who left his native Holland for Poland, "to pour water on the hands and to sit at the feet of the great ones of the Second Palestine."

It was in Poland that Yiddish grew to rich maturity. The medieval Germanic dialect (Middle German) of the Central Rhine region was transplanted and transformed, absorbing Hebraic and Slavic elements in the course of time. This friendly and familiar amalgam of many languages became known as Yiddish, mother tongue of successive generations, second only to Hebrew in its influence on the Jewish masses of Eastern Europe and on the Diaspora at large.

The Jewish community paid dearly for its privileges. Every Jew paid a capitation tax of one Polish gulden per head, as well as income tax. In addition, he paid a "purchase tax" on most of the commodities of daily life, including meat, needles, and liquor. Jews also contributed substantial sums toward national defense.[7]

During the seventeenth century, Jews were paying annual taxes amounting to 100,000 gulden, and by 1717 they were contributing 220,000 gulden a year. Yet, despite this heavy taxation, there was still some truth to the saying that Poland was "heaven for the nobleman, purgatory for the citizen, hell for the peasant, and paradise for the Jew."

A Short-Lived Paradise

The duration of the golden epoch was lamentably brief. In the seventeenth century the Ukrainian Steppes, that enormous stretch of prairie between the Dnieper and Dniester Rivers, came under Polish sovereignty. The Polish nobility cruelly exploited and virtually enslaved the Ukrainian peasants. Their burdens were many and their rights nonexistent. They were subject to numerous abuses, and the landlords farmed out their territories to agents who wrenched exorbitant rents from the hapless peasantry.

Inevitably, Polish oppression of the Ukraine culminated in catastrophe. The climax came under the leadership of a peasant named Bogdan Zinov Chmielnicki (1593–1657), whose grievances against an arrogant Polish overlord galvanized his campaign of revolution. Encouraged by their priests, an unholy alliance of Tartars, Cossacks, and peasants wreaked a terrible vengeance "with fire and sword" on the defenseless Jews, whom they regarded as the agents and allies of their oppressors. Hell was unleashed and a reign of terror began for the "heretical Pole and unbelieving Jew." In the battle of Kniazhey Biarak on May 6, 1648, the Polish army was annihilated. With the ill-timed death of the Polish King, Wladyslaw, the way was clear for Chmielnicki to march unopposed through the Ukraine, White Russia, Lithuania, and Poland.

A Russian historian describes the blood-lust of the savage hordes:

> Killing was accomplished by barbarous torture–the victims were flayed alive, split asunder, clubbed to death, roasted on coals, or scalded with boiling water. Even infants at the breast were not spared. The most terrible cruelty was shown toward the Jews. They were destined to utter annihilation, and the slightest pity shown to them was looked upon as treason. Scrolls of the Law were taken out of the synagogues by the Cossacks, who danced on them in drunken frenzy. Then the

> Jews were placed upon the Scrolls and butchered without mercy. Thousands of Jewish infants were thrown into wells, or buried alive.[8]

Wholesale Slaughter

The atrocities committed by the raging Cossacks were bestial beyond description. The massacres at Nemirov, Tulchin, Zaslav, Ostrog, Narol, and Kremenetz added crimson pages to the already overflowing volumes of Jewish martyrology. In Polonnoye alone, 10,000 Jews perished. Among the victims was Samson of Ostropol, the renowned Kabbalist. In the Ukraine, over 100,000 Jews were slain and many communities were all but extinguished. In the Ukrainian cities situated on the left bank of the Dnieper, the region populated by the Cossacks, the Jewish communities almost completely disappeared. In the localities on the right shore of the Dnieper or in the Polish parts of the Ukraine, such as those of Volhynia and Podolia, wherever the Cossacks had made their appearance, only about one-tenth of the Jewish population survived. Some 700 Jewish communities were sacked between 1648 and 1658. Only one-tenth of the Jewish population survived in the Ukraine.[9] Manasseh ben Israel, petitioning Oliver Cromwell to readmit the Jews to England in 1655, gave the number of Jewish victims as 180,000.[10] The genocidal devastation of *Gezerot Tah Vetat* ("The Fateful Events of 1648–1649"), as the Chmielnicki massacres were known, ranks with the destruction of the Second Temple as one of the major disasters of Jewish history, to be surpassed only by the Holocaust of World War II.

Destruction, Displacement, and Dire Need

As if the cup of suffering was not already brimming, murderous gangs continued to ravage the grievously depleted communities. Rabbi Moses Rivkes (d. 1671) wrote: "Throughout the whole of Lithuania, there then roamed bands of Russians and Cossacks, who devastated the cities and occupied, among other places, Plock, Vitebsk, and Minsk. Whenever the Cossacks appeared, in their lust for spoil, they seized all the belongings of the Jews, whom they slaughtered in masses."

For the first time in history, Polish Jewish refugees, later to become a familiar sight, began to make their way to different countries; to Holland, England, Italy, Turkey, and even Egypt. All the *kehillot* were in debt. Poverty was widespread, and in 1657 the Jews were threatened with mass expulsion.[11] On March 19, 1658, King Jan Casimir recorded the following:

> Many of the Jews were robbed or killed by our soldiers, and others were despoiled or massacred by foreign troops; many lost their lives under torture. Those who survived cannot find peace in the towns and at the marts. They cannot expect security. Those who sought refuge outside the Polish boundaries are afraid to return. I know that many of the belongings of the Jews who had been plundered by the citizens are still hidden by the pillagers, and the Jews are as yet unable to recover their losses.[12]

Threats from Other Sources

The rehabilitation of stricken Jewry was impeded by the Russian and Swedish invasions of Poland (1649–1700) and by the revival of the blood libels. Sandormiersz (1698–1710), Poznan (1736), Zaslav (1747), Shepetovka (1748), Zhitomir (1753), and Yampol (1759) were scenes of murderous rampages. "Just as Poland cannot do without the *Liberum Veto,*" it was said, "so the Jews cannot have *matzot* (unleavened bread) without Christian blood." Jacob Selig sought the intervention of Pope Benedict XIV, for "as soon as a dead body is found anywhere, at once the Jews of the neighboring localities are brought before the Courts and charged with murder for superstitious purposes."[13] After accusing the Jewish Council of misadministration, the Sejm abolished the Congress in 1764. Yet before the First Partition of Poland in 1773, the Jews there numbered over 600,000, about 5.5 percent of the population. At that time 72,000 Jews in Poland were unemployed, and 9,000 were paupers.[14]

In Poland a period of endless anarchy and instability began. The fate of the "elected" monarchy depended entirely on the whims of the capricious *Liberum Veto* that became an integral part of the Polish constitution early in the seventeenth century. In their councils, the *Szlachta* placed great value on the principle of unanimity. Neither the central diet nor the regional diets could pass a resolution unless it gained the consent of all persons present. With one phrase, *nie pozwalam* ("I do not permit it"), a veto that required neither explanation nor justification, any nobleman could not only doom any bill under discussion, but could also bring about the dissolution of the diet. Of the fifty-five diets held after 1655, forty-eight produced no legislation. Upon accession, each monarch signed a pact (*pacta conventa*) which virtually ensured his complete subordination to the will of the diet, itself hardly a bulwark of strength and decisiveness. Nor was that governing body in any position to enforce its decisions, for the Polish army numbered no more than 16,000 men at most. "If this is liberty," commented the British envoy, "then the Lord preserve me from it."

Chapter 2

From the Mists of Mysticism

Mysticism virtually defies verbal definition. Perhaps it could be called "the fight of the Alone to the Alone." In essence it represents man's yearning to unravel the Divine mystery. To some, mysticism is synonymous with the occult, with spiritualism, clairvoyance, magic, visions, and revelations. To others, it is "experimental wisdom," "knowledge of God through experience," or "the immediate awareness of the relation with God."

Jewish mysticism in its various forms represents an attempt to interpret the religious values of Judaism in terms of mystical values. It concentrates on the idea of the living God Who manifested Himself in the acts of Creation, Revelation and Redemption.[1]

Graetz, Geiger, and Zunz considered *Kabbalah* degenerate and even "unJewish." Graetz maintained that *Kabbalah* could not be considered a legitimate part of Judaism.

Kabbalah's *Antecedents*

The term *Kabbalah* is found in the work of the philosopher Solomon ibn Gabirol (c. 1021–1056), *Tikkun Middot Hanefesh* ("Improvement of Moral Qualities"). Yet it was not until the fourteenth century that it was generally associated with mysticism. The literal meaning of *Kabbalah,* which derives from the Hebrew root *kabbel* (to receive), is "tradition" or "acceptance." But although the mystical associations of the word *Kabbalah* are of medieval origin, the mystic tradition goes back to the very origins of Judaism. Not content with pondering the literal meaning of the Scriptures, the sages delved deeply into *sitrei Torah* (the secrets of the Torah). Every Biblical word was minutely explored, and the Bible provided ample scope for mystical flights. Thus, an intricate web of folklore was spun around the story of the Creation *(Maaseh Bereishit)* in the first chapter of the Book of Genesis and around the Divine Chariot (*Maaseh Merkavah*) described in Ezekiel's dream.

Every reference was closely scrutinized and a complete hierarchy of angelic beings was envisioned. The diligent and devout searchers wove layer upon layer of inspired conjecture around the power and significance of the very name of the Lord, the mighty and mysterious *Shem Hameforash* (the ineffable Name of God).

The path of the mystic is terrifying and tortuous, and men are repeatedly warned to follow a smoother, straighter road. "Seek not things that are too hard for thee," counsels Ben Sira, author of *Ecclesiasticus,* "and search not things that are hidden from thee."[2] According to the Mishnah, *Maaseh Bereishit* may not be expounded in the presence of two, neither may *Maaseh Merkavah* be expounded in the presence of a person who is not a sage and, therefore, incapable of understanding. "Whosoever speculates upon four things, what is above and what is below, what is ahead and what is behind, such an individual should never have been born, for he dishonors his Creator."[3]

The philosopher Philo (c. 20 B.C.E.–50 C.E.) believed that the narratives in the Bible could not be understood literally. Thus, for example, Abraham's journey and the Exodus were not simply historical events, they were allegories of the soul's journey toward God.

Warnings did not discourage the passionate pilgrims, and many embarked on the perilous passage toward the Great Unknown. Not all the voyagers could navigate the strange and stormy seas, and relatively few arrived safely at their destination. The Talmud records the fate of four celebrated scholars. "Four men entered the *Pardes* (Garden), Ben Azzai, Ben Zoma, Aher, and Rabbi Akiva . . . Ben Azzai looked and died. Ben Zoma looked and lost his senses. Aher "cut the plants" in the garden of faith (became a heretic). Only Rabbi Akiva entered safely and emerged unharmed."[4]

The Masters of Kabbalah

Among the fabled masters of mysticism were Rabban Johanan ben Zakkai and his disciples, Rabbi Joshua ben Hannaniah and Rabbi Jose; Rabbi Phinehas ben Yair and Rabbi Nehuniah ben Hakaneh. Many legends sprang up around the mystics. We are told that Rabbi Oshaiah and Rabbi Hanina ben Dosa created a 3-year-old calf[5] and that Rabbi Joshua ben Levi transformed cucumbers and pumpkins into deer and fawns.[6]

Although some authorities were opposed to mystical speculation, others regarded it as an integral element of Judaism. "On Judgment Day," declared Rabbi Ishmael, "the Great Judge will ask each scholar: 'My son, since you have studied the Talmud, why have you not also studied the *Merkavah* and perceived My splendor?' "[7]

"The *Kabbalists* received their tradition from the Prophets," affirmed Rabbi Jonathan Eibeschütz (1696–1764).[8] Post-biblical literature is rich in mystical concepts. Philo developed an intricate symbolism around these concepts. His aim was to harmonize Hellenistic and Jewish cultures. The Philonic concept of Logos (the Greek for "word," "speech" or "reason") sought to bridge the gap between the transcendent God and the world: Philo asserted that the most exemplary life was a life of contemplation (*via contempliva),* wherein man experiences the presence of God. Through his intellect, man has affinity with the Divine Being.

Terminology and Traditions

There are numerous terms used to define mysticism and its practitioners. Among them are *Hokhmah Nistarah* ("Hidden Wisdom"), *Razei Torah* ("Secrets of the Torah"), *Yordei Merkavah* ("Riders of the Chariot"), *Yodei Hen* ("Knowers of Grace"), *Baalei Hasod* ("Bearers of the Secret"), *Dorshei Reshumot* ("Searchers of Scriptures"), *Hakhmei Hatushiah* ("Students of Profound Knowledge"), *Yodim* ("Gnostics"), *Anshei Maaseh* ("Men of Action"), and *Baalei Avodah* ("Masters of True Worship"). The mystical tradition can be traced from the martyred *tanna,* Rabbi Akiva (c. 40–135), to the late Chief Rabbi of the Holy Land, Abraham Isaac Kook (1865–1935). Printed works or treatises on the *Kabbalah* number nearly 3,000, with an equal number in manuscript form in private and public collections.

Kabbalah exists in two forms: contemplative or theoretical *Kabbalah (Kabbalah iyunit)* and practical *Kabbalah (Kabbalah maasit).* Theoretical *Kabbalah* concerns itself with the nature of God and the cosmos and with the tenets of dogma and ethics. God is the *Ein–Sof* ("The Infinte," "The Endless," "The most Hidden of all Hidden," "The Boundless," and "The Transcendent"). The link connecting the *Ein–Sof* to the visible world, is formed by emanations of the ten *Sefirot.* This differs from the doctrine of emanations found in Neoplatonic philosophy, for in *Kabbalah* the emanations are all contained within the Godhead.

How does one relate God, Who is perfection, to the world, which is manifestly imperfect? The answer takes us back to the very dawn of Creation. In the Kabbalist's view, the world was created by emanations, *Sefirot* (a Hebrew word meaning either "to count," "brilliancy," or "luminary"). These emanations or agencies are *Keter* ("crown"), *Hokhmah* ("wisdom"), *Binah* ("understanding"), *Hesed* ("lovingkindness"), *Gevurah* ("power"), *Tiferet* ("beauty"), *Netzah* ("victory"), *Hod* ("majesty"), *Yesod* ("foundation"), and *Malkhut* ("sovereignty"). When Adam was exiled from Eden, the *Shekhinah* ("Divine Presence") was exiled from the *Ein–Sof.* This schism accounts for all the world's evils, and thus the mystics sought to reunite the *Ein–Sof* with the *Shekhinah.*

The Holy Land was the birthplace of *Kabbalah,* and it was there that a number of studies were written by talmudists. The *Hekhalot* ("palaces") literature, as the mystical *midrashim* written in the early rabbinic and geonic periods are known, describes in astonishing detail the halls and palaces, the *Pamaliah shel Maalah* (the household of the upper world), the *Malakhei Hasharet* (ministering angels), the *Malakhei Habbalah* (angels of destruction), the *Shedim* (roving spirits), *Ashmedai* (king of the demons), *Lilit* (demon of the night) and *Dumah* (guardian angel of the souls in the nether world).

Kabbalah*'s Texts*

A major work of mysticism is the short book *Sefer Yetzirah* ("Book of Creation"), which contains only six brief chapters. According to legend, it was written by the Patriarch Abraham, but there is reason to believe that it was in fact written in Palestine or Babylonia between the third and sixth centuries of the Common Era. Both Saadia Gaon of Sura (882–942), father of Jewish philosophy and the Gaon Elijah of Vilna (1720–1797) wrote commentaries on it. The chief premise of this intriguing treatise is that the world was formed through the "thirty-two ways of wisdom," the twenty-two letters of the Hebrew alphabet plus the ten *Sefirot.* Other topics are the *tzeruf* (esoteric alphabetical combinations), the *gematriah* (calculations based on the numerical value of the letters), *notarikon* (acrostics), and *temurah* (changing the meaning of a word by transposing its letters).

We learn from Eleazar ben Judah of Worms (c. 1160–1238), author of *Sefer Haroke'ah* ("The Book of the Spice Dealer"), that it was the scholar Aaron ben Samuel of Baghdad who introduced the study of mysticism to Italy in the ninth century. His pupil, Moses ben Kalonymos of Lucca, carried his teachings to Germany, where during the twelfth and thirteenth centuries, the *Hasidei Ashkenaz* (the pious men of Germany) made their contributions to kabbalistic lore: *Sefer Hasidim* ("The Book of the Pious") in which Samuel Hehasid and Judah Hehasid of Regensburg (d. 1217) dealt with both the soul's strivings and the body's need for a life of devotion. The book has been described as "a noble commentary on the verse 'Love thy neighbor as thyself' (Leviticus 19:18) that exemplifies the highest moral teachings of the ages."[9]

Notable contributions to mysticism were made by the pseudo-Messiah, Abraham ben Samuel Abulafia (1241–after 1291). After failing to convert the anti-Semitic Pope Nicholas III to Judaism, Abulafia journeyed to Sicily, where he proclaimed himself the Messiah. The author of twenty-six works, the majority still in manuscript form, Abulafia propounded a "prophetical *Kabbalah*" (*Kabbalah Nevu'it*) that centered on the mystical significance of the four-lettered Name of God. He was convinced that devout contemplation of the Divine Names could produce a state of ecstasy. "They called me heretic and unbeliever," lamented Abulafia, "because I had resolved to worship God in truth."

The Zohar

"I thank God every day that I was not born before the *Zohar* was revealed," said Rabbi Phinehas of Korets (Korzec), "for it was the *Zohar* which knit my very soul to Judaism." Apart from the Torah, no other book is as highly venerated by *hasidim* as the *Sefer HaZohar* ("Book of Splendor" or "Book of Radiance"), that became the Bible of the Kabbalist.[2] The origin of this work is obscure. It was discovered in the late thirteenth century by the Spanish Kabbalist, Moses ben Shem Tov de Leon (1250–1305), who attributed authorship to the second century *tanna,* Simon ben Yohai. A midrashic and kabbalistic commentary on the Pentateuch, the *Zohar* was written in Aramaic. First published in Mantua in 1558, it was published in Krakow in 1603 and in Lublin in 1623. Many of the passages of the *Zohar* are poetic descriptions in lyrical terms of the wonders of the universe that God had fashioned. It contains a fascinating blend of metaphysics, mystical cosmogony, and esoteric psychology.

Throughout the ages, scholars have debated the authorship of the *Zohar.* Isaac of Acre, Elijah Delmedigo (1591–1655), Judah Aryeh of Modena in the seventeenth century, and Jacob Emden in the eighteenth century all disputed the *Zohar's* antiquity, and maintained that the *Zohar* could not possibly date back to the second century. Among their arguments, they cited numerous anachronisms such as references to the Crusades and to Islam, the use of vowels and accents, and linguistic formations. Graetz labeled it a "clumsy forgery," and other scholars detect the work of several hands in this complex composition.

"Every word of the Torah contains many levels of meaning and embodies a sublime mystery. The narratives of the Torah are like outer garments," declared Rabbi Simon ben Yohai. "Alas for the man who regards the Torah merely as a book of tales and profane matters."[10] In this spirit, the *Zohar* strips off the semantic screens and attempts to pierce the very core of every biblical phrase or letter. Among concepts discussed by the *Zohar* is the transmigration of souls (*gilgul*): "All souls must undergo transmigrations. . . . Men do not understand the ways of the Holy One. . . . They know not how many transmigrations and hidden trials they have to undergo, nor do they know the number of souls and spirits which enter into the world and which do not return into the palace of the Heavenly King."

The Kabbalists of Safed

After the expulsion of the Jews from Spain in 1492, the Holy Land became the scene of a remarkable kabbalistic renaissance. High on the slopes of the graceful Galilean hills, looking across to snow-capped Mount Hermon, lies the picturesque town of Safed. In the sixteenth century, it became the home of many celebrated scholars. Here lived the renowned masters of mysticism, men whose vision added new light and new dimensions to everyday life. Through self-affliction (*sigufim*), fasts (*taaniyot*), ablutions (*tevilot*), and ardent worship, they strove for a closer communion with God. For them, prayer was a means of ascent. For them every word, every gesture, every act, every thought, was fraught with untold significance. Every blade of grass, every budding flower, every element of nature, was a manifestation of the Creator.

To the mystics, the Sabbath was particularly precious, for it was, in essence, a foretaste of the world to come. With fervor, with prayer, with love, and with song, the Kabbalists welcomed the Seventh Day. It would require a Rembrandt or a Chagall to recreate the scene when, on Friday afternoons, the white-robed sages, their faces lit with holy joy, would form a procession through the winding lanes of the picturesque town, chanting the Psalms and *Lekhah Dodi* ("Come my Beloved") as they welcomed the Sabbath Bride. The practice of reciting the "Song of Songs" on Sabbath eve as well as Proverbs 31 at the Sabbath table originated in Safed. Here lived the legal codifier, Joseph Karo (1498–1575), whose diary, published under the title *Maggid Mesharim,* records mystical revelations from a Heavenly messenger (*maggid*). Here lived Moses ben Jacob Cordovero (1522–1570), the author of thirty works, among them an exposition of kabbalistic doctrines known as *Pardes Rimmonim* ("Garden of Pomegranates"), which he composed at the age of twenty-six, and *Tomer Devorah* ("The Palm Tree of Deborah").

The Holy Lion

The king of the Kabbalists was Isaac Luria Ashkenazi (1534–1572), known as the *Ari* ("lion") or *Ari HaKadosh* ("The Holy Lion"). Luria was probably born in Jerusalem and lived for a time in Cairo. He studied under Rabbi Betzalel Ashkenazi (d. 1590), author of *Shitah Mekubbetzet* ("Collected Opinions"). After his father's death, Luria's mother took him to Egypt where he lived in the home of an uncle. In 1569 or 1570 Luria settled in Safed, where he studied under Moses Cordovero to whom he refers as "our teacher whose light may be prolonged." His spiritual mentor was rumored to be Simon ben Yohai himself. Luria believed himself to be the Messiah, son of Joseph. In a letter to his son, Isaiah Horowitz (1565–1630) writes: "Three supremely great men lived here at the same time–our teacher Rabbi Joseph Karo, Rabbi Moses Cordovero, and Rabbi Isaac Luria, of blessed memory. These were veritable angels of the Lord of Hosts. The revered principals of the Academies on High, the sages of the *Mishnah,* and even Elijah of blessed memory appeared to them."[11] The angel, or *maggid,* would come to Karo on numerous occasions and speak through Karo's own voice. He described these experiences; "As I was reading the *Mishnah,* the voice of the beloved knocked in my mouth and the lyre sang of itself."

Lurianic Mysticism

It was the "Holy Lion's" chief disciple, Hayim Vital of Calabria (1542–1620) who, in his books *Eitz Hayim* ("Tree of Life") and *Shaarei Kedushah* ("Gates of Holiness"), both formulated and recorded the Lurianic doctrines. The cornerstone was the daring concept of *tzimtzum* (withdrawal or contraction), whereby God is believed to have withdrawn from Himself to Himself in order to leave space for the world to be created. The vacuum (*halal*) was illuminated by a thin light of God. When God's light reentered this space, it did so by means of the ten *Sefirot.* However, during the delicate reentry process, the lights (*orot*) of the *Ein-Sof* were shattered. This cosmic calamity is known as "the breaking of the vessels" (*Shevirat Keilim*) or the "Death of the Kings." This explains how God can be both immanent and transcendent. Holy sparks were scattered throughout all creation, and the Divine Light was trapped by *kelipot* (isolated shells). The heavenly sparks were lodged in all things. Thus the "vessels" and the "shells" are of paramount importance, for they contain minute particles of the *Ein-Sof.* It is the duty and role of man to awaken the dormant sparks, to redeem the lost ones by prayer and by *tikkun* (perfecting). Only when all the holy sparks have been released can the Messiah come and Divine harmony be restored. It is the mission of the Jewish People to bring about this reunion.

In these uncharted regions Rabbi Isaac Luria broke new metaphysical ground. He was a brilliantly original thinker, a man of far-ranging imagination, endowed with what we would today call extrasensory perception. He could sum up a man's inner essence on sight. He believed that every man left his imprint on the world. He believed that man could, if he willed it, turn "evil spirits" into "good spirits." Luria advocated asceticism, fasting, self-mortification, and humility. Every night a man should say, "Lord of the Universe, I forgive all who have angered and injured me today, whether wittingly or unwittingly, whether in deed or thoughts. May no man be punished for my sake or because of me."

Glimmer of Hope

Intrinsic to Judaism is belief in the Messiah, who will fulfill the biblical prophecies and gather together the scattered remnants of the House of Israel. The devout Jew avers daily, "I believe with perfect faith in the coming of the Messiah, and though he tarry, yet will I wait daily for his coming." This is one of the Thirteen Articles of Faith compiled by Moses Maimonides (1135–1204). And these were the poignant words *ani maamin* ("I believe") that the martyrs of the Holocaust sang with death-defying valor as they entered the valley of the shadow of death. For thousands of years, with a fidelity that never faltered and with a yearning that was never stilled, the House of Israel has believed in and has waited for its promised Redeemer.

Messianic Movements

Like shooting stars, false Messiahs flashed across the skies of Jewish history, so that the flame of Messianism glowed through the darkness of the endless exile. But in the wake of each falling star came disillusionment, despair, and disaster. Rabbinic writings clarified the veiled Messianic allusions in the Bible, the Apocrypha, and the Pseudepigrapha. Jewish eschatology envisaged a twofold Messiah: Messiah ben Joseph, who would subdue *Gog* and *Magog* (the arch forces of evil) and Messiah ben David, who would establish the Kingdom of God on earth and rule over Israel at the end of days. The Jewish Messiah is not a divinity but a man, an offshoot of the House of David, the long-awaited Prince of Peace, who would inaugurate a golden age of universal brotherhood. Many were the legends woven around the ubiquitous Elijah, precursor of the Messiah, and other dramatis personae of the Apocalyptic vision.

Again and again pretenders arose to lift and then dash the hopes of the people. Rabbi Akiva, one of Judaism's best-loved sages, hailed as Messiah Simon bar Koziba whom he renamed Bar Kokhba ("son of the star"), applying to him the verse: "There shall come forth a star out of Jacob and a scepter shall rise out of Israel" (Numbers 24:17). With the destruction of the Temple and the ruthless sacking of Judea in 70 C.E., Rome thought it had crushed the spirit of revolt. But while the rest of the ancient world had bowed to tyranny, Jews still hurled themselves against the massive forces of the Roman Empire. Bar Kokhba led the epic battle that raged for three fearful years (132–135 C.E.) in which thousands of Jews were killed and thousands more perished as a result of pestilence and famine. "All of Judea," records the historian Dio Cassius, "became a virtual desert."

Messianic Pretenders

Minor "messiahs" often appeared on the Jewish scene. Among the more flamboyant ones was David Alroy, a twelfth century native of Kurdistan, who promised to liberate Persian Jews from the yoke of Islam. However, he was murdered by his father-in-law, and his supporters faded away. Another aspirant to the messiah's throne was David Reuveni, who claimed to be the plenipotentiary of his brother, King Joseph of Habor. Reuveni sought the endorsement of the Pope and appealed to Emperor Charles V and King Manuel of Portugal for help against the Turks. Reuveni perished, probably in a Spanish prison. Yet many believed in him, and he fired the imagination of Diego Pires (1500–1532), who called himself Solomon Molkho and declared that the messianic era would commence in 1540. Unhappily, Molkho did not live to see it; he was burned at the stake by the Inquisition in Mantua in 1532.

Shabbetai Tzvi

According to Rabbi Israel Baal Shem Tov, even Shabbetai Tzvi (1626–1676), king of the pseudomessiahs, was endowed with a "holy spark." Jewry was attracted to his magnetic personality and inflamed by his prophetic imagination.

Shabbetai Tzvi was born in Smyrna in 1626. His birth date fell on the Sabbath day, appropriately enough, in view of the repercussions of his ill-fated career. It was also the Ninth of *Av,* the day commemorating the destruction of the First and Second Temples. He was the second of merchant Mordecai Tzvi's three sons. The young Shabbetai studied in Smyrna under Rabbi Joseph Eskofa, author of *Rosh Yosef.* At the age of 18, he was ordained *hakham* (sage). At the age of 20, he married his first wife whom he divorced a few months later. He suffered from a manic-depressive psychosis, alternating from feelings of sublime happiness and ecstasy to moods of dejection and melancholy. To his believers, his face was "like the face of Moses which was like the face of the sun." He uttered the ineffable Name of God, and Rabbi Joseph Eskofa excommunicated him. He was expelled from Smyrna in 1651. He journeyed to Jerusalem and Egypt. On May 31, 1665, he proclaimed himself Messiah. He stated that he heard a voice saying, "Thou art the Savior of Israel. I swear by my right hand and by the strength of my arm that thou art the true redeemer." Claiming that the Messiah ben Joseph had preceded him in the guise of the Polish Jew Abraham Alman, who was murdered by the Cossacks, Shabbetai Tzvi proclaimed himself "Messiah the son of David." Shortly afterwards he was excommunicated by the *Beit Din* (religious court) of Smyrna. Although it was hardly a vote of confidence, the verdict did not deter his followers, and his chief aide, Nathan of Gaza, continued to issue messianic manifestos. "It is difficult to describe the joy with which the reports of Shabbetai Tzvi were received in Hamburg," wrote Gluckel of Hameln.[12] "Most of these letters were received by the Sephardim, who thereupon read them to the community assembled in the synagogue. . . . Some of them unfortunately, sold everything–house, land and possessions–expecting to be redeemed immediately."

Isaac Primo, secretary to Shabbetai Tzvi, issued an edict on behalf of his master, proclaiming that the fast day of the Ninth of *Av* had been transformed into a day of rejoicing:

> From the first begotten son of God, Shabbetai Tzvi, Messiah and Redeemer of the people of Israel to all the children of Israel, peace. Since ye have been deemed worthy to behold the great

day and the fulfillment of God's word by the prophets, your lament and sorrow shall be changed into joy, and your fasting into merriment, for ye shall weep no more . . . because I have appeared.

The marriage of Shabbetai Tzvi to Sarah, a Polish orphan whose parents perished in the Chmielnicki massacres, as well as the prophecies of Nathan of Gaza and the initial enthusiasm of the Polish Kabbalist, Nehemiah HaKohen, convinced many of the doubters. Moreover, the message fell upon eager ears yearning to hear of imminent redemption. "Soon will I avenge you and comfort you even as a mother comforteth her son," Shabbetai Tzvi announced to Polish Jewry, "and I will recompense you a hundredfold for the sufferings you have endured. The day of revenge is at hand and the year of redemption hath arrived."

He conferred on his leading believers royal titles, and he distributed the kingdoms of the earth among his faithful adherents. He was arrested by the Turkish authorities who were alarmed by the messianic unrest among the Jewish population. He remained in prison in Constantinople for more than two months. He was then transferred to Abydos. He named his prison *Migdal Oz* ("the Tower of Strength"), a reference to a verse in the Book of Proverbs (18:10), "The name of the Lord is a tower of strength." Believers streamed to Shabbetai's residence. Regular pilgrimages were organized from the capital to the Dardanelles, and ferryboat trade flourished. Day and night long rows of boats plied the waters as the governor of the fortress collected huge sums from the sale of permits to visit his distinguished prisoner.

On September 16, 1666, Shabbetai Tzvi stood before the Privy Council of the Sultan in Adrianople and was offered a choice: convert to Islam or face execution. He preferred a Turkish turban to a martyr's death. After his conversion to Islam and for the remaining decade of his life, he was known as Mehmed Effendi (keeper of the palace gates). A royal pension was added to the honorary appointment. In spite of his apostasy, Shabbetai Tzvi still retained many supporters. They rationalized his actions as necessary in order to achieve the ultimate goal of retrieving the imprisoned holy sparks from the realm of evil. By converting to Islam, Shabbetai Tzvi was actually descending into that realm and personally reenacting this primal struggle.

In 1673 Shabbetai Tzvi was exiled to Dulcigno in Albania where he died on the Day of Atonement in September 1676.

The Aftermath

As the volcano subsided, the cinders were scattered far and wide as pygmies tried to tread in the footprints of the giants. Several Shabbatean supporters claimed the messianic mantle. Among them were Abraham Miguel Cardozo (1630–1706), Mordekhai of Eisenstadt (d. 1729), Judah Hasid of Dubno, Hayim Malakh, Nehemiah Hiya Hayun (1650–1726) and Heschel Tzoref (1633–1700). In 1700, some 1,500 followers of Judah Hasid emigrated to the Holy Land.

The most notorious of the pseudomessiahs was Jacob Leibowitz Frank (1726–1791) of Galicia, a one-time clerk and traveling salesman. He joined the Donmeh (Turkish for "apostates"), the Judeo-Muslim sect formed by the followers of Shabbetai Tzvi. Later, when he proclaimed himself Messiah, orgies took the place of mystic speculations, and immoral rites were the order of the day. "Poland is the country," wrote Frank, "that was promised to the Patriarchs. Were I to be given all the countries of the world filled with jewels, I would not leave Poland since it is God's legacy and also the legacy of our fathers." In 1757 Frank declared to Bishop Dembowski of Kamenetz–Podolsk, "The Talmud pretends to be an interpretation of the Bible, but it is full of lies, baseness and opposition to the Torah itself."

In that year the Bishop of Kamenetz–Podolsk forced the Jewish community to participate in a "disputation" with the Frankists. One thousand copies of single tractates of the Talmud went up in flames. It was ironic that Jewry, for whom apostasy was anathema, would sigh with relief when Jacob Frank and his 600 followers embraced Christianity in February 1759.

Social Conditions

In Eastern Europe class divisions were clear-cut. The scholars had as little in common with the unlettered masses as the Polish nobles had with the peasantry. The scholars lived in a rarefied world of their own, a world of *tanna'im, amora'im,* and *geon'im. Halakhah* sharpened their intellect and the *aggadah* broadened their spiritual horizons.

Primarily, almost exclusively, they focused upon the study of talmudics and rabbinics. The philosopher Joseph Solomon ben Elijah Delmedigo points out that "the Jews of Poland are opposed to the sciences . . . The Lord hath no delight in the sharpened arrows of the grammarians nor in the measurements of the mathematicians and the calculations of the astronomers."[13] The words of the philosopher Solomon Maimon (1754–1800) echo this theme: "Talmudic scholarship constitutes the principal object of education among us. Wealth, physical beauty, accomplishments of any kind, though appreciated by the people, do not command the same claim on any office and honorary post in the community."[14]

At this time the power of the *Kehillah* was weakening. The reins were in the hands of a few wealthy oligarchs, who were indifferent to the wretched plight of the people. In *Yesod Yosef* ("Foundation of Joseph"), Rabbi Joseph of Dubno describes the late seventeenth-century scene:

> The leaders live in luxury and splendor and do not fear the burden of taxes and other communal levies. They impose heavy burdens upon others and lighten their own burdens. They take the lion's share of all honors and distinctions . . . and the congregation of God, the children of Abraham, Isaac and Jacob, are crushed and humiliated, left naked and barefoot by heavy taxes. The tax collectors come to their homes and cruelly extort payment and rob them of all they find. They are left without furniture and without any utensils and without clothing for wife and children. Everything is removed and sold to cover the taxes. The very straw is taken out from the beds of the poor, and they are left in the cold and rain, shivering and crying, each in his corner, husband, wife and children.[15]

The *Yishuvniks* (rural population) were at the mercy of the squires. "One never sees a smiling peasant in Poland," was an adage current at the time, and it applied equally to the Jews in the Eastern provinces. Most of them were scattered throughout remote hamlets, far from the main centers of Jewish life.

Economic, Social, and Intellectual Restrictions

Social contact was restricted. The sexes were segregated. Adults prayed separately, and children played separately. Child marriages were common. It was not until 1761 that the Lithuanian Council forbade the marriage of boys under thirteen and girls under twelve. Under these circumstances the *shadkhan* (marriage broker) fulfilled a vital role. "Truth in advertising" was not a criterion and hyperbole was rampant. In vain Jonah Landsofer, a seventeenth-century writer, pleaded, "Whenever you are arranging a marriage between two parties never exaggerate, but always tell the truth."[16] The Hebrew word for *shadkhan* was taken as an acrostic of the phrase *sheker dover, kesef notel* ("though speaking falsely, he takes money"). The Polish Council fixed the commission at 2.5 percent of the dowry in a local marriage, and at 3 percent if the bride and groom had lived more than forty-five miles apart.

The rabbi in Poland was a salaried official. There was little real communication between him and his congregants. He advised them on ritual matters, but was far removed from the material problems that plagued them. It was rare for the rabbi to preach, except on such key occasions as *Shabbat HaGadol* (the Sabbath before Passover) and *Shabbat Shuvah* (the Sabbath before the Day of Atonement). At such times he usually delivered a *pilpul* (dialectical discourse) on some abstruse talmudic passage, or he would attempt to reconcile two conflicting exegetical statements. "They make it their custom to display the subtleties of their learning and their hair-splitting casuistries," complained Rabbi Jacob Joseph of Polonnoye. Fellow scholars may have been spellbound, but the masses were unimpressed. "Everyone is hungry for power," testified Rabbi Jacob Joseph sadly, "and everyone cries out, 'I want to rule, for I am a scholar.' "[17] It was not until much later that the masterly *maggidim* (popular preachers) arose, men like Rabbi Jacob Krants, the *Dubner Maggid,* whose discourses stimulated, enlightened, and even entertained attentive multitudes.

An Unschooled, Superstitious Folk

In the eighteenth century only a very small minority was privileged to attend a *yeshivah.* For the great majority, the sole source of instruction was the *heder* or the *Talmud Torah,* where instructors were not of the highest caliber. Solomon Maimon offers this description of the *heder:*

> The school is a small and smoky hut, and the children are scattered, some on benches, some on the bare earth. The master, in a dirty blouse, sits at the table, holding between his knees a bowl in which he grinds tobacco into snuff with a huge pestle like the club of Hercules, whilst at the same time he wields his authority. . . . Here the children are imprisoned from morning to night without an hour for themselves, except on Friday and half-holidays and on the New Moon.[18]

Rabbi Jacob Joseph of Polonnoye censures the teachers in similar terms: "They find it more profitable to flatter and amuse the parents than to teach the children," he lamented.[19] So the Torah was a closed book to most of the country folk. Superstition was rife in Podolia and Volhynia, where the massacres were still fresh in the minds of men, bewildered by the smoldering trails of the pseudo-messiahs. "There is no country," it was said, "where the Jews are as much given to mystical fancies, devil-hunting, talismans, and exorcisms of evil spirits as they are in Poland."[19] Some believed in the power of amulets (*kami'ot);* others believed in magic. Stories of devils and *dibbukim* (disembodied spirits of the dead that entered the bodies of the living) were current. "The masses," records Rabbi Moses Isserles, "have taken to the study of the *Kabbalah.* Students of *Kabbalah* include simple men who do not know their right hand from their left hand, people who live in darkness and cannot explain the meaning of the weekly portion of the Torah or understand a passage of Rashi."[20]

Rabbi Isaiah Horowitz and Nathan Nata Spira (1584–1633), author of the Kabbalistic work *Megalleh Amukkot* ("Revealer of Hidden Matters"), were the torch-bearers of *Kabbalah* in Eastern Europe. And so highly was *Kabbalah* esteemed, that Rabbi Joel Serkes declared: "He who denies the truth of the wisdom of *Kabbalah* is called a heretic." People avidly read the ethical book *Kav HaYashar* ("Measure of Righteousness") by Rabbi Tzvi Hirsch Kaidanover (1654–1712), with its stories of demons and *gilgulim* (wandering souls). "Oh, man," warns the author, "were thou to know how many demons thirst for thy blood, thou wouldst abandon thyself entirely, with heart and soul, to Almighty God."

Among the people wandered *baalei shem* ("Masters of the Name"), itinerant teachers who seemed to perform miracles, heal the sick, and drive out *dibbukim* by means of the Divine Name. Such men were Elijah ben Judah of Chelm (1514–1583), Elijah ben Moses Ashkenazi Loanz of Worms (1555–1636), Joel ben Isaac Heilprin of Ostrog (mid-seventeenth century), and Seckel Loeb Wormser (1768–1847), the Baal Shem of Michelstadt.

Simultaneous Awakenings

The eighteenth century was known as the Age of Enlightenment, a period in Western civilization when traditional concepts concerning the nature of man and society were being scrutinized, challenged, and reappraised. The European mind was dominated by man's belief in himself. In a humanistic framework, man divorced the Creation from the Creator and saw himself in control of the Universe. Yet this same era saw the rise of Methodism and Christian pietism as well as Hasidism. The Pietist movement in Germany, led by Count Ludwig von Zinzerdorf (1700–1760), was specifically an antirationalist reaction, and similar developments took place in other countries. The Polish Socinians, anti-Trinitarians of the sixteenth and seventeenth centuries, fought for the simplification of dogma as well as for social justice. At the same time, the Quakers in England and the Moravians in Central Europe stressed inwardness as the key to faith.

The Jews of Podolia, Volhynia, and Moldavia were surrounded by a sea of hatred, and the sky was darkened by clouds of medieval superstition. They needed a guide to lead them through the maze of misery, to comfort and to strengthen them. In answer to this need, the Baal Shem Tov arose and walked the earth.

Chapter 3

The Master of the Good Name

More legends have been woven around Rabbi Israel Baal Shem Tov, "Master of the Good Name," than around Moses, father of the Prophets. Only 200 years have passed since his death, yet he seems to belong to antiquity. Fact and fable are so intertwined that biographers find it difficult to distinguish between them. So it happens that despite the lack of authentic data regarding his parentage and personal life, the picture of the Baal Shem Tov (known by his acronym: the Besht) is both colorful and convincing, for we see him clearly through the eyes of his disciples.

Israel was born in 1698 or 1700 in Okopy,[1] a small town near Kamenetz on the borders of Podolia and Moldavia. For a time (1672–1698), Podolia belonged to Turkey. Later, under the terms of the Treaty of Carlowitz, it was returned to Poland.

Hasidic tradition records that Israel's father, Eliezer, lived in captivity for many years. Yet, throughout his exile, he remained loyal to his religion and true to his wife. And so he was rewarded with a son who was destined to "enlighten the eyes of Israel."[2] Another legend offers a different version of Israel's birth: it relates that Eliezer's hospitality was proverbial, and that in the spirit of the Patriarch Abraham he received all men, the destitute, the unlettered, and the impious, with the same warmth that he extended to scholars. One day the host's lovingkindness was put to the test. In the guise of a mendicant bearing a staff and bundle, the Prophet Elijah appeared at Eliezer's door on the Sabbath day. Although this desecration of the Holy Sabbath must have grieved Eliezer sorely, he did not by word or deed betray his displeasure. On the contrary, he took special care to make his guest feel at home. "Because you did not put a sinner to shame," Elijah assured his forbearing host, "you will father a son who will be a light to the House of Israel."[3]

His Early Years

Eliezer died when that beloved son was still very young. He left the small child few worldly possessions, but Israel was heir to his father's piety and wisdom. From his father he inherited a deep love of nature and genuine concern for his fellow man. "Always remember that the Lord is with you and therefore fear nothing, fear no one," were the dying words of the aged Eliezer. Israel often knew hunger, but he never knew fear, and he never felt alone. The *Shivhei HaBesht* ("In Praise of the Baal Shem Tov") records:

> And it came to pass, after the death of the Besht's father, that the lad grew up, and the Jews of the community dealt kindly with him because his father had been very dear to them. They therefore put him in the charge of a teacher for instruction, and he made rapid progress in his studies. It was a habit of his, however, to study for several days and then to run away from school. Then they would have to search for him and would find him sitting alone in the forest. They ascribed this to the fact that he was an orphan, and that he had no one to look after him and so had to make his own way in the world. They would, therefore, bring him back again to his teacher. And so it happened a number of times; he would run away to the woods in order to be alone until, finally, they lost interest and abandoned the plan of giving him to a teacher. And thus the lad grew up in an unusual manner.[4]

Meanwhile, Israel applied himself secretly to mystical studies, particularly to practical *Kabbalah.* The writings of Rabbi Isaac Luria and of Rabbi Hayim Vital became his *vade mecum.* Hasidic legend maintains that Israel even had access to the writings of the mysterious Kabbalist, Rabbi Adam, "whose identity has eluded all historians."[5]

A Beloved Teacher

Outwardly Israel lived an unremarkable life. Since he loved children, he became a *behelfer* (teacher's assistant) at Horodenka near Brody, and with kindness he controlled his little charges. No longer were the diminutive scholars dragged or forced to attend school. Every morning they sang as they followed their spirited leader to class. *Hasidim* say that this daily procession of singing children was as pleasing to the Almighty as the songs of the Levites in the Temple.

Later, Israel worked as a *shamash* (beadle) and *shohet* (ritual slaughterer). But it was as a patient and gentle teacher that he won the affection of the community. They even asked him to settle local disputes, for he was by nature a peacemaker; and it was in the course of an arbitration that he met Rabbi Efraim Kutower of Brody, who happened to be passing through Horodenka. A shrewd judge of character, Rabbi Efraim offered the youthful adjudicator his daughter Hannah in marriage. Israel readily accepted, with the provision that the betrothal be kept secret and that he be referred to in the betrothal document as "Israel ben Eliezer." But Rabbi Efraim died before he reached home, and the betrothal document baffled the prospective bride, since it contained no clue as to the whereabouts or identity of the bridegroom.

Later, when Israel arrived to claim his bride, the bride's brother, Abraham Gershon, a well-known Kabbalist and member of the *beit din,*[6] whom Rabbi Jonathan Eibeschütz called "the pious rabbi,"[7] was somewhat less than enthusiastic. His prospective brother-in-law seemed uncultured and uncouth. However, he could not persuade his sister to annul the betrothal. "Since our dear father made this arrangement," Hannah insisted, "we need not hesitate. Surely this is the will of God."

Earning the Title "Baal Shem Tov"

After the marriage, Rabbi Gershon attempted to "educate" Israel, but his attempts were not very successful. To end the increasing friction, the newly-wedded couple left Brody. Israel then spent a number of years in seclusion in mystical study and meditation. For him the vast and solitary grandeur of the Carpathian

Mountains reflected the power and glory of the Creator. *Hasidim* relate that Israel's teacher at that time was none other than Ahijah the Shilonite, prophet during the reign of Solomon and teacher of Elijah (I Kings 11:29). There is no evidence that Israel ever received rabbinical ordination. Nature, however, endowed him with qualities that more than compensated for the lack of formal qualifications. He also acquired a useful knowledge of the healing qualities of various herbs, and people began to come to him for medical advice. By 1736 he was known as Baal Shem Tov ("The Master of the Good Name") or by the acronym "Besht."

At first, the Besht followed the pattern of the wandering wonder-workers who wrote *kami'ot* (amulets), exorcised demons, prescribed *segulot* (magical healing aids), and healed the sick. But soon he began to chart his own highly individual course.

After a short stay at Tluste (in Eastern Galicia), Rabbi Israel settled in Medzibozh, near Brody in Podolia, and rarely visited outlying communities. Now he was able to concentrate on propounding his principles and setting them into practice. In context, some of these doctrines were little short of revolutionary.

Returning Kabbalah *to the People*

It must be stressed that *Kabbalah* is a double-edged weapon, dangerous in the hands of charlatans and megalomaniacs. Its theories are often esoteric and its doctrines complex and obscure. Inevitably, *Kabbalah* had become the jealously guarded province of an intellectual élite, who revelled in its mind-intoxicating and mind-illuminating profundities. This was the rich inheritance that the Besht wished to share with the masses. He believed that all the Children of Israel were entitled to enter the spiritual kingdom, and he threw open the heavy gates. It was not enough that this knowledge be available. It had to be intelligible. The privilege of the few had to become the prerogative of the many. Just as the "dry bones" in Ezekiel's vision were restored to life, so the Besht fashioned *kabbalistic* abstractions into a living reality.

The Beliefs and Purposes of the Besht

The fame of the Besht spread far and wide. Even his brother-in-law, formerly so hostile, became a devoted follower. For three years before his departure to the Holy Land, Rabbi Gershon lived in Medzibozh, and was a close companion of the Besht. For a time he even taught Tzvi, Israel's only son. In a letter written to his brother-in-law in the Holy Land, the Besht makes this startling revelation:

> On *Rosh Hashanah* (The New Year) 1747, I experienced an uplifting of the soul and I asked the Messiah, "Let me know, Master, when thou wilt appear on earth," and the reply was: "This shall be a sign unto thee, when thy teachings shall become known . . . when all other men shall have the power of performing the same mysteries as thyself, then shall all impurity disappear, and the time of great favor and salvation shall arrive."[8]

"I have come into this world," maintained the Besht, "to show man how to live by three precepts: love of God, love of Israel, and love of the Torah." According to the Besht, there are no divisions between the sacred and the secular, and there are no veils between Man and his Creator. A man's every act must reflect the worship of the Creator (*avodat HaBorei*). The verse, "I place God before me always" (Psalms 16:8) served as the Besht's guiding principle. The *Shekhinah* permeates all four orders: inanimate things, plants, and living creatures as well as man. God revealed himself to Moses in a bush of thorns as proof that His radiance might be glimpsed anywhere and everywhere. For those who have eyes to see, the world is a mirror reflecting the glory of God.

The Besht in Contrast with Spinoza

The Besht has often been described as a pantheist. However, the pantheism of the Besht had little in common with the pantheism of Benedict Spinoza (1632–1677). Spinoza died thirty-two years before the Besht was born, and the Besht was probably unaware of his existence. Yet it is interesting to compare their antithetical viewpoints. Spinoza believed in *Deus sive Natura,* the oneness of God and nature. He rejected traditional views of the nature of prophecy, the miracles, and the Divine origin of the Torah. To Spinoza, God is immanent. To the Besht, He is both immanent and transcendent. Spinoza sees a world without a purpose. The

Besht sees a world created to fulfill the Divine plan. Spinoza's God dwells in the world. The Besht's world dwells in God. For the Besht, God, whom the sages call *HaMakom* ("The Place"), is the place of the world and the world is part of His essence. Martin Buber elucidates these opposing beliefs:

> Spinoza's world is a world which goes on existing beyond the life which the individual man or woman has lived and beyond the death which the individual man or woman is going to die. . . . The hasidic world is the concept of a world as it is in this moment of a person's life; it is a world ready to be a sacrament, ready to carry out a real act of redemption.[9]

Far from being a casuistic philosopher, the Besht was not concerned with speculative metaphysics. He spoke directly to the masses in a language they understood, and he taught them what may be called "practical piety." Of course, his teachings were not novel, but his methods were. The anecdote, the parable, the metaphor, and the aphorism took the place of *pilpul* (dialectics), appealing to the heart as well as to the mind. Not since the development of *aggadah* and *midrashim* had the "story" been given such importance. To speak of the Baal Shem Tov is to speak in stories and legends that glow like beacons in the darkness.

A Rejection of Sadness

Although he was a child of the *Kabbalah,* the Besht rejected its asceticism. In his eyes, self-mortification was devised by Satan to afflict man both physically and spiritually. "The body must be strong for the worship of the Lord: therefore one must not weaken the body."[10] The Besht admonished his disciple, Rabbi Jacob Joseph of Polonnoye in this regard.

The Importance of Joy

Joy was the keynote of the Besht's philosophy. He wrote, "our Father in Heaven hates sadness and rejoices when His children are joyful. And when are His children joyful? When they carry out His

Commandments."[11] This immediate, worldly joy is the true reward, the greatest reward, for the performance of a good deed and the fulfillment of a commandment (*mitzvah*). Rewards to be received in the world to come are incidental, for a *mitzvah* should be performed for its own sake. Tears of joy are permitted and are even desirable. In contrast, a man should subdue sadness and raise himself to the higher realms of joy. Should a man err, he is urged not to brood over his transgression, lest he sink further into a morass of melancholy. He should demonstrate the sincerity of his repentance by returning instantly, and with renewed ardor, to the service of God. He should understand that the evil impulse (*yetzer hara*) and the good impulse (*yetzer hatov*) were created at the same time. God can be served by the evil impulse if the flame is directed toward Him.

Prayer

The Besht maintained that the secrets of the Upper World were revealed to him not because of the intensity of his studies but because of the intensity of his prayers. For man must pour his very essence into every word, into every God-directed thought. Prayer is part of the *Shekhinah,* which may be why the *Shekhinah* itself is called prayer.

But how can a man divest himself of the distracting influences and desires that constantly assail him? Song and dance are potent aids. For a man is like a ladder, his feet are on the ground but his head can reach the heavens.[12] Through *bittul hayesh* (negation of existence) man can rise above himself. Even *mahashavot zarot* (unworthy thoughts) can be harnessed to Godly purpose. When Rabbi Israel prayed, it seemed that all Creation listened in awe. His son Tzvi related that his father once appeared to him in the shape of a burning mountain. "Why do you appear to me in this form?" inquired Tzvi. "In this form I serve the Lord," was the reply. On another occasion, the Besht refused to enter a house of worship. "I cannot go in; the sanctuary is crowded with prayers," declared the Rabbi, standing on the threshold. He explained to his puzzled listeners that "the prayers have been recited in a lifeless and mechanical manner. They have no wings with which to fly upwards to the higher spheres. Those poor prayers, lifeless, fill every corner of this House of God. So you see, there is no room for me to enter."

Worshipping with spontaneity was more important than worshipping at prescribed times. *Hitlahavut* (enthusiasm) and ecstasy replaced formalism. The verse, "All my bones say, Lord who is like unto thee!" (Psalms 35:10) was taken literally, and when *hasidim* communed with their Heavenly Father it seemed as if every fiber of their being was actively involved.

The Good in Every Jew

In every Jew Israel perceived a spark of holiness, though it was sometimes dormant. He looked upon his people with boundless love and compassion. Rabbi Israel once told a friend, "I believe that I love the most sinful member of the House of Israel more than you love your only son." For the Besht evil did not exist. "What shall I do with my son, he is so wicked?" asked a despairing father. "Love him all the more," was the characteristic counsel of the Besht.

Wherever he went the Besht sought the straying lambs, fearful lest a single sheep be lost from the fold. He believed that "God dwelleth with them in the midst of their uncleanliness." The Besht deeply lamented the apostasy of the Frankists. "I hear the *Shekhinah* grieving and mourning," he once said. Yet he refused to give up the hope of their ultimate return to Judaism. "As long as the limb is attached to the body, there is still hope that it will be healed. But after the limb is amputated, then everything is lost. Every member of the House of Israel is a limb of the *Shekhinah*."

Descriptions of hell and its horrors, "fire and brimstone," were the stock in trade of many *maggidim* (itinerant preachers), whose harsh castigations he forthrightly condemned. "Woe unto those," the Besht declared, "who dare to speak evil of Israel. Dost thou not know that every Jew, when he utters even a brief prayer at the close of day, is performing a great work before which the very angels in heaven bow down in homage." Reprimands were not the way of the Besht. "God does not look on the evil side," he explained, "how dare I do so?"

The Role of the Tzaddik

The Besht was the prototype for the *tzaddikim* who were to play so unique a role in Hasidism. Martin Buber explains the *tzaddik*'s task:

> A helper is needed, a helper for both body and soul. He can heal both the ailing body and the ailing soul, for we know how one is bound up with the other, and his knowledge gives him the power to influence both. It is he who can teach you to conduct your affairs so that your soul remains free, and he can teach you to strengthen your soul, to keep steadfast beneath the blows of destiny. . . . The *tzaddik* must make communication with God easier for his *hasidim,* but he cannot take their place. . . . The *tzaddik* strengthens his *hasid* in the hours of doubting, but he does not infiltrate him with truth. He only helps him to conquer and reconquer it for himself. . . . He develops the *hasid's* own power for right prayer. He teaches him how to give the words of prayer the right direction, and he joins his own prayer to that of his disciple, and therefore lends him courage, strengthening his wings.[13]

A ceaseless striving for communion with the Creator, a constant cleaving to the Divine, is known as *devekut,* and this is the focus of the *tzaddik's* life. Even seemingly ordinary conversations are conducted in such a way that the *devekut* is not disrupted. When he is performing a *mitzvah,* his absorption in the actual deed does not lessen his consciousness of its true purpose and ultimate end, the glorification of God. *Hasidim* were convinced that the *tzaddik* could bring earth closer to heaven, that his power was unlimited, that he could even abrogate evil decrees.

The Real Value of Study

It is a popular misconception that the Besht disapproved of study. The fact is that he put a different emphasis on study. It was not simply an intellectual exercise. He believed that the Torah, the living words of the Most High, should transform the student, for man "must study the Torah to become a Torah." In the words of the *Mishnah,* it should "clothe him in meekness and reverence; it fits him to become just, pious, upright, and faithful; it keeps him from sin, and brings him near to virtue."[14] *Kavanah* (sincerity) and *hitlahavut* (enthusiasm) were as essential in study as in prayer. Humility was important too, and the scholar must guard against intellectual pride. The Besht's comments on the Torah were penetrating, and his knowledge of Talmud and *Kabbalah* was equally impressive. According to legend, Rabbi Israel was one of the three scholars who participated in the public disputation between the Frankists and the rabbis that was held in Kamenetz-Podolsk in 1757. "They shall not take the Torah from us," he exclaimed, "for without it how shall we survive among the nations?" Yet, as we have noted, Rabbi Israel did not spend his boyhood in *yeshivot* (talmudical colleges), nor did he write learned books. This was the task of his successors, who faithfully recorded the words and deeds of their master. This was a man with rare qualities of mind and soul, with profound sensitivity and vision.

In Praise of the Baal Shem Tov

Rabbi Israel exercised great influence over his followers. No one could meet him without falling under the spell of his unique personality. His disciples loved him, revered him, and all but worshipped him. "If he had lived in the time of the Prophets, he would have became a prophet," Rabbi Leib Sarah's, a contemporary of Rabbi Israel, averred: "If he had lived in the age of the Patriarchs, he would have ranked with them, so that just as one says, 'God of Abraham, God of Isaac and God of Jacob,' one would also say 'God of Israel.'" The Besht's devoted disciple, Rabbi Meir Margolies (d. 1790) testified, "All secrets were revealed to him."

The kindest and most approachable of men, the Besht won the hearts of the poor and the humble. He communicated on equal terms with Rabbi Dov Baer, the learned *Maggid* of Mezhirech and with the scholarly Rabbi Jacob Joseph Katz of Polonnoye, but he was equally at home with a cobbler who could neither read nor write. Just as the codifiers, Rabbi Moses ben Maimon, Rabbi Joseph Karo and Rabbi Asher ben Jehiel systematized the Oral Law and rendered it accessible, so the Master of the Good Name simplified *Kabbalah,* constructing a road along which all could travel safely.

The Death and Legacy of Rabbi Israel

On the 7th day of *Sivan* 1760,[15] the second day of *Shavuot,* Rabbi Israel died in the presence of his family and disciples. With joyful anticipation he went to meet his Maker. "I do not lament my fate," he said to comfort the mournful bystanders, "I know full well that I shall leave through one door and enter through another. . . . Let not the foot of pride overtake me." With this verse from the Book of Psalms (36:12) on his lips, he was gathered to his fathers.

"In Praise of the Baal Shem Tov" (*Shivhei HaBesht*) was first published in 1815 in Kopyss and Berdichev. The work is comprised of legends collected by Baer ben Samuel, the son-in-law of the Besht's first scribe. A collection of the sayings of the Besht, *Keter Shem Tov* ("The Crown of a Good Name"), compiled by Aaron ben Tzvi Kohen of Opatow, was printed in Zolkiew in 1794. Important too among the works of the Besht, is *Tzavaat HaRibash* ("Testament of the Besht") and *Hanhagot Yesharot* ("Upright Rules of Conduct"). Compiled by Isaiah of Yanov and published in 1793, it has since appeared in twenty-six different editions and it summarized basic ideas of Hasidism.

In the eighteenth century, while scientists were demonstrating that the earth is not the center of the universe but simply a small planet revolving around the sun, the Besht maintained that humanity constituted the center of Creation. "Once in a thousand years," declared Rabbi Aaron of Karlin (1736–1772), "does a soul like that of the Besht descend into the world."

Chapter 4

The Magic Circle

So Hasidism took root, but it was a tender plant. At first the movement was local, confined mainly to Podolia, Volhynia, and Galicia. In order to spread its message to Poland and Lithuania, a new kind of leader was needed, for only a talmudist could influence the Jewish classicists. Fortunately, among the sixty-nine disciples that tradition ascribes to the Besht, there were many outstanding talmudic scholars, bound to their master by unbreakable bonds of love and loyalty.

The Besht's only daughter, Udel, was the mother of three children: Moses Hayim of Sudlikov (1748–1800), author of *Degel Mahneh Efraim* ("The Banner of the Camp of Efraim"), a source book of hasidic lore; Rabbi Barukh of Medzibozh (1757–1810), and Feiga, mother of Rabbi Nahman of Bratslav (1772–1811). Tzvi, the only son of the Besht, was of too retiring a disposition to be his father's spiritual heir. But the survival of Hasidism was more important to the Besht than the perpetuation of his own dynasty. Like Moses, his successor was a stranger not a son, and the "Joshua" of the Besht was Rabbi Dov Baer, *Maggid* of Mezhirech (Miedzyrzec). The son of a Hebrew teacher, Abraham Dov Baer was born in 1710 in Lukatsch, Volhynia. The boy showed great aptitude for learning, and he was soon sent to a *yeshivah* at Lvov, where he studied under Jacob Joshua ben Tzvi Hirsch Falk (1680–1756), author of *Penei Yehoshua,* a commentary on the Palestinian Talmud.

The Maggid *of Mezhirech*

Rabbi Dov Baer married the daughter of Rabbi Solomon Shakhna of Torchin where he eventually settled, and where he became first a teacher and then a preacher, a *maggid,* in Korets and Dubno. It was as a *maggid* that he became renowned, for he was both potent and persuasive. With vivid parables, he illuminated abstruse texts that suddenly became meaningful and relevant. A diligent student of *Kabbalah,* the *Maggid* rigidly adhered to ascetic Lurianic practices that gravely undermined his health.

The Heir of the Baal Shem Tov

From the Besht, Rabbi Dov Baer sought healing for his stricken body and received instead an elixir for his soul. His first visit was brief, but the second visit lasted six months. "Your interpretations are correct," the Besht told his new disciple, "but they lack inspiration." Dov Baer recognized the truth of this statement. Humbly, thirstily, the preacher of Dubno crouched at the feet of the Besht to listen and to learn. "He taught me the language of the birds and the trees. He revealed to me the secrets of the sages and the mystical meaning of many things," recorded Dov Baer with awe. "Once, while we were studying the *Maaseh Merkavah* (the narrative concerning Ezekiel's Divine Chariot), we heard mysterious thunder and perceived flashes of lightning that continued for nearly two hours. I was terrified, and I almost fainted."

The Master perceived that Dov Baer would be a suitable successor. After the death of the Besht the disciple assumed the mantle of leadership and settled in Mezhirech. "What can be done?" asked Rabbi Jacob Joseph, submitting to the inevitable, "since the day the Besht ascended to heaven, the Shekhinah has moved from Medzibozh to Mezhirech, and we are forced to bow our heads in obedience."

Rabbi Dov Baer not only inherited the mantle of the Besht, but also his master's love of Zion. For Rabbi Dov Baer, Zion was the spiritual center of the world. The *Shekhinah,* which accompanied the Jews into exile after the destruction of the Temple, had shared the tribulations of the children of Israel. Rabbi Dov Baer taught that one should not be totally preoccupied with one's own sufferings, for it should be remembered that the *Shekhinah,* too, suffers and yearns for redemption. He defined the connection between the *Shekhinah's* exile and the Jews' own:

> The role of the *tzaddik* is to help restore the *Shekhinah* to its original glory. Liberation from Egypt did not signify the end of bondage. As long as we are in exile, we are still in Egypt. Spiritual redemption and physical redemption are interwoven. We are all responsible for the exile and the fact that it has lasted so long. By purifying ourselves and overcoming our faults, we can hasten the redemption.

The Maggid's *Court*

Failing health restricted Dov Baer's travels and confined him mainly to Mezhirech, but what he was unable to do in person, he achieved through his disciples. His court was the center of a conclave of remarkable men, who later became the founders of distinguished dynasties. Seldom had so much talent been gathered in so small a town, for the *Maggid's* court was a college, a spiritual training ground for future hasidic leaders. From the Ukraine came Levi Isaac of Berdichev, Menahem Mendel of Vitebsk, Nahum of Chernobyl and Ze'ev Wolf of Zhitomir; from Lithuania came Aaron of Karlin, Shneur Zalman of Liozno (later of Liady) and Rabbi Hayim Heikel of Amdur.

Zealous endeavors to attain adherents was never a primary concern of Judaism but in their efforts to sway their fellow Jews, Hasidism became a "missionary movement." Rabbi Dov Baer's emissaries spread hasidic fervor to remote villages and far–flung townships throughout Poland and Lithuania. Solomon Maimon testifies to the success of these mystical missions and describes one such encounter:

> As I was quite captivated by this description, I begged the stranger to communicate to me some of these Divine teachings. He clapped his hands on his brow, as if he were waiting for inspiration from the Holy Spirit, and turned to me with solemn mien, his arms half-bared, which he brought into action somewhat like Corporal Trim, when he was reading

the sermon. Then he began as follows: 'Sing unto the Lord a new song; and his praise in the assembly of saints' (Psalms 149:1). Our teachers explained this verse in the following way. The attributes of God, the Perfect Being, must surpass by far the attributes of every finite being; and consequently His praise, as the expression of His attributes, must likewise surpass the praise of any other being. Till the present time, praising God consisted of ascribing to Him supernatural powers, such as discerning that which is concealed and foreseeing the future. Now, however, the hasidic rabbis are able to perform such supernatural actions themselves. Accordingly, it is necessary to find new praises that are applicable to God alone.[1]

Maimon then describes his own visit to the *Maggid:*

At last I arrived at Mezhirech, and, after having rested from my journey, I went to the house of the Master, under the impression that I would be introduced to him at once. I was told, however, that he could not speak to me at this time, but that I was invited to his table on the Sabbath along with the other strangers who had come to visit him. . . . Accordingly, on Sabbath, I went to this solemn meal, and found there a large number of respectable men who had come from various districts. At length, the awe-inspiring Master appeared clothed in white satin. Even his shoes and snuff box were white, this being among the Kabbalists the color of grace. He greeted every newcomer in turn. After the meal was over, the Master began to sing a melody awesome and inspiring. Then he placed his hand for some time upon his brow, and began to call upon such and such a person of such and such a place. Thus he called upon every newcomer by his own name and the name of his residence, which excited no little astonishment. Each recited, as he was called, some verse of the Holy Scripture. Thereupon the Master began to deliver a sermon for which the verses recited served as a text, so that, although they were disconnected, verses taken from different parts of the Holy Scripture, they were combined with as much skill as if they had been formed as a single whole. What was still more extraordinary, every one of the newcomers believed that he discovered, in that part of the sermon which was founded on his verse, something that had special reference to the facts of his own spiritual life. At this we were, of course, greatly amazed.[2]

The Passing of the Maggid *of Mezhirech*

For a short time the *Maggid* lived in Annopol, where he died on December 15, 1773, thirteen years after the Besht's passing. In his "Last Will and Testament" he wrote to his son: "For Heaven's sake, do not seclude yourself for solitary meditations more than once a month, but on that one day, do not speak even with members of your household. On the anniversary of my death, do not fast. On the contrary, you are to make a festive meal and give charity beyond the norm. When opponents provoke strife, remain silent and let God requite them."

The following words were inscribed on the *Maggid's* tombstone:

> Here lies concealed our Master, Guide and Teacher, Teacher of the whole Diaspora, that great luminary, Gaon in the Exoteric and Esoteric. No secret was hidden from him, the Divine Eagle, the Holy Light, a Man of Wonder, our Teacher and our Master Rabbi Dov Baer, son of Rabbi Abraham. His memory is for a blessing for the life of the world to come. He passed away on the year 5533, the 19th of *Kislev.*

He was survived by a son, Rabbi Abraham the *Malakh* ("the Angel"), who died on the 12th of *Tishri* 1776. Rabbi Abraham's teachings were published in *Hesed LeAvraham* (Czernowitz, 1851).

There are conflicting figures regarding the number of the *Maggid's* disciples: estimates range from thirty-nine to 300. By this time there were *hasidim* in many parts of the country, even in Vilna, the mitnagdic (anti-hasidic) stronghold.

The Contrast between Founder and Disciple

What the Besht had achieved through parable, the *Maggid* achieved through discourse. Like the Besht, he himself did not write books. His discourses were published by his disciple, Rabbi Solomon of Lutsk (d. 1813), in three volumes: *Maggid Devarav LeYaakov* ("He Declareth His Words Unto Jacob") also known as *Lekkutei Amarim* ("Collection of Sayings"), *Or Torah* ("Light of the Torah"), wherein he expounds on the weekly portions of the Pentateuch, and *Or Ha'emet* ("Light of Truth"). In these works, the *Maggid* explained his conception of the Deity, cosmology, and the role of the *tzaddik*. If the Besht was the soul of Hasidism, the *Maggid* was its body. He created the hasidic court. Unlike his master, who is reported to have visited at least fifty localities, the *Maggid* was homebound. Like the Besht, he taught that there is an element of the Divine in all human deeds or thoughts. One should be self-critical even when performing good deeds, scrutinizing one's actions for ulterior motives. One should pray not merely for one's own material needs, but also for the end of the sufferings of the *Shekhinah* in exile.

The *Maggid* developed further the hasidic concept of the *tzaddik*. He believed that the *tzaddik* could bring heaven and earth closer; that, unlike a cedar, mighty but barren, the *tzaddik* is as a palm tree that produces fruit and fills the air with fragrance. He also believed that in every human being there is a trace of Cain as well as of Abel.

The Conversion of Rabbi Jacob Joseph of Polonnoye

While the Besht gave birth to the movement and the *Maggid* developed and organized it, Rabbi Jacob Joseph Katz of Polonnoye formulated its literature.

Like the *Maggid*, he received a traditional Torah education. The descendant of such renowned scholars as Rabbi Samson ben Pesah of Ostropol (d. 1648); Rabbi Yom Tov Lipmann Heller (1579–1654), author of the commentary on the Mishnah *Tosefot Yom Tov* ("The Additions of Yom Tov"); and Joseph Katz, author of *Yesod Yosef*, the youthful Jacob Joseph was renowned for his mastery of both the Talmud and *Kabbalah*. He became rabbi in Sargorod, where he remained until 1748. Like the *Maggid*, he initially resisted the growing influence of the Besht. But finally he, too, entered the magic circle.

It is told that when the Besht once visited Sargorod, the entire community flocked to meet him. Rabbi Jacob Joseph was already in the synagogue awaiting the worshippers for morning service, but he waited in vain. When he sent the beadle to investigate, the messenger hurried to the marketplace and promptly forgot his mission, remaining to listen with the others. So Jacob Joseph prayed in exasperated solitude, finding it harder than usual to concentrate. Later he summoned the Besht and demanded, "Are you the one who disturbed the communal prayer?" "Your Excellency, I am the one," answered the Besht mildly, "but I entreat you not to be angry with me. Let me tell you a story. . . ." Rabbi Jacob Joseph listened to the words of the Master and many things became clear to him. Thereafter, he became a fervent disciple.

The sudden conversion to Hasidism of the revered rabbi of Sargorod was regarded with marked disfavor by the community. Rabbi Jacob Joseph was the first hasidic leader to suffer indignities, persecution, and even expulsion. He moved to rabbinic posts in Rashkov (1748–1752) and Nemirov (1752–1770) finally settling in Polonnoye (1770–1782).

The Besht and His "Yossele"

The Besht was aware of his new adherent's potential. "The Blessed One will thank me for finding Him a Yossele (little Joseph – an affectionate term) like this." On another occasion, he remarked: "All Jacob Joseph's works are pleasing to the Creator, Praised be His Name, and all his doings are in the Name of God."

Rabbi Jacob Joseph followed the practices of the Lurian Kabbalists. He fasted each day until nightfall, a habit he continued for five years. In the sixth year, during one of Rabbi Jacob Joseph's week-long fasts, the Besht heard a heavenly voice urging: "Hasten to your Jacob Joseph, otherwise he will die." The Besht rode with such speed that his good horse fell exhausted and died on the way. On arrival, the Besht caused his ascetic disciple to break his self-destroying fast: "My horse died on the road for your sake. Let this be an atonement for you."[3]

Rabbi Israel wrote to him in his effort to have Jacob Joseph cease this practice:

> Behold, I have received the letter composed by your unsullied hand and saw from its first two lines that his eminence believes

fasting necessary. This shocked me to my innermost soul. By the counsel of God and His *Shehkinah,* I order you not to bring yourself into this danger, for this way is dark and bitter and leads to depression and melancholy. The glory of God does not dwell where there is depression but where the joy in performing His *mitzvah* prevails. "Hide not thyself from thine own flesh" (Isaiah 58:7). God forbids unnecessary and excessive fasting. If you hearken to my words, God will be with you.

Unfortunately, few letters of the Besht have been preserved. But one of these rare letters expresses the Master's deep affection for his "Yossele." It opens with the salutation: "From the community of Medzibozh . . . to my beloved, beloved of my soul, the Rabbi, the great luminary, right-hand pillar, strong hammer, renowned in piety, perfect scholar, he who is full of wonder and works wonders, who is bound up in the chambers of my heart, more close to me than a brother–our teacher Joseph Hakohen."[4]

"Each day," records the *Shivhei HaBesht,* "Rabbi Jacob Joseph used to study wearing *tallit* and *tefillin.* Before eating, he would master seven pages of the Talmud. Not one night passed, winter or summer, weekday, Sabbath or holiday, that he did not rise at midnight to study. His study of Torah, his prayers and his holy acts were performed with such vigor that his very flesh trembled."

When Rabbi Israel Baal Shem Tov died in 1760, he was succeeded by Rabbi Dov Baer, the *Maggid* of Mezhirech. At first Jacob Joseph resented the successor, but he quickly came to acknowledge the wisdom of "our teacher, the *hasid* Dov Baer."

The Scholarly Works of Rabbi Jacob Joseph

After the death of the Besht, Rabbi Jacob Joseph devoted himself to writing, and he produced four monumental works. His first work *Toldot Yaakov Yosef* appeared both in Medzibozh and Korets in 1780. *Ben Porat Yosef* was first printed in Korets in 1781, *Tzafnat Pane'ah* in Lvov in 1782, and *Ketonet Passim* in Lvov in 1866. *Toldot Yaakov Yosef* appeared without any scholarly endorsements. "Because of preoccupation with the printing," wrote Rabbi Abraham Samson Katz, head of the *beit din* in Rashkov and Rabbi Abraham Dov Baer, head of the *beit din* in Chmelnick, "we have not been able to acquire *haskamot* (endorsements) from the great scholars of the land, but we are certain that all of them would express appreciation for this precious book." The *Toldot* is a commentary on the Torah and on the 613 Commandments.

Ben Porat Yosef is divided into two sections. The first part is a commentary on Genesis, and the second part contains responsa and discourses delivered on *Shabbat Shuvah* and *Shabbat Hagadol.* It also contains the letter that the Besht wrote to his brother-in-law, Rabbi Gershon of Kitov.

Tzofnat Pane'ah is a commentary on Exodus. In his writings, Rabbi Jacob Joseph quotes Rabbi Israel Baal Shem Tov 556 times, and he cites Rabbi Dov Baer, the *Maggid* of Mezhirech, fifty-seven times. In addition to the books that were published, Rabbi Jacob Joseph wrote a number of other works that have been lost. In his preface to the *Toldot,* he refers to "the preface of my *siddur.*" However, there is no trace of this *siddur.*

The keen intellect and phenomenal erudition of Rabbi Jacob Joseph enriched the movement. Myths gave way to perceptive homilies and illuminating *midrashim.* The Baal Shem Tov had brought *Kabbalah* to the hearts of the people, and his disciple opened the minds of the scholars to the profundities of Hasidism. Scrupulously, he acknowledged his debt to the Besht. The formula, "I heard from my master," or "I heard from my master of blessed memory," occurs numerous times in his writings.[5]

Protecting the Vineyard of the Lord

Patience and forbearance were not among his qualities. He believed that attack was the best form of defense, and to defend Hasidism it was necessary "to demolish the citadel of the rabbinate." He censured the rabbis severely, calling them the "little foxes who despoil the vineyard."[6] He chastised them for their sophistry, materialism, and inaccessibility. He considered them poor successors to the pious scholars of previous generations:

> In former times when men were engaged in piety and learning for their own sake and not for the sake of honors and rewards, the scholar would seek the company of the uneducated and would conduct himself with modesty and humility so as to

draw the plain folk nearer to their Father in Heaven; but it is not so in this generation when there is no bond of feeling and unity between the learned and their less cultivated brethren.[7]

Teachers were castigated by Rabbi Jacob Joseph for their lack of dedication.[8] Slaughterers were reproved for relying solely on technical knowledge of the laws of *shehitah.* Scholars were accused of pride and egotism: "Each one puffs up, saying: 'I shall rule. I am a greater scholar.' "

Who, then, could counterbalance the hypocrites, the sycophants, the false prophets, the "satyrs," the "demons in the vineyard of the Lord?" Why, the *tzaddik,* of course. He would serve as mediator between man and fellowman, as well as between God and man. For Jacob Joseph, as for the *Maggid,* the *tzaddik* was a medium through which the Creator works. His feet must be firmly rooted in reality, but, like Jacob's ladder, his thoughts must soar to the heights. Humility was essential, for he must walk and work in harmony with plain folk in order to set aflame their "holy sparks" and raise their spiritual status. The *tzaddik* resembled Abraham, who pleaded for the doomed cities of Sodom and Gomorrah. He was unlike Noah, who was indifferent to the fate of his generation and built an ark for himself and his family, without uttering a single prayer for the rest of the world.

Rabbi Jacob Joseph died in Polonnoye in 1782. He had added new dimensions to hasidic lore, and his works form a valuable guide to Jewish socio-religious life in the eighteenth century. From his prolific writings, the student can determine the hasidic attitude to almost any problem. The opponents of Hasidism burned his books, but *hasidim* revered them. Rabbi Phinehas of Korets declared, "There have never before been books like these in the world." A second hasidic scholar added similar words of praise: "Even in the days of the Messiah, there will not exist a mind like this."

Rabbi Phinehas of Korets

Among the many planets orbiting around the brilliance of Rabbi Israel Baal Shem Tov's sun was Rabbi Phinehas of Korets (Korzec). He was a descendant of Rabbi Nathan Nata Spira (1584–1633) who, in 1617, had been called to the rabbinate of

Krakow. The wealthy Rabbi Spira refused to accept a salary. He offered 252 interpretations of the prayer of Moses (Deuteronomy 3:23) under the title *Meggaleh Amukkot* (printed in Krakow in 1637 and in Fürth in 1691).

The son of Rabbi Abraham Abba, a learned Lithuanian rabbi, Rabbi Phinehas was born in Shklow in 1726. In addition to studying rabbinics, the young Phinehas applied himself with particular passion to mystical studies, and the *Zohar* became the light of his life. "The *Zohar*," stated Rabbi Phinehas, "has kept me alive. The exile is very painful for me to bear, and I can only find relief from it during the hours that I study the *Zohar*."[9] The *Zohar* was important to him because it had originated in the Holy Land and not in the Diaspora. "Be heedful," he urged his followers, "not to allow three days to pass without studying the *Zohar*," and he urged his *hasidim* to complete the study of the entire *Zohar* in the course of each year. He repeatedly thanked the Almighty that he had not been born prior to the discovery of the *Zohar*.

Rabbi Phinehas also diligently pondered the words of Rabbi Moses ben Jacob Cordovero, the *Remak* (1522–1570), author of *Pardes Rimmonim* (Krakow, 1591) and the works of Rabbi Isaac Luria. Another book that rarely left his desk was *Maggid Mesharim* on the Torah (printed in Lublin in 1646) by Rabbi Joseph Karo, containing the secrets divulged to the author on 135 occasions by his heavenly mentor, an angel (the *maggid*). Rabbi Phinehas was reluctant to accept a rabbinical post and lived in dire poverty. To earn a minimal livelihood, he taught children in the vicinity of Polonnoye. Eventually, he settled in Korets, a town in the Rovno district of the Ukraine. It was one of the oldest Jewish communities in Poland. Between 1766 and 1819 four Hebrew printing presses were established there, printing nearly 100 books, mostly works of *Kabbalah* and Hasidism. In Korets, Rabbi Phinehas came under the influence of Rabbi Isaac ben Joel Hakohen, author of the Kabbalistic work *Brit Kehunat Olam* (Lvov, 1848). Although Rabbi Phinehas later moved to Ostrog and Shepetovka, he remained known as "Rabbi Phinehas of Korets."

Rabbi Phinehas and the Besht

Rabbi Phinehas met Rabbi Israel Baal Shem Tov three times and these meetings changed his life. The Besht made him realize that self-deprivation was not the only path to the service of God. Unlike Rabbi Israel Baal Shem Tov, he would don his *tefillin* on the intermediate days of the Festivals, though without the customary benedictions. He believed that prayers should be recited at the prescribed times (*tefillah bezmano*).

Rabbi Phinehas favored Rabbi Jacob Joseph of Polonnoye as the successor of Rabbi Israel Baal Shem Tov. He greeted the writings of Rabbi Jacob Joseph as "Torah from the Garden of Eden," classifying them with the *Zohar* and the *Eitz Hayim* (Korets, 1784) by Rabbi Hayim Vital. Among Rabbi Phinehas' disciples were Rabbi Jacob Samson of Shepetovka, Rabbi Ze'ev Wolf of Zhitomir, Rabbi Aaron Samuel ben Naftali Hertz Hakohen and Rabbi Raphael of Bershad. His discourses were published in various collections: *Midrash Phinehas* (Bilgoray, 1931), *Pe'er La-yesharim* (Jerusalem, 1921), *Nofet Tzufim* (Lvov, 1864), *Geulat Yisrael* (Lvov, 1864), and *Likkutei Shoshanim* (Czernowitz, 1857). Many of his unpublished works are to be found in private and public collections in Jerusalem and in the Hebrew Union College Library in Cincinnati. His first wife, Treina, gave birth to two sons, Rabbi Meir and Rabbi Moses. When she died, he married Yuta who bore, in the course of time, two sons, Jacob Samson and Ezekiel, and one daughter, Reizel Sheindel.

Turbulent Times

During the years 1708–1770 the Haidemaks, lawless paramilitary bands violently disrupted Jewish life, reviving grim memories of the Chmielnicki massacres of the previous century. Jewish merchants traveling on the highways were robbed and murdered; Jewish tenant farmers living in isolated places were brutally assaulted. The onslaughts of these wild Ukrainian bands in the provinces of Kiev and Podolia culminated in the Uman massacres on June 19, 1768. According to some authorities, the number of victims reached 20,000. The Jews in the entire southern part of Poland were seized with terror and many fled the Ukraine. Rabbi Phinehas urged them to remain in their homes. "Were it not for me," he later asserted, "not one Jew would have remained there." The revolt was ultimately suppressed by Russian and Polish troops under the command of General Ksawery Branicki, and a special prayer was composed in his honor.

Rabbi Phinehas followed political developments closely and grieved over the disintegration of the Polish State. Throughout his life, he prayed for the continuance of Poland. "I am not strong enough," he once remarked, "to prevent the danger. As long as Rabbi Nahman of Horodenka was there, this nation (i.e., the Russians) could not cross the river Dnieper. When Rabbi Nahman, however, crossed the river Dniester (on his way to the Holy Land), I remained alone, for only Rabbi Nahman of Horodenka was mighty enough to prevent this disaster."[10] Rabbi Phinehas despised the Russians whom he regarded as "mice" and felt that they "do not know the meaning of truth."

Rabbi Phinehas did live to see the First Partition of Poland. In August of 1772, Poland's three neighbors, Russia, Prussia, and Austria entered into an agreement and proceeded immediately to occupy the provinces that they had allocated to themselves. Russia's share was the most extensive, comprising all that still remained of the Polish Republic beyond the Dvina and the Dnieper. Austria appropriated the whole of Galicia, and Frederick the Great obtained West Prussia. Rabbi Phinehas, together with the rabbi of Dworna, traveled extensively in an effort to collect money for Jews held in prison (*pidyon shevuyim*).

Charity, Truth, and Devotion to the Flock

When Rabbi Phinehas was told of the great misery among the needy, he listened, sunk in grief. Then he raised his head. "Let us draw God into the world," he cried, "and all need will be quenched. A prayer which is not spoken in the name of all Israel is no prayer at all." Commenting on Moses' prayer: "Let me go over I pray You, and see the good land" (Deuteronomy 3:25), Rabbi Phinehas remarked, "Moses said to God, 'I do not want to be like the ten spies who brought back an unfavorable report. I want to see only the good aspects.' " In order to have a constant reminder of the destruction of the Temple, he lived in a room that was virtually windowless.

He once told his *hasidim,* "I have found nothing more difficult in life than to overcome lying. It took me fourteen years. I broke every bone in my body, and at last I found salvation. For the sake of truth, I served twenty-one years: Seven years to find out what truth is, seven years to drive away falsehood, and seven years to absorb truth." Rabbi Phinehas had a high regard for music and song. Once, he said, "Lord of the Universe, if I could sing, I should not let You remain up above. I should pursue You with my song until You came down from Heaven and stayed with us on earth."

Rabbi Phinehas collected money for the support of the poor in the Holy Land, and in 1791 he himself set out on pilgrimage. However, he died on the journey. He did not get further than the Russian frontier at Shepetovka. Rabbi Phinehas felt that anyone who was in a position to settle in the Holy Land should do so. Yet, he understood why so many *tzaddikim* did not actually go: It was because the Diaspora still needed them. In this regard he said, "The areas near the King's residence do not need special protection. The presence of the King is sufficient. More distant places, however, are garrisoned with troops."

A fitting tribute to Rabbi Phinehas might include the following story:

> When Rabbi Israel Baal Shem Tov lay dying, his disciple Rabbi David of Ostrog asked him sadly: "Rabbi, how can you leave us alone?" Comfortingly, if cryptically, the Great Master replied: "The bear (i.e., Rabbi Dov Baer, the *Maggid* of Mezhirech) is in the woods and Phinehas is a sage."

Rabbi Isaac of Drohobycz

Among the outstanding personalities, contemporaries of Rabbi Israel Baal Shem Tov, who helped to disseminate the teachings of Hasidism during the eighteenth century was Rabbi Isaac of Drohobycz.[11]

Parentage and Ancestry

Rabbi Isaac was a descendant of Rabbi Isaac Hayon, author of *Appei Ravravi* (Krakow, 1591). Rabbi Uri of Strelisk maintained that "Rabbi Isaac of Drohobycz was the ninth generation of those who were endowed with the 'Holy Spirit' (*ruah hakodesh*).[12] Rabbi Joseph of Yampol went further in asserting that seventy-two generations of Rabbi Isaac's family were endowed with 'Divine Spirit.'"

Rabbi Isaac's father, Joseph Virnick, was renowned for his honesty. The Jews called him "Rabbi Joseph, the man of truth," while the gentiles described him as "prawdziwi" (true). According to legend, he traveled in the Holy Land toward the end of his life. When Rabbi Israel Baal Shem Tov set out on his abortive journey to the Holy Land, Rabbi Joseph wanted to join him, but was not allowed to do so by the Besht's companions. "You are heading for the Holy Land," Rabbi Joseph told the Besht, "but you will not reach it. You are preventing me from accompanying you, yet eventually I will get there." Rabbi Joseph's father, Rabbi Moses Pistin, rabbi of Swiercz in Galicia near Przemysl, died a martyr's death. Rabbi Isaac's most prized possession was the Pentateuch that his father sent him from the Holy Land inscribed, "For these do I cry, for my father, Rabbi Moses, who died as a martyr."

Rabbi Isaac's mother was known as "Yente the prophetess." Once, while she was sweeping the house, she recited the *Keddushah.* "I heard the Angels reciting *Keddushah,*" she later explained, "and so I too had to respond."

Personal Life

We know little about the personal life of Rabbi Isaac. He was probably born shortly before 1700. An excellent speaker, he is known as the *Maggid* of Drohobycz, where he lived for a number of years. An itinerant *maggid,* he often took up the wanderer's staff, traveling to Galicia, Volhynia, and even to Slutzk in Lithuania. He lived for a time in Brody, which was also the home of Rabbi Ezekiel ben Judah Landau (1713–1793), known as the *Noda BeYehudah,* who became rabbi in Prague in 1755. Rabbi Abraham Gershon of Kutov, brother-in-law of the Besht, was also living in Brody. Later, Rabbi Isaac lived in Ostrog (Ostraha), Volhynia, where he stayed in the home of the wealthy Rabbi Joseph (Yozfe), the rabbi of Ostraha. Rabbi Joseph built a two-story building, the ground floor serving as a synagogue and the upper floor as a *beit hamidrash.* He also supported a *kollel* for advanced students that produced outstanding rabbis and judges, among them Rabbi Isaac. Eventually Rabbi Isaac became *maggid* and *dayan* in Horochow, Volhynia.

Becoming a Hasid

Rabbi Isaac was often involved in controversy. At first, he was an opponent of the Besht. It was Rabbi Isaac's custom to fall asleep the moment he uttered the phrase, "In your hand, I commend my spirit." But one day he made a derogatory reference to the Besht, and on that day sleep eluded him. He then traveled to Medzibozh, the home of the Besht. The Besht greeted him with warmth and affection. "Peace be upon you, my master and teacher," said the Besht, "you have come a long way to ask forgiveness for having mocked me. I forgive you wholeheartedly."[13]

The Besht believed that the support of Rabbi Isaac would strengthen the hasidic movement. He invited his visitor to a meal, and insisted on bringing the dishes to the table. "To serve Rabbi Isaac," said the Besht, "was like serving the High Priest in the Temple."

Rabbi Isaac at first opposed the amulets (*kami'ot*) prepared by the Besht and was reassured only when told that the only words inscribed were "Israel the son of Sarah." (Sarah was the name of the Besht's mother.) "What can I do?" the Besht said, "Rabbi Isaac is the *tzaddik* of this generation."[14]

On Prayer, Preaching, and Penitence

Once, when the daughter of Rabbi Joseph was very ill, the distraught father urged everyone to fast and pray for her recovery. Rabbi Isaac, however, ordered a festive meal. This conduct puzzled Rabbi Joseph. Rabbi Isaac explained: "If I were to fast, it would not be unusual. But the fact that I am having a festive meal on an ordinary day will cause a commotion in the celestial spheres. This will give me an opportunity to pray for your daughter's speedy recovery."

Rabbi Isaac maintained that a preacher should consider three things before delivering a discourse: that the spirit of the Torah should permeate the soul of every listener, that the discourse should be for the benefit of the whole community, and that it should not be delivered unless the preacher had heard it from the Almighty Himself. Rabbi Isaac would say,

> When I am setting out to preach in different communities, the Evil Angel comes to me and says: 'Isaac, you had better stay at

> home and study Torah. Why do you want to dissipate your energy? Why do you want to neglect the study of the Torah?' I reply, 'I am only going to preach in order to make money.' The Evil Inclination then leaves me alone. However, the moment I begin to preach, I cast away all material considerations and concentrate on imbuing the audience with love of Torah and fear of the Almighty.[15]

Rabbi Isaac once remarked, "People usually become reconciled on the Eve of the Day of Atonement. This is not right. How can we bear a grudge against a fellow Jew for a whole year? How can we wait a whole year before making peace? Reconciliation should take place every day and not just on the Eve of the Day of Atonement." It is not surprising that Rabbi Isaac was highly esteemed by his contemporaries. Rabbi Israel Baal Shem Tov said of him, "Rabbi Isaac has a saintly soul. He was given a tiny soul, the tiniest soul in existence, but he stretched and expanded it to such an extent that it became almost tantamount to the soul of Rabbi Simon bar Yohai."

Rabbi Isaac died in 1768. His son was Rabbi Jehiel Michael of Zloczow (1731–1786), author of *Mayim Rabbim* and a disciple of Rabbi Dov Baer, the *Maggid* of Mezhirech.

Chapter 5

The Great Defender

"A noble and holy soul has descended into the world, and it shall be an eloquent advocate for the House of Israel." Rabbi Israel Baal Shem Tov is said to have greeted the birth of Rabbi Levi Isaac of Berdichev (1740–1809) with this prophetic proclamation. And the prophecy was fulfilled.[1]

Levi Isaac's Introduction to Hasidism

Levi Isaac was born in 1740 in Husakov near Przemysl in Galicia into a family renowned for scholarship. His mother, Soshe Sarah, was a descendant of Rabbi Samuel Edels (1555–1631). His father, Meir, was rabbi in Zamosc. From his early years, the boy showed a phenomenal aptitude for study. He studied in the nearby town of Jaroslav and soon he was known as a prodigy, the "illui of Jaroslav."[2]

Upon marriage to the daughter of Samuel Israel Peretz of Lubartow (near Lublin), he took up residence in his father-in-law's town. There he met scholars like Rabbi Joseph ben Meir Teomim (1727–1793), author of the *Peri Megadim,* a commentary on the codes *Orah Hayim* and *Yoreh De'ah.* It was there that he also came in contact with Rabbi Shmelke Horowitz of Nikolsburg (1726–1778), then rabbi in Richwal, who introduced Levi Isaac to the philosophy of Rabbi Israel Baal Shem Tov. Both Rabbi Shmelke and his brother Phinehas (1731–1805), who became rabbi in Frankfort-on-Main, were remarkable men and devoted followers of the *Maggid* of Mezhirech. Rabbi Shmelke was noted for his singular religious devotion. To guard against oversleeping, he would endeavor to choose the most uncomfortable sleeping positions. He often sat upright with his head resting on his arms, a lighted candle in his hand. When it burned low, the heat of the flame would wake him, and he would instantly resume his studies. His prayers were often impassioned improvisations. "Alas, Lord of the Universe!" he exclaimed one New Year's Day, "all the people cry out to you, but what of all their clamor! They think only of their own needs, and do not lament the exile of Your glory!"

In 1778, while on his death bed Rabbi Shmelke confided to his disciples: "Today is the day of my death. You should know that the soul of the prophet Samuel is within me. For this there are three outward signs: my name is Samuel, as his was; I am a Levite, as he was; and my life has lasted fifty-two years, as his did."

Rabbi Shmelke instilled in Levi Isaac a strong desire to meet the *Maggid* of Mezhirech. Levi Isaac's father-in-law, Israel Peretz, objected and placed many obstacles in his way to thwart his wishes. However, fate intervened and it was a reversal in the fortunes of Israel Peretz that ultimately led his son-in-law to the *Maggid* of Mezhirech: He had suffered severe financial losses and had fallen in arrears with his payments to the local squire. The official had Israel Peretz imprisoned in punishment. In order to effect his father-in-law's release, Levi Isaac traveled to various towns trying to raise redemption money. One of these journeys brought him to the *Maggid.* At once, a new world opened for the ardent young scholar, a world in which he felt immediately at home. Thereafter he frequently came to Dov Baer to drink deeply from the fountain of Hasidism.

At the age of 21, Rabbi Levi Isaac succeeded Rabbi Shmelke as rabbi in Richwal and shortly thereafter in 1771, he became rabbi of Zelechow. But fierce and mounting opposition to Hasidism forced him to leave. For a time he stayed with Rabbi Israel of Kozienice, and in 1775 he became rabbi in Pinsk,[3] Lithuania where he stayed for five years. In 1781, he took part in a notable debate at Praga, near Warsaw and forcefully defended Hasidism against his opponent, the fanatic *mitnagged* Rabbi Abraham Katzenellenbogen of Brest Litovsk.

In 1785 Levi Isaac finally found peace in Berdichev, "the

Jerusalem of Volhynia," where he lived for the rest of his life, loved and honored by that community. There he died on the 25th day of *Tishri* in 1809. It seemed to Rabbi Nahman of Bratslav that "the light of the world had been extinguished." Just as Vilna could not replace Elijah Gaon, so Berdichev could not replace Levi Isaac.

The "Righteous Defender"

Levi Isaac was a *meilitz yosher* ("righteous defender"), an advocate par excellence, a mediator who tempered justice with compassion. Suffering did not embitter this eternal optimist, who harbored a passionate belief in the inherent goodness of humanity. He certainly earned the title, the *Darbarimdiger* ("the merciful one"). With abundant and overwhelming love, he gazed upon his people. He could not behold "iniquity in Jacob nor perverseness in Israel" (Numbers 23:21). He regarded every member of the House of Israel as a letter in a *Sefer Torah* ("Scroll of the Law"), sacred and above reproach.

Even the most blatant transgressor was given the benefit of the doubt. When he happened to meet a young man eating in public on the Fast of *Tisha B'Av* (the anniversary of the day on which both the First and the Second Temples were destroyed) the rabbi asked him mildly, "Have you forgotten that today is the Ninth of *Av*? Or are you perhaps unaware that it is forbidden to eat on the Ninth of *Av*?" "I have not forgotten what day it is and I am well aware of the prohibition," answered the young man. "Possibly, my son, you are not in good health and have been advised by your doctor to eat?" the rabbi of Berdichev inquired further. "No, I am in excellent health," was the reply. "See, O Lord," exclaimed the sage with joy, "how admirable Your children are! Even when they transgress Your Commandments, they do not stoop to falsehood."

Observing a coachman clad in a *tallit* and *tefillin* (prayer shawl and phylacteries), reciting Psalms as he oiled the wheels of his wagon, the Rabbi of Berdichev's comment was in character: "How noble is this people that You have chosen. Even when they oil the wheels of their wagons, they are mindful of You and commune with You." When the rabbi overheard a thief bragging to confederates of the size of his haul, the rabbi murmured: "It is still a long time until *Selihot* (special penitential prayers recited from the Sunday before *Rosh Hashanah* until *Yom Kippur*), yet this man has already begun to confess his sins." To one inveterate evildoer, the rabbi confided: "I envy you, for if you would only repent and return wholeheartedly to the Almighty, a ray of light would stream forth from every one of your transgressions, and you would be altogether luminous."

It was only on behalf of the House of Israel that his anger was aroused. He fiercely defended the people against the itinerant *maggidim* who harangued and tormented them. Yet even this wrath was tempered. Once, in semihumorous fashion, he "explained" the situation: "Lord of the Universe! This poor *maggid* reviles and rebukes Your people, because that is how he earns his livelihood. Give him, I beg of You, his daily bread, so that it will no longer be necessary for him to defame Your holy people." It distressed him to hear another rabbi publicly admonish a congregant for worshipping in a hasty and seemingly indecorous manner. "It is wrong to criticize a Jew on such grounds," maintained the rabbi. "God will surely understand him, just as a loving mother understands the often unintelligible mumblings of her little child."[4]

The Advocate before the Heavenly Court

On the solemn Days of Judgment, *Rosh Hashanah* (the New Year) and *Yom Kippur* (the Day of Atonement), when the House of Israel was on trial before the Heavenly Court, Rabbi Levi Isaac prepared his case and presented it with the skill of an experienced lawyer. He was once asked, "Why do you say your prayers after the proper time?" He replied, "We have not heard that there is a clock in Heaven.[5] I, Levi Isaac, believe that each moment of the day a Jew should rise and proclaim that we have one God. He should worship the Lord at all times, not just when the clock tells us to."

He longed for the coming of the Messiah. At his granddaughter's engagement, he inserted in the betrothal contract the words, "The wedding will take place, God willing, in Jerusalem, the Holy City. However, if, God forbid , the Messiah should not come during the coming year, the wedding will take place in Berdichev."[6]

Like many great advocates, he would frequently use an anecdote to illustrate his argument. Sometimes he would call witnesses.

On the Day of Atonement, he once urged the town's humble tailor to speak up in front of the whole congregation; the man publicly made his confession: "I, Yankel, am a poor tailor who, to tell the truth, has not been too honest in his work. I have occasionally kept remnants of cloth that were left over, and I have occasionally missed the afternoon service. But You, O Lord, have taken away infants from their mothers, and mothers from their infants. Let us on this Day of Days, be quits. If you forgive me, then I will forgive you." At this the rabbi sighed: "Oh, Yankel, Yankel, why did you let God off so lightly?"

Levi Isaac's Relationship with God

Sometimes the rabbi took the offensive and even dared to question the very validity of the Heavenly Tribunal. "Do not our sages tell us that a childless person may not be appointed a member of the *Sanhedrin,* since he may be devoid of pity? How then are the Angels qualified to constitute a tribunal and to sit in judgment upon mortals?"[7]

A rare rapport seemed to exist between Rabbi Levi Isaac and his God, with whom he communed in terms of remarkable intimacy and warmth. His famous monologue, which has been set to music, reads as follows:

Good morning to you, Lord of the Universe.
I, Levi Isaac, son of Sarah of Berdichev,
Have come to You to plead on behalf of Your people Israel.
What have you against Your people Israel?
Why do you oppress Your people Israel?
No matter what happens, it is "Command the children of Israel"!
No matter what happens, it is "Speak to the children of Israel"!
Dear Father, I ask You, how many other peoples are there in the world?
Babylonians, Persians and Edomites among others.
The Germans – what do they say? "Our king is the king"!
The English – what do they say? "Our Sovereign is the Sovereign"!
And I, Levi Isaac, son of Sarah of Berdichev, say:
"Hallowed and magnified be the name of God"!
And I, Levi Isaac, son of Sarah of Berdichev, say:
Lo azuz mimkomi! I will not stir from here!

There must be an end to the sufferings of Your people Israel.
Hallowed and magnified be the Name of God.[8]

Israel's advocate would diligently seek evidence that could be used on his client's behalf. Once, on the eve of the Day of Atonement, he searched the streets for a Jewish drunkard: since Jews are specifically enjoined by the rabbis to eat and drink on the day before *Yom Kippur,* it might be expected that some would fulfill this particular precept with overenthusiasm and overindulgence. Yet not a single drunkard could be found in the entire town of Berdichev. The Rabbi marveled at the sobriety of his people and brought this astounding testimony to the attention of the Supreme Judge.[9]

"Master of the World," said Rabbi Levi Isaac, "look down from Heaven and see who is like unto Your people Israel, 'a kingdom of priests and a holy nation.' You have commanded us to eat and drink today before the fast. Indeed, is it not written, 'All who eat and drink on the ninth of Tishri will be counted as if they had fasted on the ninth and tenth'? If a commandment such as this had been given to other nations of the world, by the time evening came, many would be drunk, many would be rolling in the gutters, many would have bruises and pains. Not so Israel. This day they fulfilled Your command to eat and drink at specially prepared tables. And now while the sun still shines, they have all hastened here to the synagogue and none is drunk or asleep. They stand upon their feet, all holy and pure, all prepared to take upon themselves the hardships of the holy day to confess before You and to turn to You in truth and with a full heart. Surely, Your children are deserving of forgiveness for all their sins, of being inscribed and sealed for life, and of being granted a good year, a year of redemption."[10]

On the Day of Atonement, Rabbi Levi Isaac would present his heartfelt plea to the Almighty: "I have no strength to pray, but surely You have the strength to say, '*salahti* (I have forgiven).' "

Levi Isaac's Prayers and Poetry

Rabbi Levi Isaac composed many moving prayers. Among them is *Gott vun Avraham* ("God of Abraham"), a touching farewell to the Sabbath, that Jewish women took instantly to their hearts. In the soft Sabbath twilight, pausing on the threshold of a new week, hundreds of thousands of devout wives and mothers have recited these weighty words:

> God of Abraham, of Isaac and of Jacob, protect in love Your beloved people Israel from all evil for the sake of Your name. Now that this beloved Sabbath is departing, may the new week come to us with complete faith, with faith in the sages, with love for our fellow men, with attachment to the Creator, Blessed be He, so that we may truly believe in Your thirteen principles, in speedy redemption in our days, in the resurrection of the dead, and in the prophecy of our teacher Moses, peace be upon him. Lord of the World, Who gives strength to the weary, give strength also to Your dear Jewish children, who praise only You and who serve only You; so that the new week will come to us with health, with good fortune, with success, with blessing, with peace, with the gifts of children, life and sustenance, for us and for all Israel and let us say, Amen.[11]

Equally famous is the *Dudele* (the "You" song) based on the 139th Psalm:

> Master of the Universe,
> I will sing a song to You.
> Where will I find You?
> And where will I not find You?
> Where I go, there are You,
> Where I stay, there are You
> Only You, You only
> You again and only You
> When I am gladdened–You!
> And when I am saddened–You!
> Only You, everywhere You!
> You, You, You!
> Sky is You!
> Earth is You!
> You above! You below!
> In every trend, at every end
> Only You, everywhere You!
> You! You! You![12]

His prayer was full of ecstasy. When he was about to pour forth his prayers before the Almighty, he would tremble violently, in awe of the glory of the Lord. If he was praying in one corner of the room at the beginning of the service, he might well end his prayers in the opposite corner an hour later, without ever being aware that he had changed position. "When Rabbi Levi Isaac began his services and uttered the call to prayer, *borekhu* ("Bless you the Lord who is to be blessed")," a disciple Rabbi Samuel Kaminer reported, "he stood on the same rung of fervor as did the *Maharsha* (Rabbi Samuel Eliezer Edels, 1555–1631) when he composed one of his celebrated responsa."[13]

Rabbi Barukh of Medzibozh, the grandson of the Besht, once watched Rabbi Levi Isaac recite his prayers, and then remarked: "Rabbi Levi Isaac, my friend, if Aaron the High Priest had performed his service in such a manner when he kindled the lights of the *menorah,* surely he would have upset the oil and broken the *menorah* itself."[14]

"Flaming fervor (*Hitlahavut*) should pervade all our prayers," maintained the Rebbe. "Alas, in this generation, however, our transgressions have so weakened our spirits that we are unable to reach such a rung until half the service is over. But when the Messiah appears–may he come soon–it is written: The earth will be filled with the knowledge of the Lord as the waters cover the earth. Then shall we all able to begin our prayers with *Hitlahavut.*"[15]

Levi Isaac's Legacy

Rabbi Levi Isaac encouraged Hebrew printing in the Ukraine. During a period of thirteen years, Samuel, the son of Issahar Segal, printed twenty-eight books, each carrying the *haskamah* (endorsement) of either Rabbi Levi Isaac or one of his sons. Apart from Rabbi Abraham Joshua Heschel of Opatow, no other hasidic rebbe gave as many *haskamot* as Rabbi Levi Isaac. His son, Rabbi Meir, author of *Keter Torah* on Genesis (Mezirow, 1803) and on Exodus (Zhitomir, 1803) died in 1806. His grieving father wrote: "I returned his soul in the pure state I received it." His second son, Rabbi Israel, rabbi of Pikow, was the author of *Toldot Yitzhak ben Levi* (Berdichev, 1811), and his third son was Rabbi Dov Berish.

Levi Isaac was venerated by his contemporaries. Rabbi Abraham Joshua Heschel of Opatow described him as *rabbenu shel kol bnei hagolah* ("leader of all the children of exile"). Rabbi Levi Isaac was the first person to whom Rabbi Shneur Zalman of Liady wrote after his deliverance from prison in St. Petersburg in 1798. Rabbi Levi Isaac's disciples included Rabbi Aaron of Zhitomir, and Rabbi Abraham David of Butchatch, Moses of Savran, Yosef of Nemirow and Abraham Mordekai of Pinczow.

He wrote *Kedushat Levi,* which was first printed in Slavuta in 1798. It contains discourses on *Hanukkah* and *Purim* by his father as well as selected discourses by his sons Meir and Israel. The second edition was printed by his son in Berdichev in 1836. *Kedushat Levi Hashalem* (Jerusalem, 1964) contains 533 printed pages: discourses on the Torah, on Talmud, on Midrash, on the Ethics of the Fathers, and on festivals.

In *Kedushat Levi* the rabbi stresses the importance of inwardness and authenticity. "When we perform the *mitzvot* with great enthusiasm the Holy One blessed be He, plants in our hearts thereby the desire to do another, like a father, observing that his son has learned something new, asks him a further question on the basis of it. When a man craves wealth or fame, he should reason thus: 'If I have such a strong desire for things that are ephemeral, how much stronger should be my desire for God, who is eternal and the source of everlasting joy?' "[16]

When the time came for him to join his fathers, Rabbi Levi Isaac was prepared. Apparently, he even received a brief extension, for at the end of the Day of Atonement he told his community, "My life has now run its course, and I should be leaving the world at this very hour. Yet, since I grieved at not being able to fulfill the *mitzvah* of dwelling in a *sukkah* and reciting the benedictions over the *etrog,* I prayed that my time might be extended until after the Festival of Tabernacles, and our merciful Master granted my prayer."

A fitting epitaph for Rabbi Levi Isaac is that he loved God and he loved Judaism, but that the rabbi's love for his fellow Jews was his all-consuming passion. "Every day I set aside a time to thank our Heavenly Father," said Rabbi Jacob Isaac of Lublin, "for sending the world a soul as unique as Levi Isaac of Berdichev." "The Holy One Blessed be He is the *Tzaddik* in Heaven," remarked Rabbi Shneur Zalman of Liady, "but Rabbi Levi Isaac of Berdichev is the *tzaddik* on earth."

Chapter 6

The Wrath of Elijah

Elijah ben Solomon, the Gaon of Vilna (*Der Vilner Gaon*), has left a remarkable imprint on Jewish history. Although he spent most of his life within the "four ells of *halakhah*," he wielded extraordinary power as the greatest rabbinic authority of East European Jewry. Venerated by his contemporaries, he became a legend in his lifetime. By reason of his intellect and personality, he loomed like a colossus over the great men of his generation.

A Promise of Greatness

Legends and miracles were not a hasidic monopoly. Just as the *Shivhei HaBesht* ("In Praise of the Baal Shem Tov") weaves a garland of legends around the founder of Hasidism, so *Aliyot Eliyahu* ("The Ascent of Elijah") gathers together the stories that grew around the Gaon. Elijah was born on the first day of Passover, April 23, 1720, in Vilna or in nearby Seltz. A descendant of such renowned rabbis as Moses Kramer (d. 1688) and Moses Rivkes, Elijah was a prodigy in an age when *illuyim* (prodigies) were almost commonplace. He is reputed to have delivered a talmudic discourse of astounding profundity at the age of six and a half. One of his teachers was probably Moses Margolies, rabbi of Kaidan and commentator on the Palestinian Talmud (*Yerushalmi*). At a very early age Elijah married Hannah, daughter of Rabbi Judah Leib of Kaidan, and she bore him two sons, Aryeh Leib and Abraham.

When Elijah was about 20 years old, he began an incognito journey through Poland and Germany that lasted eight years. This act was part of a self-inflicted penance known as "going into exile" (*golut uprichten*). From Königsberg he wrote to his family a letter of such ethical content, that it was later published under the title *Alim Leterufah* ("Leaves for Healing"). The fatherly admonitions include the suggestion that his daughter should only recite her prayers at home. In the synagogue she might be distracted by the finery of her friends and envy them.

An Encyclopedic Knowledge

Elijah's capacity for study was almost superhuman. One of his maxims was: "In this world only those things that are acquired by hard labor and through struggle are of value." Unswervingly, without any deviation, he followed the path of the Torah. This was the sum total of his life, and to its study he dedicated mind, heart, and soul. His general knowledge was encyclopedic and his range of interest wide. In addition to Hebrew grammar, he also studied biology, astronomy, trigonometry, algebra, and medicine. Furthermore, he encouraged Barukh of Shklow (1740–1810) to translate into Hebrew the six books of Euclid's *Geometry*. "If one is ignorant of the secular sciences, one is a hundredfold more ignorant of the wisdom of the Torah," maintained the Gaon, "for the two are inseparable."[1]

The Gaon aimed at literal interpretation (*peshat*) rather than dialectics (*pilpul*). In this regard, it was said of him that "with a single shaft of the light of truth he would illumine the darkness, and with a single word could overthrow heaps of *pilpulim* hanging by a hair."[2] In his eulogy of the Gaon, Rabbi Abraham Danzig (1748–1820), author of *Hayei Adam* ("Human Life"), credited him with the authorship of seventy books,[3] among them commentaries on the Bible, The *Mishnah,* the Palestinian Talmud, *Sefer Yetzirah,* the *Zohar,* and the *Shulhan Arukh.* He also wrote critical notes on *tanna'itic midrashim,* as well as treatises on astronomy, trigonometry, algebra, and Hebrew grammar. Not all his works have seen the light of day, and many have been lost. A number of his manuscripts, including parts of the *Mishnah* commentary, have not been traced.

Almost a century before the *Jüdische Wissenschaft* (scientific inquiries into Jewish history, literature, and religion), the Gaon of Vilna was analyzing rabbinic texts with scientific skill, resolving problems that had baffled scholars for centuries. His intuition compensated for his lack of original manuscript material.

The Gaon declined a position of rabbi and lived on a small legacy from his great-great-grandfather, Moses Rivkes. Unlike the physician and scholar, Maimonides, whose days were occupied at the court of the Vizier Al-kadi al-Fadil, with private patients, and with communal affairs as well as with philosophic study and research, the Gaon lived in virtual isolation. When Jonathan Eibeschütz, rabbi of the three communities of Altona, Hamburg and Wandsbeck, was accused of Sabbateanism by Rabbi Jacob Emden, he applied to Elijah for support. But firmly and with humility, the Gaon remained aloof. "I wish I had wings like a dove. I would then fly to restore peace and quench the terrible flames of dissension. But who am I that people should listen to me?" the Gaon humbly replied. "If they ignore the instruction of their own rabbis and heads of holy congregations, how will they listen to the voice of an unknown person who lacks even the virtue of age?"[4]

Elijah's rather revolutionary advice to his disciples was, "Do not regard the views of the *Shulhan Arukh* as binding, if it is your opinion that they are not in agreement with those of the Talmud."[5] Nevertheless, the Gaon reflected the intolerance of his generation. When a *maskil,* Abba of Hlusk, commented that the authors of the *midrash* occasionally infringed upon the rules of grammar, Elijah would not let him go unpunished. "I was sentenced to forty strokes," writes Abba to Moses Mendelssohn. "I was led to the threshold of the synagogue and my neck was enclosed within the iron rings attached to the wall. . . . Everybody who had come for the afternoon service stopped and called to me: 'Traitor to Israel.' But even more, they nearly spat into my face."[6]

Hasidism's Bitter Enemy

It is one of the ironies of history that the Gaon, who was called "the *hasid*" and who was the author of works on mysticism, became one of the most bitter antagonists of Hasidism. Small hasidic groups had been established in Brest-Litovsk, Grodno, Troki, and Lutsk, and the fiery activities of Rabbi Aaron of Karlin (b. 1736) near Pinsk sent sparks flying far and wide. Some of these sparks reached Vilna. There, too, the "*Klaus* of the Karliner," headed by Rabbi Isser and Rabbi Hayim, was beginning to attract attention. It also drew the attention and roused the ire of Elijah who became its arch-opponent, the *mitnagged* of Hasidism. For more than two decades he waged a bitter battle against the upstart group.

Although firmly and faithfully rooted in Jewish tradition, Hasidism was in a sense a rival movement. It was not differences of principle but differences of practice that created discord and inevitably met strong opposition from the establishment. For instance, the *hasidim* adopted *nusah Ari,* the liturgy of the Kabbalist Isaac Luria, in preference to *minhag Ashkenaz,* the German–Polish ritual. Thus they had to establish their own houses of worship. The Gaon feared that such separatist tendencies would disrupt and demoralize the House of Israel.

Elijah Gaon insisted upon meticulous observance of the minutiae of all rabbinical laws and regulations. To him it was intolerable that some *hasidim* should disregard the prescribed hours of worship. He did not believe that *devekut* and *kavanot* could make up for belated services, and he remained unconvinced when the *Hasidim* reasoned, "Can a child be told when to approach his father?" Neither did he accept the thesis that spontaneity ranks higher than punctilious recitation.

The Gaon was deeply concerned with the conduct of synagogue services. He himself deleted many *piyyutim* (liturgical compositions) in order to shorten the lengthy services, and he encouraged communal singing. But he abhorred the undisciplined way in which many *hasidim* worshipped, swaying and dancing, singing, sighing, sobbing, or laughing as the mood seized them.

To the eyes of the unsympathetic outsider, the hasidic way of prayer appeared unusual, even strange. The philosopher Solomon Maimon reported:

> They are engaged in all sorts of mechanical operations, such as movements and cries to bring themselves back into the state of ecstasy once more, and to stay in that state without interruption during the whole time of their worship. It was amusing to observe how they often interrupted their prayers with all sorts of extraordinary tones and comical gestures, that were meant

> as threats and reproaches against their adversary, the Evil Spirit, who tried to disturb their devotion.[7]

To Maimon, the way of the *hasidim* was amusing. But the Gaon was not amused. To him this behavior was not only unseemly but utterly abhorrent. It is said that the *hasidim* in and around Vilna did, in deliberate defiance of their persecutors, conduct themselves somewhat indecorously: "They poured scorn on the students of the Torah and upon the learned, inflicting all manner of ridicule and shame on them, turning somersaults in the streets and marketplaces of Kalisk and Liozno, and generally permitting themselves all sorts of pranks and practical jokes in public."[8]

The Threat to the Survival of Judaism

Dr. Solomon Schechter describes the Gaon as *Der Ewige Student* (the perpetual student). For him the "Torah is to the soul of man what rain is to the soil."[9] To a man so dedicated to scholarship, no amount of Torah study could be adequate, let alone excessive, and in his eyes the criticism of intensive study expressed by some of the hasidic leaders threatened the very survival of Judaism. Neither the vast erudition of the *Maggid* nor the intellectual brilliance of Jacob Joseph of Polonnoye could allay Elijah's fear that "the Torah would be forgotten in Israel." He vehemently opposed the advice of the hasidic rabbis that "a man must not pass all his time in study," and he was probably in complete disagreement with the observation of the Besht that the "evil inclination (the *yetzer hara*) might persuade a man to concentrate upon the study of the Talmud and all its commentaries in order to prevent his following other studies which might lead him to the fear of God."[10]

In counterattack the hasidic leaders accused their rabbinic opponents of "exhibitionism, hypocrisy, sophistry, and learning not for the sake of Heaven." Rabbi Jacob Joseph let fly sharply-pointed arrows, and many were on target. "There are rabbis," he wrote, "who do not accept the Torah interpretations of another scholar but only their own, and when they hear the Torah of others, they pass it off as something of no interest."[11] Similarly, Rabbi Judah Leib, preacher of Polonnoye (d. 1770) and author of *Kol Aryeh*

("The Voice of a Lion"), censured the talmudists for their pride and intellectual arrogance. "They are wise, understanding, and God-fearing in their own estimation." These counterattacks were bitterly resented.

The cult of the *tzaddik* was also alien to the Gaon, for it produced a new type of teacher, whose powers stemmed from the heart rather than the head. His training ground was the court of his rabbi rather than the *yeshivah,* since knowledge was not the chief qualification of leadership. Discourses about *tzaddikim* took the place of discussions on the Talmud. Instead of poring over the tractates of the Talmud, instead of exploring the highways and the byways of Jewish Law, *hasidim* discussed with awe the miracles wrought by their wonder rabbis, and a rich new folklore sprang up. The eighteenth century saw the emergence of many remarkable rabbis. Many of the *tzaddikim* lived on a lofty spiritual plane to which they could raise their followers. Among them were such outstanding personalities as Rabbi Meir Margulies, Jehiel Michael of Zloczow, Ze'ev Wolf of Zbarazh and Mordecai of Nezhizh. Yet the Gaon of Vilna was neither able nor willing to concede that such men deserved recognition. For him they barely existed.

Mystic though he was, the Gaon failed to discern in Hasidism a new and momentous phase in the evolution of Jewish mysticism. In taking isolated thoughts out of context, the Gaon misunderstood and distorted them. "All accusations by the Gaon against the *Maggid,*" wrote a hasidic teacher, "based on quotations referring to God as residing in material things, are without foundation. These statements are not to be taken literally, for they are intended only to indicate the extent and intensity of God's providence."[12] The Gaon associated Hasidism with Sabbateanism and Frankism rather than with Lurian *Kabbalah.* Elijah's knowledge of hasidic doctrines and dogma came to him through indirect sources and were, therefore, frequently unreliable and invariably biased. To the Gaon, the acquisition of learning was an intellectual exercise; it had broadened his knowledge but not his outlook. He was intolerant of anyone whose views differed from his own. The forces against Hasidism were now marshalled under the banner of the Gaon and a *causus belli* was soon found.

In 1771 an epidemic broke out in Vilna and many children died. A scapegoat had to be found, and the community chose the *hasidim* for this role. The hasidic leaders were accused of "defaming the Gaon of Vilna," and the hasidic Rabbi Hayim was compelled to do public penance. He pleaded in vain with the Gaon for forgiveness. The Gaon would not relent. Rabbi Hayim was forced to leave Vilna, the hasidic synagogue was closed, Rabbi Isser was imprisoned and the following year hasidic works were burned. Harsh though these penalties were, the Gaon was still not content.

The Herem *of Vilna*

The *kehillah* of Vilna, with the consent of the Gaon, issued a *herem* against the "heretical sect." The *herem* (the decree of excommunication) was the most powerful weapon which the Jewish authorities possessed, and it was used primarily to maintain communal discipline. In a bygone age, when the synagogue was the center of the community, the mere threat of the *herem* would often subdue unruly elements. The strange ceremony, complete with the lighting of candles and sounding of the ram's horn, was designed to strike terror in the heart, and the recitation of the appropriate formula was as chilling as a death sentence.

The *herem* was widely used and by all accounts even more widely misused. It was not unheard of for scholars to invoke it against one another, and the rabbi who did not raise the threat against recalcitrants was the exception. The most celebrated cases of excommunication in the seventeenth century were those of the noted rationalist Uriel da Costa (1585–1640) and of the philosopher Benedict Spinoza (1632–1677), who was formally excommunicated on July 27, 1656, by the *Sephardic* community of Amsterdam. In eighteenth-century England, the *herem* helped enforce the *askamot* (the civil laws of the congregation).

The *herem* of Vilna was not merely against an individual, but against a whole movement. Even this mass excommunication of the *hasidim* did not satisfy the Gaon. "Had I the power," he declared, "I would have punished these infidels as the worshippers of Baal were punished of old."[13] A month after the proclamation of the *herem,* a letter was circulated through all the communities in Lithuania and White Russia:

> Our brethren in Israel, you are certainly already informed of the tidings whereof our fathers never dreamed, that a sect of

> the 'suspects' (*hashudim* instead of *hasidim*) has been formed . . . who meet together in separate groups and deviate in their prayers from the text valid for the whole people. . . . They are the same who, in the middle of the *Shemoneh Esrei* prayer, interject obnoxious alien words (Yiddish) in a loud voice, conduct themselves like madmen, and explain their behavior by saying that in their thoughts they soar into lofty worlds. . . . The study of the Torah is neglected by them entirely, and they do not hesitate to constantly emphasize that one should devote oneself as little as possible to learning and not grieve too much over a sin committed. . . . Every day is for them a holiday. . . . When they pray according to falsified texts, they raise such a din that the walls quake . . . and they turn over like wheels, with the head below and the legs above. . . . Therefore, do we now declare to our brethren in Israel, to those near as well as far. . . . All heads of the people shall robe themselves in the raiment of zeal, of zeal for the Lord of Hosts, to extirpate, to destroy, to outlaw, and to excommunicate them. We, here, have already, with the help of His name, brought their evil intention to nought; and as here, so should they everywhere be torn up by the roots. . . . Do not believe them even if they raise their voices to implore you . . . for in their hearts are all seven horrors. . . . So long as they do not make full atonement of their own accord, they should be scattered and driven away so that no two heretics remain together, for the disbanding of their associations is a boon for the world.[14]

The scribes of Vilna were kept busy. A second circular followed almost before the ink on the first was dry, adding more fuel to the raging fire. It purported to supply additional proof of heresy.

> A manuscript has been found in the possession of a certain Isser that pointed out the misdeeds of which he had already made a full confession, and that 'soul-snatchers' such as these were destroyers in a double sense, as they not only beguiled people to forsake the Torah, but sought to seize the money of their youthful followers, whose dowry (i.e., of their wives) was squandered in wandering from town to town and in orgies.[15]

The Vilna authorities wrote urgently to Brody pleading with the community to take immediate action, and the town responded without delay. On the 20th day of *Sivan,* the Brody leadership excommunicated the *hasidim.* All the curses of the Pentateuch were heaped in Hebrew and in Yiddish on those who deviated from the "established custom."[16] Similar steps were taken by other communities. The *hasidim* were forbidden to set up separate places of worship and were even barred from celebrating *se'udah shelishit* (the third Sabbath meal) together.[17]

The Hasidim *Respond*

That same year (1772) saw the publication of *Zemir Aritzim Veharbot Tzurim* ("Uprooting of Tyrants and Flinty Swords") by Aryeh Leib ben Mordekhai, a collection of all the bans issued against the *hasidim.* In 1775 two of Hasidism's finest scholars, Rabbi Shneur Zalman of Liady and Rabbi Menahem Mendel of Vitebsk, came to Vilna and sought a personal interview with the Gaon. Rabbi Shneur Zalman recorded what followed:

> We set out toward the saintly Gaon's house to discuss the whole matter with him in order that all misunderstanding might be removed. I myself took part in this mission as well as our saintly master the deceased Rabbi (Menahem) Mendel. But twice the Gaon locked the door against us. The leaders of the community approached him saying: "Our Master, their chief spokesman has come to discuss the matter with you, and when he is convinced of the error of his ways assuredly peace will again prevail in Israel"; but the Gaon gave evasive replies. When his followers started to plead with him, the Gaon left the city and stayed away until we returned home.[18]

However, there is little accuracy in Solomon Maimon's assertion that "scarcely any trace of the *hasidim* can be found."[19] The *herem* could be devastating when wielded against individuals, but was ineffectual when applied to large groups of people who could ignore with impunity threats that could not be enforced. The publication of the *Toledot Yaakov Yosef* gave additional ammunition to its opponents. Hasidic presses sprang up in Medzibozh, Slavuta, and Korets specifically for the printing and reprinting of hasidic and Kabbalistic works.

Severe Measures against Hasidim

In 1781, nine years after the proclamation of the first decree of excommunication, Vilna proclaimed a second *herem* against the *hasidim.* Once more the Gaon was in the forefront. "Although it was not my custom to trespass beyond my province," wrote the Gaon, "yet I also gave my signature, being mindful of the saying: 'When the Torah is being annulled, it is time to act.' "[20] Two envoys, Rabbi David and Rabbi Joshua Segel, were sent from Vilna to warn people throughout Lithuania against the *hasidim.* Most communities followed the leadership of Vilna. On the 3rd of *Elul* 1781, the Rabbinical Assembly at Zelva (near Grodno) endorsed the *herem.*[21]

In Shklow and Mogilev in White Russia, a circular was issued condemning the *hasidim* in the most severe terms:

> Because of our many sins, worthless and wanton men who call themselves *hasidim* have deserted the Jewish community and have set up a so-called place of worship for themselves. And there, as every one knows, they worship in a most insane fashion, following a different ritual that does not conform to the religion of our Holy Torah, and they tread a path which our fathers did not tread. In addition to this, the works of their teachers have, unfortunately, recently been published, and it is obvious to us that all of their writings are opposed to our Holy Torah and contain misleading interpretations. The exaggerations and stories of miracles that are described in their books are particularly transparent and obvious lies, and far be it from us to place any trust in any such exaggerated statements. And behold, as a result of this great misfortune, a fire has been kindled in the midst of Jewry, and there is a breaking away from the obligations imposed by the Torah.
>
> Therefore, we, the undersigned, are in agreement that every community is most urgently bound to adopt rigorous measures–carrying with them every possible penalty–in order to put into effect all the protective and defensive measures described below. And these details are to be officially recorded in the minute books of every community and city that they may serve as a charge and as a memorial for future generations, so

that our Jewish brethren may avoid the evil customs and laws of the *hasidim.*

The following are the protective measures that were adopted in our session:

1. A day of fast and public prayer is to be instituted on January 15, 1787.

2. All possible measures are to be adopted to put an end to the prayer meetings of the heretics in all communities, so that they will be deprived of the means of common assembly.

3. Careful watch is to be maintained that no one should study their literature, and search is to be made with this purpose in mind.

4. We fully confirm the validity of the ordinances that were issued in Brody and Vilna dealing with the prohibition of pilgrimages to the heads of the sect.

5. That which their ritual slaughterers kill may not be eaten; the meat of such slaughtering is to be considered carrion, and the instruments used are to be considered polluted and forbidden. Meat brought into one city from another place is to be considered carrion, unless it is accompanied by a certificate from a reliable person who is not a member of the hasidic group.

6. In every city supervisors should be appointed to see that all the above mentioned provisions are carried out.

7. No one is to shelter any member of this sect.

8. No member of the above mentioned sect may bring a suit in a Jewish court. No community may permit any one of them to hold a position as cantor or rabbi, and it goes without saying that no one of them may teach our children.

9. It is to be announced in all communities that anyone who knows anything, good or bad, about the *hasidim* must bring this information to the court.[22]

In 1794 both the *Toledot Yaakov Yosef* and the *Testament of the Besht* were burned in public in front of the Great Synagogue in Vilna. Hitherto peaceful communities were rent by hatred and bitterness. Even acts of physical violence were not uncommon.

In May 1796, it was related in Vilna that a *hasid* was journeying through the country, purporting to be the son of the Gaon, publicly proclaiming that his father deeply regretted his harshness towards the *hasidim* and was now making atonement for his grievous errors. The wrath of the Gaon in response to this rumor was awesome. In letters, dated June 22 and October 14, 1796, Rabbi Elijah thundered: "These dolts who have sown so much evil should be chastised before the assembled people with whips and scorpions and brought to reason. No man should have pity upon them and take their part, but rather they should be cast out from all the tribes of Israel as evildoers."[23] Clearly the Gaon saw himself in the role of his namesake, the prophet Elijah. The *hasidim* were to the Gaon of Vilna what the worshippers of Baal were to Elijah the Tishbite.

Reactions to the Gaon's Death

On the third day of *Sukkot* (October 9, 1797) the Gaon died, and "the joy of the festival was turned into mourning and all the streets of Vilna resounded with lamentation."[24] Some of the *hasidim,* however, would not allow the death of the Gaon to diminish "the Season of Rejoicing," particularly since "the Light of the Exile" had been their most pitiless persecutor. The *Kehillah,* incensed at what they considered "this heretical conduct" of the *hasidim,* set up a special committee to deal with it. But two decades of relentless warfare, waged by the greatest exponent of talmudic Judaism in modern times, had failed to destroy or even weaken the movement. Stronger measures were necessary.

The Involvement of the Russian Government

With the connivance of the *Kehillah's* special committee, a certain Hirsch son of David (Davidovich) of Vilna drew the attention of the Prosecutor-General in St. Petersburg to the "political misdeeds perpetrated by the chief of the Karliner (hasidic) sect, Zalman Borukhovitch (son of Borukh)."[25] The Russians acted on this information with practiced speed. In October 1798, Rabbi Shneur Zalman of Liady and twenty-two of his followers were arrested. The other *hasidim* were soon released, but Rabbi Shneur Zalman was taken to St. Petersburg. In a Hebrew memorandum, which had to be sent to Vilna to be translated into French, Rabbi Shneur Zalman protested his innocence. He must have pleaded with convincing eloquence. On the 19th of *Kislev,* (Dec. 15, 1798), the *Yahrzeit* of the *Maggid,* he was released and recited the verse from Psalms 4:19: "He hath redeemed my soul in peace."

The ordeal did not alter the temperament or outlook of the compassionate sage, who still urged his followers to be patient and forbearing with their opponents. His pleas were in vain. The *hasidim* of Vilna, outraged by the tactics of the *Kehillah,* responded with counteraccusations. They accused the *Kehillah* of diverting to other purposes monies collected for taxation, and on this charge the elders of the *Kehillah* were arrested on February 4, 1799. The charges were soon disproved. Subsequently, eight *hasidim* were elected to the *Kehillah,* and for a time a *hasid,* Meir ben Raphael, was actually head of the community.[26]

The hasidic victory was cut short by the actions of Avigdor ben Hayim (Haimovitch), a vindictive and unscrupulous man, formerly rabbi in Pinsk, who had alienated the *hasidim* and had been deposed by them in 1793. When his demands for restitution and compensation were unsuccessful, the ex-rabbi turned informer. In a lengthy report to the Russian Emperor Paul I in St. Petersburg, he described the *hasidim* as a "pernicious and dangerous sect," supporting his accusations with a wealth of distorted data and malicious misquotations. "I endeavored through preaching to persuade them to return from their errors to the right way," wrote Avigdor to the Czar, "but when I saw that this effort had no effect on them at all, and when there came into my hands their clandestinely printed books in which law and justice were most insolently distorted, I was perplexed in mind, for I did not know how to frustrate their designs."[27]

A second warrant for the arrest of Rabbi Shneur Zalman was issued on October 30, 1800, and once more the rabbi of Liady was taken to the prison of St. Peter and Paul at St. Petersburg. Here he was confronted with nineteen charges, all of which he successfully refuted. Three weeks later, on November 17, Rabbi Shneur Zalman was released from prison. Yet it was not until March 29, 1801, that he was free to leave the Russian capital and return home.

The End of the War

The internecine war was finally settled, ironically enough, by State intervention. In January 1800, the civil governor of Lithuania,

Ivan Friesel, stated that the hasidic group was to be tolerated. "The Statute concerning the Organization of the Jews" of December 9, 1804, granted every Jewish community the right to build separate synagogues and to choose its own rabbis. The rabbis were authorized to supervise all religious ceremonies and to settle all disputes relating to religion, but without recourse to "anathemas" and "excommunications." The struggle was over. *Hasidim* and *mitnagdim* had to learn to coexist and to allow each other the freedom to worship as each saw fit.

Chapter 7

The Legacy of Lubavitch

Rabbi Shneur Zalman ben Barukh, *"der alte rebbe,"* as he was affectionately called, was born in 1747, in Liozno, White Russia. In sharp contrast to the wealth of detail that surrounds every aspect of his adult life, little is known about his parentage and early upbringing. "This young lad," said one of his teachers, Issahar Baer Kobilink of Lubavitch, "is fit to be my friend and companion, not my disciple. He needs no guidance in the study of Talmud. His intellect is such that he can make his own way through the 'sea of the Talmud' and its commentaries."

A Passion for Knowledge

At the age of 13, Shneur Zalman became an associate of the *Hevrah Kaddisha* ("The Holy Society"), that supervised burial arrangements. He had a methodical mind and systematically set about acquiring knowledge. He described his youthful method of study:

> When I was 13 years old I studied by myself most of the time, devoting eighteen hours a day to my studies. For three consecutive years, I allotted two-thirds of my time during the week to the study of the Talmud and the Codes and utilized the rest of the time for the study of Scripture, *Aggadah, Midrash,* and *Kabbalah.* On the Sabbath, I divided the day equally between

the Talmud, Codes, Scripture and *Aggadah,* and finally *Midrash,* the *Zohar,* and *Kabbalah.*[1]

Soon men of wealth were competing for this young scholar as a desirable son-in-law and at the age of 15, on the eve of *Shabbat Nahamu,* 1860, he married Sterna, daugther of a businessman, Judah Leib Segal of Vitebsk. He continued to study with single-minded passion. By the age of 18, the youthful scholar had mastered the Talmud with all its commentaries, and still he studied with unmitigated ardor that seemed excessive to his materialistic father-in-law. In mean and petty ways, Judah Leib Segal gave vent to his resentment and even begrudged Shneur Zalman the candles he needed for his nighttime studies. Still, Shneur Zalman was undaunted, pursuing his far-ranging explorations of rabbinical and mystical Judaism by moonlight. At midnight and in the otherworldly stillness of the dawn, the city of Vitebsk could hear the musical voice of the wakeful *matmid* (diligent student) as he chanted to himself.

Shneur Zalman Makes His Choice

Like the Gaon of Vilna, Shneur Zalman applied himself to the study of astronomy and trigonometry, and he paid special attention to Hebrew grammar, which he regarded as essential to the understanding of the Torah. Alone, without colleagues or teachers, the 19-year-old became restless. He became aware that there were "two luminaries shining in the world," the light of Mezhirech, the rallying ground of the *hasidim,* and the light of Vilna, the *mitnagdic* stronghold. "In Vilna the Torah is studied, but in Mezhirech they learn how to pray. My soul," he declared, "desired Torah, so I set out for Vilna. But, on the way, I changed my mind. A little knowledge of the Torah I had already acquired, but of the principle of true worship I had yet learned nothing. I needed a guide who would show me how to serve God. Such a counselor would I find in Mezhirech."[2]

In 1765, at the age of twenty, he left Vitebsk, armed with little but intellectual curiosity and the six rubles that his brother had given him for provisions on that arduous journey. But, in Mezhirech, at journey's end he found the guidance he was looking for. "Blessed be the Lord," he exclaimed, "who hath led me along the true path." The *Maggid,* with his rare power of discernment, immediately recognized the brilliance of his new disciple. *Hasidim* related that, as the *Maggid* was passing through the students' dormitory one night, he paused at the bed of Rabbi Shneur Zalman. "Miracle of miracles," he remarked softly, "that so much spiritual strength resides in so frail a dwelling! This young man, sleeping so serenely, will one day become the rabbi of all the provinces of Russia, with multitudes listening to his voice."

Shneur Zalman and the Maggid

Just as the master honored the disciple, so the disciple honored the master and repeatedly acknowledged his indebtedness. "When we learn Torah from the *Maggid,* it is as though he teaches us the Written Law." The bonds between them were close. "The Besht I see only in a dream, and then only on the Sabbath and on Festivals," Rabbi Shneur Zalman remarked, "but my teacher, the *Maggid,* I behold both when I dream and when I am awake."

For three years, Rabbi Shneur Zalman studied with the *Maggid,* following him from Mezhirech to Annopol. There he found colleagues of the caliber of Rabbi Elimelekh of Lyzhansk, Rabbi Levi Isaac of Berdichev, and Rabbi Nahum of Chernobyl. Such fellowship was stimulating and instructive for the youthful Shneur Zalman. "Torah," he gratefully acknowledged, "I learned from the *Maggid,* who was my counselor in ethics. From Rabbi Phinehas Shapiro of Korets, I learned to seek truth and to value humility. And from Michael (Jehiel Michael) of Zloczow (1726–1786), I absorbed melodies which he had heard from the Besht himself."

Shneur Zalman also benefited from his role as companion and tutor of Rabbi Abraham (1741–1777), the *Maggid's* son, who was known as *Avraham HaMalakh* ("Abraham the Angel"). "Not in vain," commented Rabbi Levi Isaac of Berdichev, "did they call him 'the Angel,' for he is as pure as his deeds." Though heir to the nonascetic traditions of Hasidism, "the Angel" spent his time in fasting, self-affliction, and solitude. But for six hours each day, the young ascetic and Rabbi Shneur Zalman studied together, devoting three hours to Talmud and three hours to *Kabbalah.* "Let my son go his own way," instructed the *Maggid.* "Explain the Torah to him as you understand it, and he will interpret it according to his own conception. Show him the Talmud according to the letter, and he will explain its meaning to you according to the spirit."[3]

The New Shulhan Arukh

Although one of the youngest and newest of the disciples, Rabbi Shneur Zalman was encouraged by the *Maggid* to compile a new *Shulhan Arukh* ("A Code of Jewish Law"). "Our dear Shneur Zalman's immediate grasp of any problem is tantamount to minor prophecy," was the *Maggid*'s exalted evaluation of his disciple's potential. Rabbi Shneur Zalman was qualified for this challenging task. His phenomenal familiarity with rabbinic literature was united with a gift for lucid exposition. His logical and highly-trained mind could not tolerate ambiguity or obscurity. Rabbi Shneur Zalman was 25 when he completed the section *Orah Hayim* ("Way of Life").

He marshaled ancient authorities with masterly skill and thoroughness, and the "Rav's *Shulhan Arukh*", as his magnum opus was called, won high praise from his contemporaries, who called him "Prince of the Torah" and "unique in his generation." "He is like an iron pillar," they said of him, "on whom one can depend." The work was published in three parts: *Hilkhot Talmud Torah* (Shklow, 1814), *Yoreh De'ah* (Kapust, 1814), and *Hilkhot Pesah* in 1814. The work in its entirety was published in Kapust in 1816.

In general, Rabbi Shneur Zalman followed Ashkenazi scholars rather than the Sephardic school, just as he opted for the halakhic authorities in preference to the mystics. Thus, the *Rav's Shulhan Arukh* was weighty evidence that contrary to the accusations of the *mitnagdim,* the *hasidim* were not attempting to lighten the "yoke of the *mitzvot.*" Rabbi Shneur Zalman stressed that minor precepts were to be fulfilled as meticulously as major ones.

After the death of the *Maggid* in 1773, the disciples dispersed, and many established their own courts. Rabbi Shneur Zalman settled in Liozno, a loyal supporter of his former pupil, young "Abraham the Angel." He was also a follower of the venerable Rabbi Menahem Mendel of Vitebsk, who had actually beheld the glory of the Besht. Yet, it was not long before Rabbi Menahem Mendel made his way to the Holy Land, and Rabbi Abraham died at the age of 36. With this double bereavement, Rabbi Shneur Zalman reverted for a time to the solitary life he had led before entering the home of the *Maggid.* Caring little for honor or recognition, he withdrew from the world of people into the world of books. It is related that even at the age of 40, he shrank from the homage of the *hasidim* who flocked to him. His wife, however, made this homage more acceptable. "They are coming," she explained with subtlety, "to hear the Torah of the *Maggid.*"

The "Suffering Servant" of Hasidism

It was at this time that the Gaon of Vilna launched his mighty offensive against Hasidism. Maligned and menaced, the movement desperately needed a powerful leader. From afar, Rabbi Menahem Mendel realized this, and he wrote from the Holy Land urging his followers to enlist the aid of Rabbi Shneur Zalman: "Revere him. . . . Honor him. He has labored hard to hear the words of the living God. We have anointed him a teacher of righteousness in the country, so that the Congregation of the Lord should not be like sheep without a shepherd. For, as guide and teacher, there is none to compare with him." During that time of crisis there was no room for hesitation or excessive humility. Rabbi Shneur Zalman rose to the occasion. Before long, he was the acknowledged head of the hasidic communities in White Russia, and his followers were numbered in the thousands. Yet he continued to live in a modest, almost Spartan style, for he attributed the sufferings of the Diaspora to the people's yearning for material things.

From Rabbi Menahem Mendel came empathy and encouragement. "We have heard," he writes, "the groaning of the children of Israel. By His Name I swear that our doctrines and beliefs are blameless. We forgive those who provoke us and harm our person."[4] Rabbi Shneur Zalman preached patience and advocated forgiveness. However, peaceful overtures were neither appreciated nor reciprocated by the enemies of Hasidism. Rabbi Shneur Zalman became Hasidism's "suffering servant." Twice arrested, his detention in St. Petersburg gave rise to many legends. His bearing impressed the mistrustful dignitaries, and his ready wit stood him in good stead. During one of his interrogations a state prosecutor asked the prisoner to explain the meaning of the Biblical verse: "And the

Lord God called unto the man and said unto him: 'Where art thou?' " (Genesis 2:9). "Surely," reasoned the prosecutor, "the Lord knew where Adam was, so why did He ask his whereabouts?" Rabbi Shneur Zalman replied: "The question, 'Where art thou?' did not apply only to Adam in the Garden of Eden. The question is of timeless relevance. Whenever a man sins and deviates from the right path, God calls him to repentance with the searching words, 'Where art thou?.' "

An Effort toward Reconciliation

Rabbi Shneur Zalman worked tirelessly for reconciliation with his opponents. To the leaders of Mogilev, he lamented, "We have been sold alive. We cannot even be ransomed for money. We implore you not to cast us aside." Not all his *hasidim* were conciliatory, and some employed provocative tactics that caused him great distress. He pleaded repeatedly that the movement should not suffer because of the misdeeds of individual members. Rabbi Shneur Zalman urged his *hasidim* to conduct themselves in an honorable manner in order to demonstrate to the *mitnagdim* that their accusations were unfounded. Rabbi Shneur Zalman himself made friendly contact with mitnagdic scholars, and many of the opponents were won over by his erudition, passion, and fiery eloquence. So, to a certain extent, he personally succeeded in mitigating the schism in the House of Israel.

He also tried to appease his antagonist Rabbi Barukh of Tulchin who objected to Rabbi Shneur Zalman: "Why should there be any misunderstanding between us? Have I not suffered martyrdom and twice been dragged in chains to St. Petersburg, all so that the name of your grandfather might be vindicated? Might I not have said: 'There is his grandson Rabbi Barukh in Medzibozh. Send for him, that he may come and answer for his grandfather.' "[5]

The Arrival of Napoleon

Yet, Rabbi Shneur Zalman was not destined to enjoy the tranquility for which he yearned. The phenomenal exploits of Napoleon brought about a radical change in the status of European

Jewry. As the Napoleonic armies marched through Italy, the "walls of the ghettos began to dance." The Yellow Badge gave way to the tricolor cockade, and the gates of the ghettos were torn off their hinges. In 1799, while Napoleon was in the East, he is said to have invited the Jews of Asia and Africa to rally to his standard in order to regain possession of Palestine. Eight years later, on February 8, 1807, he summoned a *Sanhedrin,* commanding it to "reveal again to the people the true spirit of its laws and render proper interpretations of all mistaken conceptions." The *Sanhedrin* obliged by releasing soldiers in the French army from their religious obligations. Although few Jews accepted the pronouncements of the *Sanhedrin* as authoritative and binding, the Emperor was for the moment satisifed with his experiment. "To me at least, the *Sanhedrin* is useful," was his comment.

Although Napoleon was the hero of Polish Jewry, who regarded him as their liberator, Poland's hasidic rabbis were divided on this issue. Among staunch Napoleonic supporters was Rabbi Menahem Mendel of Rymanow (d. 1815). While Rabbi Menahem Mendel baked *matzot* (unleavened bread) for the festival of Passover, he would exclaim each time he put fresh dough into the oven: "Another Muscovite regiment goes into the fire." On the other hand, Rabbi Jacob Isaac of Lublin and Rabbi Israel of Kozienice prayed for the victory of the Czar. Rabbi Naftali of Ropczyce (1760–1827) also opposed French dominion, regarding Napoleon as the symbol of heresy and agnosticism.

Grateful for his relatively humane treatment in St. Petersburg, Rabbi Shneur Zalman aligned himself with the anti-French faction. To Rabbi Moses Meisels he wrote: "It was revealed to me during *Musaf* ("The Additional Prayer") on *Rosh Hashanah* that if Bonaparte is victorious, there will be great material prosperity in Israel, but the Jews will become estranged from God. But should *Adonenu* (our Lord) Alexander be victorious, even though they would suffer great poverty, the Children of Israel would draw closer to their father in Heaven."[6] According to a Lubavitcher legend, Napoleon used to say: "Whenever I ride, that blond Jew rides before me." (Rabbi Shneur Zalman was fair-haired.)

In 1812, in order to elude the advancing French armies, Rabbi Shneur Zalman hastily left home with his entire family, twenty-eight souls in all, leaving most of his possessions behind. Their arduous journey took them from Liady to Krasny and then to

Smolensk. "I would die rather than live under him (Napoleon)," wrote Rabbi Shneur Zalman. He arrived in Piena on the 8th of *Tevet.* On the 18th of *Tevet* he fell ill and on the 24th of *Tevet* he died. He was buried in Hadiacz in the district of Poltava.

The Literary Legacy of Rabbi Shneur Zalman

The *"alte Rebbe"* left a vast literary treasure house: *The Rav's Shulhan Arukh; Torah Or* ("Torah's Light"), homilies on Genesis, Exodus, *Hanukkah,* and *Purim, Likkutei Torah* ("Gleanings of Torah"), homilies on Leviticus, Numbers, and Deuteronomy; *Be'urei HaZohar* (Commentary on the *Zohar*), and a Kabbalistic commentary on the Prayer Book. His most important contribution to Jewish philosophy was, however, the *Tanya* (the title's literal meaning is: "It has been taught"). The first edition, printed in Slavuta in 1796, carried the title *Likkutei Amarim* ("Collected Essays") but was published as the *Tanya* in Zolkiew in 1798. The *Tanya* met with instant acclaim. His contemporaries greeted it with reverence. "With the *Tanya,*" declared Rabbi Zusya of Annopol, "The Israelites will go forth to meet the Messiah."

The *Tanya* is divided into five sections. Section one consists of fifty-three chapters. Section two, *Shaar HaYihud VehaEmunah* ("Portal of Unity and Repentance") and section three, *Iggeret HaTeshuvah* ("Epistle of Repentance"), each contain twelve chapters. Section four, *Iggeret HaKodesh* ("The Holy Letter"), has thirty-two chapters. Section five is called *Kuntres Aharon* ("Final Discourse"). Fifty-five editions have so far appeared, and the *Tanya* has been translated into Yiddish and English.[7] The fifty-three chapters of part one correspond to the weekly Torah reading, and *Habad hasidim,* to this day, religiously study a chapter of the *Tanya* every week.

The Maimonides of Hasidism

Rabbi Shneur Zalman has been described as the Maimonides of Hasidism, for he represents the synthesis of Lithuanian scholarship and hasidic fervor. In his works emotion and *hitlahavut* (ardor), rich legacies of the Baal Shem Tov, are fused with philosophy and intellectualism. Yet, while Maimonides sought to harmonize Mosaic teachings with Aristotelian principles, the main concern of Rabbi Shneur Zalman was to guide "those who are in pursuit of righteousness and seek the Lord . . . whose thoughts are confused as they wander about in darkness in the service of God, and who are unable to perceive the beneficial light that is buried in books."[8]

Rabbi Shneur Zalman devoted twenty years to the preparation of the *Tanya.* Part one clearly demonstrates his mystical orientation, for he refers to the *Zohar* no fewer than forty-nine times, to Isaac Luria ten times, and to Hayim Vital twenty-nine times.[9] He anlayzes the various facets and components of the soul, differentiating in true Kabbalistic tradition between the Divine soul (*nefesh Elohit*) and the animal soul (*nefesh habehamit*). He examines the role of man in the cosmic order, the purpose of human existence, the concept of the Messianic era, the resurrection, the qualities of fear and love in relationship to God, and the Lurian doctrine of *tzimtzum* ("contraction")

Habad

According to Rabbi Shneur Zalman, the intellect consists of three kindred faculties, *Hokhmah* (wisdom), *Binah* (understanding) and *Daat* (knowledge), the first, second and third of the ten *Sefirot.* The first letter of each of these three Hebrew terms form the acronym *Habad,* as Rabbi Shneur Zalman's doctrine was called. The prophets and the rabbis taught that "God desires the heart." Rabbi Shneur Zalman stressed that God also desires the mind. Reason was elevated above emotion. "It is well-known to all who have basked in the fragrant doctrines of the Besht and his disciples," wrote Shneur Zalman, "that understanding is the mother of children. These 'children' are love and fear, born of knowledge and profound contemplation of the greatness of God."[10]

He taught that man is neither a static nor a passive entity. He is a dynamic being who must strive to develop his potential and perfect himself. For here there is no aristrocracy of birth, and all men are capable of scaling the heights. Every Jew has the making of a *tzaddik.* In every soul there are sparks of goodness, but often these are in a state of "suspended animation." These sparks can be reclaimed, for the "gates of repentance never close." He believed that "within the soul dwells the light of God, which is not subject to the variations and determinations of time."

The Philosophy of Habad

Within the framework of *Habad,* the *tzaddik* is not an intermediary. He is a supervisor rather than a superior, a teacher of morality rather than a worker of miracles. It is permissible to lean on a friend for support, but it is better to stand by oneself. Trained to spiritual self-sufficiency and not to total dependence on the *tzaddik, Habad hasidim* visit their rabbi regularly for guidance and instruction. They pay him respect rather than homage, for the bond between them is one of mutual affection and esteem.

Habad attached great importance to Torah study and regarded it as equal to the observance of all the Commandments. Through the study of the Torah, man can reach the highest stage of development and self-perfection, for the Torah illuminates and elevates the mind. It is food for the soul, and the soul cannot live without it. Rabbi Shneur Zalman once remarked to Rabbi Joshua Zeitlin of Shklow: "The *hasidim,* too, set aside time for study. The difference between them and the *mitnagdim* is this: the latter set time for study and they are limited by a time factor, whereas the former make the Torah their path of life."

From every chapter that a man studies and from every *mitzvah* that he performs an angel is created. When the Torah is studied with ardor and when a *mitzvah* is performed with joy, animated angels are created. When there is no ardor, the angels are joyless and dispirited. The "animal soul" emanates from the *Kelipot* (shells), known as *Nogah* (light), which is an amalgam of good and evil, and man cannot entirely escape from its source. The concern of Rabbi Shneur Zalman was not with the *tzaddik* (righteous person), nor with the *rasha* (wicked person), but with the *beinoni* (average man).

While the eighteenth-century philosophers grappled with doubts and perplexities, Rabbi Shneur Zalman formulated his philsophy of Judaism with clarity and cogent conciseness. Moreover, his style is both lucid and lively, avoiding technical terms, and his material is presented with freshness and originality.

No other hasidic rabbi left such a distinctive imprint on the movement as this "suffering servant." He established a dynasty, Lubavitch; he formulated a philosophy, *Habad;* he added fuel to the fire kindled by the Besht, and the flames burned with a new brilliance.

Chapter 8

Hasidism's Great Storyteller

"The Holy One Blessed be He sends the cure before the malady," so says the *Midrash.* This saying comes to mind when one considers the life and works of Rabbi Nahman of Bratslav, for Nahman was born a year before the *Maggid* of Mezhirech died, the year during which the Gaon of Vilna issued his *herem* against the *hasidim.* Poet and seer, one of the most remarkable of all the hasidic rabbis, Rabbi Nahman was the greatest storyteller in the annals of Hasidism. Indeed, the stories of Rabbi Nahman rank with the classic tales of Jacob Ludwig Carl (1785–1863), Wilhelm Carl Grimm (1786–1859), and Hans Christian Andersen (1805–1875).

Nahman was born in Medzibozh on the 4th of April, 1772. His mother, Feige, was the daughter of Udel, the only daughter of the Besht. His father, Simha, was the son of Rabbi Nahman of Horodenka (Gorodenka), a devoted follower of the Besht and a reader in the Besht's synagogue. Together with Rabbi Meir of Przemysl, Nahman of Horodenka emigrated to the Holy Land in 1764. The younger Nahman's grandmother, Udel, also had two sons, Barukh of Medzibozh and Moses Hayim Efraim of Sudylkow. The brothers were totally different in temperament. Rabbi Moses Hayim was a fine scholar of retiring disposition, while the turbulent Rabbi Barukh was quarrelsome, boastful, and exceedingly vain.

Growing Up in the Shadow of the Besht

Nahman was brought up in conditions of great poverty, but the glory of the Besht had not departed from Medzibozh. It was crowded with memories of his great-grandfather, and Nahman spent many hours at the ancestral tomb lost in dreams. For little Nahman, the Besht lived on. An assiduous student, the child learned fast. With increasing eagerness he applied himself to Talmud, Bible, the *Zohar,* and the writings of the Kabbalists. *Halakhah* and *aggadah* were equally dear to him. Almost from the cradle, he absorbed the legends and the wonder tales of the Talmud and medieval literature, as well as the stories of the Besht. *Halakhah* sharpened his intellect, while *aggadah* fired his imagination. When Nahman was but 13 years old, his uncle, Rabbi Moses Hayim, predicted that he would be "the greatest of all the *tzaddikim.*" That year, Nahman married Soshia, daughter of Efraim of Zaslav, and settled with his youthful bride in Husiatyn, Podolia.

Marriage did not change his way of life. Nothing could divert him from his studies. "Great was his mastery," records his disciple Nathan, "of the Bible, of *Ein Yaakov* (an annotated compilation of the aggadic sections of both the Palestinian and Babylonian Talmud by Jacob Ibn Haviv, 1460–1516), of Lurianic literature, and of the *Zohar.*" Nahman did not believe in short cuts to Heaven. He chose the long, hard, and narrow way. "No limits are set to the ascent of man and each can scale the very highest peaks," he believed. Heir of the Besht though he was, he adopted the austere practices of Luria.

Personal Habits and Challenges

The frail Kabbalist indulged in prolonged fasts. Often he abstained from food for days on end. In one year he fasted eighteen times "from Sabbath to Sabbath," and these fasts were followed by immersions in ice-cold *mikva'ot* (ritual baths). Often he wandered alone for days through the fields and in the forests, meditating on the mysteries of mortality, contemplating undisturbed the wonders of nature. In sharp contrast to his indifference to his own health was the deep concern he displayed for the physical, as well as the spiritual well-being of his *hasidim.* Premonitions of a short life span were always with him. Not an hour was wasted, not a minute lost. He regarded each day as if it were his last. He never rested on the spiritual laurels of his distinguished ancestor. "The world imagines," he said, "that I have attained a high status because I am a descendant of the Besht. It is not so. I have succeeded because I have afflicted my body. Whatever I have achieved is due to my own endeavors."

To broaden his experience, Nahman tried new ventures and new challenges. He knew nothing about boats, but without hesitation stepped into one and sailed for hours down the river. Through trial and error he learned what other people learn from teachers. Thus, it was from personal experience that he could say: "Everyone can reach the top, provided that he strives and works for it."

It was said that King Solomon understood the language of the flowers, birds, and animals. In a different way, nature spoke to Nahman and through nature spoke God. "When a man becomes worthy to hear the songs of the plants, how each plant chants the praises of God, how beautiful and sweet it is to hear their singing! And therefore, it is good to serve God in their midst, roaming over the fields among the growing things, pouring out one's heart before God in truthfulness."[1]

The remarriage of his father-in-law spelled the end of financial security for the young scholar and his family. He settled in Medvedevka near Uman, and there at the age of 18, Nahman became a rebbe. But he was in every way a non-conformist rebbe. "I shall make a path through the desert," he proclaimed. "I shall hew down one by one the trees which have stood for thousands of years, so that no obstacle stands in our path."[2]

The Pilgrimage to Eretz Yisrael

With an overwhelming passion, Rabbi Nahman, Hasidism's staunchest Zionist, yearned for the Holy Land. "All holiness is concentrated in the Holy Land. Only there is it possible to ascend the ladder of holiness. The holiness of *Eretz Yisrael* strengthens a man's faith and helps him to subdue anger and to banish melancholy."[3] Aphorisms were no substitute for action. At the age of 26, on the eve of Passover 1798, he decided to undertake this momentous journey. "In this year," he announced, "I shall certainly be in the Holy Land. . . . I shall set forth immediately, whatever the conditions, and even without money. Perhaps those who take pity on me will aid me."

The decision distressed his family. In vain his daughter pleaded, "Who will look after us while you are away in the Land of Israel?" He was unswerving in his determination. So powerful was the call of the Holy Land that nothing could dissuade him, and he steeled himself against the plaintive pleas of his children. "Go to your relatives," he replied, "your older sister will become a servant. People will have compassion for your younger sister. Your mother will become a cook. I shall sell some household goods to raise money for the journey. My heart is already there." The knowledge that the Besht did not succeed in visiting the land of his fathers strengthened the resolve of the Besht's forceful great-grandson. "I know that I will have to surmount innumerable obstacles. As long as my soul is within me and the breath of life is in my nostrils, I will not give up. I am willing to die in order to reach the Land of Israel."

In poor health, and almost penniless, ready to face the untold hazards that lay ahead, Rabbi Nahman set out on his journey. First he went to Kamenetz, where he celebrated *Shavuot* (The Feast of Weeks). He embarked at Odessa, and four days later, after a stormy voyage, he reached Istanbul. Great were his sufferings in Istanbul. A plague was ravaging the community, and Rabbi Nahman barely escaped infection. "Before one rises," he commented with resignation, "one must first fall." It was only with difficulty that he managed to obtain passage on a boat. Eventually (some four months after leaving home), he arrived in Haifa on the eve of *Rosh Hashanah,* September 10, 1799.

Now the young mystic was in his element. After walking only four cubits on the hallowed soil, he felt that he had already attained a high degree of spirituality. Rabbi Nahman visited Tiberias and Safed, the homes of his spiritual counselors, the Kabbalists. Wherever he went, he was honored and made many friends, among them Rabbi Abraham of Kalisk. He even assumed the role of peacemaker and brought about a reconciliation between Rabbi Abraham and Rabbi Jacob Samson of Shepetovka. Mindful of his family obligations, Nahman betrothed his daughter to the grandson of Rabbi Menahem Mendel of Vitebsk. Reluctantly he returned home, via Rhodes, where he spent Passover. But he always spoke with love and with longing of the Holy Land. "My place," he declared, "is only in the Land of Israel. If I travel anywhere, I shall travel only thither." He constantly relived every detail of the visit. "The Holy Land," he stressed, "is the nerve center of the Jewish people. Each Jew has a share in it as long as he honors the Lord. If he desecrates God's name, he loses the association with the Holy Land and becomes a source of quarrels. I survive only because I have been in the Land of Israel."

The Anti-Rationalist

In an age of rationalism, the age that produced Moses Mendelssohn (1729–1786) and Solomon Maimon, Rabbi Nahman valued faith above philosophy and simplicity above sophistry. Nahman, whose instinct was sure and whose intuition was reliable, had little patience for subtle dialectics. "It is better to be a believer, although unlettered, than a scholar and a skeptic." He despised philosophy. "Happy is he who knows nothing of their books, but who walks uprightly and fears retribution." Even Maimonides, the greatest Jewish philosopher of all time, did not escape censure.[4] "He who looks into the *Moreh* (Maimonides' *Moreh Nevukhim,* "Guide to the Perplexed")," pronounced Rabbi Nahman severely, "loses the Divine image of his being."[5] "There are some who pass today for great philosophers," he added, "but in the world to come it will be revealed that they were in reality nothing more than heretics and unbelievers."[6]

Confession occupied a significant place in Nahman's world. Rabbi Nahman's *hasidim* were called *vidduiniks* (confessors) because they went to confess their sins to the *tzaddik.* The private prayer of the *vidduiniks* was: "In Thy mercy make me worthy to confess before the *tzaddik,* in order that he may make atonement for me by means of his wisdom and humility."

Beliefs and Prejudices

In physicians, as in philosophers, Rabbi Nahman had little faith. Healing came from God.

> Even where there are distinguished doctors, one should neither rely on them nor put one's life in their hands. They are liable to err and can easily do damage which can never be rectified. How much more is this the danger with the majority of doctors that are to be found in our country, who cannot

distinguish their right hand from their left and are veritable killers. . . . It is well to avoid them.[7]

Jestingly he remarked: "It was difficult for the Angel of Death to kill the whole world by himself so he appointed deputies–the doctors."[8]

Although he did not glorify poverty, he disapproved of the acquisition of wealth and advocated modesty. In many ways Rabbi Nahman himself was modest and unassuming, yet he was deeply conscious of his own special qualities and unique mission. "Since the Jews were dispersed from the Holy Land," he declared, "there have been four great periods of learning, and at the center of each epoch stood a chosen one. There are four chosen teachers: Rabbi Simon bar Yohai, Rabbi Isaac Luria, the Besht, and myself."[9] "All *tzaddikim,* after reaching a certain degree of spirituality, remain static; I, however, with the help of God, become another person every day." "In the world to come," he told his disciples, "you may be worthy to understand the hidden meaning that underlies my most casual remark."[10]

He warned against the heretical *maskilim* and the new ideas that were infiltrating from Germany. "Heresies are spreading," he said. "Happy is he who strengthens himself by faith."[11] His prayers reflected these concerns: "Master of the Universe, help us to resist the temptations that are to be found in the writings and languages of the Gentiles. . . . Annul the evil decrees, especially the decrees that compel our young people to study ungodly writings."[12]

Rigorous, indeed, were the standards that Rabbi Nahman set for the *tzaddik,* for the role of the *tzaddik* was of transcendent importance. Rabbi Nahman believed that only through the *tzaddik* could a man attain understanding of the Divine. The *tzaddik* could perform miracles in heaven and on earth. The words of the *tzaddik* were more precious than the "words of the Torah and prophets." Thus for the *hasid* to visit his *rebbe* sporadically was not enough, for close communion between the two was essential. So exalted was Nahman's concept of the *tzaddik* and so exacting were his criteria that few of his contemporaries passed muster. "The evil spirit finds it hard to lead all of mankind astray, therefore he appoints pseudo-*tzaddikim* in various places to help him."[13]

Nahman was no false prophet to cry "Peace! Peace!" when there was no peace. His criticism was scathing when he felt that criticism was called for, and he was not concerned with repercussions. No one could ignore this dynamic, maverick descendant of the Besht, this great rebel of Hasidism.

The Enmity of the Shpoler Zeide

His contemporaries, for their part, either loved or loathed him. Among his adversaries was Rabbi Aryeh Leib (1725–1812) of Shpola, known affectionately as the *Shpoler Zeide* ("the Grandfather of Shpola"). To him the Besht attributed the lofty soul of Rabbi Judah Löw ben Betzalel (*Der Hokhe* Rabbi Löw) of Prague. "You were sent to redeem lost souls. There are many outcasts in the world," said the Besht, "you alone can reclaim them." The *Shpoler Zeide* lived to the age of 87 (he died in 1812), and was well advanced in years by the time Rabbi Nahman came to live nearby. Having known the Besht, Rabbi Phinehas of Korets, and the *Maggid,* Rabbi Aryeh Leib was regarded as the "Lion of the *tzaddikim.*" Yet, friendly and unpretentious, he traveled from village to village, bringing a message of hope to the people. He was a popular *tzaddik,* with many miracles to his credit.

In 1800, eighteen months after his return from the Holy Land, Rabbi Nahman settled in Zlatopol, which was near Shpola. Repeatedly, the older *tzaddik* clashed with the turbulent newcomer. Rabbi Aryeh Leib regarded Rabbi Nahman as irresponsible and presumptuous, seeking to destroy from within what the Gaon of Vilna had failed to destroy from without. "This is not the way a *tzaddik* should conduct himself," he remarked, "nor is this the manner in which a *tzaddik* should converse." The mantle of the Gaon of Vilna had fallen on the octogenarian of Shpola. The struggle between the *mitnagdim* and the *hasidim* was over, but now "civil war" broke out within the hasidic movement itself. Its aim had been the close fellowship of *hasid* with *hasid,* but now it was torn by jealousies and hatreds. Rival factions exchanged recriminations, and the accusations once leveled at the founder of *Habad* were now hurled at Rabbi Nahman. He was even accused of following Shabbetai Tzvi and Jacob Frank. "Curse Nahman," urged the sage of Shpola, losing much of the serene benevolence that had characterized his life, "and I will assure you a portion in the world to come."[14]

Rabbi Levi Isaac of Berdichev tried to make peace. He did not succeed, for, having antagonized his contemporaries, Rabbi Nahman made no attempt to pacify them. He accepted persecution and vilification as almost inevitable. He asked,

> How is it possible that they should not quarrel with me? I am not really of this world, and therefore the world cannot understand me[15]. . . . All that has been before is as the life within the fruit before it is ripe. . . . There has never been anyone like me in the world. . . . I am like a fruitful tree whose branches and foliage are fresh and green. . . . I have kindled a torch that will never be put out. . . . The righteous redeemer will be one of my descendants. . . . In the world to come all men will be *hasidim* of Bratslav."[16]

Such sentiments were hardly conciliatory. Clearly, he was not destined to live a peaceful life, nor did he seek it. "I assure you," Rabbi Nahman told his followers, "I could live at peace with everybody, but I am not fated to do so. There are certain steps that one cannot take without causing dissension." Rabbi Nahman did not stand completely alone. Among his supporters were Barukh of Medzibozh, Abraham of Kalisk, and Hayim of Krasny. "If only I knew that the world would listen to me," declared Rabbi Levi Isaac of Berdichev, "I would cry aloud, in a voice that could be heard from one end of the universe to the other, that whosoever wishes to be upright and to serve the Lord in truth should attach himself to Rabbi Nahman."

In 1802, Nahman settled in Bratslav, Podolia, on the banks of the River Bug. There he met Rabbi Nathan ben Naftali Sternhanz (1780–1895) of Nemirov, who became his Boswell. "Had I come to Bratslav merely to find you, that in itself would be reward enough," he once remarked. "Nathan, Nathan," he exclaimed, "you have the power to make my Torah live forever." It was Rabbi Nathan who minutely recorded the aphorisms, the discourses, and the tales of his master. "Great mysteries are contained in these fables," maintained the scholar-scribe, Nathan, to whom every word was sacred.

Relationship with Hasidim *and* Mitnagdim

The relationship between Rabbi Nahman and his followers was an intimate one. They needed a charismatic leader, and he needed their loyalty and devotion. "How can I ever forget you?" he writes. "Every one of you has a place in my heart. Every one of you has a share in my Torah." "Eat or do not eat, sleep or do not sleep, pray or do not pray, one thing you must do," he told his followers, "and that is to come to me." For mysterious reasons that he hinted at but did not divulge, Rabbi Nahman traveled from place to place. He visited Lvov, Ostrog, and Zaslav. "If the people only knew the purpose of my journeys, they would kiss my footprints," he confided to his followers.[17]

By 1808, Nahman's health had deteriorated still further, and he began to suffer from tuberculosis. The following year, when his house in Bratslav was burned down, he settled in Uman, scene of the notorious Haidemak massacre led by the Cossack Zhelyeznyak in the spring of 1766. There Nahman became acquainted with such notable *maskilim* as Hayim Heikel Hurwitz (c. 1749–1822) and his son, Hirsch Baer Hurwitz (Hermann Bernard, 1785–1861), who later settled in England and was appointed "Praeceptor Linguae Sacrae" at the University of Cambridge in 1837. "Hirsch Baer Hurwitz read and explained the German classics to Rabbi Nahman," writes a contemporary *maskil,* "and Nahman listened with great eagerness. When pleased by an idea, he immediately incorporated it into his work and attributed it to a *tzaddik.*"

Rabbi Nahman's days were now numbered, and for three years he lived in the shadow of death. But for him, death was merely a change of activity. "After my demise," he told his *hasidim,* "any man may come to my grave and recite ten chapters from the Book of Psalms and contribute to charity on my behalf. Then, even if his sins are many, I will do my utmost to intercede for him." With deep sorrow, Nathan watched his beloved mentor fade. "Rabbi, Rabbi, with whom are you leaving us?" he asked in anguish. The master comforted his *hasidim.* "I am not, God forbid, leaving you. I will be with you always." He died on the third day of *Hol Hamoed Sukkot* October 15, 1810, and was buried in Uman.

After Rabbi Nahman's Death

Seven children were born to Nahman, two sons and five daughters. His elder son, Solomon Efraim, died in infancy. His younger son, Jacob, born in 1796, died at the age of 10. Thus, there was no son to succeed Nahman. And he had no successor. His disciples became known as the *Toite Hasidim* (Dead *Hasidim*) because they remained so faithful to the living memory of their departed *rebbe* and never found another leader to replace him.

Yet the intra-movement feud did not end with the death of Rabbi Nahman, and for some time the leaderless *hasidim* were still vilified and persecuted. Rabbi Moses Tzvi of Savran, the leader of the opposition, called them "sinners who caused others to sin," and warned his followers not to intermarry with them. "Moreover, a *hasid* of Bratslav should not instruct your children. . . . A *shohet* (ritual slaughterer) of Bratslav is disqualified from *shehitah* (ritual slaughter)." Rabbi Nathan of Nemirov pleaded with Rabbi Moses Tzvi, "Do not shed innocent blood," but he pleaded in vain.

Bratslav *hasidim* scattered, but they made it a practice to gather together once a year to recall in fellowship the days and the ways of their remarkable *tzaddik*. "Before the New Year, each *hasid* lays aside his business and often makes a financial sacrifice to come to Uman, where he worships, weeps, and remembers. The extent of the joy, weeping, and dancing in the holy chapel cannot be described. It is a time of mutual enlightenment and inspiration." After the Russian Revolution of 1917, the gatherings of Uman came to an end. Until the outbreak of the Second World War, the "Dead *Hasidim*" met regularly in Lublin.

The Works of Rabbi Nahman

Rabbi Nahman was a prolific author, but most of his books appeared posthumously. They were lovingly edited and transcribed by Rabbi Nathan, who opened a printing press in Bratslav in 1821 for this purpose. These works include *Likkutei Tefillot* (Bratslav, 1822), *Likkutei Halakhot* (Jerusalem, 1909), *Sefer Hamodot* (Mohilev, 1811), *Sippurei Maasiyot* (Ostrog, 1815), *Alim Leterufah* (Berdichev, 1896), and *Sihot Haran* (Ostraha, 1816).

The Tales of Rabbi Nahman

It is only recently that Nahman has been accorded his rightful place in Yiddish literature, particularly with regard to his contribution to folklore. He has been described as "the greatest storyteller of the Jewish people" and the "classical storyteller of all time, not only in Hasidism, but in the whole range of Jewish lore, with few, if any, equals in other literatures."[18]

It was in Bratslav that Nahman began to tell his stories. A gifted narrator, he spoke in Yiddish, and the stories were faithfully recorded in Yiddish by Nathan of Nemirov. "Every word written in this holy book is sacred," wrote Rabbi Nathan, "these stories emanated from the mouth of the great *tzaddik* himself." Undoubtedly, Rabbi Nahman gathered material from many far-flung sources, recasting it in a form original and fresh, unmistakably the product of his own fertile mind. His knowledge was encyclopedic. He shows familiarity with animal life, with marine life, and with many branches of natural science.

Some tales were brief; others were virtually novelettes. Altogether some thirteen long stories and twenty-one short stories have been preserved. Among the most famous are: "The Lost Princess," "The Broken Betrothal," "The Cripple," "The King's Son and the Servant's Son," "The Wind That Overturned the World," "The Bull and the Ram," "The Prince," "The Spider and the Fly," "The Rabbi's Son," and "The Seven Beggars."

Often Rabbi Nathan describes the event that inspired a particular story; the rise of Napoleon, for instance. "We were astonished by the exalted position to which that one (Napoleon) had been raised, so that from a lowly man (literally "servant") he had become an emperor. We spoke with our Master about it. And he said: 'Who knows whose soul is his? In the Castle of Transformations souls are at times exchanged.' And he began to tell the tale of the king's son and the maid's son whose souls were exchanged."[19] The story of the "Lost Princess" was probably inspired by the death of his daughter, Sarah.

On another occasion, Rabbi Nahman saw a reader of a synagogue wearing torn garments. "Are you not a master of prayer, through whom the blessings are brought down to earth?" he asked. He then told the story of "The Master of Prayer." These narratives reveal the storyteller's own views and attitudes. "The Sage and the Simpleton" reflects his attitude towards the *maskilim,* for in this story he maintains that wealth leads to idolatry and that the truly pious do not strive for riches. For those who pursue wealth are always in debt, "slaves to their desires and ambitions and the slaves of others.

Would it not be better if they turned away from their idols of gold and silver and learned to serve God?"

These allegorical narrations are sometimes perplexing and sometimes illuminating. In his comments on "The Seven Beggars" the writer Meyer Levin states:

> Each tale is an intricate maze. The reader follows several different paths, only to find himself suddenly standing still, bewildered and triumphant, at their common crossroads. The meaning is hidden, yet shining clear, for each person in each tale is a symbol, as abstract as a numeral, and in the end, the symbols seem miraculously to have taken their places in the pure formula of a given theorem.[20]

The tales have been printed in innumerable editions in Hebrew, Yiddish, and English. In the twentieth century they have been edited by S. A. Horodezky, David Kahana, and Eliezer Steinman.[21] In 1906 Martin Buber was the first to introduce Nahman to the Western world. He translated the tales into German. These were translated into English by Maurice Friedmann.[22] "I have not translated these stories," Buber confesses, "but retold them with full freedom, yet out of his spirit as it is present to me." Some of Nahman's stories are to be found in Meyer Levin's *Golden Mountain.*[23] However, no verbatim translation of the stories has yet appeared.

"By strengthening their hearts and clinging to my advice," said Rabbi Nahman, "my followers will ultimately cause others to recognize the truth of my teachings. The fire which I have kindled will burn until the coming of the Messiah."

Chapter 9

"The Second Baal Shem Tov"

Chronic constitutional weaknesses rendered the Polish State an easy prey for its predatory neighbors. The Three Partitions (1772–1795) erased the name of Poland from the political map of Europe, and the subjugated territory was divided among the mighty encircling triumvirate of Russia, Prussia, and Austria. Galicia was acquired by Austria in 1772, and the 1789 census revealed 178,072 Jews among the 3,039,391 inhabitants; Lvov, Krakow, Brody, and Tarnopol had sizable Jewish communities. In all, there were nearly 400,000 Jews living under Austrian dominion.

The civil emancipation of the Jews began in the last decades of the eighteenth century. In his Edict of Tolerance (*Tolerantzpatent*) of January 1782, Joseph II, Emperor of Austria, proposed "to grant to all his subjects, Jews as well as Protestants, freedom of worship." He abolished the yellow patch, the "Jews' Badge," and repealed discriminatory laws that dated back to the Middle Ages. Jews were permitted to send their children to State schools "to learn, at least, reading, writing, and arithmetic." They became liable for military service and were no longer prevented from pursuing careers in industry.

This period saw the rise of the Enlightenment (*Haskalah*) movement, aimed at integrating Jews into the mainstream of modern European culture. One of the Enlightenment's most famous exponents was Moses Mendelssohn, the "German Socrates," who wished to lead the Jews "out of the narrow labyrinth of ritual theological casuistry into the broad highway of human culture."

Armed with Mendelssohn's translation of the Bible into German with a Hebrew commentary, known as the *Biur,* the *maskilim,* as men of the enlightenment were called, launched vitriolic attacks upon talmudists and *hasidim* alike. The hasidic leaders were caricatured as ignorant magicians whose followers "walked in the darkness." Such invective was largely ineffective. In a rationalistic era, the era of Voltaire, Rousseau, and Locke, East European Jews in surprising numbers sought to enter the moonlit gardens of Hasidism.

Elimelekh of Lyzhansk

"And a river went out of Eden to water the garden; and from thence it divided and became four streams." This verse from Genesis (2:1) has been interpreted by Rabbi Meshullam Zusya of Annopol as meaning: " 'Eden' represents the Baal Shem Tov; 'the river' is the *Maggid* of Mezhirech; 'the garden' is Rabbi Elimelekh of Lyzhansk, and the four streams are Rabbi Israel of Kozienice, Rabbi Mendel of Rymanow, Rabbi Joshua Heschel of Opatow, and Rabbi Jacob Isaac of Lublin."

Elimelekh of Lyzhansk was born in 1717 in Lapacha, near Tiktin, one of the seven children of a wealthy landowner called Eliezer Lipmann. The family traced its descent back to the commentator Rashi (1040–1105), and even farther back, to the second-century *tanna* Johanan Hasandelar ("the shoemaker"). Eliezer and his wife, Meresh, were kindly, charitable people, who tried to ease the poverty of their hard-pressed neighbors. Their house was always open and all were welcome. "My mother," said her son Zusya, "did not pray from a prayer book, because she could not read. But she knew by heart how to recite the benedictions. And she recited them with such fervor that, where she had recited the blessings in the morning, in that place the radiance of the Divine Presence rested the whole day."[1]

Early Influences

Elimelekh and his brother Zusya studied in Tiktin, where they met Rabbi Shmelke Horowitz, who was then living with his grandfather, Meir HaLevi Horowitz. From Rabbi Shmelke, one of Hasidism's great scholars, Elimelekh learned to study with single-minded diligence. Elimelekh was also influenced by Rabbi Shmelke's brother, Rabbi Phinehas (1730–1805), author of *Sefer Hamikneh,* novella on Tractate *Kiddushin.*

The most dominant force in Rabbi Elimelekh's life, however, was his own brother, Meshullam Zusya of Annopol (d. 1800), a remarkable man even in an age of remarkable men. Although he lived in unmitigated penury, he would say, "I have never experienced suffering." His humility was equalled by his kindheartedness and his total devotion to the service of God and man. "No matter when I lift my soul to Heaven," said Rabbi Nathan Adler (1741–1800), the German Kabbalist of Frankfurt-on-Main, "Zusya is always ahead of me." But Zusya was never content with his spiritual achievements and he strove ceaselessly to improve and perfect his way of life. His favorite saying was, "In the world to come, they will not ask me: 'Why were you not Moses?' They will ask me, 'Why were you not Zusya?' "

The Travels of the Two Brothers

"Exile atones for everything," said Rabbi Johanan in the Talmud.[2] So Elimelekh decided to go into "exile" with his brother Zusya, to atone for their misdeeds and to bring others to repentance. Traveling incognito, for three years they suffered the rigors of the road, often weary and hungry, often endangering their lives. Generally, communal leaders were reluctant to permit unknown "wanderers" to occupy the pulpit, and it was only infrequently that Elimelekh preached in a local synagogue. They traversed Poland and reached as far as Ushpitzin on the border of Germany, spreading hasidic teachings wherever they went. Rabbi Noah of Kobryn defined the effects of their travels: "You will find *hasidim* up to the point that the brothers Rabbi Zusya and Rabbi Elimelekh reached in their long journeyings. Beyond that you will not find *hasidim.*"

Hasidim delight in recounting the adventures of the two roaming *rebbes.* It is told that they once arrived at an inn. Rabbi Elimelekh lay down to rest against the wall, with Rabbi Zusya beside him. A crowd of drunken peasants entered, grabbed Zusya and began to pummel him. After a while, they let him slide to the floor. Anxious to shield his brother, Elimelekh said to him: "Dear Zusya, now let us change places. Let me lie in your place and you sleep in my corner. It is time for you to rest. It is my turn to suffer their blows." They quickly changed places. However, after another round of drinking, the peasants said to one another, "It is not fair to beat only one. Let the other have his share." So they dragged Zusya out and again rained blows upon him. "If a man is destined to receive blows," philosophized Zusya, "he will receive them, no matter where he puts himself."[3]

Zusya and Elimelekh shared their thoughts as well as their sufferings, and their dialogues were instructive. "Dear brother," Zusya once said, "we believe that the souls of all men were contained in Adam. So we, too, must have been present when Adam ate of the Tree of Knowledge (Genesis 3:6). How could we have permitted him to commit such a sin?" "I could easily have prevented it," replied Elimelekh, "but I refrained from doing so. Had Adam not eaten, the poisonous suggestion of the serpent would have haunted him for all eternity, for he would have believed that, had he eaten, he would have become like God himself."[4]

Rabbi Elimelekh and the Maggid

When the Besht died, Rabbi Elimelekh was 43 years old. Medzibozh lost its attraction for him. He devoted himself completely to his studies and to ascetic practices, fasting from Sabbath to Sabbath for a period of fourteen years. At Zusya's urging, Elimelekh visited the *Maggid* Dov Baer at Dubno. The *Maggid,* whom Rabbi Elimelekh hailed "my teacher," became his mentor. At Dubno, Elimelekh renewed his acquaintance with Rabbi Shmelke, and there he also met Rabbi Levi Isaac of Berdichev and Michael of Zloczow.

The "Uncrowned" Leader of Hasidism

After the death of the *Maggid* in 1773, Elimelekh reigned for the next thirteen years as the "uncrowned" head of Hasidism. He was supported by most of the *Maggid's* great disciples. Among them were Rabbi Jacob Isaac, the "Seer," whom Elimelekh called "Messiah, son of Joseph," Rabbi Israel of Kozienice, Menahem Mendel of

Rymanow, the witty Rabbi Naftali of Ropczyce, and Rabbi Kalonymos Kalman Epstein, the author of *Ma'or VaShemesh* ("The Light and the Sun").

Elimelekh's home town, Lyzhansk, became the Jerusalem of Hasidism, and Elimelekh proved to be an ideal rebbe. Like the Besht, Elimelekh could establish instant rapport with both scholars and the masses. The *Maggid* had remained at home, waiting for the people to come to him. But like the Besht, Elimelekh took up the wanderer's staff and visited many villages and distant hamlets. In this way he came to understand the economic struggles, as well as the spiritual needs, of the people. He was deeply concerned about the plight of orphans, and it gave him particular pleasure to arrange marriages for them. There was never any money in his home, for all gifts were immediately distributed among the poor.

Faith in God and in the Tzaddik

Paramount, of course, was the need for faith, an unfaltering faith in God. But it was also necessary to have faith in the *tzaddik*. With the cessation of prophecy, the *tzaddik* was the true heir of the prophets. Who, then, is a *tzaddik*? According to Rabbi Elimelekh, he is any man who observes the Sabbath with true devotion. The role of the *tzaddik* is to strengthen his followers in their struggle against the Evil Inclination.

A key weapon in this struggle is prayer, for all that the *tzaddik* can achieve is through the power of prayer. Rabbi Elimelekh himself composed a special prayer to be recited before the statutory services:

> May it be Thy will to remove all barriers between our souls and Thee, our Father in Heaven. Keep us from conceit, anger, ill temper. . . . Plant Thy Holy Spirit within us and save us from all envy and jealousy. Endow us with vision to see in each individual his good qualities and to close our eyes to his defects. Then shall our prayers cause us to rise to even higher levels and bring us nearer to Thee.

Many *hasidim* recited these words regularly. In the court of Biala, it was the custom to recite this petition just before *Kol Nidrei* on the eve of the Day of Atonement.

A Standard of Conduct and of Study

At a time when Hasidism was suspect and *hasidim* were regarded as renegades, Rabbi Elimelekh drew up a code of conduct for his followers. "He who adopts this liturgy (*Nusah Ari*)," his son Eliezer reported in his father's name, "should not utter falsehood or curse his neighbor in his heart. . . . He should not be guilty of pride or jealousy, nor should he covet wealth." Rabbi Elimelekh counseled moderation in all things, and abstinence as far as liquor was concerned.

Under the direction of Elimelekh, Torah study was intensified at Lyzhansk. *Hasidim* were exhorted to apply themselves, each according to his ability, to Scripture, *Mishnah,* and *Gemara,* with the commentaries of Rashi and *Tosafot.* The curriculum included the books of *Musar* ("ethical literature"), the *Shelah* (*Shnei Luhot HaBrit*) by Isaiah Horowitz, and *Hovot HaLevavot* ("Duties of the Heart") by the religious philosopher, Bahya ben Joseph Ibn Pakuda (c. 1050–1120).

A perfectionist, he was tormented by self-doubts and feared that he had not fulfilled his mission. "I am old," he grieved, "I am nearly sixty years of age, and I have not managed to carry out even one *mitzvah* with proper devotion. A new *Gehinnom* (hell) will have to be created for me. The hell that now exists cannot purge my sins and transgressions." It did not seem to the self-doubting *tzaddik* that he could possibly be worthy of inheriting the world to come. "If I were asked in the world to come 'Have you studied Torah?' I would have to answer, 'no.' To the question, 'Have you prayed properly?' I would also have to answer negatively. All that could be said in my favor would be that I had told the truth." He pondered the matter constantly. "If I am directed to enter *Gehinnom,* I will ask, 'Who ordered this?' And if they tell me, 'The Almighty,' I will hasten into hell to fulfill the will of God."

Despite the opposition of both the Besht and the *Maggid* to asceticism, Elimelekh never entirely discarded the Lurianic way of life, although he did persuade Rabbi David of Lelov to discontinue such practices. Elimelekh agreed with the *Maggid* that "learning two pages of the Talmud with the commentaries of Rabbenu Asher ben Jehiel (1250–1327) is preferable to fasting, and reciting the Book of Psalms thrice daily is more beneficial than fasting a whole week." Elimelekh stressed that repentance was not to be associated with melancholy, for "sadness prevents a man from serving his Creator."

A Voice for Moderation

When the Vilna authorities excommunicated the *hasidim,* Elimelekh, like the *Maggid,* advised restraint. Even when he was physically assaulted by an over-zealous *mitnagged,* his reaction was mild: "Master of the Universe! I forgive him with my whole heart. Let no man be punished on my behalf." But when Rabbi Levi Isaac of Berdichev was persecuted, Elimelekh rallied to his support. Similarly, Elimelekh was helpful, too, when Rabbi Shmelke's defense of Hasidism caused yet more controversy and criticism. Shmelke insisted that "the *hasidim* are dedicated to the service of God. They pray and study Torah at every available moment. . . . Have we not all one Father? Has not one God created us? Why do we deal treacherously every one against his neighbor?"[5] Elimelekh traveled to Nikolsburg, delivered passionate discourses, and was able to reconcile the rabbi and his community.

Two letters, written at this time and included in Elimelekh's book, *No'am Elimelekh* ("The Pleasantness of Elimelekh"), throw some light on the "civil war" that was raging so fiercely in Galicia between *mitnagdim* and *hasidim.* In one letter, his son refutes the accusations of Rabbi Abraham Katzenellenbogen of Brest-Litovsk, and justifies the adoption by the *hasidim* of the *Nusah Ari* ("The Lurian Liturgy"). Another letter stresses the high caliber of the *tzaddikim.* "They serve God in truth without any pride. . . . They engage ceaselessly in the study of the Torah for its own sake. They study in order to fulfill the Commandments. . . . Their whole purpose is to purify themselves and their thoughts."

Elimelekh died on the 21st day of *Adar* 1786. His grave became a place of pilgrimage. For over 150 years, until the outbreak of World War II, *hasidim* would place *kvitlekh* (petitions) at the tomb.

No'am Elimelekh

Rabbi Elimelekh's most important work, *No'am Elimelekh,* a commentary on the weekly Torah readings, is one of the classics of hasidic literature. It was first printed in Lvov two years after Elimelekh's death by his son and successor, Rabbi Eliezer. The book is divided into four parts: 1) expositions of the Torah; 2) *Likkutei Shoshanim,* brief comments on biblical passages and rabbinic sayings: 3) letters of Rabbi Elimelekh, his son, and his disciples, and 4) lists of religious exercises (*Hanhagot Yesharot*). In the first edition, only two letters appeared, but in subsequent editions further letters were included.

The book was instantly acclaimed for its power and profundity and has since appeared in over forty editions. The name of the author is omitted in the first edition. Rabbi Menahem Mendel of Rymanow used to say that only on the eve of the Sabbath, after emerging from the ritual bath, was he able to grasp the full meaning of *No'am Elimelekh.*[6] Rabbi Hayim of Kosow went further, declaring that "only a person who is able to revive the dead is able to understand this book."[7]

There is also an epilogue, *Tzetl Katan,* that advises the reader to repeat it at least twice a day and to understand every word in Yiddish. Among Rabbi Elimelekh's rules were: "A Jew should guard himself against hating any Jew, except for one who is so wicked that no excuse can be found for him. A Jew should not engage in any conversation at all before prayer, not even to utter a single word, because talk is a hindrance to concentration. He should speak gently to all men. He should see to it that his clothes are always clean." Rabbi Elimelekh was survived by his daughter, Meirush, and by three sons: Rabbi Eliezer, Rabbi Lippa of Hmelnick, author of *Orah LaHayim,* and Rabbi Jacob of Moglienice.

In the course of thirteen years, Elimelekh provided his followers with weapons that enabled them to survive the onslaught of the *mitnagdim* and the *maskilim.* The weapons were prayer, study, kindness, and compassion. Not undeservedly was he called "The Second Baal Shem Tov."[8]

Chapter 10

The Polish Pioneers

During the last quarter of the eighteenth century, the period of the Partitions of Poland (1772–1795), over 700,000 Jews lived in Poland and in Lithuania,[1] and their lives were fraught with hazard and hardship. Under the terms of the First Partition, Russia secured parts of White Russia. The Second Partition (1793) gave Russia half of Lithuania and the rest of White Russia. In the Third Partition (1795), Russia took Courland and the rest of Lithuania. The decree of December 23, 1791 set up the so-called Pale of Settlement, consisting of the western and southwestern provinces, to which the Jews were confined in very straitened circumstances.

Much of their social misery, ironically enough, stemmed from the corruptness of the community leaders. A rabbi recorded their abuses:

> They consume the offerings of the people and drink wine for the fines imposed by them. Being in full control of the taxes, they assess and excommunicate their opponents. They remunerate themselves for their public activity by every means at their disposal, both openly and in secret. They take no step without accepting bribes, while the destitute carry the burden. . . . The learned cater to the rich, and, as for the rabbis, they have only contempt for one another. . . . The rich value the favor of the Polish lords above the good opinion of the best and the noblest among the Jews.[2]

It was inevitable that although the Polish Constitution of May 1791 improved the lot of the Polish peasantry, it in no way bettered the situation of the overburdened Jews.

Home to Great Torah Scholars

Despite its impovireshment, Poland was still *akhsaniah shel Torah* (Home of the Torah), and her *yeshivot* produced some of Jewry's greatest talmudists. Many of Europe's key rabbinical posts were occupied by Polish scholars: Rabbi Jacob Joshua ben Tzvi Hirsch (1660–1756), rabbi of Frankfurt-on-Main and author of *Penei Yehoshua,* novella on the Talmud, was born in Krakow as was Rabbi Jonathan Eibeschütz; Rabbi Ezekiel ben Judah Landau, rabbi in Prague, was born in Opatow; Rabbi Joseph ben Meir Teomim (1727–1800), author of *Peri Megadim,* a commentary on the *Orah Hayim,* and rabbi of Frankfurt-on-Oder, was born in Lvov; Tzvi Hirsch, son of Aryeh Leib (Hart Lyon), rabbi of the Great Synagogue in London (1758–1764), was born in Rzeszow.[3]

The Early Years of Rabbi Israel Hopstein

Many great scholars dwelled in Poland itself. Among them were Efraim Zalman Margoliot (1762–1828) of Brody and Rabbi Jacob Meshullam Ornstein (d. 1839) of Lvov. However, the scholarly élite had little contact with the masses, who were, to a large extent, far removed from the Torah, drowning in a dark sea of suffering and superstition. Desperately, they grasped at a lifeline, and the lifeline was Hasidism. One of the earliest leaders was Rabbi Israel Hopstein, *Maggid* of Kozienice. Israel was born in 1733 in Opatow near Sandormiersz. His father was Shabbetai, a poor bookbinder. His mother, Pearl, had been childless for many years, and Israel was born only after she had received a blessing from the Besht. The boy received his early talmudic training from the rabbi of Opatow, Dov Berish Katz, a grandson of Rabbi Shabbetai ben Meir HaKohen (1621–1662) author of *Sifsei Kohen.* One of Israel's fellow students, Isaac Abraham Katz, author of the Responsa *Keter Kehunah* ("Crown of the Priesthood") and rabbi of Pinczow, recalls the diligence with which Israel pursued his studies. Later, Israel studied in Ostrowiec under Rabbi Ezekiel and in Horochov, Volhynia, under Mordekhai Tzvi Hurwitz, son of Isaac Halevi Hurwitz, rabbi of Altona and author of *Metaamei Yitzhak* (Piotrokow, 1907).

Studies and Training

After the death of his father on the 25th of *Shevat* 1761, Israel settled in Przysucha. There he came under the influence of Rabbi Abraham of Przysucha (d. 1800), from whom he acquired not only knowledge of Talmud and *Kabbalah* but also training in *maggidut* (homiletics). He was a gifted student, and even the *mitnagged* Hayim ben Isaac of Volozhin (1749–1821), founder of the *yeshivah* of Volozhin (a townlet in Lithuania), testified to Israel's phenomenal mastery of Talmud and the Codes.

Like his namesake, Rabbi Israel Baal Shem Tov, Israel became a teacher. He loved and understood children, and many of his pedagogical ideas were far in advance of his time. Rabbi Shmelke Horowitz became Israel's guide to Hasidism, and Israel quoted him frequently, often referring to him as "the Gaon, the *Hasid,* the Prince of God." The time came for Israel to journey to Mezhirech, then the Zion of the movement. "I studied 800 books of the Kabbalah," the newcomer to Mezhirech remarked humbly, "but when I arrived in the presence of the *Maggid,* I realized that I had not yet begun to study."[4]

"Our teacher, the *tzaddik,* interprets the Torah through the Holy Spirit which rests upon him," wrote Rabbi Israel. The *Maggid's* response was instant and ardent. "Blessed be the Holy Name!" he exclaimed. "The Almighty has provided a young man who can edit the manuscript of Rabbi Isaac Luria's Prayer Book." The *Maggid* realized that Israel would be more than an inspired editor and that through him Hasidism would spread throughout Poland. "Now that you have arrived," he prophesied, "the prayer *Keter Yitnu* ("They will give a Crown") will be recited in Warsaw as well," (meaning that more people would adopt the Lurian Liturgy and become *hasidim*).

After the death of the *Maggid,* Israel came under the influence of Rabbi Elimelekh of Lyzhansk. "My knowledge of the *Kabbalah* may be superior to that of my teacher Elimelekh," Rabbi Israel admitted, "but I am not able to serve God in the way that he does, in a spirit of self-sacrifice, love, and awe." Rabbi Israel often refers in his own writings to *No'am Elimelekh*, the "holy book of our rabbi and teacher."[5] Before his death and with touching symbolism, Elimelekh bequeathed his "heart" to Rabbi Israel. To his colleague, Menahem Mendel of Rymanow, the dying sage bequeathed his brain; his intellect he gave to Rabbi Abraham Joshua Heschel, and to the Seer Rabbi Jacob Isaac, he gave his vision.

The Fatherly Maggid *of Kozienice*

In 1765, Rabbi Israel became *Maggid* in Kozienice, a small town northeast of Radom, with a population of only 1300 Jews. To supplement his meager stipend, Rabbi Israel preached in the neighboring towns of Magnuszew and Grice, and multitudes flocked to hear him. His tone was gentle and persuasive, his use of Torah texts apt and illuminating. His love of learning and the depths of his scholarship were apparent in every word he spoke. "He who studies Torah for its own sake," he once said, "becomes a chariot riding in the Name of God. Holiness rests upon him and all the angels listen to him."

The Author of Many Works

Rabbi Israel wrote prolifically, and among his sixteen published works are *Avodat Yisrael* (Yosefow, 1842), discourses on the Torah, and *Pirkei Avot,*[6] *Or Yisrael* (Czernowitz, 1862), *Nezer Yisrael* (Vilna, 1822), *Beit Yisrael* (Warsaw, 1864) on *Pesahim, Beitzah, Haggigah,* and *Moed Katan, Tehilot Yisrael* on Psalms.[7] He was particularly fascinated by the personality of Rabbi Judah ben Betzalel Löw, of Prague, the reputed creator of the *Golem,* and Israel wrote *Ge'ulat Yisrael* ("Redemption of Israel") about him. The writings and responsa of Rabbi Israel demonstrate the mastery of *halakhah* that earned him the respect of his contemporaries. Rabbi Israel was scrupulous about acknowledging his sources, giving credit wherever it was due. His literary productivity and manifold communal commitments are the more astonishing when one considers that Rabbi Israel was fragile in physique and beset by many ailments. Often, he was too weak to rise from his bed, and many blankets were needed to warm him. Every day he was carried to the synagogue by his attendants, but his indomitable spirit overcame his physical disabilities.

A Father and Friend to the Poor

Rabbi Israel never forgot the poverty of his early days. He was virtually a father to many orphans and brought up a number of them in his own home. All the money he received from his *hasidim* was promptly distributed among the needy. When a fire ravaged the Jewish quarter of Kozienice in 1778, he financed the rebuilding of an entire street, allocating its new houses to the poor. The street then became known as "the *Maggid*'s Street." Although the *Maggid* himself lived in austere surroundings, he did not prescribe such austerity for others. "Tell me," he once asked a wealthy *hasid,* "what do you eat every day?" "Very little," replied the rich man, "my needs are simple. Bread with salt and water are enough for me." "Your way is not a good way," reproved the *Maggid,* "You should eat fattened chickens and drink wine. For if you eat well, you will give bread to the poor. But if your menu consists of dry bread, you will begrudge the poor even stones." Kozienice became a place of pilgrimage and the frail *Maggid* won many adherents to the movement.

Unassuming and devoid of worldly ambition, Rabbi Israel was revered by colleagues as well as by *hasidim.* "I have heard a *bat kol* (a heavenly voice)," declared the Rabbi of Rymanow, "proclaim that 'he who lives in the generation of the *Maggid* and has not looked upon his face will not be worthy to welcome the Messiah when he comes.' " The *Maggid's* fame spread beyond the Jewish community, and he was visited by such Polish nobles as Adam Chartoryski, Josef Poniatowski, and Prince Radziwill. Rabbi Israel offered special prayers on behalf of the childless Chartoryski. "Oh, Master of the Universe," he reasoned, "You have so many Gentiles, let there be another one." Chartoryski was subsequently blessed with a child and never forgot his debt to the rabbi. There are allusions to the *Maggid* in the works of the Polish writers, Anna Potocka and Leon Dembowski.[8]

Rabbi Israel was deeply concerned with the welfare of Jewry as a whole. He was one of the twenty-four delegates who urged the Government to abolish the state tax on *shehitah* (the ritual slaughter of animals). When military service for Jews between the ages of 24 and 28 was arbitrarily instituted, Rabbi Israel was among the community leaders who negotiated for exemption, and arranged instead for the payment of 700,000 gulden. In many such situations, Rabbi Israel's connections with the Polish nobility proved advantageous.

The Effects of Napoleon's Triumphs on Polish Jewry

The *Maggid* watched the ever-changing political map closely, as each change drastically affected, but seldom improved, the situation of the Jews. "I like the Poles," declared Napoleon at Verona in September 1796, "The Partitioning of Poland was an iniquitous deed that cannot stand. When I have finished the war in Italy, I myself will lead the French troops and will force the Russians to reunite Poland."[9]

These were not idle words. Under the treaty of Tilsit (1807), Napoleon's reconstituted Poland was styled the Grand Duchy of Warsaw. The Duchy covered 30,000 square miles with a population of over 2,000,000.

The new regime started on an admirably democratic footing by abolishing serfdom and legislating civil equality. Predictably, however, the nobility opposed the Bill of Civil Rights, and on October 17, 1809, Duke Frederick Augustus decreed that: "Those inhabitants of our Varsovian Duchy professing the Mosaic religion are barred for ten years from enjoying the political rights that they were about to receive, in the hope that, during this interval, they may eradicate the distinguishing characteristics which mark them off so strongly from the rest of the population." Assimilation was the price of emancipation, and for Rabbi Israel, this was too high a price. In common with most of his hasidic contemporaries, he opposed Napoleon.

Rabbi Menahem Mendel of Rymanow was a notable exception. *Hasidim* believe that, just as the High Priest Simon the Just (fourth-third centuries B.C.E.) was considered the guardian angel of Alexander the Great, so the Rabbi of Rymanow provided spiritual support for Napoleon. "I see the Red Jew (the rabbi of Rymanow) walking by my side through the heat of the battle," Napoleon allegedly declared, "assuring me of victory." When Napoleon stood at the gates of Moscow, Menahem Mendel prayed for him. On the other hand, Naftali of Ropczyce mobilized *hasidim* against the Corsican. According to hasidic legend, the fate of Napoleon was decided not on the battlefields, but in the courts of the hasidic rabbis. *Hasidim* relate that Napoleon came in disguise to plead with Rabbi Israel, but his pleas were unavailing, for the rabbi interpreted the verse of Exodus (28:18), *navol tibbol* ("thou wilt surely wear away"), as *Napol* ("Napoleon will fall.")[10]

Wealthy and Influential Supporters

Rabbi Israel attracted to his court influential magnates who negotiated for and represented the Jewish community. Josef Mandelsburg of Kazimierz obtained a salt monopoly, and over 5,000 Jewish families were employed in his various enterprises. Another powerful *hasid* was Samuel Zbitkover (1758–1801), the "Rothschild of Polish Jewry," who lived in a district of Warsaw called *Targo Wash,* where he owned houses, wine cellars, and inns. This district was later called *Szmulowizna* in his honor, for Samuel financed the forces of King Frederick of Prussia and of Poniatowski. In 1794, during Tadeusz Kosciuszko's rebellion, Samuel provided financial backing for a volunteer battalion of Jewish cavalry organized by Berek Joselewicz (c. 1765–1809). During the upheavals that followed, Samuel saved the lives of hundreds of Jews. His son Berek Dov Bergson was equally committed to Hasidism, and his wife, Tamarel, was a devout follower of the *Maggid.* A number of the *Maggid's* disciples, among them Simha Bunem of Przysucha and Rabbi Isaac of Warka, were in the employ of the benevolent Bergsons.

A passionate bibliophile, Rabbi Israel rejoiced in a fine collection of early prints. He was instrumental in having hitherto unobtainable volumes reprinted, and it was through him that a number of *Kabbalistic* manuscripts first appeared in print.[11]

A Personal Relationship with God

Like Levi Isaac of Berdichev, Rabbi Israel communicated with God on friendly terms. He even spoke to Him in Polish, crying out in ecstasy *"moi kochanka"* (my darling). Like Rabbi Levi Isaac of Berdichev, Rabbi Israel was persecuted and forced to take refuge at Zelichow. But his faith never faltered. "Perchance, Almighty God," he pondered, "You withhold Your mercy from the children of Israel because of the dearth of true *tzaddikim* to plead for them. Behold in Rymanow You have Rabbi Mendel, who is equal to all the *tzaddikim;* You have the Seer, who is equal to the *Urim Vetumim* (sacred means of Divination used by the early Hebrews), and finally you have me. I most sincerely repent and plead for forgiveness for all Your children."[12]

Rabbi Israel died in 1815 on the eve of the Festival of Tabernacles. He was succeeded by his son, Rabbi Moses Elikum Berish. Rabbi Israel's *hasidim* interpreted the verse, "And it came to pass when the Ark set forward that Moses said" (Numbers 10:35), to mean that "when the Ark set forward (i.e., when Israel of Kozienice died), then 'Moses said,' meaning that the leader was succeeded by his son Moses."

A father to his *hasidim* and to all Jewry, a statesman as well as a scholar, the *Maggid* of Kozienice was one of the towering pillars of Polish Hasidism.

The Sad-eyed Seer of Lublin

Early in the nineteenth century, Lublin and Przysucha replaced Medzibozh and Mezhirech as the key centers of Hasidism. The influence of the Besht, the *Maggid* of Mezhirech, and Rabbi Shneur Zalman had been restricted to the Jews of Podolia and the Ukraine; the influence of Rabbi Elimelekh of Lyzhansk was confined to Galicia; now, from Lublin and Przysucha, Hasidism spread to Polish Jewry.

The father of Polish Hasidism was Rabbi Jacob Isaac Hurwitz, known as *HaHozeh* ("The Seer") of Lublin. He was born in 1745, son of Eliezer Halevi Hurwitz, rabbi in Josefow. A brilliant and restless student, Jacob Isaac was 15-years-old when the Besht died. Shortly afterward, he made his way to Mezhirech. "Such a soul has not made its appearance since the time of the prophets," the discerning *Maggid* declared.[13]

After the death of the *Maggid* in 1773, Jacob Isaac became a disciple of Rabbi Shmelke Horowitz (1726–1778) of Nikolsburg, immersing himself in his studies to the exclusion of all else. Even his teacher thought such single-mindedness excessive. Rabbi Shmelke urged his colleague Zusya of Annopol to "make our Itzikel (little Isaac) a little lighter of heart." Like the *Maggid,* Rabbi Shmelke held the young man in high esteem: "When Jacob Isaac recites the benedictions," remarked Rabbi Shmelke reverently, "the entire Heavenly court responds, Amen." Rabbi Zusya could not change the youthful Seer's meditative disposition, but he did persuade him to make his way to Lyzhansk. "Only in the court of my brother," declared Rabbi Zusya, "will you find perfection."[14]

Under the Influence of Elimelekh of Lyzhansk

At Lyzhansk, Jacob Isaac found such like-minded associates as Menahem Mendel of Rymanow and Abraham Joshua Heschel of Opatow. Rabbi Elimelekh took a paternal interest in the newcomer, stating emphatically, "He is my equal." Jacob Isaac did indeed seem to acquire his master's spiritual vision. Rabbi Elimelekh had lived a life of extreme self-denial, and his disciple followed this rather unhasidic model. To avoid seeing unseemly things, he literally shielded his eyes for seven years, and his eyesight was seriously impaired. However, he acquired the title "seer" because of his inner vision, and because he seemed to have acquired his master's spiritual insight.

The Move to Lublin

Within the lifetime of Elimelekh, Jacob Isaac had established his own court at Lancut near Lyzhansk. In 1800, no doubt in deference to Rabbi Eliezer, Elimelekh's successor, he moved to Lublin, which had been the meeting place of the "Council of Four Lands" (*Vaad Arba Aratzot*). It has also been the home of Rabbi Jacob Pollak, Rabbi Shalom Schakhna, and Rabbi Meir ben Gedaliah, the *Maharam.* Seroka 28, the street where Rabbi Jacob Isaac established his *Beit Hamidrash,* vied in popularity with the *Maharshal's Shul* (the synagogue of Rabbi Solomon ben Jehiel, the *Maharshal* (1510–1573). Lublin became the training ground for hasidic leaders. Gifted young men flocked there, as did the founders of the most illustrious hasidic dynasties in Poland and Galicia. The dynasties of Przysucha, Kotzk, Ger, Ropczyce, and Dynow were all greatly influenced by the life and doctrines of the Seer. Even the iconoclastic Menahem Mendel of Kotzk, generally no respecter of persons, referred to the Seer as *Urim Vetumim.* Rabbi Uri of Strelisk, known as the "Seraph" (d. 1826), declared: "Lublin is *Eretz Yisrael;* the court of the *Beit Hamidrash* is Jerusalem; the *Beit Hamidrash* itself is the Temple; the study of the Seer is the Holy of Holies, and the *Shekhinah* speaks from his mouth." Rabbi Elimelekh of Dynow compared his visionary gifts with those of the Prophet Samuel.

It was said that the moment a *hasid* arrived, the Seer would take out his soul and cleanse it carefully, remove all the rust and restore it to a state of pristine purity, so that its owner became as sin-free as a newborn babe. People left his presence comforted and hopeful. However, this was not a reciprocal process, and the *tzaddik* himself was generally of a somber disposition. Although he inspired confidence in others, he had little self-assurance. While there was always a smile on his face, there was no joy in his heart, for he was always afraid; afraid of sin, afraid of his own power. "There can be no man less worthy than I am," he sighed, "the lowliest workman is more deserving."[15] "Woe to the generation," he lamented, "that looks to me for leadership."

The Seer ministered to his community with diligence and devotion, and from this he derived special satisfaction. "I do not know what merit I have definitely acquired. Maybe I can rejoice that I have performed at least one good deed in this life," reflected the self-effacing Seer. "I arranged the marriage of forty orphans. Whenever I arranged a marriage for a member of my own family, I also provided for a fatherless child." The Seer habitually brought home poor wayfarers and waited on them himself, for "is not carrying the spoons and the coal-pan from the Holy of Holies part of the services of the High Priest on the Day of Atonement."

The Seer took nothing for granted and even explained that there was a good reason for the acceptance of *pidyonot* (presents of money). "When a *tzaddik* petitions God on behalf of a *hasid,* it is possible that this may be regarded as presumptuous. People may ask him, 'Why does not the *hasid* pray for himself?' Now, when the *tzaddik* accepts money, he has a ready response: 'I am praying on his behalf because he has given me a *pidyon.*' "[16]

The Books of the Seer

He was the author of three works: *Divrei Emet,* printed by his grandson, Rabbi Jacob Isaac, carries the *haskamot* of Rabbi Abraham Joshua Heschel of Opatow and Rabbi Meshullam Zalman Ashkenazi of Lublin. It was printed in Zolkiew in 1808 and has since been reprinted eighteen times. Apart from the discourses, there are writings on the talmudic tractates *Shabbat* and *Hullin.* Another work, *Zot Zikkaron,* was first printed in Lvov in 1851 and has been reprinted twelve times, and *Zikkaron Zot,* on the weekly portions of the Torah, received the *haskamot* of Rabbi Jacob Aryeh Guterman of Radzymin, Rabbi Dov Berish Meisels, and Rabbi Joseph Saul Nathanson of Lvov. It was printed in Warsaw in 1869 and has since been reprinted nine times. The *Hozeh* himself gave *haskamot* to eleven works, among them *Divrat Shlomo* (Lvov, 1899) and *Likkutei Maharan.*

In Lublin, Rabbi Jacob Isaac faced great opposition from the *mitnagdim,* especially from Rabbi Berish Shveshaft (c. 1824) and Rabbi Azriel Halevi Horowitz (d. 1819) known as *Der Aizener Kop* ("The Iron Head"). From his second marriage to Tehilla Sprinza, daughter of Rabbi Tzvi Hirsch of Lancut, the *Hozeh* had four sons (Rabbi Israel, Rabbi Joseph, Rabbi Abraham, and Rabbi Tzvi Hirsch) and two daughters.

On the night of *Simhat Torah* 1814 after the Torah processions, the Seer left the *beit hamidrash* and retired to his room on the first floor of his house. The room had only one small window. At midnight a *hasid,* Rabbi Eliezer of Hmelnick, passed the *rebbe's* courtyard and saw a body lying on the ground. "I am Jacob Isaac the son of Motel," the Seer whispered to him. He was taken into the house. "The evil powers pursued me," he told Dr. Bernard of Piotrokow. He was seriously injured, and died on *Tisha B'Av* 1815. His mysterious fall has never been explained.[17]

Chapter 11

The Way of Przysucha

Rabbi Jacob Isaac was also the name of the greatest of all the Seer's disciples. He was commonly known as the Holy Jew, the *Yehudi HaKadosh,* or the *Yid HaKodesh.* He was a giant among giants, regarded with affection and with awe. Many explanations have been offered for the appellation of "Holy Jew." Some explain that it was given to distinguish between the Seer and his student, in compliance with the rabbinic ruling that forbids a disciple to call himself by the same name as his teacher.[1] Others maintain that the soul of the disciple, Jacob Isaac was the soul of Mordekhai, the hero of the Book of Esther, who is referred to in the Book of Esther (10:3) as "Mordekhai the Jew" (*hayehudi*). The Talmud asks rhetorically why Mordekhai was called *hayehudi* (the Jew) and answers, "because he repudiated idolatry. Anyone who repudiates idolatry is called a Jew."[2] Pride, anger, avarice, slander, and lying are synonymous with idolatry. Throughout his life, the Holy Jew shunned such negative qualities, and for this reason he merited the title "Yehudi."

According to yet a third theory, Jacob Isaac would scrupulously identify all authorities he cited in his discourses and would even attribute his own ideas to others, with the modest disclaimer: "I heard it from a Jew." Perhaps the truth is that the "Holy Jew" was simply an apt description of this remarkable rabbi, for every day of his life Jacob Isaac strove to be a Jew in the fullest sense of the term.

Early Influences

He was born in 1765 at Przedborz, a town in the Kielce province of Central Poland. His father was Asher Rabinowicz (d. 1798) at one time the rabbi in Grodzisk. Like Rabbi Israel Baal Shem Tov, the boy studied and prayed in secret, spending hours alone in the deserted *Beit Hamidrash* without the knowledge of his parents or his teachers. At the age of 14, he studied under Rabbi Aryeh Leib Charif Heilprin, who afterwards served as rabbi in Sochaczew and Warsaw. Jacob Isaac attended the *yeshivah* at Leszno in western Poland, under Rabbi David Tevele ben Nathan (d. 1792), rabbi of Horochow and author of *Nefhesh David* and *Mikhtav LeDavid* (Przemysl, 1878).

It was not only from his rabbis that Jacob Isaac learned wisdom. He liked to tell of the lesson taught him by his neighbor, a blacksmith. Late one night, when the weary scholar was preparing to set aside his books, he heard the smith still hammering away. "If my neighbor can labor so industriously for material things," he reflected, "then surely I can work even harder in the service of the Lord." And at dawn the knowledge that the smith was already at the anvil drove slumber from the scholar's eyes. In these long hours of study, he mastered Talmud and rabbinics to such high degree that he asserted that in the classical work, *Urim VeTumim* by Jonathan Eibeschütz (1690–1764), he only found "three remarkable passages."

At Opatow

While Jacob Isaac lived in Opatow (Apta) with his parents-in-law, he acted for a time as principal of the Talmudical College. Opatow was the home of Rabbi Moses Leib of Sasow (1745–1807) author of a noted novella on the Talmud.[3] The rabbi of Sasow was called "the father of widows and orphans," because he worked tirelessly to raise funds to sustain the poor and to redeem captives. At Opatow, Jacob Isaac established cordial relations with Rabbi Moses Leib and also came into contact with the extraordinary rebbe, Abraham Joshua Heschel (d. 1835), a disciple of both Rabbi

Elimelekh of Lyzhansk and Rabbi Jehiel Michael, the *Maggid* of Zloczow.

Under the Wing of the Rabbi of Lelov

Jacob Isaac became a teacher and wandered from place to place in search of pupils. In the course of his wanderings, he encountered the kindly Rabbi David of Lelov (1746–1814), a disciple of the Seer, known for his patience and for his forbearance, for his love of children, and his concern for animals. During country fairs, he would bring water to thirsty horses neglected by their owners. Rabbi David brought a number of talented men under the wings of Hasidism and the Yehudi was his greatest acquisition.

Rabbi David brought Jacob Isaac to the Seer who considered the newcomer an answer to his fervent prayer: "Let God, the Master of the spirits of all flesh, set a man over the congregation who will go out before them and who will come in before them" (Numbers 27:16). The Yehudi was the answer to his prayer. The Seer was quick to recognize the quality of his new disciple, and he lavished him with praises. "His soul had already appeared three times: in our Patriarch Jacob, in Mordekhai, and in Rabbi Jacob ben Meir Tam (1100–1171)." Other contemporaries acclaimed him with equal warmth. "The rabbi of Lublin," said Uri of Strelisk, "can be compared to the phylacteries of Rashi. Jacob Isaac can be likened to those of Rabbenu Tam."[4]

A Gentle Disposition and a Sharp Wit

To Hasidism, Jacob Isaac applied the dialectic approach of the talmudists. Allied to his quick wit was a gentle disposition, for he would expound his precepts to colleagues and disciples with humility. He regarded pride as the source of all evil, and there was not a trace of it in the unassuming *tzaddik.* "Why," he asked, "is the word 'justice' repeated twice in the injunction, 'justice, justice shalt thou follow' " (Deuteronomy 16:20). "Because," he explained, "only just means should be used to secure the victory of justice. Moreover, a man should never cease to pursue justice."

The Enmity of the Seer

Yet the mild master had his detractors, among them the Seer himself, whose attitude towards him was, to say the least, ambivalent. Although he occasionally delegated authority to senior disciples, the Seer came to resent the growing influence of Jacob Isaac. Since the Seer ministered to the masses, he had little time for the "graduate" disciples. Consequently, men like Menahem Mendel of Kotzk, Simha Bunem of Przysucha, and Dov Baer of Radoszyce transferred their allegiance to Jacob Isaac, who established his own court in Przysucha. This aroused the antagonism of the Seer, and the hostile flames were fanned by such mischief makers as Simon Ashkenazi and Judah Leib of Zelichow. Jacob Isaac's every action was misrepresented and his visits to Lublin misconstrued. "He comes only to woo *hasidim* away from me," was the Seer's unperceptive reaction, as he virtually banished Jacob Isaac from Lublin. Although yearning with all his heart for reconciliation, Jacob Isaac practiced patience and restraint, but to no avail. He even traveled to Rymanow to seek Menahem Mendel's intervention as peacemaker. But nothing helped. "Let it be," the Yehudi then said to Hayim Meir of Moglienice, "No good will come of our talk. They will soon say that I am acting like a *rebbe*."[5]

On one occasion, the Seer presented Jacob Isaac with one of his shirts as a mark of esteem, and the gift was precious in the eyes of the disciple. But on his way to the bath house, a ragged beggar fell at the feet of the Yehudi and wept bitterly. The compassionate sage had no money at hand, so he took the shirt that the Seer had given him and handed it to the beggar. News of this incident quickly reached the Seer, who was angered at the apparent slight. Grieved by the misunderstanding, Jacob Isaac turned to the Seer. "Look into my heart," he pleaded. "Can you see there any anger or evil intent?" The Seer gazed at him long and earnestly and turned away abashed. "There is neither anger nor evil intent in your heart."

It was revealed to Jacob Isaac that, according to the hidden auguries in the mystical book of *Raziel* (a composite kabbalistic book supposedly delivered by the Angel Raziel to Adam), he was destined to die after *Rosh Hashanah,* and when the time came the Seer was distraught. "Stay with me," he implored, "and we will keep you alive." But Jacob Isaac declined. "The Seer could have kept me alive," mused the Yehudi, "but my soul would have paid a high price."

An Unhappy Home Life

Jacob Isaac's domestic life, too, was not free from dissension. His wife, Sheindel, was difficult and quarrelsome. It is related, for instance, that once, on the first night of Passover, she refused to allow Jacob Isaac's aged mother to sit at her accustomed place next to her son, claiming this prerogative for herself. A tempestuous scene ensued. The dismay of the Yehudi and the chagrin of the *hasidim* disrupted the serenity of the evening. The Yehudi died on the 19th of *Tishri* (the third day of *Hol Hamoed Sukkot*) 1814.[6] He was survived by three sons, Rabbi Jerahmiel, Rabbi Nehemiah, and Rabbi Joshua Asher, and one daughter, Rebecca Rachel, who married Rabbi Moses Biderman of Lelov. The Yehudi's discourses are found in *Nifla'ot HaYehudi* (Piotrokow, 1908) *Torat HaYehudi* (Bilgoray, 1911), *Tiferet HaYehudi* (Piotrokow, 1912), and *Keter HaYehudi* (Jerusalem, 1929).[7]

The Philosophy of Przysucha

The Przysucha doctrines, like *Habad* philosophy, brought about a new orientation in Hasidism. What Rabbi Shneur Zalman had done for White Russia and the Ukraine, Jacob Isaac did for Polish Jewry. The Hasidism of Elimelekh of Lyzhansk, of Israel of Kozienice, and of the Seer of Lublin was concerned with the masses. The *rebbes* were preoccupied with the material, as well as the spiritual, well-being of their followers. Like faithful shepherds, the *rebbes* could not be deaf to the cries of the flock. The *rebbes* were practical idealists. They were concerned with helping as many as possible as much as possible.

The *rebbe* is not "merely" a miracle worker. Indeed it is considered no great effort to work miracles. It requires greater effort–and is a greater accomplishment–to be a good Jew. Therefore, it is important to learn to be a good Jew. Through study of *Gemara* (Talmud) and *Tosafot,* the mind is purified and ennobled.[8]

"Ye shall not lie to one another" (Leviticus 19:11) enjoins the Torah, but it is equally essential for a man not to lie to himself. With all his strength, the Yehudi fought against superficiality, stressing sincerity and total involvement in prayer, study, and every human relationship. For Rabbi Shneur Zalman it was possible to acquire the love of God and the fear of God only through the contemplation of the almost ineffable grandeur of Creation. Jacob Isaac, however, was not concerned with speculative research, but with action and motivation. Neither parental merit nor the mediation of teachers could bring one to the highest pinnacle. It could only be reached through painstaking personal striving. Every deed should be performed in the spirit of truth, for truth is the seal of God. Falsehood and deceit must be completely eradicated. The Besht believed that there was a spark of divinity in every Jew. Jacob Isaac went even further maintaining that every Jew could be a Moses and should be satisfied with nothing less than aiming for the highest goal.

The Yehudi's Prayers and Views on Prayer

In Przysucha, services were not always recited at the prescribed times, for it was believed to be better to pray late than to pray without *kavanah.* Regular hours are acceptable under normal conditions, but during an emergency, unconventional methods must be used. For the *hasid,* life is always a battlefield, for there can be no armistice between those mortal enemies, good and evil. The teachings of the Yehudi would seem to be in the mainstream of hasidic thought, yet just as Rabbi Shneur Zalman was opposed by Rabbis Barukh of Medzibozh, Mordekhai of Lehowitz, and Abraham of Kalisk, so too, Jacob Isaac had many adversaries who rejected his teachings as novel.

"The prayer of Jacob Isaac," commented Rabbi Jacob Aryeh of Radzymin, "was like the prayer of the Besht. The prayer of the Besht was like the prayer of Isaac Luria. The prayer of Isaac Luria was like the prayer of Rabbi Simon bar Yohai, and the prayer of Rabbi Simon bar Yohai was like the prayer of Adam before he sinned." Not only did Jacob Isaac establish a famous dynasty, but he also blazed a new trail through the complex maze of hasidic lore.

Rabbi Simha Bunem

In the early history of Hasidism, sons did not automatically succeed their fathers. The Yehudi had three sons, Jerahmiel, Nehemiah, and Joshua Asher. Yet his *hasidim* appointed Rabbi Simha Bunem, the Master's favorite disciple, as their leader.

Simha Bunem Bunehart was born in Wodzislaw in 1765. His father, Tzvi, was *maggid* of the town and a scholar of note.[9] On his mother's side, Simha Bunem was a descendant of Joel ben Samuel Serkes (1561–1640). From his father Simha Bunem acquired a basic grounding in Rabbinics and homiletics. Later, to widen and deepen his knowledge, he studied in Mattersdorf under Rabbi Joab ben Jeremiah (d. 1807) and at Nikolsburg under Mordekhai Benet (1753–1829), Chief Rabbi of Moravia. Benet was famous for his wide-ranging erudition. Every day he would either lecture on Maimonides' work *Yad Hahazakah* ("The Mighty Hand") or his *Mishneh Torah* ("The Second Law"), the Hebrew compendium of the *halakhah.* He paid particular attention to Hebrew grammar and to the medieval Jewish philosophers.

A Cosmopolitan Rabbi

Upon his return from Hungary, Simha Bunem married Rebecca of Bendin, and the young scholar soon became attracted to Hasidism. Rabbi Moses Leib of Sasov, the Seer, Rabbi David of Lelov, and Rabbi Israel of Kozienice became his spiritual fathers. At the suggestion of the *Maggid* of Kozienice, Simha Bunem began to work for the industrialist, Berek Dov Bergson, and his wife, Tamarel, and he traveled widely as their representative. The cosmopolitan rabbi frequently visited the Danzig and Leipzig trade fairs. He wore European clothes, spoke Polish and German, visited the theater occasionally, and enjoyed playing cards.

After a few years as a timber merchant, Simha Bunem qualified as a practicing chemist (*magister pharmaciae*) in Lvov. He opened an apothecary's shop in Przysucha, where he soon acquired a large clientele. He even supplied medicines to the Napoleonic forces in Russia.

An Unlikely Heir to the Court of Przysucha

His business preoccupations did not lessen his interest in Hasidism. He visited the rabbis of Kozienice, Opatow, Lelov, and Lublin regularly. "Stay with me," pleaded the Seer, "and I will endow you with the Holy Spirit."[10] In Przysucha and in Lublin, Simha Bunem fell under the spell of Jacob Isaac, and the master loved him dearly. "This young man," remarked Jacob Isaac, "is the core of my heart." Every night Simha Bunem would close his store and hasten to the Yehudi, where new stores of wisdom were opened for him. He accompanied the Yehudi to Rymanow, and when the Yehudi died, Simha Bunem was his heir apparent. Some could not forget his background. "How can he call himself rabbi," sneered Rabbi Meir of Opatow. "Did he qualify for that in Danzig, in German theaters, or in the pharmacy?" "Rabbi Meir does not know what sin is, and he does not know how to sin," retorted Rabbi Simha Bunem. "I can understand temptation and can help men to withstand it. I can inspire my *Hasidim* with the fear of God."[11]

Just as Rabbi Dov Baer developed the doctrines of the Besht, so Simha Bunem interpreted the ideas of Jacob Isaac. He too surrounded himself with a band of selected young men to whom he dedicated his life. They responded with equal dedication, forsaking all material interests (sometimes even wife and children) for his sake. "He never speaks an idle word," testified one disciple. Regular periods were set aside for the study of Talmud, medieval philosophy, and cognate subjects. *Kabbalah* did not figure prominently in the curriculum. The school of Simha Bunem concentrated on Maimonides' *Guide to the Perplexed,* Judah Halevi's *Sefer HaKuzari* ("Book of the Khazars"), Jedidiah Berdesi's *Mivhar Peninim* ("Choice of Pearls"), and the works of Judah ben Betzalel Löw, the *Maharal* of Prague, whom Simha Bunem regarded as his "Heavenly Teacher."[12]

Rabbi Simha Bunem thought highly of the commentary on the Pentateuch by Rabbi Abraham Ibn Ezra (1089–1164), whose textual analysis was the forerunner of Biblical criticism. "Through Ibn Ezra," asserted Simha Bunem, "one can acquire fear of God." It was quite possibly to counter the growing influence of the *Haskalah* movement that Simha Bunem focused attention on the primary sources of Judaic faith and inspiration: the Bible, Talmud, and the medieval philosophers.

Defender of His People and His Faith

Rabbi Simha Bunem did not lead an isolated life in Przysucha. He distrusted the "enlightened absolutism of Nicholas I." He boldly told high Russian officials that "it was not the business of the State to interfere in the internal affairs of Jewry. These matters could safely be left in the hands of rabbis and spiritual leaders. As far as the Jews were concerned, the duty of the State was to improve their economic position and to alleviate the poverty that prevailed among them." He vehemently opposed the Committee of the Old Covenant (*Komitet Staroza-konnych*) and its assimilationist program, particularly its emphasis on secular education for children, censorship of Hebrew books, translation of the Talmud, and the establishment of a rabbinical training college. Supporters of this committee, which was founded in Warsaw in 1825, included the mathematician, Abraham Stern, representing the *maskilim* and Jacob Zunberg Bergson, son of Tamarel.[13]

In his later years, Rabbi Simha Bunem became blind, an affliction that he accepted with courage and faith. "I prayed to God," he said, "that He should deprive me of my sight in order that I might see the inner light. . . . What is good for me to see I see with the inner light. What is not good to see, I do not wish to see at all."

On Truth, Humility, and Prayer

Rabbi Simha Bunem held that truth must permeate every thought, every word, and every deed. Any action that is not based on truth has no validity. A man must be faithful to God and to his people. But first of all he must be faithful to himself. Preparation is the basis of prayer and study. A man must first cleanse his heart and mind. It is futile to pray when preoccupied with sensual desires and worldly thoughts, and it is useless to perform *mitzvot* for ulterior motives. Doing so would be tantamount to idolatry. In order to strike the proper balance between pride and false humility, "an individual should believe simultaneously, 'I am dust and ashes', and 'for me alone the world was created.' "

The *hasidim* of Przysucha did not stress congregational prayers nor did they conform rigidly to regulated hours of worship. On the words of the morning prayer, "Let a man at all times revere God in private as in public, acknowledging the truth in his heart," Simha Bunem commented: "Only if a man acknowledges the truth and speaks the truth is he able to 'rise early' and pray at the appointed times laid down by the sages."[14]

On Miracles and Tzaddikim

Miracles had no place in Rabbi Simha Bunem's philosophy. He tried to curb the cult of the *tzaddik.* "A fur hat and an illustrious father," he pointed out, "do not make a *tzaddik.* No doubt, Esau, too, wore silk garments and recited Torah at *Shalosh Se'udot* (the third Sabbath meal)."[15]

The Parables of Rabbi Simha Bunem

Apart from the Besht, no other *tzaddik* had created as many parables as Simha Bunem. The parable of the false *tzaddik* is an illustrative example. The authorities seized a drunken peasant and decided to have a little sport with him. They washed him, dressed him in the garb of a high Church dignitary, and brought him, still unaware, to the episcopal palace. The dazed villager awoke from his stupor, found himself dressed as a bishop and treated with deference and addressed with respect. Servants bowed and the public accorded him great honor. Eventually, he became convinced that he really was a bishop. True, he could not understand the theological tomes that lined his study, but then he reasoned that in all probability, neither could any of the other bishops. Similarly, the *rebbe* pointed out, that not all who dress like *tzaddikim* are actually *tzaddikim.* They may appear to be *tzaddikim,* but they are far removed from the path of godly fear and love, and thus the people are misled.[16]

In another story, he related how Rabbi Eizik Yookil of Krakow dreamed that he should go to Prague, where he would find a great treasure near the Palace. When the same dream kept recurring, Rabbi Eizik went to Prague in search of the treasure. On the third day, one of the guards approached him. "Stranger," he said, "I have been watching you these three days, walking aimlessly around the palace. What are you looking for?" The rabbi revealed his purpose. He explained: "I had a remarkable dream. I was told that if I dug beneath the royal palace, I would discover a great treasure. But now I am here I do not know what to do." The soldier smiled. "You believe in dreams? Look at me! I, Dimitri Massarek, one of His Majesty's guards, dreamt the same dream for two consecutive nights. Go to Krakow, said a voice to me. Dig in the yard of a Rabbi Eizik the Hebrew teacher, and you will discover a treasure. But I take no heed of such foolishness. I would not waste my time or money journeying to Krakow. I do not believe in dreams."

According to Rabbi Simha Bunem, the wiser a person is the more humble he should become. To consider the greatness and glory of Creation is to become aware of one's insignificance. But it is not enough to be outwardly self-effacing. A man may appear unassuming, while his heart is filled with arrogance. Before prayer it was particularly important to be free of all feelings of egoism and self-importance.

Ironically, the teachings of Rabbi Simha Bunem aroused the antagonism not only of the *mitnagdim,* but also of a number of *hasidim.* Rabbi Naftali of Ropczyce went as far as to describe him as "dangerous." "I am not saying anything against the rabbi personally," Naftali rather unconvincingly explained, "he is a true *tzaddik,* yet his way is dangerous to those who follow him." In an equally enigmatic vein, Rabbi Uri of Strelisk commented, "Rabbi Simha Bunem is a great *tzaddik* who wishes to show the world a new way to God, but he traveled the new path before the work was completed. As a result of this, those who followed him have taken a wrong course."

A Failed Effort to Undermine Rabbi Simha Bunem

Many *tzaddikim* attended the wedding in Ustilug of the son of Rabbi Dan ben Isaac of Radziwillow and the daughter of Joseph ben Mordekhai of Neshitz. Such opponents of Rabbi Simha Bunem as Simon Ashkenazi, Moses of Kozienice, and Meir of Opatow, seized the opportunity to seek the support of Rabbi Abraham Joshua Heschel of Opatow in undermining the status of Simha Bunem. But the Rabbi of Przysucha sent five of his disciples, among them Isaac Meir of Ger, Alexander Zusya of Plock, Issahar Dov Horowitz, Rabbi Feival of Grice, the son-in-law of Bergson, Eliezer Dov of

Grabovitz, to present his side of the story to the Apter. As a result, the opponents of Simha Bunem met with a stern rebuke. "If you were living in a forest," the Rabbi of Opatow admonished them, "you would have quarrelled with the trees."[17]

Rabbi Simha Bunem died on the 12th of *Elul* 1827. As he lay dying, he heard his wife Rebecca weeping. "Why do you weep?" he comforted her, "All my life I have been learning how to die." A sepulcher (*ohel*) was built over his grave in Przysucha. He was succeeded by his son, Rabbi Abraham Moses (1800–1829). Rabbi Simha Bunem's discourses are found in *Hedvat Simhah* (Warsaw, 1930), edited by Rabbi Jonathan Halevi Eibeschütz; *Kol Simha* (Przemysl, 1876); *Ramataim Zoffim* by Rabbi Samuel Shinover (Warsaw, 1908); and *Niflout Rabbi Bunem* (Warsaw, 1908).

"Rabbi Simha Bunem," said Rabbi Isaac Meir of Ger, "had the keys to all the firmaments. He could have quickened the dead but he did not take what was not his."

Rabbi Naftali Tzvi of Ropczyce

Among the hasidic *rebbes* who left an imprint on Galician Hasidism was Rabbi Naftali Tzvi of Ropczyce who was renowned for his humor, his wit, and his glittering aphorisms. Many called him "the wisest of the *rebbes.*" He once remarked, "I would rather sit next to a wise man in purgatory than next to a fool in paradise." Like Rabbi Israel Baal Shem Tov, Rabbi Naftali believed that a person could transcend his limitations in the joy and service of the Creator.

Naftali was born in Leshnev on the sixth of *Sivan* 1760. His father, Mendel Rubin, was rabbi in the town. His mother, Beila, was the daughter of Yitzhok Horowitz of Hamburg. At first, Naftali studied under his father and then in the *yeshivah* of his uncle, Rabbi Meshullam Igra (1752–1802) of Tysmenitsa and Pressburg. Naftali quickly made a name for himself as a brilliant speaker and his *bon mots* earned him renown. He became a disciple of Rabbi Elimelekh of Lyzhansk, Rabbi Menahem Mendel of Rymanow, and of the Seer of Lublin.

On the death of his father, on *Simhat Torah* 1804, Rabbi Naftali succeeded him as rabbi of Linsk but continued to reside in Ropczyce. A follower of the school of Przysucha, Rabbi Naftali opposed unnecessary delay in the recitation of the statutory prayers and believed that the services should be held at the appointed times as laid down in the Codes.[18] He set high standards for his followers. "The main aim of a *hasid,*" he stated, "is to study Torah diligently and the Talmud diligently until at least the age of 25 and only then should Hasidism be studied."

Beliefs and Customs

By means of his prayers, a *tzaddik* can annul the decrees of the Almighty. Through prayer, a *tzaddik* can create a new world in which evil does not prevail. Moses said, "I prayed to the Almighty at that time,"[19] implying that a Jew can and should pray to the Almighty at all times. Faith is superior to wisdom, because wisdom has its limits while faith is infinite. In every aspect of life, a person must serve the Almighty. The primary motive for eating and drinking should be to gain strength in order to study and to pray. By our service to the Almighty, we are rebuilding Jerusalem daily. One of us adds a row, another only a brick. Each contributes according to his strength. And when Jerusalem is completed, the Redemption will take place. A man should avoid anger, because it can only be counterproductive. Had Boaz become angry when Ruth sought him out, he would not have married her and King David would not have been born. Rabbi Naftali stressed truthfulness. The last letter in the Torah (Deuteronomy, 31) is a *lamed.* The first word in the Book of Genesis is a *bet.* A *lamed* and a *bet* stand for the Hebrew word *Lev* (heart), sincerity.

Once, on *Shabbat HaGadol,* he returned home exhausted after delivering an impassioned discourse on the great *mitzvah* of *Ma'ot Hittin,* (providing the poor with Passover necessities). "Were you successful?" asked his wife. "I have succeeded in accomplishing half the task," replied the rabbi. "The poor are willing to take, but the rich are not yet willing to give."[20] He pointed out that the lot of the spiritual leader was not an easy one. Moses, who established his tent "outside the camp," was criticized for his "aloofness." Aaron who mingled freely with the community was censured for being "too accessible."[21] Rabbi Naftali urged his followers to study works of *Musar* such as *Tanna Devei Eliyahu.* He would blow the *Shofar* on *Hoshana Rabba.* On the Eighth day of *Tishri,* he would recite the Book of Psalms twice, because there are 150 Psalms, and the sum of twice that number (300) is equivalent to the numerical value of the Hebrew word *kapper* (forgive).[21]

Rabbi Naftali's discourses are recorded in *Zera Kodesh,* part one on Torah and part two on Festivals. It was first published in Lvov in 1868 with the endorsements of Rabbi Joseph Saul Nathanson and Rabbi Hayim Halberstam of Sanz. His second work, *Ayalah Sheluhah* on Genesis and Exodus, was printed in Lvov in 1863. His third work, *Imrei Shefer* on the Torah, was printed in Lvov in 1884. *Ohel Naftali* (Lvov, 1911), edited by Abraham Hayim Simha Bunem Michelson, contains many of Rabbi Naftali's stories.

Rabbi Naftali died on the 11th of *Iyyar* 1827 and was buried in Lancut, near Rzeszow. He was survived by three sons. His successor as rabbi of Ropczyce, however, was his son-in-law Rabbi Asher Isaiah Rubin, the author of *Or Yeshu* (Lvov, 1870). He died on the eve of Passover 1845.

The Ohev Yisrael

After the death of the *Maggid* of Kozienice, Rabbi Abraham Joshua Heschel "the *Ohev Yisrael*" ("the Lover of Israel") became the spokesman for Hasidism. He was known as the peacemaker. Dissident hasidic sects at odds on ideological grounds accepted his authority.

Rabbi Abraham Joshua Heschel implored his children not to inscribe extravagant epitaphs upon his tombstone. He pleaded, "Write only that I loved the House of Israel." His teachings are reflected in his books, *Ohev Yisrael* ("Lover of Israel") and *Torat Emet* ("The True Law"), both published posthumously. Although not a *kohen* (of priestly descent), the rabbi of Opatow believed that he had been a High Priest in an earlier life. In the order of service of the High Priest, recited during the additional service (the *Avodah*) on the Day of Atonement, the rabbi would change the prescribed text: "Thus did he (i.e., the High Priest) say," to "And thus did I say." Sincerity characterized his life, and he strove to serve God with selfless dedication.

Venerated by his *hasidim,* he also won the admiration of his teachers and his peers. "He is as kindhearted as our Father Abraham," declared Rabbi Elimelekh of Lyzhansk. The *Ohev Yisrael* was born in 1748 in Zmigrod, near Rzeszow. His family tree could be traced back to Rabbi Abraham Joshua known as "Rabbi Reb Heschel" of Krakow. In 1788, he became rabbi of Kalbaszow, near Rzeszow, Western Galicia, where he lived in dire poverty.[23] In

1800, he became rabbi of Opatow. He tried his utmost to bring the different hasidic groups together. He defended the *hasidim* of Bratslav against the onslaught of their implacable enemy Rabbi Moses Tzvi of Savran. He acted as a conciliator at the famous hasidic wedding of Ustilug. The opponents of Rabbi Simha Bunem of Przysucha met with stern rebuke.[24]

It is not clear why the *Ohev Yisrael* left Opatow in 1808 and assumed the rabbinate of Jassy in Moldavia. He saw special symbolism and a good, personal omen in the Hebrew spelling of the name of his new home: In Hebrew, Jassy is spelled "Yas" (*Y*od, *A*lef, *S*amekh), which, he maintained, stood for *Sof* (samekh) *Eretz* (alef) *Yisrael* (yod), a phrase that means "the borders of the Land of Israel."[25] Jassy, however, soon proved to be an unhappy place for him. The man of peace, the conciliator, was beset by hostility and antagonism. As conditions in Jassy became untenable for him, the *rebbe* revised his acronym and said that the name "Yas" stood for *Yesh* (yod) *Omrim* (alef) *Sedom* (samekh), meaning "some would call it (the town) Sodom.[26] In fact, in order to escape his persecutors, he fled the city in the dead of night. His final abode was Medzibozh, the "Jerusalem of Hasidism" where he lived for twelve years. He died on the 5th day of *Nisan* 1825 at the age of 77. His work, *Ohev Yisrael* (Zhitomir, 1863), was acclaimed by the *hasidim*. Twelve editions have since appeared. Rabbi Hayim of Sanz studied a portion of the *Ohev Yisrael* every day and declared that "A Jew should even pawn his Sabbath garments to acquire a copy of this book." The *Ohev Yisrael* was opposed to asceticism. He pointed out that in the *Sidrah* of *Ekev,* it is twice written, "And you shall eat and be satisfied" (Deuteronomy 8:10 and 11:15). He saw no point in enduring unnecessary hardships. He quoted the passage from the Talmud (*Berakhot* 8a), "Eating and drinking on the ninth of *Tishri* (the day before the Day of Atonement) is equivalent to fasting on the ninth and tenth (i.e., on the Day of Atonement itself). Purposeful fasting was a different matter when Czar Alexander I issued anti-Jewish decrees on the 14th of January, 1824, the *rebbe* immediately proclaimed a fast day. The rebbe maintained that it is a positive commandment to love every Jew. Love of the Jewish People is bound up with love of the Almighty. Both are equal since he who loves the Almighty loves His people. One should attempt to love one's fellowman with true concern for his welfare and for his future.

Chapter 12

The Holy Rebel

Menahem Mendel of Kotzk is one of Hasidism's greatest enigmas.[1] He mystified his contemporaries, terrified his followers, baffled his biographers, and intrigued hasidic historians. Biographies, essays, novels, and plays have been written about him, yet very little is known. So, while it is not easy to analyze his teachings, it is even harder to unravel the complexities of his character. The light of research has not dispersed the clouds in which he deliberately enveloped himself. But from innumerable anecdotes, aphorisms, and discourses, gathered and transmitted by able disciples, there emerges the outline of a tragic and powerful figure.

Like the prophets of old, he became the great protester and challenger of religious behavior within the hasidic movement. If classical Hasidism emphasized love, joyfulness, and emotionalism, the rebbe of Kotzk invoked constant tension and militancy. A lonely man and an original thinker, he lived in dissent and continuously questioned accepted habits of thought. He was the embodiment of protest against the trivialization and externalization of religious life. Rabbi Mendel saw the shallowness of the prevailing religious mood, fought against it, and remained all his days at war with himself and society. He did not yield. He lived in a state of permanent agitation and ferment and could not bear the complacency and indifference that led to decay. He was out to intellectualize the mind and deepen the outlook. Thought had to take preference over emotion, analysis over imagination.

"Black Mendel"

Menahem Mendel (Heilprin) Morgenstern was born in 1787 in Bilgoray, near Lublin. His father, Leibish, was a poor glazier who earned an inadequate livelihood by traveling to remote villages. From infancy, Mendel was a determined, headstrong child to the point of being almost unmanageable. Educating this brilliant but unruly boy was no easy matter. He lived in a world of his own–a world of books and dreams, never wasting a moment in play or childish pursuits. He developed into an organized student and a highly independent thinker. An introvert, he was cold and reserved, unwilling to confide in anyone. "I am alone," he wrote rather sadly, "even when I am surrounded by friends and colleagues."

He studied at the *yeshivah* of Rabbi Joseph Hochgelernter (1740–1807), author of *Mishnat Hakhamim* (Lvov, 1792), at Zamosc. His fellow students nicknamed the youthful introvert "Black Mendel," because of his personality and because he devoted himself with complete absorption to his studies. He had little concern for family or friends. Only his teachers mattered to him. He was particularly respectful of his first instructor, the one who had taught him the alphabet, upon which all subsequent studies are based. As he pointed out, the teachers of Scripture, Mishnah, Talmud, and the Codes deal with controversial matters, but there is no controversy over the *Alef Bet* (the first two letters of the Hebrew alphabet).

His academic prowess impressed and awed his instructors: "Mendel does not make even a gesture without premeditation. His words are deep. His ways are hidden." Later his disciples spoke of him with even greater reverence. "What I have labored over for many days," marveled Rabbi Isaac Meir, "the rabbi grasps in seconds. My knowledge does not even reach his doors." "He is the source of all wisdom and understanding," averred Rabbi Abraham of Sochaczew.

At the age of 20, Mendel married Gluckel Nei of Tomaszow. After giving birth to a son, David (who later succeeded him), Gluckel Nei died. One year later Rabbi Mendel married Haya Lipshitz, the sister-in-law of Rabbi Isaac Meir Alter. Two sons (Rabbi Benjamin and Rabbi Moses Jeruham) and two daughters (Sarah Zina and Berakhah) were born of this union. Afterwards, he made his way to Lublin. "An old man in Gorey," related Mendel, "was telling hasidic tales in the *Beit HaMidrash.* He told what he knew, and I listened. I became a *hasid.*" When his father reprimanded him for associating with a hasidic rabbi, Mendel replied, "We read in the Torah (Exodus 15:2) 'This is my God and I will glorify Him'. My spiritual father takes precedence over my physical father." But it was not easy to be a spiritual father to this determined youth. "What sort of rabbi do you want?" the Seer of Lublin asked him. "I seek a rabbi who is a good Jew, a plain Jew, and one who fears God," was Mendel's forthright reply. The Seer responded, "Your way is the way of melancholy. Forsake it, for it has not found favor in my eyes."

The Influence of the Court of Przysucha

Mendel did not change his ways, but his *rebbe.* In Jacob Isaac of Przysucha, he found a leader who was a kindred spirit, a *rebbe* who scorned the elaborate ritual of the hasidic court. For the first and only time in his life, he felt that he was no longer alone, for Przysucha was a training ground for the perfection of the soul.

With Jacob Isaac's death, Mendel was left a spiritual orphan. *Hasidim* relate that the *rebbe* appeared to his bereaved disciple in a dream. "Now that I have been called to the 'Academy on High,' you know not who will be your teacher, but be not dismayed. In the celestial spheres I shall continue to be your guide." Mendel, who was afraid of no man, living or dead, replied, "I do not want a dead teacher."

Like most of his colleagues, Mendel transferred allegiance to Rabbi Simha Bunem, the successor of Jacob Isaac. But peace of mind eluded him. In self-imposed penance he wandered through the countryside, suffering many hardships. In turn he visited Kozienice, Lelov, and Szydlowiec. Rabbi Simha Bunem was drawn to the brooding and intense young man. One Passover at the *Seder* table, Rabbi Simha Bunem handed him a handsome silver goblet saying, "This fine goblet belongs to the man who has the finest brain."

A Leader in His Own Right

After the death of Simha Bunem, Mendel settled in Tomaszow, where he became a legend in his lifetime. "A fire is burning in Tomaszow," *hasidim* used to sing, "a new light is burning there." Toward this new light streamed *hasidim* of all kinds, both the erudite and the unlearned, including those who virtually abandoned family and business. The deserted women pleaded and wept in vain. "Tears were created for women," the *hasidim* unrelentingly rejoined, for they could not tear themselves away from the "burning bush" that blazed in Tomaszow. In the simple, austere synagogue they led a materially comfortless existence. Their clothes were threadbare. They were often hungry. But their hunger for knowledge was abundantly satisfied. Regularly their *rebbe* delivered discourses on the Talmud and Maimonides, and all the *hasidim* were involved in the mind-illuminating discussions that followed. There were no onlookers at Tomaszow. All were participants.

Two years later the Rabbi moved to Kotzk, where he was welcomed by his disciple, Mattathias Koroner, the rabbi of the town, and to Kotzk his devoted *hasidim* followed. "To Kotzk one does not travel," they used to sing, "To Kotzk one ascends. For Kotzk takes the place of the Temple, and to the Temple one ascends."

An Iconoclastic Rebbe

Mendel was not a *rebbe* in the accepted sense of the word. The stereotyped life that many of his fellow *rebbes* led was not for him. He despised the humble *hasidim* who begged for his blessing. He had just as much contempt for the wealthy followers who showered him, or were willing to shower him, with money or gifts. A man was not necessarily poor if he had no money, nor was a man rich if he had money. Mendel had a different sense of values. There were, according to him, only two categories—"poor in knowledge" and "rich in knowledge."

Mendel's discourses were terse, each weighed word requiring a commentary. Provided that his train of thought was clear to him, the rebbe of Kotzk cared little whether others understood him. Yet despite his aloofness and detachment, or perhaps because of it, he could not keep the throngs away. "Oxen, horses," he shouted at his *hasidim*, "what do you want from me?" But the less they were welcomed, the more they came. His very protestations provoked and attracted them. Men made considerable sacrifices to finance a pilgrimage to Kotzk. And there, in the shadow of the Master, they tarried for weeks or for months, forgetful of family and responsibilities. The avowed aim of their Master was to redeem the entire House of Israel and to make it "a kingdom of priests and a holy nation." And to do this he needed a *corps d'élite*, a small group of handpicked aides.

Rabbi Mendel, like Maimonides, preferred one discerning disciple to a thousand ignorant men. "Would that I had ten white *kaftans* and no more," he prayed. Through this small ruling class, an aristocracy of scholarship and piety, all Israelites would be led through the gates of knowledge and along the path of truth.

Usually impatient, often cruelly candid, Rabbi Mendel saw himself as a general deserted by his army in the heat of battle. He seemed to be fighting single-handed for truth and basic values. Naturally, his outspokenness did not endear him to his colleagues, nor did he court their friendship. "Do you think that I shall enjoy the world to come?" a rich follower once asked him. "You do not enjoy this world for which you have toiled so incessantly," came the forthright reply, "so how can you expect to enjoy the world to come for which you have made no preparations at all?"

Following the traditions of Przysucha, the rebbe of Kotzk attached no importance to miracles, believing that to transform a man into a real *hasid* was the greatest miracle of all, more important and more difficult than creating a *golem* (homunculus). The God-given injunction, "By the sweat of thy brow shalt thou eat bread" (Genesis 3:19), applies even more to spiritual bread. Nothing could be achieved without effort, but if the effort was strenuous enough, anything could be achieved. "If a man laments that he has striven but has not found," remarks the Talmud, "do not believe him." Mendel interpreted the talmudic adage as follows: "Do not believe that he has really striven with sufficient diligence, for, had he really exerted himself, he would undoubtedly have achieved his purpose. Why did the second Tablets of the Law survive, whereas the first Tablets were shattered?" The only reason, according to the rabbi's interpretation, was that as far as the first Tablets were concerned, Moses was simply the recipient. The first Tablets were given "ready made," and no human effort was needed. But Moses himself, with tremendous labor and earnest prayers, actually fashioned the second Tablets, and his supreme effort ensured their survival.

An Enemy of Compromise and Complacency

"All or nothing" was the credo of Kotzk, and its adherents scorned half measures and compromises. They believed that the half-way house is a resting place only for the indolent soul. Man must aim high, for he was created so that he might lift up the heavens. Only horses walk in the middle of the road. It was better to be thoroughly wicked than to be half a *tzaddik.* A perfect Gentile is better than an imperfect Jew. Sincerity is of the utmost importance, for God's name is truth. A rabbi is neither a king nor a high priest, but an ordinary human being who strives, as every man should strive, to achieve perfection. A man should increase his knowledge, even though by doing so he will inevitably lose his peace of mind. Mendel hated complacency. "He who learns Torah and is not troubled by it, he who sins and forgives himself, and he who prays today because he prayed yesterday–a very scoundrel is better than such a man."

"Where does God live?" Mendel was asked. "Wherever He is admitted," was his reply. Mendel was a dreamer. Aiming at the summit attained by the Besht, he plunged himself into the depths of melancholy. His dreams had strange dimensions, magnificent and megalomaniacal. "I am the seventh. I am the Sabbath. Six generations preceded me: the first was Rabbi Dov Baer, the second was Rabbi Shmelke, the third was Rabbi Elimelekh of Lyzhansk, the fourth was the Seer of Lublin, the fifth was the Holy Yehudi, the sixth was Rabbi Simha Bunem, and I, Mendel, am the seventh." "My soul," he said, "is one of those that were created before the destruction of the Temple. I do not belong among the people of today. And the reason for my coming into this world is to distinguish between that which is holy and that which is profane." Rabbi Mendel severely censured his hasidic colleagues. None lived up to his standards. "All the week they do what is right in their own eyes. Comes the Sabbath, they attire themselves in *kaftans* and fur hats and, wearing piety like a mantle, they exclaim: 'Come, my beloved.' "

Like the Yehudi and Simha Bunem, Rabbi Mendel did not always pray at the appointed hours. "In Kotzk," he said, "we have a soul and not a clock." To him proper preparation was as vital as prayer itself. He compared readying oneself for prayer to the actions of a woodcutter, who may spend most of the day sharpening his tools and laying the groundwork. Often it is not until the very end of the day that he actually proceeds to chop the wood that is to earn him his wages. If a man feels that by praying in private, he can concentrate better than in public, then he should do so. Lengthy services were not held in Kotzk. On the New Year and the Day of Atonement, for instance, the *piyutim* (liturgical poems) were omitted and the focal passages, the *Unetanneh Tokef* prayer of the *Amidah Musaf,* were recited quietly and quickly.

Among his many unsparing assessments and sayings was the following:

> The seal of the Holy One is Truth. The seal must be in writing, which does not lend itself to forgery, and it is indeed impossible to falsify the truth since falsified truth is not truth. What is the difference between a *hasid* of Kotzk and the rest of the *hasidim*? The latter perform the *mitzvot* openly but commit transgressions in secret, whereas the *hasidim* of Kotsk commit transgressions openly and the *mitzvot* in secret.[2]

Like the Besht, Rabbi Mendel was fired by lofty idealism. Unlike the Besht, he isolated himself from his contemporaries. He regarded himself as a reformer, a revivalist, a man with a mission. And the knowledge of his own superiority kept him apart. He did not find in his fellow men "the image of God." He saw only their faults, their weaknesses. "The whole world is not worth a sigh," was his misanthropic verdict. But neither reality nor dreams could still his spiritual *wanderlust* or satisfy his restless soul. His life was one long struggle with himself, an unceasing attempt to attain his impossible ideals.

In Support of Revolution

The *rebbe* of Kotzk supported the Polish revolt of 1830–1831, although his patriotism waned when the Minister of War, Morawski, declared, "We cannot allow Jewish blood to mingle with the noble blood of the Poles. What will Europe say when she learns that, in fighting for our liberty, we have not been able to manage without Jewish help." In spite of this, Joseph Berkowicz (1789–1846), son of Berek Joselewicz, urged the Jews of Poland to enlist, and similarly Rabbi Mendel urged wealthy Jews to aid the rebels. After the suppression of the revolt, he lived for a time in Galicia, changing his name to Morgenstern to deflect vicious Russian retaliation.

"That Friday Night"

One Friday night in 1840, on the eve of *Shabbat Toledot,* an extraordinary incident took place in the rabbi's house. It is one of the great mysteries in the history of Hasidism. The followers of Kotzk never discuss the subject, referring to it merely as "that Friday night," but *mitnagdim* and *maskilim* have no such scruples. They allege that in a crowded *Beit Hamidrash* at midnight, Rabbi Mendel cast aside the *Kiddush* cup that was held out to him by his faithful beadle, Tzvi Hirsch of Tomaszow. As if shattering the invisible chains that bound him, he cried out, "I demand justice. Have we not suffered enough? Why are you afraid, you flatterers and liars? Get away from here and leave me alone." Others assert that he shouted, "Get out of here, you fools. I am neither a rabbi nor the son of a rabbi."

The outburst exhausted him, and he fainted. He was carried from the *Beit Hamidrash* to an adjacent room, where he was revived with difficulty. On *Shemini Atzeret* 1840, Rabbi Mordekhai Joseph Leiner of Izbica, author of *Mei Hashillo'ah* ("The Waters of Siloam"), threw off the yoke of Kotzk. "The *Shekhinah* has departed from Kotzk," mourned the *hasidim.* A day after *yom tov,* together with a number of disenchanted *hasidim* Rabbi Mordekhai Joseph departed for Izbica, where he established his own court. "In Kotzk they worship the broken tablets," was Rabbi Mordekhai Joseph's cryptic comment.

A Nineteen-Year Seclusion

The majority remained loyal to their *rebbe.* Among the faithful were: Rabbi Isaac Meir of Ger, Rabbi Mendel's brother-in-law; Rabbi Abraham of Sochaczew; Rabbi Jehiel Meir, the "Psalm Jew of Gostynin"; Rabbi Isaac of Warka and Rabbi Henokh of Alexander. For nineteen years, until his death in 1859 at the age of 72, the rabbi of Kotzk remained secluded in his study. There he prayed, studied, ate, and slept. Through an opening in his door, he listened to the Reading of the Law and took part in congregational prayers. Even on the *Seder* nights, he sat alone in his room, alone with his God. At first, the beadle would bring out *shirayim* (morsels left over from the *rebbe*'s meal), but gradually this was discontinued. Only a very select number of disciples, such as his brother-in-law and his son-in-law, were able to enter the "Holy of Holies." Only once a year, on the day before Passover, did he leave his chamber so that it might be prepared for the festival. He seldom appeared in public. On the rare occasion when the double doors were opened and he entered the *Beit Hamidrash,* terror-stricken *hasidim* fled or hid under the tables. Yet, for nearly two decades, *hasidim* from all over Poland, outstanding rabbis and scholars among them, continued to make their way to Kotzk. Even a number of defectors returned, preferring the curses of Kotzk to the blessings of Izbica.

Neither Rabbi Mendel's terrifying silences nor his furious outbursts deterred them. They clustered in the *Beit Hamidrash,* studying, meditating, and gazing at the closed doors of the rabbi's room, hoping against hope to behold the countenance of the stormy petrel of Hasidism. They believed that their *rebbe,* in his self-imposed isolation, was fighting a great and fearful battle against all the massed forces of evil. They believed that, in his small room in Kotzk, the rabbi soared through the seven heavens, struggling desperately to hasten the coming of the Messiah.

A Radical Philosophy

It was a religious radicalization in which the late, great philosopher and mystic Professor A. J. Heschel saw an affinity between Rabbi Menahem Mendel's philosophy and the doctrine of the great Danish thinker, Soren Kierkegaard. Both of them independently took up a position of no compromise. To the Kotzker *Rebbe,* it meant either full religious dedication or satisfying the needs of daily life. Like Kierkegaard (of whom he had never heard), he saw the gulf between service to God and involvement in the world and its daily affairs, between piety and expediency, sanctity and self-interest. Judaism, observed Dr. Heschel, demanded everything of man, the whole man. But what the Kotzker saw around him "was fractional piety, bits and pieces of ritual floating in the vortex of disordered lives." Rabbi Mendel saw the shallowness of the prevailing religious mood, fought against it, and remained all his days at war with himself and society.

In his burning passion for truth, Rabbi Mendel saw the disease of man in falsehood, in self-pity, and in self-delusion. The heart of man is blocked and ossified. It is natural that his distrust of the world was great. He saw the world dominated by powers of falsehood and deception and demanded that at least religious existence should not give in or compromise. Religion was to him, according to Heschel, not a mere convenience, a pattern and routine, but a test and trial to man. Aiming high, Rabbi Mendel did not go out to reach all the Jews, but only the select, the few, the spiritual élite.

The Influence of Kotzk

Rabbi Mendel destroyed all his manuscripts. Methodically, each year on the eve of Passover, as he cleared out the leaven, he destroyed everything he had written. His teachings, however, left a permanent imprint on the courts of Sochaczew, Ger, and Alexander and on Polish Hasidism in general. The slight corpus of Mendel's work contrasts sharply with its powerful originality and consequent influence. His disciples were ardent and extravagant in their praise of this most turbulent of the *tzaddikim.* "It is not possible to find another like him, he is as great as the Besht," avowed Rabbi Isaac Meir of Ger. "Just as there was thunder and lightning when the Torah was given on Mount Sinai, so there was thunder and lightning when the Torah was received in Tomaszow. There is no one to grasp the quality of his genius and the degree of his greatness."

As Rabbi Mendel lay dying, he quoted the biblical passage, "With Him I speak mouth to mouth, even manifestly and not in dark speeches and in the similitudes of the Lord doth he behold" (Numbers 12:8). The dream of Rabbi Mendel of Kotzk was that every single Jew might speak face to face with his Maker, echoing the prayer of Moses, "Would that all the Lord's people were prophets and that the Lord would put His spirit upon them" (Numbers 11:29). Rabbi Menahem Mendel died on Thursday, the 22nd day of *Shevat* 1859. Rabbi Isaac Meir of Ger eulogized him: "The world is not aware of its loss. There is no one to grasp the qualities of his genius and the degree of his holiness. 'The *tzaddik* perished and no one layeth it to heart'[3] (Isaiah 57:1). Worse than that there is no one to lay the words of the *tzaddik* to our hearts." Rabbi Abraham of

Sochaczow went even further. "He is an angel of the Lord of Hosts. From him I learned wisdom and understanding." Rabbi Mendel's discourses are to be found in the manifold works of his disciples, in *Emet Ve'emunah* by Rabbi Israel Jacob Arton (Jerusalem, 1940) and in *Ohel Torah* (Lublin, 1909).

The rabbi of Kotzk was an enigma in his lifetime as he remains an enigma today. He baffled his contemporaries, and all that has been written in later years about him, both by those who knew him best and those who did not know him well at all, has not solved the mystery.

Chapter 13

The Royal Rebbe and the Militant Masters

The nineteenth century was Hasidism's golden era. This was the time when many Eastern European villages had their own hasidic courts. Many a remote little *dorf* (hamlet) in Russia and Poland owes its immortality to the hasidic rabbi who lived there and adopted its name as his title. So it was with Belz, Ruzhin (Rizhyn), and Ger. From these hamlets, brilliant luminaries lit up the souls of men and added a new luster, a new richness, a new depth to the hasidic constellation. For more than 100 years Ruzhin and Sadgora were focal centers–cities of refuge for *hasidim* in Eastern Europe.

Israel Friedmann, founder of the Ruzhin-Sadgora dynasty, was born on the 3rd day of *Tishri* 1797 in Predzborz near Kiev. His father, Rabbi Shalom Shakhnah (1771–1802), was the son of Rabbi Abraham "the Angel," and the grandson of Rabbi Nahum of Chernobyl (d. 1795). Shalom Shakhnah was 6 years old when his father, Abraham, died, and Israel was but 5 years old when he was orphaned. The child was brought up by his elder brother, Rabbi Abraham, who had succeeded his father. At the age of 13, he married Sarah, daughter of Rabbi Moses, head of the Talmudical College of Berdichev and later rabbi in Butchan. When his brother, Abraham, died childless in 1813, the 16-year-old Israel was his heir. The youthful *rebbe* settled first in Skvira and then in Ruzhin, where he established his court.

A Resemblance to the Besht

According to legend, the Besht once said, "My soul will return to earth after forty years," and many *hasidim* believed that this did, in fact, happen and that the soul of Israel Baal Shem Tov found a second home in Ruzhin.

In many ways, Rabbi Israel did resemble his great namesake. Like the Besht, he lost his father at an early age. Life was his teacher and nature his inspiration. Like the Besht, he was a man of joyous faith. "He who does not serve the Lord with joy," he stated, "does not serve the Lord at all." He opposed asceticism, believing that to afflict one's body was to endanger one's soul. Tolerant and kindly, he held the humblest individual in high esteem. "When a Jew takes his *tallit* and *tefillin* and goes to the synagogue to pray, he is as important today as the Besht and my great-grandfather the *Maggid* were in their day." Rabbi Israel further maintained that "just as the letters of the alphabet are mute without the vowel signs and just as the vowel signs are meaningless without the letters, so *tzaddikim* and *hasidim* are bound up with one another."

The Admiration of Hasidim *and Rabbis Alike*

Rabbi Israel did not write learned books nor did he make any notable contribution to hasidic thought. It was neither scholastic discourses nor exegetical homilies that attracted people. As errant children come to a loving and all-forgiving father, so the people came to Rabbi Israel. He identified himself with the problems of each *hasid,* and in his hospitable house the doors were never shut. *Hasidim* from all walks of life mingled in true fellowship.

Even among the rabbis of the day, there was remarkable unanimity in their affection for him, and almost all his colleagues felt a reverential regard for the rabbi of Ruzhin. At the famous hasidic wedding at Ustilug in 1814, Rabbi Abraham Joshua Heschel, "the Moses of his generation," once bound Israel's *gartel* (belt) around his *kapote* with the words, "Heaven hath honored me with *gelilah* (the *mitzvah* of binding the *Sefer Torah*).[1] Israel has not forgotten what he learned in his mother's womb. We, his elders, should we not abase ourselves before this young man of Ruzhin because of his nobility and uprightness?" Even the rationalist Rabbi Samson

Raphael Hirsch (1808–1888), leader of Jewish Orthodoxy in Germany, remarked after meeting Rabbi Israel, "It is difficult to perceive how such a man could be born of woman, for the light of the *Shekhinah* shines in his face." "No one can compare with him," said the Seer of Lublin, "he has the soul of King Solomon."

When Rabbi Hayim Halberstam (1793–1876) visited Rabbi Israel, he offered these words of praise:

> Why was the Temple built on Mount Moriah (where the binding of Isaac took place) and not on Mount Sinai (where the Torah was given to Israel)? Because the place where the Jew is willing to offer his life for the Sanctification of God's Name is more sacred than the place where the Torah was given. At all times Rabbi Israel is ready to offer himself for the Sanctification of God's Name.

Hasidic Royalty

Ruzhin spelled royalty. The rabbis of Ruzhin were, virtually, the Exilarchs of Hasidism. They dressed with elegance and lived in the style that befitted descendants of the House of David. "If one appears before a king, one dons fine garments, how much more so should one prepare for the presence of the king of kings?" Rabbi Israel adopted the life and style of a Polish landowner or a Russian nobleman. His residence was palatial. "Like the house of a prince," notes Professor B. Mayer in *The Jews of Our Time,* "and his clothes were costly." His coach was drawn by four horses, and he employed a large retinue of servants. In *Brama Pakulu* ("The Gates of Repentance") the non-Jewish writer Braniecki, noted that "the greatest architects, painters, and decorators came especially from Paris and Italy to the little town of Ruzhin in order to build and decorate the rabbi's house. The residence was most impressive from without, and valuable materials were used to adorn the interior."

On July 13, 1866, the London *Jewish Chronicle* reported: "The luxury of the palace is truly royal. Among other things there is a silver room full of the most splendid articles of all types and various shapes, the value of which is estimated at several hundred thousand rubles. The apartments contain most splendid Turkish and Persian carpets as well as most heavy damask hangings . . . his sons and sons-in-law wear the most magnificent *kaftans.* The smallest children and grandchildren have French, English, German, and Russian nurses and governesses, and, moreover, have tutors like young princes."

"What can I do?" asked the rabbi. "It is not my choice. I am forced from above to take the road of honor and glory, and it is impossible for me to deviate from it." The poor were not intimidated by the aura of royalty; they thronged to him and found him approachable and unassuming. The aristocracy was impressed and non-Jews often sought his guidance. Such were the claims on his time, that Rabbi Israel slept only three hours a day. "One must not waste the time of the kingdom," he said. He would rise at dawn and spend many hours in prayer and study. He opposed asceticism, however, for when a man fasts, he harms himself not only physically but also spiritually. "When there is a little hole in the body," he said, "it eventually makes a hole in the soul."

An Outlook of Benevolence and Tolerance

The Russian ukase of 1827, whereby boys were conscripted into the army at a tender age, caused the rabbi of Ruzhin considerable grief. He wept for the young boys, little more than children, whom the ruthless recruiting officers often snatched off the streets. When the little conscripts, known as Cantonists, sadly confessed that they were forced to desecrate the Sabbath and to contravene the Dietary Laws, the rabbi comforted them tenderly; "When the Messiah comes," he answered them, "it is you who will take precedence over all the *tzaddikim.*" Rabbi Israel's outlook might well be called ecumenical. Benevolent and flexible was his approach. He believed that many, if not all, roads lead to Heaven. Some make their way heavenwards through study, others through prayer, some through teaching, others through learning, some through fasting, and others through eating.

In prayer, Rabbi Israel preferred the "still, small voice." He once whispered to a *hasid* praying loudly and violently, "My friend, try first the quiet way." He urged his followers to pray at the times prescribed by the Codes.

A Prisoner and a Refugee

In the winter of 1836, two notorious Jewish informers, Isaac Uksman and Samuel Swartzmann were assassinated in Nuvay,a Oshitsa, Podolia.[2] As a result, many Jews were arrested, including Rabbi Israel, whom the governor of Kiev, General Bibikov, regarded as "wielding almost the power of a Czar." For twenty-two months, despite prodigious efforts by his *hasidim,* the rabbi languished in the prisons of Kiev and Kamenetz-Podolsk, accepting his fate with resignation and realism. "Am I better than the head of our family, King David, who suffered persecution at the hands of kings and princes?" he asked. In 1840, on the day after *Purim,* he was released and allowed to return to Ruzhin. He was, however, under strict surveillance. To forestall banishment to Siberia, Rabbi Israel escaped to Rumania, where he stayed first in Jassy and later in Scala. Meanwhile, he advised his family in Russia, though they were not in immediate danger, to escape to France or England.

Unhappily, peace eluded the refugee rabbi. The Russian Government demanded his extradition. To save their leader from imprisonment and possible banishment to Siberia, the *hasidim* maintained that Rabbi Israel was an Austrian citizen, born in Sadgora (Sadagura) to Hertz and Feige Donnenfeld. Eight people, both Jewish and non-Jewish, corroborated this claim, while the Russian Government produced documentary evidence to counter it. Austria's Salomon Mayer von Rothschild (1774–1865), interceded with Count Metternich, and the Austrian Government refused to accede to the Russian demands.

Rabbi Israel acquired an estate, Zolotoi Potok, in Sadgora, near Czernowitz and there the glory of Ruzhin was revived.

Rabbi Israel wanted to have a synagogue built in Jerusalem, but there were many obstacles to overcome before it could be built. It was no wonder that Rabbi Israel stated that he was not destined to see the erection of the synagogue and that "his son would have to build a house, for my name." In a public proclamation, Nisan Bak pleaded that "it is already twelve years since we acquired the site to erect a magnificent structure," but the synagogue remained unbuilt. He was supported in his efforts by Rabbi Abraham Jacob of Sadgora and by the family of Ezekiel Reuven Sassoon. When the Emperor Franz Joseph (1830–1916) visited Jerusalem on November 14, 1869, he noticed the unfinished building. "Where is the roof of the synagogue?" asked the Emperor. "Your Excellency," replied Nisan Bak, "even the synagogue is happy to welcome you and has taken off its cap in deference to your Majesty." The Emperor took the hint and donated 100 franks to complete the structure.[3]

The beautiful synagogue, with thirty windows facing the Temple Mount and a twelve-windowed dome, was consecrated on *Shabbat Nahamu* 1870. It was known alternately as *Tiferet Yisrael* in honor of Rabbi Israel of Ruzhin or *Beit HaKnesset Nisan Bak.* Together with fifty-seven other historic synagogues, it was wantonly destroyed by the Jordanians in the years following 1948.

The Succession

Rabbi Israel died on the 3rd day of *Heshvan* 1851. "Everyone leaves behind books," he mused, "I leave sons." Each of his six sons established his own hasidic dynasty, each attracting a large following. They were Rabbi Shalom Joseph (1813–1851) of Sadgora, Rabbi Abraham Jacob (1819–1883), Rabbi Menahem Nahum (1827–1869) of Stefanesti, Rabbi Dov (1827–1876) of Leove, Rabbi David Moses (1828–1900) of Chortkow, Rabbi Mordekhai Shraga (1834–1894) of Husyatin. There were also three daughters (Leah, Toba, and Miriam). Rabbi Israel's discourses are found in *Irin Keddishin* (Bertfeld, 1907), *Knesset Yisrael* (Warsaw, 1907), *Beit Yisrael* (Piotrokow, 1913), and *Nifla'ot Yisrael* (Warsaw, 1924).

The Militant Masters of Belz

During the nineteenth century, Belz, a small town in the Lvov area of Galicia, with a Jewish population in 1921 of 2,104 souls (50.7 percent of the total population), became the court of a famous hasidic dynasty. The founder of the Belz dynasty, Rabbi Shalom, was born in Brody in 1803. Rabbi Shalom's father, Rabbi Eleazar, a disciple of Rabbi Hayim Zantzer of Brody, was a direct descendant of Rabbi Eleazar ben Samuel (1665–1742) of Amsterdam, author of *Sefer Maaseh Roke'ah* (Amsterdam, 1740). A medal was designed in the Rabbi of Amsterdam's honor. On one side was exhibited his head in relief, surrounded by the words "Eleazar ben Samuel"; the other side contained chosen verses from Psalms. Rabbi Shalom's mother, Rebecca Heni, was the daughter of Rabbi Judah Zundel of Brody, a descendant of the talmudist and Kabbalist, Rabbi Todros ben Joseph Halevi Abulafia (1220–1290), author of the Kabbalistic work *Otzar HaKavod* ("Treasury of Glory"), a Kabbalistic interpretation of *aggadot* ("homilectica portion") in the Talmud printed in Nowydwor in 1808 and *Shaar HaRazim* ("Gates of Secrets"), a commentary on the nineteenth Psalm.

The Early Years of Rabbi Shalom

Rabbi Shalom's beginnings were spectacularly unpromising. His father Eliezer, died at the age of thirty-two in Warsaw and was survived by three sons and two daughters. Shalom's mother remarried, and young Shalom was brought up by his uncle, Rabbi Issahar Baer, rabbi of Sokol. As he grew, he became known as the "*illui* of Rava," and eventually married Malka, the daughter of the rabbi of Sokol.

Even before daybreak, the dutiful Malka would wake her husband with the words: "Shalom, arise to the service of the Creator." She would urge him, "all the laborers are already at their appointed tasks." Inspired by his wife, Shalom needed little urging, but in appreciation he applied to her the verse in Genesis (14:18), "And Melchitzedek, king of Shalem," interpreting it, "If Malka (his wife) is *tzeddeket* ("righteous"), then Shalom is king."

Hasidic Influences on Rabbi Shalom

Through Rabbi Solomon of Lutzk (d. 1813), a disciple of the *Maggid,* Shalom was drawn to Hasidism. Rabbi Solomon became, in effect, the Boswell of the *Maggid* of Mezhirech. He devoted his life to collecting and collating the sayings and discourses of the *Maggid.* Two important works, *Divrat Shlomo* ("The words of Solomon") and *Maggid Devarav LeYaakov,* ("He declareth his words unto Jacob") are the results of his labors.

Rabbi Shalom visited many of the leading hasidic rabbis of his day, including Rabbi Abraham Joshua Heschel of Opatow, Rabbi Uri of Strelisk, and the *Maggid* of Kozienice. Yet, while he appreciated the rare qualities of all the great *tzaddikim* he met, he remained an ardent devotee of Rabbi Jacob Isaac of Lublin. "He who knew the Seer glimpsed the heights to which a mortal could attain, and he who knew the Holy *Maggid* of Kozienice realized how much the love of God meant to the Jew." Whenever Rabbi Shalom left Kozienice for Lublin, the *Maggid* would release him with reluctance. "Stay here," the *Maggid* pleaded, "and you will see the prophet Elijah." "Stay with me and you will behold the Patriarchs," the *Maggid* promised further. But Rabbi Shalom withstood these temptations, and the reward was a warm welcome from the Seer. "He who deprives himself of the privilege of beholding Elijah and the Patriarchs, in order to return to his teacher," glowed the Seer, "he is indeed a true *hasid.*"

The Seer predicted that this young disciple would be "the head and leader of thousands," and honored him in many ways, such as allocating to him *shishi* (the sixth portion of the Reading of the Law), a *mitzvah* much sought after by the *hasidim.* Once, after Rabbi Shalom had recited the *Megillah* ("The Book of Esther"), the Seer commented: "I have heard this tale told many times but never as movingly as this." It was at the suggestion of the Seer that Rabbi Shalom agreed to become rabbi in Belz, a small town forty miles north of Lvov, and there he remained for forty years.

The Rabbi's Wife

Rabbi Hayim Halberstam of Sanz and his son Rabbi Barukh once visited Rabbi Shalom. He found Rabbi Shalom and his wife sitting in a bare room with plain walls. On their departure, Rabbi Hayim inquired of his son what impression the couple had made on him and how the room in which they were seated appeared to him. "As we entered," replied Rabbi Barukh, "they seemed like Adam and Eve before they sinned and as if their room was paradise." Rabbi Shalom consulted his wife Malka on almost every problem, and his example was followed by his *hasidim.* Once, when a man complained of a painful leg, she advised him to light a candle every day in the synagogue. He did so, and made a complete recovery. To her awed husband she explained, "It is written in the Psalms, Thy word is a lamp unto my feet" (119:105).

"Lord of the World! If I had the strength to waken her, would I not have done so by now?" exclaimed Rabbi Shalom when she died. "I am simply not able to do it. But You, Lord of the World! You have the power to awaken the dead. Why do You not awaken Israel?"

The Leader of Belz

Belz had always been fortunate in its spiritual leaders. Among its renowned rabbis were Rabbi Joel Serkes and Rabbi Zekhariah Mendel ben Aryeh Leib, a well-known commentator on the Codes. Under Rabbi Shalom, Belz maintained its academic leadership. People came to him from Galicia, from Hungary, and from Poland. He had many followers, and among his outstanding visitors were Rabbi Shalom Halevi Rosenfeld of Kaminka, Rabbi Hayim of Sanz, Rabbi Ezekiel of Sieniawa, and Rabbi Joshua of Leczna. From the Rabbi of Belz they learned the importance of sincerity and simplicity.

The rabbi of Belz[4] did not dress in white garments, nor did he distribute *Kamaot* (amulets), but he was widely known as a worker of miracles. Men, sick in mind or body, hastened to him. Apparently, none were disappointed, for they came as supplicants and remained as *hasidim*. "In Belz we discovered," *hasidim* would say, "that a man can be a rebbe without a *zipice* (the traditional white kaftan). They observed Rabbi Shalom at prayer and discovered the meaning of devotion. He worshipped with such intensity that phrases seemed to tumble over one another, and prayers were recited at lightning speed. Similarly, his discourses were brief and to the point.

The Danger of the Haskalah

The Edict of Toleration did little to improve the severe economic problems of the Jewish community, and taxes continued to mount. A tax on kosher meat was introduced in 1784 and increased in 1789, in 1810, and in 1816, a year that saw the introduction of a candle tax. Enforced secularization began in 1836, with the Government decree that no rabbi should be appointed who had not taken an academic course. Galicia became the center of the *Haskalah* ("Enlightenment") movement, with Letteris, Krochmal, and Rapoport as its key protagonists.

With seemingly disproportionate virulence, the *maskilim,* as the enlightened were called, assaulted Hasidism as "a cancer that has to be eradicated from its very source." In his satires, *Megalleh Temirin* ("Revealer of Secrets") and *Bohan Tzaddik* ("The Test of the Righteous"), ridicule was the weapon of satirist Joseph Perl (1774–1839). The *tzaddikim* were described as men who were ready to commit every crime. Hasidic discourses and homilies were distorted and misrepresented. But the assaults were not only verbal. A number of the *maskilim* even became "informers," hurling accusations, true and false, at the *hasidim,* accusing them of evading the candle tax, of illegally maintaining synagogues, and of printing hasidic literature.

The high incidence of apostasy among the *maskilim* convinced Rabbi Shalom that the *Haskalah* represented a danger to Judaism. There is no half-way house in Judaism. "In the Codes of the *Shulhan Arukh,* in the *Orah Hayim* ("The Way of Life"), in the *Yoreh De'ah* ("The Teacher of Knowledge"), and in *Even HaEzer* ("The Stone of Help"), works dealing with the relationship between God and man, the term 'compromise' is not to be found. Only in the *Hoshen Mishpat* ("The Breastplate of Judgment"), which deals with monetary matters, does the word occur." Thus, the rabbi of Belz refused to temporize with the reformers, categorizing as rank heresy the slightest deviation from the traditional path.

Rabbi Shalom was by nature a fighter. All his life he had fought spiritual battles. From boyhood he had excluded from his life all activities that might distract him from his studies and his struggle for spiritual self-betterment. Now he devoted himself single-mindedly to the fight against the *maskilim.* One way in which he did this was to stress the need for the thorough training in Torah for young children. "Days are coming," he warned, "when to rear a son in the Torah and in the fear of God will be as hard to accomplish as the Binding of Isaac."

Rabbi Shalom's Death and Legacy

Rabbi Shalom is quoted in the halakhic responsa by Rabbi Solomon ben Judah Aaron Kluger (1783–1869) of Brody in his work *Ha'elef Lekha Shlomo* (part 3, no. 100) and by Rabbi Joseph Saul Nathanson (1810–1875) of Lvov in his work *Sho'el UMeishiv* (part 3, no. 119).

Toward the end of his life he became blind. He died on the 27th of *Elul* 1855. His last words were: "O Lord, I am oppressed, be Thou my surety" (Isaiah 38:14). In conformity with the traditions of Belz, no *ohel* was built over his grave. He was survived by five sons (Rabbis Eleazar, Samuel, Moses, Judah Zundel, and Joshua) and two daughters (Freida and Eidel). His fifth and youngest son, Rabbi Joshua, succeeded him.

Rabbi Shalom was greatly revered by his colleagues as well as by his disciples. Rabbi Israel Friedmann of Ruzhin said: "The rabbi of Belz is the Master (*Baal HaBayit*) of the World." His discourses were collated by Rabbi Abraham Hayim Simha Bunem Michelson in *Dover Shalom* (Przemysl, 1910).

Rabbi Joshua Rokeah of Belz

Rabbi Joshua, the fifth and youngest son of Rabbi Shalom Rokeah, succeeded to the spiritual throne of Belz. Rabbi Joshua was born in Belz in 1825. He was renowned both for his phenomenal rabbinic knowledge and for his worldly wisdom. He married Rebecca Miriam, daughter of Rabbi Samuel Ashkenazi, son-in-law of Rabbi Isaac Meir of Zinkov (1775–1855) who was in turn the son of Rabbi Abraham Joshua Heshel of Opatow (1776–1825), the *Ohev Yisrael.* On the death of his father in 1855, Rabbi Joshua became the rebbe of Belz. When a *hasid* pleaded, "Help me die as a Jew," Rabbi Joshua pointedly replied, "You are making the request that Balaam made. Balaam the wicked prayed, 'Let me die the death of the righteous and let mine end be like his' (Numbers 23:10). This is understandable, for Balaam was a gentile but wished to die like a Jew. Try to live the life of a Jew first. The rest will come naturally."

Marshaling the Forces of Hasidism

Rabbi Joshua believed that a Jewish spiritual leader is obliged to devise ways and means of attracting those who are not *hasidim* and turn them into sympathizers. From distant lands men traveled to him, and all felt rewarded by the forthright counsel he offered. For him no Jew was beyond redemption. Rabbi Joshua was one of the first hasidic rebbes to engage in politics. The majority of Galician

Jews were *hasidim,* and his aim was to enlist and coordinate this reservoir of hasidic strength. Only in this way could he counteract the activities of the assimilationist organization, the *Shomer Yisrael* Association (founded in 1868), and its journal *Der Israelit* which was founded to disseminate the doctrines of the *maskilim.*

Defending the Faith

Rabbi Joshua met with opposition from all sides but despite this, he formed the *Mahzikei HaDat* organization in Galicia and Bukovina. It was the first attempt of Orthodox Jews to unite for political action in order to protect their traditional way of life. The founding conference of *Mahzikei HaDat* took place on March 13, 1879. A bimonthly paper *Mahzikei HaDat* appeared in both Hebrew and Yiddish. The *Mahzikei HaDat* published a list of Orthodox candidates standing for election to the Austrian Parliament of 1879. Of the four candidates only one, Rabbi Simon Sofer (1821–1883) of Krakow, was elected. Rabbi Simon was the son of Rabbi Moses Sofer, known as the *Hatam Sofer.* Rabbi Joshua of Belz urged his *hasidim* to vote for him. Rabbi Simon had been appointed rabbi of Mattersdorf in 1848. In 1861 he moved to Krakow, where he served as rabbi until his death. He was the author of *Mikhtav Sofer* (Jerusalem, 1952–1955). Like his famous father, Rabbi Simon believed that *Hadash asur min HaTorah* (any innovation is strictly forbidden).

In 1882, the *Mahzikei HaDat* convened a large conference that was attended by 200 rabbis and 800 representatives of different communities. The purpose of the conference was to safeguard the religious character of the Jewish communities from the pernicious influence of the Reform and the progressive movements. The conference passed a resolution that only Jews meticulously observing the precepts of the *Shulhan Arukh* were to be granted full voting rights at Jewish communal elections. "We have 613 commandments. Every one is holy and dear to us. We cannot forget even one of them," declared the rabbi of Belz to the *maskilim.*

In his fight to preserve traditional Judaism, Rabbi Joshua enlisted the help of such leading rabbinical authorities as Rabbi Joseph Saul Nathanson, rabbi of Lvov, Rabbi Isaac Aaron Ettinger, known as *"Reb Itsche"* (1827–1891), rabbi of Przemysl, and Rabbi

Meshullam Issahar Horowitz of Stanislaw. In Eastern Galicia during the 1850s, Jews accounted for one-third of the population in cities such as Lvov (Lemberg), Drohobycz, Stry, Kalish, Tysmenitsa, Jaroslaw, and Przemysl. Jews formed an absolute majority in the cities of Tarnopol, Kolomyya, Turka, and Rzeszow, and the bulk of them were *hasidim* of Belz.

Concern for Hungarian Orthodoxy

The *rebbe* of Belz was also concerned with developments in Hungary. The bitter polemics between the Orthodox and the reformers (who in Hungary were referred to as Neologists) came to a head at the General Jewish Congress, convened by the Government in 1868. It was attended by 220 delegates (126 Neologists and ninety-four Orthodox). The Orthodox left the Congress as the Hungarian Government would not initially recognize their privileges. It was only in 1870 that the Austrian Parliament permitted the Orthodox section to establish independent communities.

In an 1886 letter addressed to the Hungarian community of Sighet, the *rebbe* of Belz strongly condemned the appointment of a *shohet* (ritual slaughterer) without the consent of the local rabbi, and he stated that the animals slaughtered by this man should be classified as not fit for Jewish consumption. In a second letter, Rabbi Joshua stressed that no good would emerge from the reformers, and under no circumstances should one associate with them. The *rebbe* was in sympathy with the convention held in 1865 in Michalve, a town in Northeast Slovakia, that decided on the secession of the Orthodox congregations. The *rebbe* used to say, "When you are overtaken by tribulation, know that you are being tested by the Almighty to see how you will accept it. If you endure and adhere to the teachings of Nahum Ish Gamzu (a second century *tanna*) that this too is for your good, your distress will vanish. You will have to endure further, and you will then see that the misfortune was indeed for your good."

Like his father, Rabbi Shalom, Rabbi Joshua corresponded on halakhic matters with his contemporaries. He is quoted in the responsa *Birkat Retzah* by Rabbi Tzvi Hirsch Orenstein (1775–1839), author of *Yeshuot Yaakov* on *Shulhan Arukh, Orah Hayim* and by Rabbi Hillel Lichtenstein of Kolomyya (1815–1891), author of *Avkat*

Rakhel and *Beit Hillel* (Satmar, 1906). Like his father, Rabbi Joshua continued the building and extensions of the *Beit HaMidrash* of Belz, and it became one of the traditions of every rebbe of Belz to enhance the structure of the *Beit HaMidrash.* The rebbe wore a *tallit* both for *Minhah* and *Maariv* on the eve of each Sabbath even when not officiating at the reader's desk. He permitted *hasafot* for even the *kohen* and *levi* portions of the Reading of the Law.

Rabbi Issahar Dov Rokeah of Belz

Rabbi Issahar Dov, the third rebbe of Belz, was born in Belz in 1854. He was the second son of Rabbi Joshua and Rebecca Miriam, a granddaughter of Rabbi Abraham Joshua Heschel of Opatow. At the age of 14, Rabbi Issahar Dov married Batya Rehuma, daughter of Rabbi Isaiah Meshulam Zusya Twersky, son of Rabbi Aaron Twersky of Chernobyl. For ten years, Rabbi Issahar Dov stayed in Chernobyl and was known as the "*illui* of Chernobyl." In 1894, he succeeded his father as *rebbe.*

The *Mahzikei HaDat,* founded by his father, was weakened by the death of Rabbi Simon Schreiber (Sofer) in 1883. In 1908, the *rebbe* of Belz revived the *Mahzikei HaDat* by publishing a proclamation *Kol Mahzikei HaDat.* In it he denounced any attempts to introduce a divisive spirit influenced by arid nationalism into the communities. After World War I, when Poland became independent, a section of the Orthodox community, under the influence of the rabbi of Belz, was guided by the *Mahzikei HaDat.* A conference attended by representatives of many communities took place in Grojec Jugdellonski (Gorodok) on December 22, 1931. Its influence was confined to Galicia. Rabbi Abraham Mordekhai Alter of Ger was anxious to enlist the rebbe of Belz in the ranks of the *Agudah.* In a letter written in 1921 by Rabbi Abraham Mordekhai Alter on his return journey from the Holy Land, he stated, "I was anxious to go to Munkacs and see the rebbe of Belz, but in Vienna I was made aware of his views by Rabbi David Schreiber and consequently refrained from going."

A Courteous and Courageous Man

Rabbi Issahar Dov was gifted with the "common touch." He was kind, courteous, and humane. His displeasure was however quickly stirred against those who deliberately flouted Jewish Law. His manner was forceful in all things, and he favored the direct approach. When it was decreed that rabbis should take state examinations, he reasoned with the governor of Lvov as follows: "If your Excellency wishes to construct railways, would he not call in engineering experts to guide and to advise him? Surely in such matters he would not consult shoemakers? Similarly, in matters affecting the welfare of the rabbinate, only rabbis should be consulted."

With the outbreak of the First World War, Rabbi Issahar Dov moved first to Ratzford (Usfeherte) where he resided from 1914–1918, then to Munkacs (1918–1921) and then to Holshitz, near Jaroslav. In 1925 the *rebbe* returned to Belz, where he lived for the rest of his life. He employed a personal attendant, Jacob the *maggid,* whose only duty it was to rebuke his master at regular intervals. When they were dining together one day, Jacob the *maggid* taunted him: "The rabbi is seated and is unmindful of townsfolk who have no food." Immediately Rabbi Issahar Dov left the table to collect money for the poor.

His wife, Batya Rehuma died young. They had one son (Rabbi Aaron) and one daughter. After an interval of many years, the *rebbe* of Belz married Chayah Devorah, daughter of Rabbi Abraham Samuel, son of Rabbi Joseph of Brezany, a descendant of Rabbi Aaron Twersky of Chernobyl. There were three sons and three daughters from this marriage. Rabbi Issahar Dov is quoted in the learned works of Rabbi Isaac Schmelkes of Lvov in *Beit Yitzhak,* by Rabbi Meir Shapiro in his work *Or HaMeir,* and by Rabbi Tzvi Ezekiel Michelson.

Belz and the Beit Yaakov *Movement*

What Ger was to Poland, Belz was to Galicia. "The whole world," as *hasidim* of Belz were wont to say, "journeys to Belz." The rebbe of Belz underlined simplicity and sincerity as the fundamentals of the good life. In October 1922, Count Galecki, governor of Lvov, urged the rebbe of Belz to direct his *hasidim* to vote against the Minority Block. Unequivocally, the *rebbe* of Belz refused.

Sarah Schenirer, a dressmaker and the founder of the *Beit Yaakov* movement, was the daughter of Betzalel Hakohen of

Tarnow, a devoted *hasid* of Belz. In 1917, when she returned to her native Krakow, the dressmaker's fantasy become a fact. With the blessing of the *rebbe* of Belz, she started a school for twenty-five girls in a tiny room at Katarzyna Street, in the Jewish quarter of Krakow. Thus was founded the *Beit Yaakov* movement, whose alumnae were to become the "anti-assimilationists, the upholders of Jewish tradition, and the opponents of the subversive socialism which is spreading among the Jewish youth in Eastern Europe." By 1924, there were nineteen schools with 2,000 students. By 1937, there were 250 *Beit Yaakov* schools with a student population of 38,000. To supply the teachers for this mushrooming movement, the *Beit Yaakov* Teachers' Seminary was built in Krakow in 1925. One hundred–twenty young women began their training in 1925, and fifty students graduated each year. "The Seminary is a sunny isle that sends its rays out to the whole *Beit Yaakov* movement," a religious journalist, A. M. Ragawy, wrote in lyrical praise.

Descriptions of the Court of Belz

Jiri Mordekhai Langer (1894–1943), the Czech poet and author, visited Belz in 1913 and remained for some time at the court of the *rebbe*. When he returned to Prague, he continued to wear hasidic garments. At the outbreak of the First World War, he again visited Belz and wrote "Nine Gates," a volume of hasidic tales that have been translated into many languages. Langer gives a detailed description of Belz. "The *rebbe* is a patriarchal figure dressed in a *kaftan* of fine silk and wearing a *shtreiml*." He describes the recitation of the Psalms to welcome the Sabbath: "It is as though an electric spark has suddenly entered those present. The crowd, which till now has been completely quiet, almost cowed, suddenly bursts forth in a wild shout. None stays in his place. The tall black figures run hither and thither round the synagogue, flashing past the lights of the Sabbath candles. Gesticulating wildly, and throwing their whole bodies about, they shout out the words of the Psalm. They knock into each other unconcernedly, for all their cares have been cast aside; everything has ceased to exist for them. They are seized by an indescribable ecstasy."[5]

On *Rosh Hashanah* and *Yom Kippur* the *rebbe* himself officiated before the reader's desk. The mood of elevation reached its peak when he recited *Min HaAmakim* ("Out of the depths," Psalm 130) before the *shofar* was sounded. He would recite one verse weeping so bitterly, that no one present could fail to be moved. Immediately afterwards, he would recite the next verse with such joy and exultation, that it was hard to believe that only a moment before he was in tears.

The *rebbe* died the 24th of *Heshvan* 1925 and was buried in Belz. Two years later, a London rabbi, Rabbi Jacob Joseph Spiro, (father of Rabbi Melekh Spiro of the Willesden Synagogue) published a booklet in London entitled *Millei Dehespeid,* a moving eulogy on the great *rebbe.*

Chapter 14

The Nineteenth Century–Age of Development and Dissent

In the nineteenth century outstanding personalities arose, men of vision and vitality who molded and remade the lives of men. Many of the *tzaddikim,* as they were called, maintained huge households, receiving and entertaining hundreds of visitors. The role of the *tzaddik* was multifaceted. He was the attorney (*meilitz yosher*), who pleaded for his clients before the august assembly of the Heavenly Court; and he was *guhter yid,* the friendly father figure, in whom his children could confide. Whether they needed spiritual strengthening or *gezunt und parnossa* (health and sustenance), the *rebbe*'s blessing and his assurance that "the Almighty would help" fell like water on the parched lips of the afflicted Jews sunk in the deep valley of despair. His power was far-reaching. His most casual utterances were invested with many layers of mystical meaning, and his considered judgments were counsels beyond cavil. He wore infallibility like a silken *kapote,* and his endorsement was thought to "guarantee" the success of any project.

The *hasidim* lived in a world of their own. They were known by their apparel, their speech and their songs. In the eyes of a Gentile observer, they formed an "immense mass of squalid and helpless poverty."[1] This may well have been true, but a faith as immovable and immortal as the mountains enabled them to inhabit an inner invisible world that was a foretaste of the Golden Age to come.

The Spread of Hasidism in Russia

Although in many ways diametrically opposed in their philosophy, Chernobyl and Lubavitch were the two dynasties primarily responsible for the expansion of Hasidism in Russia during the first half of the nineteenth century.

Rabbi Nahum of Chernobyl

One of the earliest disseminators and pioneers of Hasidism in the Ukraine was Rabbi Menahem Nahum of Chernobyl, known as "Rabbi Nahum the Great." "All his words," wrote Rabbi Levi Isaac of Berdichev, "are the words of the living God, causing the human soul to rise upwards, setting the heart aflame in the service of the blessed Creator."

Uncompromising and often uncommunicative, this highly individualistic master independently pursued his own course. He was born in the year 1730, either in Nurinsk or Gurinsk, in the region between Berdichev and Kiev. He was named after an uncle who had died young. His father, Tzvi Hirsch, died when Nahum was but a child, and he was brought up in the home of another uncle. He married Sarah, a granddaughter of Rabbi Isaac Shapira, rabbi of Kovni, near Lublin. Rabbi Nahum studied *Kabbalah* diligently, especially the words of Rabbi Isaac Luria, the *Ari HaKadosh.* His way of life was ascetic in the extreme. The Hebrew word *teshuvah* (repentance) was, according to his interpretation, a mnemonic for "studying, fasting, sackcloth, ashes, weeping, and mourning." To support his family, he became a teacher, but his meager earnings were quite inadequate. He was attracted to the teachings of Rabbi Israel Baal Shem Tov and visited him twice in Medzibozh. In fact, Rabbi Nahum is mentioned in the *Shivhei HaBesht.* After the death of Rabbi Israel Baal Shem Tov, Rabbi Nahum became a disciple of Rabbi Dov Baer of Mezhirech.

Eventually, Rabbi Nahum accepted the position of preacher at Chernobyl on the river Pripet in the Ukraine. In 1765, Chernobyl had exactly 695 Jewish taxpayers. It was not a thriving community, and Rabbi Nahum's financial position showed no improvement. Rabbi Shneur Zalman appealed to his followers to help Rabbi Nahum: "Afflicted by the hand of God for quite some time, his expenses have been in the thousands. Even now he bears the sufferings of love. May God heal him. I am certain that in your great and faithful kindness you will hear these words of mine. 'May the words of my mouth be acceptable' (Psalms 19:15), and for the sake of this may the Lord doubly bless you."[2]

Choosing the Life of "Hardship and Labor in the Torah"

His followers responded generously. They were willing and indeed eager to provide him with a properly appointed home, but Rabbi Nahum declined, citing the rabbinic reference to a life of poverty, found in the Ethics of the Fathers. "This is the way that is becoming for the student of the Torah, a morsel of bread with salt thou shalt eat and water by measure thou must drink and thou must sleep upon the ground and live a life of deprivation" (6:4). Throughout the week, the abstemious *tzaddik* refrained from eating meat or drinking wine. It was his habit to recite *Tikkun Hatzot* (the special penitential service recited at midnight, prayers generally consisting of Psalms 97, 102, 137, the *Viddui* (confession), the Thirteen Attributes, and dirges commemorating the destruction of the Temple).

In his work *Hanhagot Yesharot* ("Upright Practices"), he urges his followers to do likewise. "Rise from your sleep at midnight, for that is a time when the Holy One is most accessible. Serve him diligently and devoutly by holding this nocturnal vigil."[3] Rabbi Nahum would travel regularly from town to town, not only to disseminate Hasidism but also to perform the great *mitzvah* of *pidyon shevuyim* (ransoming captives, poor Jews who were unable to pay their dues to their merciless landlords and were left to languish in unspeakable jails). Rabbi Nahum was the savior of many of these unfortunates.

Moral and Religious Teachings

"Do many acts of lovingkindness," he told his *hasidim,* "Dowering poor brides, visiting the sick." Good deeds and Torah study were to go hand in hand. "Each day, study the Torah, the prophets and the writings as well as the *Mishnah* and the *Gemara,* each one of you according to your abilities. Give as much charity as you can, fast one day each week and devote some time to the book of moral teachings, *Reishit Hokhmah* ("The Beginning of Wisdom" by Rabbi Elijah de Vidas). The proper attitude toward prayer was of particular importance:

> Take care, in so far as it is possible, not to speak before morning prayers. Take special care to recite each word of the *Shema* with due deliberation. Do not allow yourself to be distracted, at least during the recitation of the *Shema,* but recite it with awe and with love. Each word you recite in this way will help to bring life to your limbs. The 248 words of the *Shema* are said to correspond to the number of limbs in the human body.[4]

A Way of Life

The Sabbath was the center of his existence. "Honor the Sabbath as fully as you can within your means. Do so with food and drink. The Hebrew letters of the word *Shabbat* are those of *tashev* (to return, to atone), indicating that he who keeps the Sabbath, even if he is as idolatrous as the generation of Enoch, will be forgiven" (Sabbath, 118b).

Rabbi Nahum advised his followers to live their lives in the following manner:

> Keep away from depression to the utmost degree. Thus you will be saved from several sins, especially those of anger and pride. Keep yourself from being cross toward your household in any matter. Let your speech be pleasant. Accept whatever portion the Lord gives you in love, whether it be for good or for ill and suffering. Do not glorify yourself, however great your learning or your good deeds, your wealth or your fine qualities. Do not triumph over any person. If people should come to praise you, do not let it lead you to self-importance.[5]

Many tales are told of his humility and his kindness. A poor man once asked him for money to help provide a dowry for his daughter. Rabbi Nahum gave him everything he had. Later, *hasidim* saw the man spending some of the money on alcohol, so they retrieved part of the rabbi's gift and brought it back to Rabbi Nahum. The *tzaddik* was displeased. "Please give him back the money that I gave him. Everyone should imitate the Almighty who gives to the wicked as well as to the righteous. Should I be deprived of the privilege of following the example of the Almighty?"

The Literary Achievements of Rabbi Nahum

His work was published in the year he died. *Me'or Einayim* ("Light of the Eyes") was printed in Slavuta in 1797–1798. It was acclaimed by the *hasidim.* The work carried laudatory comments by Rabbi Levi Isaac of Berdichev, Rabbi Jacob Samson of Shepetovka, Rabbi Aryeh Leib of Walchisk, Rabbi Asher Tzvi of Ostrog, author of *Maayan HaHokhmah,* and Rabbi Judah Leib Hakohen, author of *Or HaGanuz.* Eleven editions were printed in the nineteenth century and in 1966 a new edition was printed in Jerusalem. The work is divided into two parts. The first part contains discourses on the Torah; the second part contains comments on the *aggadah.* He quotes Rabbi Israel Baal Shem Tov twenty-eight times and the *Maggid* of Mezhirech fourteen times, and he includes the words of many other hasidic authorities as well. His second major work, *Yismah Lev* ("the Heart Rejoices"), was also published in Slavuta during the same year and contains a collection of homilies on aggadic passages. It was edited by his disciple, Rabbi Elijah ben Ze'ev Wolf Yurevich. In subsequent editions both works appear together. *Hanhagot Yesharot* ("Upright Practices") was printed in 1816–1817. He died on the 11th day of *Heshvan* 1797 and was survived by one daughter and twin sons. His son, Rabbi Mordekhai, who succeeded his father in Chernobyl, had eight sons. However, with Rabbi Mordekhai (1770–1837), son-in-law of Rabbi Aaron of Karlin, a disciple of the *Maggid* of Mezhirech, the pendulum swung in the other direction. Rabbi Mordekhai became one of the first hasidic rabbis to live a life of luxury. Rabbi Mordekhai's opulent way of life was financed by *Maamadot* (regular contributions from his *hasidim*), and it was a way of life that his sons continued.

The Courts of Rabbi Nahum's Grandsons

Each of Rabbi Mordekhai's sons established "courts" in different localities: Rabbi Moses (b. 1789) in Korostshev; Rabbi Jacob

Israel (b. 1794) in Cherkassy; Rabbi Nahum (b. 1804) in Makarov; Rabbi Abraham (b. 1806) in Turisk; Rabbi David (b. 1808) in Talnoye; Rabbi Isaac (b. 1812) in Skvira; and Rabbi Johanan (b. 1816) in Rachmastrivka. His oldest son, Rabbi Aaron (1787–1872), became the titular head of the dynasty and lived in Tarnopol. The sons of the rabbi of Chernobyl, especially Rabbi David of Talnoye, lived on a grand and almost regal scale and laid the foundation of Hasidism in Russia.

While the rabbis of Chernobyl were somewhat particularist in their outlook, mainly concerned with the spiritual needs of their own followers, the dynasty of Lubavitch took the whole of the House of Israel under its protective wings.

Rabbi Dov Baer of Lubavitch

> He taught the Torah in public in order to show men the way of the Lord, albeit in the Kabbalistic wisdom. He composed many works on the *Kabbalah* that have spread to many communities in Israel. He was like a father of the *Sanhedrin* when teaching the Torah in public. All his people surrounded him on every side, and they all united with one heart to hear the words of the living God flashing from his lips like sparks of fire.[6]

So Rabbi Abraham Abele of Kherson described Rabbi Dov Baer (1774–1827) popularly known as the *Mitteler Rebbe* (i.e., the "Intermediary Rabbi"), son of Rabbi Shneur Zalman of Liady.

Born on the ninth day of *Kislev* 1774, Dov Baer was named after the *Maggid* of Mezhirech. Dov Baer married Sheina, daughter of a pious teacher. He was living and studying in Kremenitug in Little Russia, when his father died on the 24th of *Tevet* 1813. Rabbi Dov Baer settled in Lubavitch (Lubavichi), a small town in the district of Smolensk which became the center of *Habad Hasidim.* The Jewish population numbered only 1,164 in 1847. They earned their livelihood mainly from the flax trade and by providing for the many *hasidim* who visited their rebbe.

Two Candidates

Rabbi Dov Baer's accession to his father's place was contested by his father's star disciple, Rabbi Aaron ben Moses Halevi of

Starosielce (1766–1829) who had been a disciple of Rabbi Shneur Zalman for thirty years. Rabbi Aaron was a direct descendant of Rabbi Israel Horowitz (c. 1555–c.1630) author of *Shnei Luhot HaBrit.* For many years, Rabbi Aaron and Rabbi Dov Baer studied together, and Rabbi Dov Baer used to say that he thought of Rabbi Aaron whenever he recited the prayer: "Guard the seekers of Thy unity as the apple of Thine eye." After the death of Rabbi Shneur Zalman, Rabbi Aaron settled in Starosielce. He was the author of *Shaarei HaYihud VehaEmunah* (Shklow, 1820) and *Avodat HaLevi* (Shklow, 1821), outstanding and original contributions to the understanding of *Habad.*[7] No doubt, Rabbi Aaron felt that he was better qualified than Rabbi Dov Baer to carry on the teachings of Rabbi Shneur Zalman. The consensus of the *hasidim,* however, was to accept the leadership of Rabbi Dov Baer who was also staunchly supported by his younger brother Rabbi Hayim Abraham (d. 1841).[8]

An Advocate of Jewish Farming

During the "benevolent paternalism" of Czar Alexander I, Rabbi Dov Baer strongly advocated agricultural settlement. By the statute of 1804, those who settled in certain areas of farmland were exempted from paying taxes for five years.[9] By 1807, four Jewish colonies had been set up in Southern Russia, and during the reigns of Alexander II and Nicholas I, 645 families, a total of 3,618 people, were settled in newly established Jewish colonies in Russia.

Rabbi Dov Baer encouraged these agricultural endeavors:

> My advice is that men, women and children should learn how to perform various types of work, such as weaving, spinning, and all the skills that are required in factories. The training of artisans should be organized in an orderly manner and should be properly regulated, especially for the children of the poor and the middle class. Furthermore, many Jews should begin to engage in agriculture. They should acquire fertile land in large or small plots, and work on the soil; and God will surely bestow His blessings on the earth, and they will at least be able to feed their children properly. But since the majority of our people are unfamiliar with farmwork, they should at first engage experienced farmers (they may be non-Jews) to tend

the soil carefully during the first few years. A Jew should not be ashamed of engaging in farm work, for were not the fields and vineyards the source of all our subsistence in the Holy Land? Why then should we be different from our ancestors?[10]

Similar to His Father in Fate and Ideals

Like his father before him, Rabbi Dov Baer was unjustly imprisoned by the Russian Government in 1826 on a false charge that he had "collected two or three hundred rubles for the Sultan of Turkey." He was ordered to appear in Vitebsk before the Governor General Chavanski, who was to conduct the investigation. Through the good offices of Dr. Heibenthal and Jan Lubormirsky, he was released and to this day the anniversary of his release, the tenth day of *Kislev* is celebrated by *Habad hasidim.*

Like his father, Rabbi Dov Baer supported the *yishuv* in the Holy Land. He warned those who were responsible for collecting for the *yishuv* not to divert the money to any other cause. He recommended placing collection boxes in every Jewish home. He yearned to settle in Hebron, the site of the Cave of Mahpelah, and even acquired a small plot of land there. He maintained that prayers recited there were particularly effective, for according to tradition this was the gateway to Paradise. He quoted the view of rabbinic authorities to the effect that a man who owned land in Hebron was spared the "tribulations of the grave." A decade later, Rabbi Menahem Mendel of Kamenetz, in his work *Korot HaIttim,* (Vilna, 1840), noted that "The *kollel* in Hebron consisted of worthy people who are charitable and hospitable." The newcomers were Rabbi Jacob Slonim, son-in-law of Rabbi Dov Baer, and his wife Menuhah Rachel known as the "grandmother of the community." Emissaries from Hebron traveled to the East for support, and they also appealed to Sir Moses Montefiore for help.

Rabbi Dov Baer would stand immobile in prayer for as long as three hours at a time, and at the end of his prayer his hat and shirt would be soaked with perspiration. A prolific writer, he was the author of twenty-two works; among them were commentaries on the *Zohar* (Kapust, 1816), *Imrei Binah* (Kapust, 1821), *Poke'ah Ivrim* in Yiddish (Shklow, 1832), which has since gone through twenty-three editions, *Kuntress HaHitbonenut* (Kapust, 1820), *Kuntress HaHitpaalut* ("Tractate on Ecstasy"), printed in Koenigsberg in 1831.

He died in Nezhin in Volhynia on the anniversary of his birth, the ninth of *Kislev* 1827, at the age of 52. He was survived by two sons, Rabbi Menahem Nahum and Rabbi Barukh, and by seven daughters. Menahem Mendel, his sister's son and the husband of his eldest daughter, succeeded him. His last words were from Psalm 36:10, "For with Thee is the fountain of life." A gifted orator, his discourses were long and complex yet lucid and utterly absorbing. None could fail to understand when he expounded the philosophy of *Habad.* "If you cut his finger," *hasidim* said in awe, "you would find that in his veins flowed not blood but Hasidism."

Rabbi Menahem Mendel of Lubavitch

It was known that Rabbi Dov Baer, the *Mitteler Rebbe* (1773–1827), preferred to be succeeded by one of his sons-in-law rather than one of his sons, and thus it was that Rabbi Menahem Mendel, known as the *Tzemah Tzedek* after the title of his works, became the third *rebbe* of Lubavitch. Rabbi Menahem Mendel, born on the 29th of *Elul* 1789, was the son of Rabbi Noah, follower of Rabbi Menahem Mendel of Horodek. His mother, Devorah Leah, was the second daughter of Rabbi Shneur Zalman of Liady.

Rabbi Menahem Mendel's diligence was phenomenal. "I generally study for eighteen hours a day," he later recalled, "which includes five hours of writing, and in the past thirty years, I have spent a total of 32,000 hours studying the works of Rabbi Shneur Zalman."

In 1803, he married Hayah Mushka, daughter of Rabbi Dov Baer, the *Mitteler Rebbe,* and after the passing of his father-in-law on the ninth of *Kislev* 1827, Rabbi Menahem Mendel succeeded him.

"With a few honorable exceptions," writes the sociologist, Jacob Lestschinsky, "the Jewish masses, together with their rabbis and hasidic leaders, were buried in such obscurantism that the plans of the government, in essence progressive and, as regards the prevailing conditions of Jewish life, revolutionary, were remote from their understanding and psychology."[11] Menahem Mendel was one of these exceptions. Like his father-in-law, he actively encouraged agriculture and, in 1844, he bought 3,600 *desyatins* (9,700 acres) of land at Shezedrin around Minsk from Prince Shezedrin, and there he established a settlement for 300 families.

Efforts on Behalf of the Cantonists

One of the first problems that faced the third rebbe of Lubavitch was the pitiful plight of the Cantonists, as the forcibly recruited child-soldiers were called. By the decree of August 26, 1827, Jews became eligible for military service and could be called up between the ages of 12 and 25. Every year the Jewish community had to supply ten recruits per thousand of the population. Among the non-Jews the proportion was seven per thousand. Recruits aged between 12 and 18 were to be placed in establishments for military training. The Jewish community was instructed to appoint three to six persons, who were to be responsible for selecting the recruits.[12] The conscripts, mostly the children of poor families, were to serve for a period of twenty-six years, a term that started when the recruit reached the age of 18. The lives and prospects of these young boys were bitter indeed. They were often snatched from their mother's arms when they were but 8 or 9 years old and sent to remote provinces. Unscrupulous agents roamed the streets in search of hapless innocents. The bodies, the minds, and the souls of these unfortunate children were at stake. They were carried to distant villages, where their families could never trace them, and turned over to brutal peasants who used them like slaves.

Rabbi Menahem Mendel set up a special council to alleviate their sufferings. The *Hevrah Tehiat HaMeitim* ransomed as many children as possible. Special Lubavitch delegates regularly visited army groups to bring comfort and moral support to the child-soldiers and to lessen the likelihood of conversion.

The Haskalah *Movement Makes Inroads in Russia*

At this time, the *Haskalah* movement raised its head in Russia, and Isaac Baer Levinsohn (1788–1860) of Kamenetz-Podolsk, known as the "Russian Mendelssohn," wrote a number of anti-hasidic works, among them *Divrei Tzaddik* and *Te'udah BeYisrael.* On

January 14, 1840, the *maskilim* opened a school in Riga under the German-trained Rabbi Dr. Max Lilienthal (1815–1882), who was aided by Mordekhai Aaron Gunzburg and Aryeh Leib Mandelstamm. In 1841, forty-five delegates of the "Lovers of Enlightenment" met in Vilna to plan an expansion campaign. The Minister of Public Instruction, Count Sergius Uvarov, welcomed these innovators, regarding the movement as a logical step towards assimilation. To win the cooperation of the Jewish community "in support of the efforts of the Government," a rabbinical conference was convened at St. Petersburg.

Among the delegates were the head of the *yeshivah* of Volozhin, Rabbi Isaac ben Hayim of Volozhin (1812–1879); banker Israel Halperin of Berdichev; Betzalel Stern, director of the Jewish school in Odessa; and Rabbi Menahem Mendel of Lubavitch. Aryeh Leib Mandelstamm (1819–1889), an adherent of the *Haskalah,* was the official translator. Sir Moses Montefiore, who had been invited, was not able to attend. The sessions lasted from May 6 to August 27, 1843, but the delegates agreed on very few issues. A law promulgated on November 13, 1844 stipulated that although they were not barred from the general school system, Jews could open their own schools provided that they were self-supporting, and could also set up two theological seminaries. In a supplementary secret circular, the Government admitted that the "purpose of educating the Jews is to bring about a gradual merging with the Christian nationalities and to uproot those harmful prejudices which are instilled by the teachings of the Talmud."[13]

Rabbi Menahem Mendel in the Forefront of Battle

Rabbi Menahem Mendel fought the *Haskalah* movement both in private and in public. He sent emissaries throughout Russia to expose what he considered fallacies in the arguments of the *maskilim.* He passionately opposed the idea of revising the liturgy and of editing the Scriptures. "The Torah," he wrote, "is from Heaven. We believe that every word of the Torah given by Moses came from God."[14]

Practical steps were taken, such as the expansion of Lubavitch *yeshivot* in Bobvorna, Pasana, Liozno, and Kalisk. Rabbi Menahem

Mendel traveled widely, and his friendship with Professor I. Berstenson, Court Physician to the Czar, often helped in delicate negotiations relating to the welfare of the community. Like many of his colleagues, Rabbi Menahem Mendel suffered from the malevolence of informers like Hershel Hosheh, Benjamin the Apostate, and Lipmann Feldman, who tried unsuccessfully to entrap him. Rabbi Menahem Mendel died on the 13th of *Nisan* 1866. He was survived by seven sons and two daughters. He was the author of forty-one works, among them *Or HaTorah* (Berdichev, 1913) and *Tzemah Tzedek* (Vilna, 1884). He was succeeded by his youngest son, Rabbi Samuel.

In the Footsteps of Rabbi Menahem Mendel

Rabbi Samuel, too, participated in discussions at St. Petersburg. This was a period of virulent anti-Semitic propaganda and fearful pogroms, and Rabbi Samuel's strenuous attempt to improve matters only resulted in his being placed under house arrest.

In the Lubavitch tradition, Rabbi Samuel's successor, Rabbi Shalom Dov Baer (1860–1920) continued to fight for equal rights for the Jewish community. He was particularly concerned with the welfare of the Mountain Jews (*Berg Yidn*) who lived in the mountains in Uzbekistan, a region far remote from the main centers of Jewish life. Rabbi Shalom Dov Baer dispatched Samuel Halevi Levitin, formerly rabbi of Rakshik, to minister to their spiritual needs, and the *Sefardim* responded gratefully, much to the gratification of the *Ashkenazim.* Rabbi Shalom Dov Baer spent the years of the First World War in Rostov-on-the-Don, and there he died.

The Ruzhin-Sadgora Dynasties

In Galicia, the dynasties of Ruzhin and Sadgora ruled supreme. Rabbi Israel of Ruzhin left six sons, known as the "Six Orders of the *Mishnah*" or the "Six Wings of the Angel" (an epithet taken from Isaiah 6:2), and three daughters. In 1851, eight months after Israel's death, his eldest son, Shalom Joseph, died and his brother, Abraham Jacob Friedmann (1820–1883), succeeded him. To Rabbi Abraham

Jacob, his loving father had applied the verse from Michah, "Thou wilt show faithfulness to Jacob" (7:20).

Thousands of *hasidim,* including rabbis and scholars, did show faithfulness to the new rabbi and Sadgora became a thriving hasidic center. Like his father, Rabbi Abraham Jacob incurred the displeasure of the authorities and was imprisoned for fifteen months in Czernowitz.

A Visit to the Royal Court of Sadgora

Sir Laurence Oliphant (1829–1888), the English proto-Zionist who propagandized for Jewish resettlement in Transjordan, described his visit to the *rebbe* in 1880.

> When I was in Vienna, people I trusted told me about the Sadgorer *Rebbe.* I wanted very much to meet him. I thought, come what may, a man who by spirit alone rules thousands of people cannot be an ordinary, commonplace creature. Since I was then situated near Sadgora, I advised the *rebbe* that my wife and I would like to meet him. Immediately, he sent us his splendid carriage. The whole Jewish community of Sadgora awaited our arrival, lining both sides of the street to see the Gentile coming to their *rebbe.* At the entrance of the *rebbe*'s house, his sons and sons-in-law, in Polish dress, greeted us. Inside, the *rebbe*'s daughters were hostesses to my wife. I was led into a room, much like a princely court, furnished with precious gold and silver antiques. There I met the *rebbe,* accompanied by two servants. Regal authority was in his face. He spoke intelligently about the situation of the Russian Jews. Though I did not quite understand his conduct, I was nevertheless convinced that he could lead and command his people with just the barest gesture.[15]

Meanwhile, Rabbi Abraham's brothers established their own courts: Rabbi David Moses (1827–1875) in Chortkov, Rabbi Mordekhai Shragai (1834–1894) in Husyatin, Rabbi Nahum (1837–1933) in Stefanesti, and Rabbi Dov in Leove (Rumania).

The Threat from Within

Having survived the assaults of the *mitnagdim,* Hasidism now had to cope with fratricidal, internal struggles. A participant in one of these unedifying episodes was Rabbi Dov (Bereinu) (1817–1866) a son of Rabbi Israel of Ruzhin.[16] Carefully educated by private tutors in almost princely style, Dov had been married at the age of 14 to Shiendel, the youngest daughter of Rabbi Motel of Chernobyl. The young couple, however, was incompatible. They were childless, and disharmony reigned in their home. After his father's death in 1852, Rabbi Dov settled in Husi, Rumania, and later he moved to Leove. He had a sensitive and brooding disposition, and was prey to fits of melancholy. The only person with whom he had any real rapport was his brother Rabbi Nahum, and Rabbi Nahum's death in 1858 was a blow from which he never recovered.

The conventional pattern of the rabbi's life was not for Rabbi Dov. He liked to gather around him a few intimates with whom he could commune and philosophize. He held himself aloof from the *hasidim.* They wearied him with their endless woes. He implored his attendants to keep the people away, but they would not be repulsed or rejected. Rabbi Dov felt himself the victim of circumstance, persecuted by his wife and by his family. His constant companions were the local apothecary and a doctor. The day came when he refused to attend the services, and on *Kol Nidrei* night in 1869, his attendants virtually carried him by force to the synagogue. Alarmed at his conduct, his wife begged several trusted *hasidim* to escort the *rebbe* to his brother in Sadgora.

The rumor that Rabbi Dov was being held against his will in his brother's house, led the lawyer Dr. Judah Leib Reitman of Czernowitz to intervene with the civil authorities. As a result Rabbi Dov came to live with Dr. Reitman, a defector from the hasidic milieu. This defection was widely exploited by the *maskilim.* In a manifesto drafted by A. Orenstein and published in the Hebrew periodical *Hamaggid,*[17] Rabbi Dov declared that though he remained true to the faith of his fathers, he sought to escape from the "foolish crowd" that surrounded him and wished to "remove the thorns from the vineyard of the House of Israel and to free Judaism from senseless customs that have no source in the Law of Israel."

This statement from a son of the rabbi of Ruzhin caused consternation among the *hasidim* and jubilation among their opponents. Rabbi Dov's brother-in-law, Rabbi Mendel, and his nephew, Rabbi Shalom Joseph, eldest son of Rabbi Isaac of Bohush, were among those who attempted to reason with the renegade *rebbe*. After eight weeks in Dr. Reitman's house, Rabbi Dov did indeed have second thoughts, and, on *Shushan Purim,* he remorsefully returned to Sadgora. It was there that, four months later, he issued a public statement (*Kol Koreh*) expressing his desire to "return to the rock from which I was hewn. . . . I will hold fast to the deeds of my holy fathers. . . . Their law is a lamp to my feet and their righteousness is a light to my path."

For six years until the day of his death in 1866, he lived in Sadgora, deserted by his wife, shunned by his brothers, and ignored by his former followers. He died as he had lived, without friends, one of Hasidism's most perplexing personalities.

But for the Sadgora dynasty, the cup of suffering was not yet full. Seven years of bitter persecution were to follow. The mantle of the Vilna Gaon fell, surprisingly enough, on a hasidic *rebbe*, Hayim Halberstam of Sanz (Nowy Sacz) who lived from 1793–1876.

The Divrei Hayim

Rabbi Hayim, or the *Divrei Hayim* as he is called, wore with ease the dual crowns of a hasidic *rebbe* with thousands of followers and a celebrated halakhist, whose rulings were regarded as law by contemporary scholars. His father, Rabbi Aryeh Leibush Halberstadt, (later changed to Halberstam) was rabbi of Przemysl and a descendant of the Codifier, Rabbi Solomon ben Jehiel Luria (1510–1573) of Lublin, known as the *Maharshal,* author of *Yam Shel Shlomo* (Prague, 1613). Rabbi Hayim's mother, Miriam, was the daughter of Rabbi David of Brody, a descendant of Rabbi Tzvi Ashkenazi (c. 1660–1718), known as the Hakham Tzvi, rabbi of the united communities of Altona, Hamburg, and Wandsbeck. Rabbi Hayim was born in Tarnogrod in 1793, the year that saw the Second Partition of Poland.

He studied under Rabbi Samuel Zanwill of Przemysl, author of a homiletical work *Divrei Shmuel* (Amsterdam, 1878), and under Rabbi Moses Joshua Heschel, author of *Yam HaTalmud* (Lvov, 1821), and Rabbi Joseph Horowitz Halevi of Tarnogrod, brother of the Seer of Lublin. At the age of 12, Rabbi Hayim, known as the "*illui* of

Tarnogrod," visited the Seer, who predicted "this lad will be a leader of his generation." The visit left a deep impression on the boy. "He who has not heard prayers in Lublin," he said, "does not know the meaning of prayers. When the passage *Hodu* ("O, Give Thanks") is reached, the walls of the *Beit HaMidrash* shake with passion. When the Seer recited one benediction, it was as if he had recited the entire service."[18] For twelve years, Rabbi Hayim continued to visit the Seer.

Rabbi Hayim married Rachel Feigele, daughter of Rabbi Barukh Teomim Frankel of Leipnik, Moravia, author of the novellae on the Talmud, *Barukh Taam* (Lvov, 1841). At the age of 18, Rabbi Hayim became rabbi of the small town of Rudnick near Brody. He made the acquaintance of Rabbi Naftali Horowitz of Ropczyce, whom he visited several times a year. There he also met Rabbi Shalom of Kaminka and Rabbi Meir of Opatow. "I have in my life," remarked Rabbi Meir of Opatow, "heard many excellent readers, but Rabbi Hayim excelled them all. He does not omit a single *kavanah* of Rabbi Isaac Luria."[19] From the *rebbe* of Ropczyce Rabbi Hayim acquired an appreciation of song and melody. "Through magic," he maintained, "one can unlock all the Heavenly Gates." In 1827, Rabbi Naftali, whom Rabbi Hayim called "the Wise Rabbi," died.

For a short time, Rabbi Hayim was rabbi in Zalin and for a while lived in Lalev (Nagykallo). Upon the death of Rabbi Barukh Moses David Landau in 1830, he became rabbi in Nowy Sacz, a city in the province of Krakow, where he lived for forty-six years. In 1880, 5,163 Jews lived in Nowy Sacz, constituting 46 percent of the population. They earned their living from the sale of agricultural produce and were also engaged in tailoring, carpentry, shoemaking, and engraving.

From Nowy Sacz to Sanz

The *hasidim* began to call the town "Tzanz," spelling it with a *tzaddik* (one of the letters of the Hebrew alphabet) to denote that it was the home of a *tzaddik*. When the "Light of the Exile," as Rabbi Hayim was called, stood in prayer, light seemed to radiate from him. It is said that he forgot the world around him. He even forgot his ailing foot, stamping it until it bled, as he poured out his heart to his

Father in Heaven. He lived in an extremely frugal fashion, distributing to the poor all the monies that he received from his *hasidim.*

He was the author of *Divrei Hayim,* printed anonymously in Zolkiew in 1864. Part one deals with the laws of divorce and with the problem of spelling the names of people and towns. Part two deals with the laws of ritual purity. His work, *Divrei Hayim,* on the four parts of the *Shulhan Arukh,* was printed in Lvov in 1875, followed two years later by *Divrei Hayim* commentary on the Torah, printed in Munkacs in 1877. He also wrote notes on the *Barukh Taam* (Warsaw, 1914). His 729 responsa reflect the social and religious life of the Jews in Galicia in the mid-nineteenth century.

Responsa

Among his correspondents were Rabbi Hayim Eleazar Wacks of Piotrokow and members of his own family. "We concentrate on the Talmud and the Codes," wrote Rabbi Hayim. "We study *Kabbalah* when others are asleep." In his responsa, he reveals himself as a great scholar and also as a staunch opponent of innovations. The introduction of machine made *matzot* in the nineteenth century sparked a violent halakhic controversy. The central issue was whether the machine process caused fermentation. Its detractors, Rabbi Hayim among them, maintained that milling by heavy machines caused the wheat to exude a moisture that resulted in fermentation, and also caused pieces of dough to stick to the machines and produce the same effect, thus rendering the *matzot* invalid.

He also opposed the institution of a choir in the community of Miskolowitz.[20] Asked whether it was permitted to bury two bodies in the same grave, Rabbi Hayim replied that according to the strict letter of the law it was not permitted. There should be a partition of six hand breadths between the graves. However, if common burial was the practice within a particular community, then it must not be forbidden, but, hereafter, proper space should be sought so as to inter the deceased in accordance with the law. Rabbi Hayim was venerated not only by the *hasidim* but even by the *mitnagdim.* Rabbi Saul Joseph Nathanson called him "Holy Gaon, light of the Exile." Rabbi Samuel Ehrenfeld remarked that "merely to gaze upon Rabbi Hayim is like studying the Torah." Rabbi Solomon Rabinowicz Hakohen of Radomsk visited Rabbi Hayim for the festival of

Shavuot, "because I want to share the experience of the Jews receiving the Torah on Mount Sinai. The atmosphere can be felt only in the presence of Rabbi Hayim Halberstam of Sanz."

The Mode of Prayer in Sanz

Rabbi Hayim would spend a long time in preparing himself for prayer. "What does the *rebbe* do before he prays?" Rabbi Joseph Epstein of Neustadt was asked. "Before reciting his prayers, he prays that he may be worthy to pray." Twice a day, the *rebbe* would distribute money to the poor. In the morning to the poor of Sanz, and in the evening to the petitioners from outside the community. On one occasion, the mail brought a magnificent donation of 100,000 gulden to the rabbi's court and within twenty-four hours all the money had been distributed among the needy. "I love the poor," Rabbi Hayim would say, "for God loves them." Rabbi Israel Friedmann of Ruzhin referred to Rabbi Hayim as the "Great *Beit Din*."

The Great Accuser

Then suddenly, "the Great Defender" as Rabbi Hayim was known, became "the Great Accuser," though the cause of this transformation is exceedingly vague. Perhaps it was because of the royal life style of the Sadgora dynasty that was so alien to him. Perhaps it was personal pique at the disrespectful behavior of Rabbi Mordekhai Shragai of Husyatin. At any rate, the temporary defection of Rabbi Dov brought matters to a head. Rabbi Hayim issued an ultimatum requiring the Sadgora brothers to "change their way of life" or suffer the consequences. In the winter of 1869, Rabbi Hayim, supported by Rabbi Shlomo Shapira (later Rabbi in Munkacs), declared war against the *hasidim* of Sadgora. "They are rebels. . . . Their scribes are apostates. . . . one must not use their *tefillin* and *mezuzot*. . . . It is forbidden to eat the meat of their slaughterers. The Almighty who preserved us from Shabbetai Tzvi should preserve us from them. They are all apostates. . . . They conduct themselves with arrogance. . . . They walk in the ways of Gentiles. . . . Their womenfolk transgress the law. . . . They should be persecuted without mercy."[21]

The Seven Lean Years

Rabbi Elimelekh of Grodzisk and Rabbi Mendel of Vishnitz rose to the defense, imploring Rabbi Hayim not "to pursue in anger this holy family." The rabbis of Sadgora refused to launch counter-attacks, and so their *hasidim* took matters into their own hands. On the 4th day of *Nisan* 1869, Nisan Bak and forty-nine other *hasidim* issued an *issur* (prohibition) known as *Mishpat Katuv* ("Written Judgment"), forbidding people to obey the dictates of the *rebbe* of Sanz. The *issur* was proclaimed at the Western Wall in Jerusalem and repeated in Safed and Tiberias.

Leading scholars, like Joseph Saul Nathanson; Rabbi Isaac Aaron Ettinger ("Reb Itsche"), rabbi of Przemysl; and Dov Berush Meisels (1798–1870), rabbi in Warsaw; now rallied to the support of Rabbi Hayim. The day after *Shavuot* (Pentecost) 1869, the followers of Rabbi Hayim publicly excommunicated "Nisan Bak and his followers." For seven years the "civil war" between the two factions raged through Galicia, dividing families and splintering communities. These were indeed the "seven lean years" of Hasidism.

Rabbi Hayim spent virtually the entire day in prayer and study, allowing himself very little time for sleep, especially on the Sabbath. "One must not sleep away the Sabbath," he observed.[22] On the 25th of *Nisan* 1876, Rabbi Hayim died. He left seven sons and seven daughters. His sons were Rabbi Ezekiel Shragai of Sienawa, Rabbi Barukh of Gorlice, Rabbi David of Kashnow, Rabbi Aaron of Sanz, Rabbi Meir Nathan of Bobow, Rabbi Shalom Eliezer, and Rabbi Isaiah.

Chapter 15

Dynamic Dynasties of the Late Nineteenth Century

Ninety percent of all the Jews in Europe and America today, and 80 percent of world Jewry find their origins in Eastern Europe. It was Poland, the main center of Hasidism, that produced the pietists, the Hebraists, the Yiddishists, the pioneers, the men of letters, and the men of action.

During the nineteenth century, Jews in Czarist Poland clustered together in closely knit communities. Differences in morals and mores set them apart from their non-Jewish neighbors, and they fought to preserve their collective identity. For the most part Polish Jewry refused to purchase civic equality at the price of assimilation, and an overwhelming majority clung with wholehearted devotion to traditional Judaism.

The spread of Hasidism marked the emergence of a Jew for whom the Torah was all-embracing and all-sufficient. It was "hard to be a Jew," but, in compensation, it was also "good to be a Jew." In an age of systematic persecution and licensed discrimination, the Jew managed miraculously to retain a spiritual *joie de vivre.* Only in the study of Torah, in the fulfillment of *mitzvot,* and in communion with his Creator, could he find refuge and the strength with which to face the decades of trauma and pain. Poland proved to be fertile soil for Hasidism, and in no other country did the movement spread so rapidly. It is possible to note only a few of the major dynasties in these pages.

Inevitably, much must be omitted. Events that merit meticulous analysis, and personalities who deserve detailed biographies must receive only passing reference. Little short of a lifetime of collation could do justice to so panoramic and densely populated a canvas.

The Radzyn-Izbica Dynasty

Rabbi Mordekhai Joseph Leiner (1800–1854) was the founder of the Radzyn-Izbica dynasty, that produced five outstanding teachers in the course of one century.[1] The rabbis of Izbica believed in informed faith rather than blind faith. God should be served with intelligence as well as with devotion. It was necessary to love not only fellow Jews but all men. Above all, man must aim to perfect himself. In this way he could help prepare for the coming of the Messiah and hasten the dawn of the Apocalyptic era.

Rabbi Mordekhai Joseph had sat at the feet of Menahem Mendel of Kotzk for thirteen years, but in 1840 he was among the disillusioned dissenters who left that hasidic court. His work *Mei Hashilloah* ("The Waters of Siloam"), written with great economy of words, maintains that the shortcomings of the biblical heroes were of minor importance and did not detract from their moral stature.

Rabbi Mordekhai Joseph's son, Rabbi Jacob (1828–1878), wrote *Beit Yaakov* ("The House of Jacob"), a work that includes commentaries on Genesis, Exodus, Leviticus, and on the Festivals; and *Sefer Hazemanim* ("The Book of Seasons"), a collection of discourses on the months of *Nisan* and *Iyyar* as well as a commentary on the Passover *Haggadah.* A gentle and kindly man, Rabbi Jacob was heir to his father's rabbinate, but not to his father's fiery temperament. The *rebbe* attracted many adherents.[2] After living in Izbica for thirteen years, he settled in Radzyn where he established his "court."

Rabbi Gershon Heinokh

Rabbi Jacob's son, Rabbi Gershon Heinokh Leiner, was one of the most original innovators, not only in the hasidic world but also in the realm of *halakhah.* Rabbi Gershon Heinokh, known as the *Baal Hatekheilet,* was born in Izbica in 1839.

Rabbi Gershon Heinokh married Hadasah, daughter of Rabbi

Joseph of Hurbiszow. The bride's father was a disciple of Rabbi Simha Bunem for nine years and of Rabbi Menahem Mendel Morgenstern of Kotzk for thirteen years.[3] He was a descendant of both Rabbi Meir Katzenellenbogen, the *Maharam Padua* (1482–1565), rabbi of Venice and then Padua; and of the merchant Saul ben Judah Wahl (1541–1617), *parnass* of Brest-Litovsk, who, according to an eighteenth-century legend was appointed King of Poland for one day. At the age of 20, Rabbi Gershon Heinokh became rabbi of Radzyn (Radzyn-Podolski) in eastern Poland, where 53 percent of the population (2,853 people) were Jewish. It was there that he prepared his grandfather's manuscript, *Mei Hashilloah* for publication. The book derives its title from the verse, "the waters of Shiloah (Siloam) that go softly" (Isaiah 8:6).

A Brilliant But Controversial Work

At the age of 18, Rabbi Gershon Heinokh had begun work on a project that was to earn him great fame. *Tohorot,* the sixth and last order of the *Mishnah,* contains twelve tractates. Apart from the tractate *Nidah, Tohorot* has no *Gemara* in either the Palestinian or Babylonian Talmuds. Rabbi Gershon Heinokh produced a monumental anthology called *Sidrei Tohorot,* a compendium of the commentaries and interpretations of the sages found in rabbinic literature. He designed his book in the form of a pseudo-*Gemara,* with a commentary resembling Rashi bordering the text on the left side of the page, and *Tosefot* on the right, flanked by the commentaries of *Messorat HaShas, Ein Mishpat,* and *Ner Mitzvah.*

The work received enthusiastic and glowing praise from Rabbi Abraham ben Joseph Ashkenazi (1811–1880), the Sephardic Chief Rabbi of the Holy Land; Rabbi Israel Joshua Trunk of Kutno; Rabbi Simon Sofer (1820–1883), founder of the *Mahazikei Hadat;* Rabbi Isaac Elhanan Spector (1817–1896) of Kovno; Rabbi Tzvi Hirsch Orenstein of Lvov; Rabbi Samson Raphael Hirsch (1808–1888) of Frankfurt; and Rabbi Meir Loeb ben Jehiel Malbim (1809–1879).[4] Similar endorsement came from Sephardic authorities such as Rabbi Ovadiah Abraham of Baghdad and Rabbi Solomon Behor. When it was first printed in Josefow in 1873, it was censored by Rabbi Betzalel and his colleagues at the *Beit Din* of Vilna who objected to a publication in the format of a *Gemara.* To placate his opponents, the subsequent edition of *Sidrei Tohorot* on *Oholot* (Piotrokow, 1903), bore on every page the words "collated from the words of the *tanna'im* and *amora'im.*"

The Petil Tekheilet

"The redemption will begin," wrote Rabbi Gershon Heinokh, "when we are permitted to rebuild the Temple. If we are worthy, permission will be granted even before the ingathering of the exiles." Jews are required to wear ritual fringes that meet very detailed specifications. Each fringe should have seven white threads and one blue (*petil tekheilet*), in accordance with the words of Numbers 15:38, "and they put with the fringe of each corner a thread of blue." The *tanna* Rabbi Meir asked, "Why was the color of blue chosen?" He then explained: "blue is the color of the sea, the sea resembles the heavens, and the heavens remind us of the Throne of Glory" (Sotah 17a). The art of dyeing the blue thread was the secret of a few families who lived on the coast of Palestine. The dye was derived from a native mollusk called *hilozon.* Ritual fringes containing the blue thread were discovered in the Bar Kokhba caves, and the dye is known to have been in use until the end of amoraic times. Reference is made to it by Natronai Gaon of Pumbedita in the early eighth century.

However, the dye had become increasingly difficult to obtain, and it soon disappeared from the ritual fringes. "Nowadays," writes the *Midrash Rabbah* (Numbers 17:5), "we only possess white *tzitzit,* the *tekheilet* having been concealed." Maimonides too, in his commentary on the *Mishnah,* maintains that it had been lost. Rabbi Gershon Heinokh was determined to rediscover the source of the dye and to restore the thread to its rightful place. He fervently believed that this restoration would hasten the redemption. *Hasidim* maintained that Rabbi Samson of Ostropol, in his work *Mahaneh Dan,* predicted that *tekheilet* would be rediscovered in the nineteenth century.

In 1887 Rabbi Gershon Heinokh wrote a thirty-eight-page booklet on the subject entitled *Maamar Sefunei Temunei Hol* (Warsaw, 1887). In it he lists the conflicting views on the number of *tzitzit* that should be dyed. Rashi maintains that four of the eight threads should be colored. Rabbi Abraham ben David of Posquieres known as the *Ravad* (1120–1198) believes that only two should be dyed. Rabbi Gershon Heinokh endorses the view of Maimonides that one is sufficient.

The Search Ends on the Coast of Italy

Accompanied by his attendant, Israel Kotzker, and his son, Rabbi Eliezer Mordekhai Joseph, Rabbi Gershon Heinokh went to Naples in 1887 and again in 1888 where he visited the aquarium four times. He studied the Italian seashore and became an expert on marine life. According to Dr. Aaron Marcus, the *rebbe* even visited the Vatican Museum where he allegedly studied the garments reputed to have belonged to the High Priest, especially the *tzitz* (a plate or crown of pure gold described in Exodus 28:36). According to the Bible, the gold plate was held in position on the forehead of the High Priest by a blue thread.

On the eve of *Shavuot* 1888, Rabbi Gershon Heinokh published his second treatise on the subject, a 206-page book entitled *Maamar Petil Tekheilet,* in which he claimed to have rediscovered *holozon* (Sepia officinalis), a member of the *cephalopod* family, that is related to the octopus and squid families. On the first day of *Hanukkah* 1889, the rebbe began to wear the blue thread on his *tzitzit.*

Support and Opposition

A factory was established in Radzyn for the manufacture of ritual fringes containing a blue thread and soon 12,000 *hasidim* were wearing the thread of blue. At the recommendation of Rabbi Abraham Bratslaver (d. 1918), the practice was adopted by the *hasidim* of Bratslav with a slight variation. While the *hasidim* of Radzyn are content to include one blue thread among the eight prescribed by the Torah, the *hasidim* of Bratslav favor two blue threads among six white ones. Many scholars, however, opposed the restoration of the blue thread. Among them were Rabbi Joshua of Kutno, Rabbi Meir Arik, Rabbi Elhanan Spector, and Rabbi Hillel Moses ben Tzvi who decried the practice in his book *Mishkanot Aviv Yaakov* (Jerusalem, 1886). In addition, hasidic *rebbes* like Rabbi Aryeh Leib Alter of Ger, Rabbi Abraham Bornstein of Sochaczew, and Rabbi Tzadok Rabinowicz of Lublin did not support him. Among his few supporters was Rabbi Akiva Joseph Schlesinger (1837–1922), author of *Lev Ivri* ("Hebrew Heart" published in 1865) and one of the founders of the city of Petah Tikvah. To win over his detractors, Rabbi Leiner wrote a third 250-page work, *Ein Tekheilet* (Warsaw, 1891), which was published posthumously.

In addition to *Sidrei Tohorot* and works on *tekheilet,* he wrote a treatise on the will of Rabbi Eliezer Hagadol called, *Orhot Hayim* (Warsaw, 1891); *Tiferet Hahanokhi,* a commentary on the *Zohar* (Warsaw, 1900); *Daltot Shaarei HaIr* on *Tikkunei Eruvim* (Warsaw, 1902); and *Sod Yesharim,* discourses on Torah (Warsaw, 1902). Among the fifteen manuscripts that remained unpublished were *Hiddushim* on the Palestinian and Babylonian Talmud, responsa on the four parts of the *Shulhan Arukh,* on *Aggunot, Pri Eitz Hayim,* on the *Sefer HaMitzvot* of Maimonides, on the lettering of the *Sefer Torah* according to *halakhah* and *Kabbalah.*

Rabbi Gershon Heinokh altered certain familiar customs in his own practice. He would drink the fifth cup of Elijah on Passover, and at circumcision ceremonies, he acted as both *sandak* (the child's sponsor) and *mohel* (circumciser). Famous for his knowledge of medicine, Rabbi Gershon Heinokh wrote prescriptions in Latin that were accepted without question by the local pharmacies.

Rabbi Gershon Heinokh's Legacy

He died on the fourth day of *Tevet* 1891 in Lublin. He was an innovator in many areas of life and learning. Asked why he did not follow in his grandfather's footsteps, he replied, "Indeed, I do follow his example. My grandfather departed from the ways of his forebears, and so I too can forge new paths." The phrase, "He creates new things and is a man of war," was accurately applied to Rabbi Gershon Heinokh, whose innovations aroused deprecation and controversy.

His son, Eliezer Mordekhai Joseph (d. 1929), was active in communal affairs. He was one of the delegates who interceded with the Russian Minister of the Interior, Peter Stolypin, with Josef Pilsudski, and with the Socialist leader, Hermann Diamond on behalf of the Jewish community. He dedicated himself to the publication of his father's voluminous writings. Nine texts were published, while fifteen remained in manuscript.

Rabbi Jehiel Meir Lipshitz of Gostynin

"King David composed the Psalms" it was said, "but the 'Good Jew of Gostynin' knew how to recite them."

Rabbi Jehiel Meir Lipshitz was born in 1810 in Opoczna, Poland. His father was Rabbi Jacob Tzvi, and his mother, Sarah, was the daughter of Rabbi Judah Leib ben Tzvi Hirsch (d. 1803). When Jehiel Meir was still very young his parents died, and he and his sister Hayah Sprintza were brought up by their uncle, Rabbi Noah Samuel Lipshitz (1800–1832). His uncle's writings included *Zeir Zahav UMinhat Yehudah,* a commentary on *Sefer HaMahriyah* (Lublin, 1897), and *Divrei Shmuel* (Lodz, 1929). Rabbi Noah Samuel was a renowned scholar. At the age of 12 he knew the first part of Maimonides's *Yad HaHazakah* by heart. He was a *hasid* of Rabbi Israel, the *Maggid* of Kozienice, and received *haskamot* from the *Maggid* as well as from Rabbi Akiva Eger and Rabbi Azriel Halevi Horowitz (the "Iron Head"). Each year, on the 15th day of *Shevat,* he made a *siyyum* (completion ceremony) for completing the entire Talmud. He studied eighteen chapters of the *Mishnah* daily.

The Qualities of Rabbi Jehiel Meir

Rabbi Jehiel Meir studied in Kutno under Rabbi Moses Judah Leib Zilberberg (d. 1865), author of *Zayit Raanan* (Warsaw, 1851) and married the daughter of Rabbi Leibish of Gostynin. Rabbi Jehiel Meir cherished the *mitzvah* of *hakhnassat orhim* (hospitality). He would not and could not sit down to a meal without an *oreah* (guest). On one occasion, after the termination of the fast on the 17th of *Tammuz,* he searched the entire town for a guest, as he would not break his fast without first fulfilling the commandment of providing hospitality.

Rabbi Jehiel Meir became a devoted *hasid* of Rabbi Menahem Mendel of Kotzk. "Fear not," the Kotzker Rebbe told the newcomer, "our purpose is not to pursue novelty. We just strive to bring out the best that is in ourselves." When Rabbi Jehiel Meir's father-in-law asked him why he traveled to Kotzk and what he learned there during the Festival of *Shavuot,* he replied, "In Kotzk I became aware of the full implication of the eighth commandment, 'thou shalt not steal' (Exodus 20:13). It means that it is not only forbidden to cheat others but that one must not steal from oneself; that is, one should not deceive oneself."[5]

The rebbe of Kotzk held Rabbi Jehiel Meir in high esteem. He lauded him as the "*Merkavah Yid,*" an expert in *Kabbalah,* and specifically on the *Maaseh Merkavah* (description of the Divine Chariot). On one occasion, Rabbi Menahem Mendel of Kotzk said to him, "Why are you giving me a *kvitl*? You have already prayed, and your prayer has undoubtedly already been answered." The rebbe of Kotzk was proud to count Rabbi Jehiel Meir among his disciples. "I have two Meirs, Rabbi Jehiel Meir and Rabbi Isaac Meir Alter of Ger," he said. He described him as a "man of truth."[6]

"The rabbi of Kotzk," said Rabbi Jehiel Meir, "labored to instill in me a love of mankind so far-reaching that I should be able to love my enemy as much as I love my friend. But I was not able to absorb all of it." In Kotzk, he befriended Rabbi Wolf of Strykow and Rabbi Abraham Bornstein of Sochaczew. After unsuccessfully engaging in business, he followed the advice of Rabbi Menahem Mendel of Kotzk and became rabbi of Gostynin, a town in central Poland with a total Jewish population in 1856 of 2,000. He maintained cordial relations with Rabbi Israel Joshua Trunk (1820–1893) of Kutno, author of *Yeshuot Yisrael* (1870) on *Shulhan Arukh Hoshen Mishpat.* "He who travels to Gostynin and does not stop on the way to see Rabbi Joshua," said Rabbi Jehiel Meir, "behaves as a man who enters a house and neglects to kiss the *mezuzah.*"

Rabbi Jehiel Meir as Rebbe

After the death of Rabbi Menahem Mendel of Kotzk in 1859, Rabbi Jehiel Meir traveled to the courts of Rabbi Isaac Meir Alter of Ger, Rabbi Abraham ben Rafael Landau of Ciechanow, and Rabbi Jacob Aryeh Guterman of Radzymin. When the rabbi of Ciechanow died in 1875, Rabbi Jehiel Meir became *rebbe.* Every *Rosh Hodesh* he conducted a *tish.* He kept the anniversary (*Yahrzeit*) of Rabbi Menahem Mendel of Kotzk not on the 22nd of *Shevat* (the day he died), but on the 23rd day of *Shevat.* "I have a tradition," he stated, "that I would die either a day before or a day after the *Yahrzeit* of Rabbi Mendel, hence I observe the *Yahrzeit* a day later. Only then, am I assured that I would survive the year."

He refused to accept *pidyonot* (monetary contributions) from his *hasidim* but charged a fee for the performance of wedding ceremonies. He believed strongly in *tefillah bezemanah* (prayers to be recited at the proper time). In this way, he differed from his mentor, the *rebbe* of Kotzk, who permitted worship outside the time limits set for prayer. Rabbi Jehiel Meir declared that it was the Almighty's desire that prayers be recited at their proper time. To support his view, he cited the verse, "observe to offer unto me in due season" (Numbers 28:2). He emphasizes this point in a letter: "I entreat you not to engage in anything prior to prayer, not even if you rise early. Your first duty is to commence to pray."

His *hasidim* often referred to Rabbi Jehiel Meir as a "miracle worker." They had great faith in his prayers, and many of the poor begged him to become a symbolic "partner" in their business. It was a rule of Rabbi Jehiel Meir that if someone offended him, he would refrain from expressing his displeasure on the same day. On the following day, he would say to the man, "I was displeased with you yesterday." Although he was renowned as a *baal mofet*, the *rebbe* himself disclaimed such powers. When a *hasid* asked the *rebbe* to bring about a cure for his ailing wife, the *rebbe* replied, "Were I able to achieve cures, I would have visited the sick of my own accord and effected their healing. All I am able to do is to pray for the sick person. You yourself can do the same. Go and do so."

The Power of the Psalm

He was also popularly known as the "Good Jew of Gostynin" and as the *tehillim yid* (a Yiddish expression meaning "the Psalm Jew"). "*Tehillim*" (Psalms), he declared, "contain the whole music of the heart of man." It was in the Psalms that the vast host of suffering humanity found the deepest expression of their hopes and fears. In his will Rabbi Jehiel Meir enjoins his followers to "study the Psalms many times with a translation. Let the Psalms be familiar to you. Utilize the commentary of Rashi. Take heed to recite at least five chapters of Psalms daily." What the *Zohar* was to Rabbi Phinehas of Korets, the Psalms were to Rabbi Jehiel Meir. "The recitation of Psalms," he would say, "removes all trouble." The *rebbe* of Sochaczew was known to remark, "The *rebbe* of Gostynin achieves more with his recitation of ten chapters of Psalms, than I do with all my fervent prayers."[7] To Rabbi Jehiel Meir, the Psalms were the best and only cure. To some *hasidim* he allocated ten chapters, to others the entire book. When a *hasid* was faced with a lawsuit, the *rebbe* told him, "I am convinced that if one follows my advice and recites the Psalms, King David himself comes and defends him." When one of the children of the *Sefat Emet* was ill, the Gerer *Rebbe* sent his brother, Rabbi Solomon, to Rabbi Jehiel Meir. "To force the rabbi of Ger to recite the whole book of Psalms is difficult," said Rabbi Jehiel Meir, "but let him at least recite ten sections daily."[8]

Rabbi Jehiel Meir signed a public appeal (*kol koreh*) imploring the people not to own or read heretical literature. "If he finds such things at home, he should burn them immediately." The *kol koreh* was also signed by Rabbi Israel Joshua of Kutno, Rabbi Hayim Eleazar Wacks, rabbi of Piotrokow, and Rabbi Elimelekh Shapiro of Grodzisk. Rabbi Jehiel Meir also strongly condemned the reading of secular works. "I have heard that there are young men who waste the Sabbath day by reading romances. The Almighty Blessed be He, enriched us with a priceless treasure which is beyond comparison. Why should we waste our precious time on trivialities. Would it not be better to recite Psalms or study the ethical work *Kav HaVashar*" ("The Measure of Righteousness" by Rabbi Tzvi Hirsch Kaidanover).

Physical and Spiritual Successors

He was survived by two sons, Rabbi Leibish and Rabbi Israel Moses of Proskurow, and one daughter, who married Rabbi Jacob Zilberstein. Jehiel Meir's teachings are found in *Meron HaRim* (Warsaw, 1892), edited by Hayim Jacob Zelig Goldshlag of Lubanitz, and *Mei HaYom* (Lodz, 1910), edited by Rabbi Simon Menahem Mendel of Gubartshow.

Rabbi Jehiel Meir died on the eve of *Shabbat,* the 21st day of *Shevat* 1888, and was buried on the following Sunday. Before his death, he instructed communal leaders to appoint as his successor Rabbi Joshua Weingarten (1847–1922) author of *Helkat Yo'av* on the four parts of the *Shulhan Arukh* (Piotrokow, 1903). Rabbi Abraham Bornstein of Sochaczew once told his grandchild, Rabbi David, "I am very sorry that I have not taken you with me to see Rabbi Jehiel Meir, for he is a true Jew."

Rabbi Isaac Kalish of Warka

"I have finally found your father, Rabbi Isaac," Rabbi Menahem Mendel Morgenstern of Kotzk told Rabbi Jacob David Kalish. "I searched for him in the Higher Regions but could not find him. I searched for him among the disciples of Rabbi Israel Baal Shem Tov. I looked for him among the *tanna'im* and *amora'im.* Eventually I found him gazing sadly at a river. 'What are you doing here?' I asked him. 'The river is full of the tears of the children of Israel and I cannot move from it,' he replied."[9] This story epitomizes the outlook of Rabbi Isaac of Warka. What Rabbi Levi Isaac of Berdichev was to Russian Jewry, Rabbi Isaac of Warka was to Polish Jewry–one of the great defenders of the House of Israel.

Rabbi Isaac was a descendant of Rabbi Mordekhai ben Abraham Jaffe (1530–1612), author of the authoritative work *Levush Malkhut* (printed in Lublin, 1590), a commentary on Rabbi Jacob ben Asher's *Tur.* Rabbi Isaac's father, Rabbi Simon, was known as "Simon the Merciful." His wife, Yuta, had given birth to seven daughters before their only son, Isaac, was born in Zlushin in the year 1779. Isaac married Rachel, the daughter of Rabbi Meir of Zarek, and for a time he lived with his in-laws.

His Mentors and Disciples

Through his teacher, Rabbi David Biderman of Lelov (1746–1814), Rabbi Isaac came to know and eventually study under several great hasidic masters. Among them were: Rabbi Jacob Isaac Horowitz, the Seer of Lublin, Rabbi Jacob Isaac Rabinowicz of Przysucha, and Rabbi Simha Bunem of Przysucha, and his son, Rabbi Abraham Moses. For a time Rabbi Isaac was employed by Tamar (Tamerel) Bergson of Warsaw, a member of a prominent family and a devoted follower of Rabbi Israel the *Maggid* of Kozienice. Later, he served as rabbi first in Gubartshow and then in Ruda. After the death of Rabbi Abraham Moses in 1829, Rabbi Isaac assumed leadership of the *hasidim* of Przysucha.

When he moved to the town of Warka, many disciples followed him there. Among his 114 great disciples were Rabbi Jacob Aryeh Guterman of Radzymin, Rabbi Dov Berish of Biala, and Rabbi Shragai Feivel of Grice, (all of whom eventually became leaders of Polish Hasidism). Rabbi Israel Friedmann of Ruzhin venerated Rabbi Isaac highly. He said that each letter of the Hebrew name *Yitzhak* (Isaac) stands for an attribute of Rabbi Isaac: *Yod* is *Yashar* (upright), *Tzaddik* (righteous), *Het* (*hasid*), and *Kuf* is *Kadosh* (holy). Rabbi Isaac maintained that the truly humble man is unable to feel anger. Even if he is interrupted when busy, a man should show no annoyance. He should always believe that the other man is more important than himself.

Rabbi Isaac was once asked to explain the response of Rabbi Zera to his disciples' question (recorded in tractate *Megillah* 29a): "In virtue of what have you reached such a good old age?" Rabbi Zera replied, "I have never rejoiced in the downfall of my fellows." Is one to understand from his answer that the other sages were guilty of this offense? "No," replied Rabbi Isaac, "What Rabbi Zera meant was that he never found enjoyment at occasions of gladness, such as weddings and the like, when he knew that at that very moment someone of his fellowmen was inevitably suffering afflictions."

A Negotiator on Behalf of His People

Rabbi Isaac was one of the most community-minded of the Polish hasidic *rebbes.* He was concerned with every facet of Jewish life as well as with the economic plight of the Jews in the Holy Land, for whom he assiduously collected funds.

In 1824, the Russian authorities in Poland closed the hasidic *shtiblekh.*[10] Rabbi Isaac enlisted the aid of Stanislav Hoga (1791–1860), an assimilated Jew whose high position in the government's censorship office made him an influential intermediary on behalf of the Jewish community. Hoga was successful in getting the edict rescinded, and the *shtiblekh* were reopened. In the year following this event, Hoga moved to England, and there he converted to Christianity. Hoga achieved some recognition for his translations into Hebrew of a number of works. Notable among them was a translation of John Bunyan's *The Pilgrim's Progress* (London, 1844). Stanislav Hoga eventually returned to Judaism.

Rabbi Isaac traveled widely to urge the hasidic *rebbes* to fight against the conscription of young Jews for military service. Rabbi Israel Friedmann of Ruzhin advised him to send a messenger, Israel Birkenfield of Krakow, to London to enlist the support of the

English philanthropist Sir Moses Montefiore. When Sir Moses visited Warsaw in May 1846, Rabbi Isaac Kalish and Rabbi Isaac Meir Alter called on Sir Moses.[11] Before arriving in Warsaw, Sir Moses had been received by Czar Nicholas I and had asked the monarch to grant the Jews "equal rights with all other subjects of the Empire." Sir Moses was partly successful: The ukase (edict) under which the Jews were to be expelled from the western frontier zone of Russia was abrogated through his intervention.

The Cantonists (Jewish children forceably drafted into the Russian army) were not Rabbi Isaac's only problem. Czar Nicholas divided the Jews of Russia into two groups: the "useful" and the "non-useful." Among the "useful" ranked the wealthy merchants, craftsmen, and agriculturists. All the other Jews, the small traders, and poorer classes (which included the bulk of the *hasidim*) were regarded as "non-useful" and were to be conscripted into the army. Furthermore, a special tax imposed in 1822 on liquor forced many *hasidim* to abandon this formerly lucrative profession.

For the Improvement of Jewish Life

Rabbi Isaac, together with Rabbi Isaac Meir Alter and Rabbi Hayim Davidsohn of Warsaw (1760–1854), were signatories to a manifesto dated the 14th of *Tevet* 1842, urging Jews to settle the land. "Not only is there no trace in the Talmud of any edict against working on land," stated the *kol koreh* (proclamation), "but on the contrary, we find in the Talmud that many of the saintly *amora'im* who lived outside the Land of Israel owned lands. It is therefore proper that every rabbi give these words the widest publicity."

On one occasion, a boat carrying many *hasidim,* who were traveling to Warka, capsized with many casualties. The rabbi of Warka went *uprehten golus* (exiled himself) as atonement and lived for a time in Natrazin. Rabbi Isaac died on the last day of Passover 1848. He was survived by two sons (Rabbi Jacob David of Amshinow and Rabbi Menahem Mendel of Warka) and four daughters (Hannah, Devorah, Tzipporah, and Bluma). Rabbi Isaac's discourses are found in *Ohel Yitzhak* (Piotrokow, 1914).

Rabbi Abraham Bornstein of Sochaczew

A hasidic *rebbe* who is considered one of the leading halakhic authorities of the nineteenth century was Rabbi Abraham Bornstein of Sochaczew. Many rabbis from far and wide turned to him to clarify and elucidate complex legal problems. *Avnei Nezer,* his voluminous correspondence of responsa on the four parts of the *Shulhan Arukh* was printed between 1912 and 1934. Each responsum reveals his complete grasp of the subject addressed by the major rabbinic authorities, medieval as well as contemporary.

What Rabbi Elijah the Gaon of Vilna was to the mitnagdic movement of the eighteenth century, Rabbi Abraham was to the Hasidism of the nineteenth century. It was with good reason that Rabbi Jehiel Meir "the Good Jew of Gostynin" referred to him as the *Torah Yid* ("the Torah Jew"). His works have become a classic source for halakhic scholars and indispensable for every codifier. It was undoubtedly the vast and irrefutable erudition of rebbes such as Rabbi Abraham Bornstein and Rabbi Isaac Meir Alter of Ger that blunted the taunts of the *mitnagdim.* No longer could the militant opponents of Hasidism allege that "Torah learning is not to be found among the *hasidim.*"

A Man of Great Heritage and Great Promise

Born in Bendin, Poland in 1839, Rabbi Abraham was the son of Rabbi Ze'ev Nahum. His father held the position of rabbi first in Bendin and subsequently in Belkish and Biala. Rabbi Abraham was known as an assiduous scholar. Like his father, Rabbi Abraham even spent *Purim* studying. It was said that because of his father's dedication and love of learning, he was deemed worthy of being blessed with such a son as Rabbi Abraham.

Rabbi Abraham's mother was a descendant of the renowned Rabbi Moses Isserles, author of *Darkei Moshe,* who was known as the *Rema.* A child prodigy, Abraham soon became known as "the *illui* of Lekish." Both Rabbi Isaac Meir Alter of Ger and Rabbi Hayim Halberstam, the *Divrei Hayim* of Sanz sought him as a son-in-law. He eventually married Sarah Zinah, daughter of Rabbi Menahem Mendel Morgenstern of Kotzk. His father-in-law became his guide and mentor, and he spent seven years in Kotzk. "I have never forgotten what I learned in Kotzk,"[12] Rabbi Abraham later declared. "The *rebbe* is comparable to an angel of the Lord of Hosts. He is the fountain of wisdom and understanding. From him I learned true concentration." The teachings of Kotzk never deserted him. "I am like a broken vessel," said Rabbi Abraham, "but when I recall Kotzk, all my bones revive. In Kotzk I discovered that the best way to reach the Almighty was through intensive and continuous study of the Torah." Rabbi Abraham was greatly venerated by his contemporaries. "In our generation," stated Rabbi Isaac Meir Alter, "the Torah is handed over to him. The *rebbe* of Kotzk has left us a great legacy."

Years of Privation

Four years after Rabbi Mendel's death Rabbi Abraham became rabbi in Parczew, a city in the Warsaw province, where the Jews formed 81 percent of the entire population. Parczew was largely a mitnagdic community wherein much of the Jewish population subsisted at poverty level. So serious were his financial problems at that time that Rabbi Isaac Meir Alter sent him a weekly stipend of fifteen rubles. Subsequently, he became rabbi in Krosnowicz (1866–1876), and at Nasielsk (1876–1883) where he succeeded Rabbi Samuel Shinover, the author of *Ramatayim Tzofim* (Warsaw, 1883). Rabbi Abraham was not happy in his rabbinical posts. He could not reconcile the lofty ideals and learning represented by Kotzk with the pettiness and strife that a communal rabbi must often contend with. He could not tolerate dishonesty in any form. He himself would examine the weights and scales of the traders in the market. When someone told him that he had avoided paying for a railway journey, the *rebbe* advised him that he should pay his debt by buying a ticket and destroying it.

Despite the wholehearted support he received from Rabbi Israel Joshua Trunk of Kutno, he suffered from opposition and conflict. For example, his enemies accused him of failing to publicly recite the prayer for the welfare of Czar Alexander III on the day of his coronation in 1881. For a time, Rabbi Abraham was suspended from the rabbinate and was even threatened with expulsion from Russia. In 1883, Rabbi Abraham became rabbi of the city of Sochaczew, near Warsaw, which had a large Jewish population. It was there that he wrote his important work, *Eglei Tal* (Piotrokow, 1905), on the laws of the Sabbath, and it was there that he founded a large *yeshivah*.

Strong Principles

Rabbi Abraham ate very sparingly, maintaining that excessive food dulled the senses. His discourses commenced at midnight. Among his great disciples were Rabbi Joshua Winegarten of Kinsk, author of *Helkat Yo'ev* (Piotrokow, 1903) and Rabbi Meir Dan Plotzki (1867–1928) of Ostrow, author of *Hemdat Yisrael* (Part 1, 1903, Part 2, 1927).

In 1884, Rabbi Abraham issued a *kol koreh* (proclamation) denouncing "heretical works published in Hebrew or Yiddish that tended to lead young people astray."[13] People were being deceived, he maintained, by the misleading titles of those works. In another *kol koreh,* he urged the rabbis to organize study circles for workers and businessmen:

> People preoccupied by the need to make their livelihood have few opportunities to study: They cannot set aside even one or two hours a day to learn. Thus, it is the duty of our spiritual leaders to allocate time between *Minhah* and *Maariv* to teach the people of their congregation some *halakhah* or whatever subject would be most relevant. It is the study of Torah that will advance the children of Israel materially as well as spiritually.[14]

He unequivocally opposed and roundly condemned the practice of purchasing rabbinical posts. He argued that the rabbis had forbidden such practices in edicts issued as early as 1587 in Lublin and 1590 in Poznan. To support his view, he quoted the condemnation of Rabbi Mordekhai ben Abraham Solomon Jaffe (1530–1612), the *Levush,* Rabbi Solomon ben Jehiel Luria (1510–1573), the *Maharshal,* and Rabbi Isaiah Horowitz, known as the *Sheloh.* Rabbi Abraham's *kol koreh* was cosigned by Rabbi Abraham Mordecai Alter of Ger and the *rebbe* of Aleksandrow.

In every halakhic judgment, Rabbi Abraham tended to take the traditional point of view. For instance, he concurred with Rabbi Joshua of Kutno and Rabbi Hayim Halberstam of Sanz in forbidding *matzot* made by machines for use on Passover. He decreed that when *etrogim* from the Holy Land were available, *etrogim* from Corfu should not be utilized. (*Avnei Nezer, Orah Hayim,* 483).

In 1883, the community of Czenstochowa wanted to introduce an innovation in their synagogue of not calling people up to the Torah by name. Instead, they wished to use the formula, "let the *Kohen* come up," etc. Rabbi Abraham wrote a letter forbidding this innovation: "Far be it for us to annul a custom that is deeply rooted. They merely wish to ape the German style. The Jewish customs were not enacted for nothing. They have sound reasons."

He corresponded with Rabbi Joshua of Kutno, Rabbi Hayim Eliezer Waks of Kalish, Rabbi Shneur Zalman of Lublin, and Rabbi Shalom Mordekhai HaKohen. Rabbi Abraham advised his students to study the Talmud with the commentary of Rabbi Nissim, the North African talmudist. "When we study the *Ran*, we fulfill the *mitzvah* of obliterating Amalek. Amalek was crooked, and the *Ran* is smooth and straightforward." Rabbi Abraham prayed without gestures, as was the custom of Kotzk, and refrained from visiting cemeteries. He maintained that "it is more constructive to study a page of the *Gemara* or *Zohar* than to visit graves." His wife, Sarah Zinah, died on the eve of *Hanukkah* 1909. "Up to now," he lamented, "I lived in the power of Kotzk. Now that she is gone, I do not know how I will survive."

He died on Sunday, the 11th day of *Adar* I 1910. Some of his discourses are quoted by his son and successor, Rabbi Samuel (1856–1920), in his work *Shem MiShmuel* (1928–1934). It is not surprising that Rabbi Jacob Guterman, the rebbe of Radzymin, eulogized Rabbi Abraham as "the last of the Men of the Great Assembly."

Rabbi Tzadok Hakohen Rabinowicz

Rabbi Tzadok Hakohen Rabinowicz or the "Kohen," as he was popularly known, was an extraordinary personality of phenomenal versatility. In fact, there are few areas of Jewish learning, biblical, talmudic, kabbalistic, halakhic, and homiletic, to which he did not make momentous and original contributions. He was one of Hasidism's most prolific, most profound, and most innovative writers. Although not one of his works was printed during his lifetime, over twenty monumental works were published posthumously. Over twenty unpublished manuscripts were destroyed during the Holocaust. In every work, he demonstrated a synthesis of the

Lithuanian style of learning (as expounded by Rabbi Hayim of Volozhin) and the emotional fervor of the hasidic school of Izbica.

Rabbi Tzadok was the son of a *mitnaged,* Jacob Hakohen Rabinowicz, rabbi of Krezburg, Courland, and a grandson of Rabbi Zalman Mireles, rabbi of the triple communities of Altona, Hamburg and Wandsbeck, who was a son-in-law of Rabbi Tzvi Ashkenazi (the *Hakham Tzevi*). Rabbi Tzadok's mother, Ita, was the daughter of Rabbi Barukh Halevi Horowitz, a descendant of Rabbi Isaiah Horowitz.

His Early Years

Rabbi Tzadok was born on the 22nd day of *Shevat,* 1823. At the age of 3, he could already read the prayer book. Tzadok was 6 when his father died, and he was brought up by his uncle, Rabbi Joseph ben Asher Hakohen Katz, author of *Kappot Zahav Shetayim* (Vilna-Horodno, 1836), who later became rabbi in Krinki near Bialystok in 1836.

Tzadok's *bar mitzvah* discourse, which was later printed in his work *Meishiv Tzedek* (Piotrokow, 1921) shows an incisive mind and an astonishing grasp of *halakhah.* As a young man he began to compile an alphabetical list of the rabbinical scholars of the post-talmudic era. "The *Illui of* Krinki," as he was known, married the daughter of the wine merchant, Samuel Hirsch of Wladovka. At the age of 17, Rabbi Tzadok celebrated a *siyyum,* the ceremony that marks the completion of the study of the entire Talmud.

Obtaining a *Hetter Me'ah Rabbanim* (the dispensation of one-hundred rabbis that is needed in certain circumstances to allow a man to remarry), was the task that, in 1847, brought him in touch with most of his great contemporaries. These included: Rabbi Jacob Ornstein, rabbi of Lemberg, author of *Yeshuot Yaakov;* Rabbi Tzvi Hirsch Chajes (1805–1855) of Zolkiew and Kalish; Rabbi Solomon ben Joseph Aaron Kluger of Brody; Rabbi Isaac Meir, author of *Hiddushei HaRim;* Rabbi Shalom Rokeah of Belz, and Rabbi Hayim Halberstam of Sanz. Rabbi Tzadok was asked by Rabbi Ornstein, "Is it true, young man, that you know the whole Talmud by heart?" "Would it not be enough" rejoined Rabbi Tzadok, "if I knew half of the Talmud?" "Which half do you know?" inquired Rabbi Ornstein. "Whichever half you wish," replied Rabbi Tzadok.

After successfully accomplishing his mission, Rabbi Tzadok married Havah Devorah, a daughter of Rabbi Israel Jacob of Ciechanow (near Lublin). Rabbi Tzadok became a disciple of Rabbi Mordekhai Joseph Leiner of Izbica, author of *Mei Hashilloah.* "In Izbica," Rabbi Tzadok would say, "they know what is *Hasidut* and what is Torah."[15]

Devotion to Study

Every day Rabbi Tzadok would conclude an entire tractate of the Talmud, and in the evening the event would be celebrated with a festive meal. On the Sabbath he concluded two tractates, the tractates of *Sabbath* and *Eruvim.* When Rabbi Joshua Heschel Ashkenazi of Lublin died in 1887, Rabbi Tzadok refused the rabbinate of Lublin. His wife had a shop selling old clothes, and her income enabled him to pursue his studies undisturbed. He interpreted the verse, "And Abram was very rich in cattle, in silver, and gold" (Genesis 13:2), to mean that Abraham's wealth was a heavy burden to the Patriarch.

When the *rebbe* of Izbica died in 1854, Rabbi Tzadok transferred his allegiance to Rabbi Judah Leib Eger, who would give his disciple (who was a *kohen*) *matnot kehunah,* "priestly dues," the "shoulder, the two cheeks, and the maw" of animals as enumerated in Deuteronomy 18:3. When Rabbi Judah Leib Eger died on the 22nd of *Shevat* 1888, he was succeeded by his son Rabbi Abraham (1846–1914). Rabbi Tzadok reluctantly became *rebbe.* His first act was to begin writing a Sefer Torah. He devoted every Friday to this sacred task, which took him twelve years to complete. He rarely accepted money from his followers. He devoted the monies he received from the ceremony of *pidyon haben* ("Redemption of the First Born") to the acquisition of books.

Like Rabbi Abraham Mordekhai Alter of Ger, he was a fervent bibliophile. His house was crammed with books that he called "my teachers." Every book bore his elaborate glosses and annotations. When his wife died a year after he became *rebbe,* he said in eulogy: "Half of my destined share in the world to come belongs to her. She encouraged me to devote myself to Torah study." His capacity for study was extraordinary. A scholarly tome was always in his hand or open before him. Not a moment was wasted. By the time he entered the synagogue on the Sabbath morning, he had already completed his study of the tractate. He corresponded with his contemporaries, Rabbi Gershon Heinokh of Radzyn and Rabbi David Tzvi Ashkenazi of Koenigsberg.

On the 28th of *Nisan* 1884 he wrote a lengthy letter to his boyhood friend, a Doctor Asher, then living in Manchester, England, about whom little is known. His friend was apparently anxious to leave "the wealthy land of silver and gold" and settle in the Holy Land. Rabbi Tzadok too was urged by his brother, Rabbi Isaac Avigdor, to settle in the Holy Land.[16]

After his second wife's death, Rabbi Tzadok married the daughter of Rabbi Fishel of Strushyn, a descendant of Rabbi Jacob Isaac, the *Yehudi HaKadosh.* She was a widow with children, to whom he became a loving father. After months of illness, he died on the ninth of *Elul* 1900, at the age of 77. He bequeathed his valuable library to the *Beit HaMidrash* in Lublin. He was buried near the tombs of Rabbi Leib and Rabbi Abraham Eger.

When asked which of the works of Rabbi Tzadok should be printed, Rabbi Abraham Mordekhai Alter of Ger promptly replied, "All of them." Among the works printed were *Peri Tzaddik* on the Torah in five volumes (Lublin, 1901–1934); *Tzidkat Tzaddik* on Hasidism (Lublin, 1902); *Dover Tzedek* (Lublin, 1911); and *Resisei Lylah* on dreams (Lublin, 1903). Unpublished works include commentaries on several books of the Bible, on the *Midrash,* on the *Zohar,* and glosses on the Talmud. In 1957 *Zikhron Larishonim* on the sages of Israel was published in Jerusalem.

Rabbi Simha Bunem of Przysucha's credo was "Love of God," that of Rabbi Menahem Mendel Morgenstern of Kotzk was "Fear of God," and the motto of Rabbi Isaac Meir of Ger was "Study the Torah." All these elements were combined in Rabbi Tzadok. It was with good reason that he was called *Kohen Gadol* (High Priest) and "Teacher of the Exile."

Chapter 16

Great Polish Dynasties

The town of Aleksandrow Lodzki (or Alexander as the *hasidim* used to call it), a town in Central Poland with a Jewish population in the 1850s of 1,000, was destined to become the home not only of the Danziger family but also of Rabbi Hanokh Heinokh Levin.

Rabbi Hanokh Heinokh Levin of Alexander

Rabbi Hanokh Heinokh Hakohen, popularly known as Rabbi Hanokh Heinokh, was born in Litomirsk near Lublin in 1798. His father, Rabbi Phinehas Hakohen Levin, a *mitnagged,* was a descendant of Rabbi Shabbetai ben Meir Hakohen, the *Shakh* (a name he acquired from the initials of his work *Siftein Kohen* on *Yoreh De'ah.*). Hanokh Heinokh's mother, Sarah Hannah, also traced her descent back to eminent rabbis.

Rabbi Hanokh Heinokh married Hannah Feigel, daughter of Jacob Yokil, a wealthy man of Przysucha. At the betrothal, he met Rabbi Jacob Isaac, the Holy Jew of Przysucha. When Rabbi Hanokh Heinokh returned home and was asked what he had learned in Przysucha, he replied, "I became aware that there is a Creator of the World."[1]

Rabbi Hanokh Heinokh studied under Rabbi Jacob Aryeh Guterman (later *rebbe* of Radzymin), Rabbi Isaac Eizig Urbach of Zluzhin (d. 1846), author of *Divrei Hayim* (Breslau, 1851), and under Rabbi Isaiah ben Meir of Przedborz (1758–1831). After his marriage, Rabbi Hanokh Heinokh lived in Przysucha. He served a long "apprenticeship" and did not become *rebbe* until he reached the age of 68. In turn, he was a disciple of Rabbi Jacob Isaac Rabinowicz, the Yehudi Hakadosh; Rabbi Jacob Isaac Hurwitz, the Seer of Lublin; Rabbi Isaac Meir Alter of Ger, the *Hiddushei HaRim;* and Rabbi Menahem Mendel Morgenstern of Kotzk.

A Modest Leader

Rabbi Hanokh Heinokh was reluctant to become a *rebbe.* After the death of Rabbi Isaac Meir of Ger, he could no longer refuse responsibility. Having subordinated his will to others for so long, he found the crown of leadership weighty and burdensome. "Woe to the generation that has me for its leader," he sighed. Yet he proved to be a conscientious and dedicated *rebbe,* who became close to each one of his *hasidim.* Underlining this individual relationship, he established the custom of handing each *hasid* a goblet of wine during the *Kiddush* on the Sabbath. Another innovation was the acceptance of *kvitlekh* (petitions) from women, which had not been the custom in Ger or Kotzk.

Prior to becoming *rebbe,* Rabbi Hanokh Heinokh served as rabbi first in Alexander, then in Nowydwor, Proshnitz, and eventually returned to Alexander. When he was asked whether he felt at home there, he replied, "There is a story that some passengers on a ship wanted to make a purchase in a foreign port. They asked a Jewish passenger to do it for them. At first, the Jew protested, 'But the place is strange to me'. The non-Jewish travelers persisted saying, 'A Jew is at home anywhere. Is it not true that God accompanies him wherever he travels?' It is indeed so with me. In any place where I commune with God, I am at home."

Many stories are told of his modesty. It is said that on one occasion a young *hasid* came to see him, and the *rebbe* told him, "Were I in your place, I would not have wasted valuable time in visiting a *rebbe* like myself." To this the *hasid* replied: "Whom else should *hasidim* recognize as their *rebbe,* if not one who holds himself to be as undeserving as yourself?" With characteristic tolerance, he defended those *hasidim* who did not pray at the appointed hours but when the spirit moved them. "In peacetime," explained Rabbi Hanokh Heinokh, "soldiers exercise according to timetables laid down in military manuals. But in time of war, the book of rules can be ignored. It is the same with the *hasidim;* for them every day is a battlefield, and when they pray they fight for the House of Israel and regulations do not apply."

The Parables of Rabbi Hanokh Heinokh

One parable much-quoted by his disciples is his interpretation of the talmudic phrase, "The world is like a wedding" (Eruvin 54a). The *rebbe* of Alexander explained this saying through the story of a country man who went to Warsaw for the first time in his life. Hearing the sounds of wedding music issuing from a certain house, he assumed that the owner of the house was celebrating the wedding of a member of his family. Days, weeks, and months passed, and the house was still the scene of wedding festivities. The villager was amazed. "Can a man have as many sons as the days of the year?" he wondered. Laughing, his neighbors explained to him that the house was a banquet hall and that every day another person celebrated a festivity there. So it is with life, pointed out the *rebbe,* "Fortune changes from day to day, and each one will have the chance of rejoicing."[2]

Another of his stories concerned a farmer who hired a *melammed* (Hebrew teacher) to teach his son the Hebrew alphabet. Later the teacher called the father to demonstrate the progress of his charge. Pointing to the first letter, the teacher asked his pupil "What vowel is under the letter *alef?*" The pupil readily replied. When the teacher reached the fifth letter of the Hebrew alphabet, the boy hesitated. He finally blurted out, "Since you ask what is under the *hey* (pronounced "hay") I have to tell you that we have hidden a calf there that my father stole."[3]

The Quality of Joy

The *rebbe* urged his followers to be joyous in their demeanor. He declared, "A Jew should be full of joy simply because he is a Jew. To be otherwise is to show that he is ungrateful to the Lord. A man who is content will see the best in his fellow man, whereas one who is of melancholy disposition stands in jeopardy. There is only a hairsbreadth between sadness and bitterness." He enjoined his followers to remember that while celebrating the festivals in a joyous manner, it was vital to ponder the moral lessons that each festival teaches. He underlined this by citing the verse in Psalms (118:27), "bind the festal offerings with cords," and explaining that unless the tailor safely knots the thread with which he works, the stitches will unravel. Similarly, unless man strives to secure the lessons during the holiday, the rabbi's work is for naught.

Hasidim who came to see the *rebbe* were often made to wait for long periods before he admitted them. The *rebbe* explained his purpose. "While they wait in the vestibule, they naturally discuss Hasidism among themselves and they learn from one another. But from me, what can they learn?"

One Code of Conduct for all Exigencies

He also urged his *hasidim* to maintain high moral standards when away from home. "When a man is on a journey," he explained, "he sometimes conducts himself according to a *Shulhan Arukh* different from the Code he follows at home." As evidence for this unfortunate tendency, he cited the Talmud's explanation of why the Torah demarcates the two verses of Numbers 10:35–36, "And it came to pass when the Ark went forth . . .," by placing an inverted Hebrew letter *nun* before and after these verses. The Torah thereby indicates that these verses constitute a separate book (with the implication that when some people leave their homes to travel, they behave as though they follow a different Torah).

After the death of his first wife, the *rebbe* married the daughter of Rabbi Asher of Porisow. He had two daughters and one son, Rabbi Jehiel Fishel (1823–1897). Rabbi Fishel was not his successor. The dynasty of Alexander was continued by the Danziger family.

Throughout his life, Rabbi Hanokh Heinokh was an ardent supporter of the poor in the Holy Land. He raised 12,000 rubles for charitable institutions there. Rabbi Hanokh Heinokh died on the 18th day of *Adar* 1872. Apart from a number of responsa and a discourse on *Shabbat Shuvah,* he did not put his thoughts on paper. Later, his discourses were printed under the name *Hashavah Letovah* (Piotrokow, 1929).

"The Heavens are the Heavens of the Lord but the earth He

gave to the children of men," says the Book of Psalms (115:16). "The Heavens are already heavenly," interpreted the *rebbe* of Alexander, "but the earth of the Lord was given to man so that he might make heaven out of it." The *Rebbe* Hanokh Heinokh of Alexander directed his life to the fulfillment of this ideal.

Rabbi Shragai Feivel Danziger of Alexander

For nearly a century the town of Aleksandrow, or Alexander, held a unique position in Hasidism. As the *Kabbalists* in the Holy Land gravitated toward Safed, so *hasidim* in Poland turned to Alexander. As Ger was the "spiritual fortress" that guarded Warsaw, so Alexander shielded Lodz. There was no other hasidic dynasty, apart from Ger, that drew so vast a multitude. And while Ger attracted the scholars, Alexander drew the *baalei battim* (responsible laity), the middle classes, the merchants, and the masses. Alexander was the third force in Poland. It stood aloof from political parties. There were few Polish towns without one or two Alexander *shtiblekh.* Rabbi Shragai Feivel, who founded the dynasty, was rebbe for little more than six months. Yet, he established branches throughout Poland.

Tzvi Hirsch, father of the founder, was the son of Barukh Danziger and was one of the most prominent *baalei battim* of Warsaw. A staunch *mitnaged* and the son of a *mitnaged,* he was related by marriage to Rabbi Levi Isaac of Berdichev. Whenever Tzvi Hirsch went to Poznan, he would visit Rabbi Akiva ben Moses Eger (1761–1837), one of the foremost rabbinical authorities in Europe. The fourth and youngest son of Tzvi Hirsch, Shragai Feivel was very young when he first met Rabbi Levi Isaac, who prophesied a great future for the diligent scholar.

At the age of 13, Shragai Feivel was sent to study under Rabbi Jacob ben Jacob Moses (d. 1832) rabbi of Kalish, Lissa, and Stry. Rabbi Jacob, who was in the forefront of the opposition to the Reform movement, was the author of *Derekh HaHayim* (first printed in Zolkiew in 1828 and subsequently reprinted in many prayer books). He had the highest regard for his new student, who he entrusted with the task of copying out the manuscript of the second part of his *Netivot HaMishpat* (Dyrenfurth, 1840), commentary on the *Shulhan Arukh.* In Lissa, Rabbi Shragai Feivel began a friendship with Rabbi Zusya, a fellow student known as the "Warsaw prodigy." On returning to Warsaw, Rabbi Shragai Feivel married Malka, daughter of a *mitnaged.* He subsequently went to Lublin, to the court of the Seer, Rabbi Jacob Isaac Hurwitz. Lublin was the nursery of the great hasidic dynasties. In Lublin, *hasidim* were fond of saying, "we see miracles and wonders rolling on the floor and no one even bothers to pick them up."

At the Seer's Court

The first discourse that Rabbi Shragai Feivel heard from the Seer was based on a verse in Exodus, "And when the people heard these evil things, they mourned and no man put on his garments" (33:7). The Seer explained that "the direct consequence of the sin of the Golden Calf was that mourning and melancholy enveloped the Children of Israel. For a time they were oblivious to the fact that despite their sins, they were still part of Creation and therefore ornaments of the Creator."[4]

Rabbi Shragai Feivel was gifted with a beautiful handwriting, and consequently he became a *sofer* (scribe). The Seer was very impressed with a set of phylacteries he had written. "This young man," said the Seer, "has correctly divined the real meaning of this section. The Torah of the Almighty is in your mouth and the letters shine like beautiful and luminous stars."[5] Rabbi Shragai Feivel attributed his skill to the fact that whenever he was engaged in the sacred art of writing Holy Scrolls, he studied the work *Urim VeTumim* (Karlsruhe, 1778) by Rabbi Jonathan Eibeschütz (1690–1764), the talmudist, Kabbalist, and rabbi of the triple community of Altona, Hamburg, and Wandsbeck. A story is told that Rabbi Shragai Feivel once mislaid his phylacteries and was greatly distressed. "Why not write another one?" asked his son. "I could not do that," replied Rabbi Shragai Feivel, "for who will give me the approval of the Seer. He is, alas, no longer alive."

A Hasid *against Many Odds*

His erstwhile teacher, Rabbi Jacob, urged Rabbi Shragai Feivel to join the rabbinate. "It is fitting that the disciples of the Besht occupy rabbinical positions in Germany, where they are needed desperately." He was anxious to enlist rabbis in the fight against the rising tide of reform and assimilation. Rabbi Shragai Feivel, however, did not wish to leave his native soil.

After the death of the Seer, Rabbi Shragai Feivel became a disciple of Rabbi Simha Bunem of Przysucha, whom he would consult whenever he visited Warsaw. His attraction to Hasidism displeased his *mitnagdic* father-in-law. He attempted to reason with the young *hasid;* and when the arguments failed, the father-in-law locked him in his room. Yet iron bars do not a prison make where a *rebbe* is concerned. Rabbi Shragai Feivel escaped through the chimney. He eventually held rabbinical positions in Gombyn, Grice, and Makova. His first post lasted only four weeks, for his authority was challenged by hostile *mitnagdim.*

Shragai Feivel's son, Rabbi Levi Isaac (named after the rebbe of Berdichev), married the daughter of Rabbi Simha Bunem. To help defray the dowry costs, Tamarel Bergson paid Rabbi Shragai Feivel 1,000 rubles to use his talents as a scribe and write a *Sefer Torah.* When Rabbi Simha Bunem died, Rabbi Shragai Feivel became a disciple first of Rabbi Abraham Moses, the son of Rabbi Simha Bunem and later of Rabbi Isaac of Warka. "Thanks be to the Master of the Universe for providing us with a saintly man like the *rebbe* of Warka," said Rabbi Shragai Feivel. The *rebbe* of Warka was a man of compassion. In teaching his followers about the importance of philanthropy, he would cite the verse, "For the poor shall never cease from the land, therefore, I command thee saying: Thou shalt open thy hand unto the poor and the needy" (Deuteronomy 15:11). He then explained that the word, "saying," is used to stress a man's obligation not only to give money to the poor but also to speak kindly and courteously. The recipient must never be humiliated or embarrassed. Rabbi Shragai Feivel said of Rabbi Isaac, "Anyone who wants to know how our Patriarch Abraham looked should gaze upon the face of the rabbi of Warka."[6]

A Life of Personal Tragedy

Rabbi Shragai Feival's personal life was beset by tragedies. Apart from one son who became his successor, his children died young. When his son Rabbi Levi Isaac died on the eve of Passover, he attempted to console his grieving wife, "Do not grieve, for our son is already in Paradise."

Rabbi Isaac of Warka died on the last day of Passover 1848. "Who will guide us now?" lamented Rabbi Shragai Feivel. The *hasidim* urged him to become their leader, and he allowed himself to be persuaded. His "reign" lasted only six months. "The hardest task," he would say, "is to help people to become God-fearing." He interpreted the adage of Hillel (*Sukkah* 53a), "If I am here, everybody is here," to mean that it was not sufficient for a leader to serve God in seclusion. The leader must take care that "everybody is here, that all the people are reaching out to their Father in Heaven."

He died on *Shemini Atzeret* 1849. His wife died the following *Hoshana Rabba* (a year less one day after his death). He was interred in Makova. Several of his responsa were published in *Peri Hadash* by Rabbi Hayim Leib Halevi of Kaluszyn and in *Kovetz Beit Shmuel* (1932). Most of his discourses are quoted in the work *Yismah Yisrael* by Rabbi Jerahmiel Israel Isaac Danziger (Lodz, 1911).

Rabbi Jehiel Danziger of Alexander

Rabbi Jehiel, the only surviving son of Rabbi Shragai Feivel, the first rebbe of Alexander, was a frail child whose health caused great concern. "Leave him in my hands," Rabbi Isaac of Warka told the worried parents, "and I will convert him into a precious vessel."[7] So the young Jehiel spent his boyhood in the home of the rebbe of Warka, a memorable experience for the impressionable boy. "I would gaze for hours at the *rebbe*'s face," recalled Rabbi Jehiel, "for my father had told me that from such contemplation I would draw strength."[8]

Rabbi Jehiel married Rosa Mindel, daughter of David of Przysucha. The young husband became a *matmid,* an assiduous student, studying throughout the night. To keep himself awake, he would place his feet in ice cold water. For a time he studied in the *Beit HaMidrash* that was formerly used by Rabbi Jacob Isaac, the Holy Jew of Przysucha. Rabbi Jehiel visited Rabbi Shalom Rokeah of Belz and once gave him a *kvitl* (petition). "Take care of Rabbi Jehiel," prayed Rabbi Shalom, "his *kvitl* is drenched with tears."

Influences and Enemies

Rabbi Jehiel also visited Rabbi Abraham Jacob Friedmann of Sadgora, Rabbi Abraham Twersky, the *maggid* of Turisk, Rabbi Leib Eger of Lublin, and Rabbi Judah Aryeh Alter, the *Sefat Emet.* Rabbi Jehiel became rabbi first in Torchin and then in Grice (where his father had once been *rebbe*). Rabbi Jehiel inherited his father's mild disposition. Despite constant provocation by his opponents, the *mitnagdim,* he remained serene and refused to retaliate. On the contrary, he avoided controversy and endeavored to make peace. For the sake of harmony and peace, he would bear all indignities.

Though forgiving and tolerant in his personal life, he was unyielding and uncompromising when religious matters were involved. He lived in a state of perpetual poverty. Every day he distributed among the poor any money that came into his house. When his father died, he was 20 years old. He then became a disciple of the rebbe of Warka. At Warka, he learned the virtue of brevity. As a result, he delivered few discourses and spoke in a concise and forceful manner. When Rabbi Menahem Mendel of Warka died in Warsaw in 1868, Rabbi Jehiel asked Rabbi Dov Berush Meisels (1798–1870), Chief Rabbi of Warsaw, to permit the body of the *rebbe* to be borne to his eternal resting place on the shoulders of his disciples (rather than in a special wagon employed by the *Hevrah Kaddisha*). "How do you know," asked Rabbi Meisels, "that this is the proper procedure for a scholar?" "It is written in the Torah," replied Rabbi Jehiel, referring to Numbers 7:8, " 'But unto the sons of Korah, he gave nothing because the service of the holy things belong to them; they bore the sacred objects on their shoulders'. Similarly, the rebbe is a sacred object, hence he deserves the honor of being carried by his disciples." Rabbi Meisels willingly gave his consent.

From Disciple to Rebbe

Rabbi Jehiel then became a disciple of Rabbi Dov Berish of Biala, who died on the 25th of *Sivan* 1870. "Rabbi Dov Berishis full of blessings," declared Rabbi Jehiel. "There is no one like him." When Rabbi Dov Berish died, Rabbi Jehiel lamented, "Master of the

Universe, it is written in Daniel 'To thee, O Lord, belongs righteousness but to us belongs humility' (9:7). When You deprive us of our righteous teacher, You leave us with inferior guides." Before Rabbi Jehiel became *rebbe,* Rabbi Jacob David of Amshinow gave him this advice: "If you become a *rebbe,* you should remember three things. First, when you sit on your chair of authority, imagine that you are actually sitting on nails. Second, before you read the *kvitl,* you should know what is written thereon. Third, when you do read the *kvitl,* you should feel as if the problems of the petitioner were your very own problems." He also received counsel from Rabbi Israel Joshua Trunk of Kutno and from Rabbi Hayim Elieser Waks, author of *Nefesh Hayim,* who told him, "If you can guide your followers in the way of the Lord, declining to become a *rebbe* would be tantamount to a sin." Rabbi Jehiel wrote to his sister in Makova entreating her to pray for him at their father's grave.

In 1870, when Rabbi Jehiel became *rebbe* of Alexander, he acquired the one time *Beit HaMidrash* of Rabbi Hanokh Heinokh Levin. This house remained the headquarters of the Alexander rebbes until it was destroyed in the Holocaust. The year that he became rebbe, he announced on the eve of the Day of Atonement, "You come to me because you are in trouble. Yet I am in even greater trouble. I must repent for my sins. I should go round the whole town, visit every single *hasid* and entreat of him to pray for me."

The Rebbe's Prayers

During prayers, the *rebbe* would weep bitterly. "I testify that when I entered the synagogue of the *rebbe,*" wrote a *hasid,* "the entire building seemed to be overflowing with holiness, and the worshippers were weeping." The *rebbe* maintained that prayer should be recited with weeping and with concentration. "I weep for all the sufferings of the Children of Israel," he averred. He quoted Rabbi Isaac ben Jacob Alfasi (1013–1103), known as the *Rif,* who said, "When a man weeps while he worships, the stars and the planets worship with him."

It is a characteristic hasidic paradox that like the *rebbe* of Warka, Rabbi Jehiel believed in joy (*simhah*) and urged his *hasidim* not to brood over their misfortunes. He claimed that joy drives away evil urges. He devoted all the monies that the *hasidim* gave him to the upkeep of orphans. He himself lived on the stipend he received as a rabbi of the town.

A *hasid* once gave him a particularly large sum of money. The rebbe looked quite dismayed. "Why are you giving me all this money?" he asked. "So that you may distribute it among the poor," replied the *hasid.* "Would it not be better if you yourself distributed it?" inquired the rebbe. "Why do you need an intermediary?"

The Last Will and Testament of Rabbi Jehiel

When Rabbi Jehiel was ill, he was visited by Rabbi Abraham Bornstein of Sochaczew. "How are things in Alexander?" asked the visitor. "All is well," replied the ailing sage. He explained that illness often prevented a man from studying and praying with total concentration. But in Alexander, study and prayer patterns were not disrupted by his illness. The *rebbe* died on the 14th day of *Shevat* 1894. In his Last Will and Testament, which was printed in his work *Tiferet Yisrael* and covers four pages, he stressed that "honoring father and mother is a precept that applies even after the death of the parents."[9] He quotes copiously from tractate *Kiddushin,* from Maimonides, the *Zohar, Sefer Haredim* (Venice, 1601), and from *Midrash Tanhuma* and *Sefer HaYashar* by Rabbi Jacob ben Meir Tam. He urged his children to pray for his soul, "for I am like a bird in a cage and cannot free myself." He also urged them to repent their misdeeds every night.

Unlike Rabbi Jacob ben Jacob Moses of Lissa (d. 1832), author of *Derekh Hahayim,* he exempted his children from fasting on the day of his *Yahrzeit.* He forbade them to put the title "*rebbe*" or "rabbi" on his tombstone. Like Rabbi Ezekiel ben Judah Landau, the *Noda BeYehudah,* he asked not to be described as either "*hasid*" or "*tzaddik,*" nor did he wish to have an *ohel* (sepulcher) erected over his grave. Instead, he requested his *hasidim* to study *Mishnah* or recite Psalms in his name.

Rabbi Jehiel left three sons: Rabbi Jerahmiel Israel Isaac, author of *Yismah Yisrael;* Rabbi Samuel Tzvi, the *Tiferet Shmuel;* and Rabbi Betzalel Ja'ir of Lodz. Rebbe Jehiel never wrote down any of his own discourses, but his sayings were quoted in Rabbi Jerahmiel's work *Yismah Yisrael,* (Lodz, 1911). Rabbi Abraham Bornstein of Sochaczew called Rabbi Jehiel "King of the *Tzaddikim*."

Rabbi Jerahmiel Israel Isaac Danziger of Alexander

Rabbi Jerahmiel Israel Isaac, son of Rabbi Jehiel, the second rebbe of Alexander, was born in Torchin in 1853. His mother, Rosa Mindel, was the daughter of a *hasid* of Przysucha. He was 5 yearsold when his father took him to Rabbi Menahem Mendel Kalish of Warka, who asked the child, "Who taught you to pray so well? Your father or your teacher?" "Neither my father nor my teacher," came the ready reply, "only the prayer book."

Rabbi Jerahmiel Israel Isaac married Devorah, daughter of Rabbi Dov (Berke) Cheitschke, a *hasid* of Porissow. The marriage was not blessed with children. Rabbi Jacob Aryeh ben Solomon Guterman of Radzymin comforted him with the thought that his soul was the incarnation of Rabbi Hayim ibn Atar, author of the commentary on the Pentateuch *Or Hahayim,* who had also been childless. The *rebbe* of Radzymin valued this disciple highly. He praised him with the words, "The grace of Joseph the Righteous rests upon him. He is destined to be a great leader. He will plant the fear of God in the hearts of his followers. Thousands will be attracted to him."[10] The *rebbe* taught him how to read a *kvitl.* He even presented him with his own walking stick, a gift the disciple cherished all his life. When he was once asked why he attached such great importance to a mere stick, he quoted the *tanna* in the Palestinian Talmud (*Nedarim* 9:1) who said, "I have the staff of Rabbi Meir (a Palestinian *tanna* who lived in the second century) in my hand, and it instructs me in knowledge."

A Scholar of Renown

Rabbi Jerahmiel Israel Isaac was renowned for his mastery of Talmud and rabbinic lore, and it was said that he knew the entire *Zohar* by heart. Rabbi Joseph (Dov) Soloveichik (1820–1892), rabbi of Brest-Litovsk (1875–1892) and author of *Beit Halevi,* said of him, "This young man is one of the foremost scholars in Poland."[11] He corresponded with halakhic authorities such as Rabbi Jacob Ridbaz (1845–1913), the "Slutzker Rav" of Safed, who told the *hasidim* that they could learn from the rebbe not only Hasidism but rabbinics as well. Rabbi Hayim Ezekiel ben Raphael Medini (1832–1904), author of the halakhic encyclopedia *Sedei Hemed* (Warsaw, 1891–1931), describes the *rebbe*'s responsum as "more precious than gold."

In a letter, the *rebbe* urged his followers to "study diligently and make progress in the Torah. He advised them to concentrate on the *Rishonim* (the early medieval authorities) and not to engage in *pilpul.* The Hebrew word of *besimhah* (with joy) is equivalent to *mahshavah* (thought)." The *rebbe* visited Rabbi Shalom Rokeah of Belz, Rabbi Hayim Halberstam of Sanz, Rabbi Abraham Jacob Friedmann of Sadgora, and Rabbi Abraham Twersky of Turisk.

The Third Rebbe of Alexander

On 14 *Shevat* 1894, Rabbi Jerahmiel Israel Isaac succeeded his father. At first he was reluctant to become *rebbe,* for he yearned to settle in the Holy Land. Rabbi Abraham Bornstein of Sochaczew, however, told the Alexander *hasidim,* "He is your *rebbe.* Do not let him go until he accepts his role." In his first discourse, the *rebbe* of Alexander frequently quoted his father's thoughts. "Let me share with you," was his introduction, "the thoughts of a sincere Jew (*an erlikher yid*)."

Aid to the Individual and the Community

"A visit to the *rebbe* for one Sabbath," *hasidim* used to say, "could provide inspiration for a whole year." The *rebbe* was greatly troubled by the many social and political problems that beset his people: legal restrictions on places of residence, the discriminatory taxation, Czarist monopolies that deprived Jews of a living, and compulsory military service, among others. People flooded him with their personal problems. They entered his study with heavy hearts and left his presence comforted. "A rabbi's most important task," he would say, "is to give the right advice, to be of real help to those who are in trouble."

During the nineteenth century, Lodz became a major textile center for the entire Czarist empire. The Jewish population grew from 27,775 in 1856 to 96,677 in 1897. Many of the textile manufacturers and workers were *hasidim* of Alexander. Many anecdotes bear witness to the wisdom of the third *rebbe* of Alexander.

When a wagoner complained that his horse refused to eat, the *rebbe* asked him, "Tell me, how do you conduct your self?" "How should I conduct myself?" replied the man, "I behave like all the other wagoners. I only wash my hands in the morning and then again only before I retire at night. I do eat bread continuously throughout the day, and I recite Grace After Meals." (An Orthodox Jew does not eat bread without first ritually washing his hands. To do so, even if he subsequently recites Grace, is a transgression.) "Now, I understand the situation," responded the *rebbe*. "You behave like an animal, so your horse acts like a human being (i.e., he will not touch food without washing first). If you reverse roles and behave like a devout Jew, your horse will revert to character, and will resume eating like a horse."

On another occasion, a *hasid* asked Rabbi Judah Leib of Ger where he should make his home. "Lodz" was the reply of the *rebbe* of Ger. When he subsequently asked the *rebbe* of Alexander the same question, he was told to reside in Warsaw. This conflicting advice worried the *hasid* until the *rebbe* of Alexander produced an explanation. "The *rebbe* of Ger, who resides near Warsaw, knows that life is difficult in Warsaw, and he advised you to live in Lodz. I, who lived near Lodz, know the conditions of Lodz better, so I advised you to settle in Warsaw. Wherever you decide to make your home, may the blessings of the Almighty be with you."

The Humble Way to Perfection

The *rebbe* stressed the need for continual striving to achieve perfection. Modesty and humility were most important attributes, since they are conducive to the Fear of God and to the love of one's neighbor. The phrasing of the precept, "Thou shalt love thy neighbor as thyself, I am the Lord" (Leviticus 19:18) indicates that love of man leads to love of God. The *Amidah* concludes with the passage, "Let my soul be unto all as dust, open my heart to Thy Torah." The *rebbe* commented, "This teaches that only the lowly can truly understand the Torah."

In a letter dated the 26th of *Elul* 1906, he urged his followers to neither read heretical works nor to engage teachers who were not imbued with the Fear of God. The gentle, mild-mannered *rebbe* never became embroiled in controversies. When Rabbi Gershon Heinokh Leiner, founder of the dynasty of Radzyn, reintroduced the *petil tekheilet* (blue thread), into the ritual fringes, the innovation caused considerable acrimony among the sages. The *rebbe* of Alexander refused to take sides. However, when Dr. Jung proposed to establish a secular school in Galicia, the *rebbe* expressed relentless opposition. In a lengthy letter, he urged his followers not be led astray by Dr. Jung. "Bring up your children in the ways of the Torah," he pleaded, "and do not try new paths."[11]

The *rebbe* was known for his phenomenal memory. He not only remembered everything he read, but he also remembered the names of the thousands of his followers and the names of their children. When a *hasid* complained that he was afflicted with forgetfulness, the *rebbe* replied, "We recite in the *Shema,* 'Go not after your own heart, and your own eyes, after which you used to go astray that you may remember. . . .' (Numbers 15:39). Obey this injunction and your memory will improve."

He refused to accept *pidyonot.* He sent money to Jerusalem for the restoration of the grave of the *Or Hahayim* on the Mount of Olives. He died on *Rosh Hodesh Shevat* 1910 at the age of 57. His brother and brothers-in-law published his discourses on the Torah in Lodz in 1911 under the title *Yismah Yisrael* ("Israel will Rejoice"), a fitting title as well for the gentle *rebbe* who served his Master and his *hasidim* with love and joy.

Chapter 17

The Greatness of Ger

How does a small town on the Vistula River achieve fame and immortality? It becomes the Jerusalem of one of the greatest hasidic dynasties. At least, this is how it was with Ger (Gora Kalwaria) near Warsaw.

Isaac Meir Rothenburg (Alter), better known as the *Hiddushei HaRim* ("Novellae of Rabbi Isaac Meir") named for the title of his works, was born in 1799 in Magnuszew, near Radom, where his father, Israel, was rabbi. He traced his ancestry to Rabbi Meir ben Barukh of Rothenburg (1215–1293). He was descended from such celebrated scholars as Rabbi Joel Serkes, Rabbi Jonathan Eibeschütz, and Rabbi Shapira of Krakow. At the age of nine, on the advice of Rabbi Israel of Kozienice, little Isaac Meir became engaged to Feigele, daughter of the wealthy banker, Moses ben Isaac Eisig Lipshitz, known as "Reb Moses Halfan." The wedding took place in Warsaw in 1811. After three months in Kozienice, Rabbi Isaac Meir settled in the flourishing Warsaw community. Some 16,000 Jews lived there in 1813; in 1831 the Jewish population had grown to 31,384, and this number had more than doubled by the middle of the century.

Rabbi Isaac Meir studied in the *yeshivah* of his relative Rabbi Aryeh Leib Zinz, later rabbi of Plock and author of ten important works. Among Rabbi Isaac Meir's fellow students were Rabbi Abraham Landau, later rabbi in Ciechanow, and Jacob ben Meir Gesundheit (1815–1878), later rabbi in Warsaw from 1870–1874. With single-minded passion, Rabbi Isaac Meir devoted himself to his studies, spending some eighteen hours a day at his books. To his worried wife, he exclaimed, "Do you know why your father chose me as your husband? Because of my aptitude for study. What I can absorb in two hours would take another man a whole day. Similarly, four hours of sleep are enough for me."

Rabbi Itsche Meir

Rabbi Isaac Meir, or "*Itsche* Meir," as he was popularly called, gathered around him young men of exceptional talent and studied with them. He had no desire for high office and declined many honors. His teachers gave him every encouragement. "If hasidic preoccupations do not distract him from his studies," predicted Rabbi Akiva ben Moses Eger (1761–1837), "Isaac Meir will reach the level of Rabbi Jonathan Eibeschütz."

Like his father, Rabbi Isaac Meir was a devoted follower of the *Maggid* of Kozienice. However, he also visited the Seer and the son of the *Maggid* of Kozienice, Rabbi Moses Eliakim Beriah (d. 1828). But when the latter embraced him, Rabbi Isaac Meir rather ungraciously exclaimed, "I do not want a rabbi who embraces me. I want a rabbi who would rend the flesh from my bones." Clearly, he needed teachers of the caliber of the Yehudi and of Rabbi Simha Bunem. Loyalty to the *Maggid*'s successor kept him in Kozienice, yet in his heart and soul, he yearned to visit the Holy Jew of Przysucha, whom he greatly revered. His great devotion is reflected in his claiming that "When the Yehudi smokes his pipe, his thoughts are the very same thoughts that were in the mind of the High Priest officiating in the Holy of Holies, on the Day of Atonement." All his life he grieved because circumstances had prevented him from studying under the Holy Jew.

His erstwhile teacher, Rabbi Moses, found it hard to forgive his favorite pupil's defection to Rabbi Simha Bunem. "Isaac Meir has spoiled a Sabbath for us," was his harsh comment, "I fear that many Sabbaths will be spoiled for him." *Hasidim* regarded this as an ominous prediction that Isaac Meir would suffer many bereavements that would take place on the Sabbath. However, in Rabbi Simha Bunem, spiritual heir of the Yehudi, Rabbi Isaac Meir found solace for his restless soul, and he visited Przysucha no fewer than seventeen times. The esteem between the *rebbe* and his disciple was mutual. "Had he lived in the time of the *tanna'im*," remarked Rabbi Simha Bunem, "Isaac Meir would have been a *tanna*."

The Ideal Haven for a Restless Soul

In Przysucha Rabbi Isaac Meir found stimulating and compatible colleagues in Rabbi Hanokh Heinokh of Alexander and Rabbi Menahem Mendel of Kotzk. Equally important, he also found there a way of life that was ideally suited to his scholarly temperament and inclinations. Actually Rabbi Isaac Meir arrived at Przysucha at a particularly auspicious moment. Rabbi Isaac Meir was one of the five delegates who were deputed to defend their Master at the wedding at Ustilug. The doctrines of Przysucha had been misinterpreted, and Przysucha devotees were estranged from their hasidic colleagues. The outstanding scholarship of Rabbi Isaac Meir helped dispel a great deal of this causeless hostility.

When Rabbi Simha Bunem died, Rabbi Isaac Meir transferred his allegiance to Rabbi Mendel of Kotzk and played a key role in establishing the hegemony of that dynasty. In 1837, Rabbi Isaac Meir's sister-in-law married Rabbi Mendel and in 1844, Isaac Meir's granddaughter (daughter of Abraham Mordekhai) married Rabbi Mendel's son, Benjamin. Although Rabbi Mendel of Kotzk was a demanding and sometimes capricious taskmaster, Rabbi Isaac Meir's devotion never waned. Perhaps their earlier camaraderie and their common apprenticeship under Rabbi Simha Bunem, helped cement the bond between the gentle scholar and the tempestuous *tzaddik*.

The World Intrudes

The Polish insurrection of 1830–1831 reduced Rabbi Isaac Meir's father-in-law to poverty. For the first time, Isaac Meir was beset with financial worries and faced the urgent need to earn a living. He opened a workshop for the manufacture of *tallitot* (prayer shawls), sold books, and turned printer. He prized his independence and refused to present himself as a candidate for the rabbinate. He himself supported the candidature of the octogenarian Rabbi Hayim

Davidsohn and later, of the Polish patriot Dov Berush Meisels as Chief Rabbis of Warsaw. It was not until 1852 that Rabbi Isaac Meir was officially appointed *dayan* (religious judge) at Warsaw with a fixed salary.

Rabbi Isaac Meir's personal life was beset by tragedy. He had thirteen children and outlived them all. In 1834, his sole surviving son, Abraham Mordekhai, died at the age of 40. "I am not lamenting my son, who died in his prime," sobbed the bereaved father, "that is the will of God. I grieve because I am now unable to carry out the precept, 'And you shall teach them (the laws) diligently unto your children' " (Deuteronomy 6:7).

Rabbi Isaac Meir Assumes the Mantle

Rabbi Mendel of Kotzk died in 1859, and reluctantly Rabbi Isaac Meir became a hasidic *rebbe,* first in Warsaw at Eisengass 56 and later in Ger. "Rabbi Simha Bunem led with love and Kotzk led with fear," he said, "I shall lead them with Torah." When a *hasid* once complained that he had no friends, the rabbi retorted, "Surely you have a *Gemara* (a volume of the Talmud) in your house?" In simple terms he set forth his objective. "I am not a *rebbe.* I do not want money. I do not care for honor. All I want is to spend my years bringing the Children of Israel nearer to their Father in Heaven."

The doctrines of Przysucha and Kotzk were combined in Ger. There was neither emphasis on miracles nor acceptance of *pidyonot* (gifts of money). "If the people who come here do not exert themselves to help themselves," the rabbi of Ger once exclaimed, "then the greatest *tzaddikim* of this generation will be powerless to aid them. There is an old proverb, 'If you cannot cross over, you do not cross over,' but I say that the more impossible a task seems, the harder one should strive to accomplish it."

In 1841, Rabbi Isaac Meir associated himself with Rabbi Hayim Davidsohn and was one of the signatories to a manifesto urging Jews to settle the land. Among others who associated themselves with enterprise were Rabbi Isaac of Warka and Zalman Posener.[1]

Sir Moses Montefiore and the Rebbe of Ger

When Sir Moses Montefiore (1784–1885) visited Warsaw in May 1846, Rabbi Isaac Meir and Rabbi Isaac of Warka called on the distinguished visitor at the Angelski Hotel in Wierzbowa Street. The same day Dr. Louis Loewe, Sir Moses' secretary, recorded the event:

> a deputation of that preeminently conservative class of the Hebrew community, known by the appellation of *Khasseedim* (sic), paid us a visit. They wore hats, according to European fashion instead of the Polish 'czapka' or the 'mycka' which is similar to that of the Circassians. They were headed by Mr. Posener, a gentleman who had done much for the promotion of industry in Poland, and his son; and he informed Sir Moses that he would, though an old man, comply with the desire of the Government and change the Polish for the German costume. Being a man held in high esteem by the Jews, and well spoken of by the Prince, his example would have a most favorable effect upon others.[2]

There are many accounts of the encounter of Sir Moses with the *hasidim*. "Behold, there is a good case to be made in favor of Enlightenment," Dr. Loewe reasoned, "Mordekhai (hero of the Book of Esther), understood the dialect of Bigtan and Teresh, two of the king's chamberlains, who sought to lay hands on King Ahasuerus (Esther 2:21). Had not Mordekhai been conversant with his native tongue, he would not have been able to discern the plot. The salvation of the Jews was due to Mordekhai's linguistic ability." Rabbi Isaac Meir countered this argument: "From the story of the Book of Esther one can prove that the Jews were not conversant with the foreign tongue. Had it been generally known that the Jews understood the native tongue, Bigtan and Teresh would never have spoken in the hearing of Mordekhai. Mordekhai, as a member of the *Sanhedrin*, was a linguist, but this did not apply to the masses." Sir Moses asked, "If you oppose the study of secular subjects, who will be qualified to protect your rights before the Government?" "We are praying for the advent of the Messiah," replied Rabbi Isaac Meir, "but until then we are well satisfied with you, honored Sir."

Sir Moses corresponded with important government leaders in an effort to reach an understanding regarding the matter of hasidic dress. Sir Moses had written:

> There is much to be done in Poland. I have already received the promise of many of the *hasidim* to change their fur caps for hats

and to adopt the German costume generally. I think this change will have a happy effect on their position and be the means of producing good will between their fellow subjects and themselves. I have received the assurance of many that they would willingly engage themselves in agriculture if they could procure land; and his Highness the Viceroy is desirous that they should do so.[3]

Sir Moses wrote to Count Kisseleff:

With respect to the peculiar costume which most of the Israelites have been accustomed to wear for many centuries, which I had an opportunity of seeing, I can assure your Excellency that most of them have already adopted the European habit and I have not the least doubt that, in the course of time, the ancient costume will have entirely disappeared. It is erroneous to suppose that the ancient custom is enjoined by or has any foundation in religion; such is not the fact. It originated from a decree of the Government in existence 300 years ago, when the Israelites were commanded under a most severe punishment to assume the garb, to distinguish them as members of the Jewish faith.[4]

The Battle against Assimilation in Study and in Dress

Together with Rabbi Mendel of Warka and Rabbi Jacob David of Amshinow, Rabbi Isaac Meir barred secular subjects from the *heder* curriculum. "It is impossible for the words of the Torah to enter into the hearts of the children," wrote Rabbi Isaac Meir, "when their minds are full of other things." Undaunted in his struggle against compulsory assimilation, he took a firm stand on the issue of the distinctive garments worn by the *hasidim*. Some rabbis were not opposed to a modification of the distinctive garments. To Rabbi Mendel of Kotzk, "the robes were merely a custom that could be modified." Similarly, the rabbi of Ruzhin pointed out that "our father Jacob received the blessings of Isaac when he was dressed in the garments of Esau." But Rabbi Isaac Meir stood firm and was duly imprisoned by Governor Paskevitch for his defiance. So great was the indignation of the entire Jewish community that he was soon released. The Government required the *hasidim* to choose between the European and the Russian way of dress. Rabbi Isaac Meir preferred the latter.

During the Crimean War (1853–1856) Rabbi Isaac Meir prayed for the victory of the allied forces, and he remained aloof when on June 22, 1863, the Poles rose in revolt against their Russian masters.

Rabbi Isaac Meir's Death and Legacy in Print

In 1866 a serious injury brought him increasing and continuous pain. But with calm fortitude, he continued his normal way of life. He died during that year. His last words, "Leibele Kaddish," were interpreted to mean that his grandson Judah Leib should recite *Kaddish* after him and should be his successor. And so it was. Rabbi Jacob ben Isaac Gesundheit (1815–1878) of Warsaw sadly voiced the popular sentiment when he said, "The *hasidim* will find another *rebbe*, but no one can take his place."

Rabbi Isaac Meir was a prolific author. Published posthumously were the *Hiddushei HaRim* (novellae) on tractate *Hullin*, and *Teshuvat HaRim* (responsa) on the Codes. His responsa pinpoint some of the day-to-day problems that Jewry faced in the mid-nineteenth century. For instance, at that time scholars debated the permissibility of baking *matzot* (unleavened bread) by machines. Rabbi Isaac Meir endorsed the view of Rabbi Solomon Kluger (1783–1869) and forbade the use of machines.

Rabbi Judah Leib Alter of Ger

Rabbi Leibele or Judah Leib, son of Rabbi Abraham Mordekhai (d. 1855) is known as the *Sefat Emet* ("Words of Truth"), because his last discourse ended with the verse from Proverbs 12:19, "The lips of truth shall be established for ever." The *Sefat Emet* became his literary pseudonym. Rabbi Judah Leib was born in Warsaw on the 28th day of *Nisan* 1847. His father died when he was barely 8 years old. To his grandfather's great joy, Leibele studied with phenomenal ardor and diligence. "Come and see," Rabbi Isaac Meir used to say with grandfatherly pride, "how my grandson studies Torah for its own sake." Whenever he went to Kotzk, he would take his grandson with him. "The journey is worthwhile, let him see a real Jew."[5]

On the 3rd day of *Adar* 1862, he was married to Yokheved Rebecca, daughter of Yudel Kaminer of Checiny, a descendant of Rabbi Barukh Frankel. After the wedding he remained in Ger. He was 19 when Rabbi Isaac Meir died on the 23rd day of *Adar* 1866, and although he inherited his grandfather's position, he had no inclination at that time to become *rebbe*.

Accepting Leadership

During the four years that followed, he became a devoted disciple of Rabbi Hanokh Heinoch Hakohen of Alexander. The *rebbe* of Alexander esteemed him highly. When the *rebbe* of Alexander died on the 18th of *Adar* 1870, Rabbi Judah Leib reluctantly assumed the leadership of the *hasidim* of Ger. Still, it was the custom of the modest young man to sit at the middle of the table rather than at the head, to demonstrate that all were equal in his eyes.

Humility and the Merits of Labor

His father, Rabbi Abraham Mordekhai, had opened a bookshop in Krochmalna Street in Warsaw in order to earn a living for his family. Similarly, a tobacco shop sustained Rabbi Judah Leib, enabling him to decline the *pidyonot* that his *hasidim* were only too willing to offer him. He lived a frugal life, content with very little, and deplored costly and elaborate celebrations. He believed in the dignity of labor and held that a rabbi who accepted money for his spiritual services forefeited his independence. The Torah was not to be studied for self-aggrandizement or material gain. Not one minute was wasted. He rose at dawn and spent the entire day in study and prayer. Even during the hours (usually between 9:30 and 11:00 A.M.) wherein he received visitors, he would hold a volume of the Codes in his hands. "How can one give advice," he would say, "unless one refers constantly to the four parts of the *Shulhan Arukh*." "Only *shiurim* (regular studies) give me strength," he asserted.

Prayers were not prolonged in Ger. The rebbe himself prayed in his own rooms, and only on the Sabbath and on Festivals did he attend the *Beit HaMidrash.* After the reading of the law he would return to his room, where he would recite the *Musaf* prayer privately.

Meanwhile the dark clouds of persecution were gathering. The assassination of Czar Alexander II in 1881 and the accession of Alexander III brought an outburst of anti-Jewish violence. It was prompted by the fact that a Jewish girl, Hessia Hellmann, had been involved in the plot. In April 1881 a pogrom took place at Elisavetgrad, followed by others in Kiev, Odessa, and Warsaw. During that period, the infamous May Laws forbade Jews to settle in rural districts, even within the Jewish Pale of Settlement and prohibited them from engaging in business activity on Sundays and on Christian holidays. Many Jews were forcibly conscripted into the Russian army, where they suffered unspeakable hardships. Unfortunate youths, potential conscripts, thronged the rabbi's court for counsel and spiritual consolation. The rabbi was also concerned in later years over the 30,000 Jewish soldiers who were involved in the Japanese war (1904–1905). All who wrote to him from the battlefield received personal letters expressing sympathy and encouragement. The rabbi spoke movingly about the Land of Israel.

The Rebbe of Ger and the Holy Land

"Just as the Jews need the Holy Land," wrote the rabbi, "so the Holy Land needs the Jews to bring out its intrinsic holiness. The bond preordained and divinely forged between the land and the people, has not been broken despite the fact that the Jews have been driven from its soil." In one responsum, he writes to a *hasid* who sent a cargo of *etrogim* for the Festival of Tabernacles to the United States via Beirut instead of Jaffa. The cargo did not arrive until after *Hanukkah,* two months after the *Sukkot* holiday. "A man must carry out his business with integrity and not apply devious means. It was wrong to divert the cargo from Jaffa to Beirut."[6] Rabbi Hayim Morgenstern of Pulawy (1870–1906), authored a booklet entitled *Shalom Yerushalayim,* in which he demonstrated that every Jew was duty bound to participate in the building of the Holy Land. Rabbi Judah Leib wrote him a letter in response, agreeing that "certainly it will be reckoned a *mitzvah* to settle in the Holy Land." Like Rabbi

Hayim Eliezer Waks of Kalish, the rebbe urged the *hasidim* to import Palestinian *etrogim*.

Dr. Theodor Herzl pleaded passionately for the cooperation of Rabbi Judah Leib:

> In the name of thousands of Jews, whose existence, threatened by hostile neighbors, grows daily more difficult. In the name of the starving multitudes who engage in all kinds of occupations to feed their children; in the name of the thousands of refugees who flee from Russia, Rumania, and Galicia to America, Africa, and Australia, where the danger of assimilation awaits them, and finally in the name of the Torah, we urge the honorable rabbi to tell us openly the sins which we have committed by espousing Zionism.

The *rebbe* did not reply.[7]

His wife Yokheved Rebecca died on the 18th of *Elul* 1901. He then married the widowed daughter of Rabbi Barukh Halberstam of Gorlice. There were ten children from his first marriage, four of whom died in infancy. He died on the 5th day of *Shevat* 1905 and left four sons and two daughters. In addition, his legacy includes such monumental works as *Sefat Emet*, a commentary on the Pentateuch, and Festivals in five parts (Piotrokow-Krakow, 1905–1908); *Likkutim* on Torah, in two parts (Piotrokow, 1934–1936); *Hiddushim* on *Seder Moed* (Warsaw, 1925–1931); Ethics of the Fathers (Piotrokow and Landsberg, 1948); Passover *haggadah* (Warsaw, 1930); commentaries on the Scroll of Esther (Jerusalem, 1952), on Ecclesiastes (Jerusalem, 1952–1953), on Psalms (London, 1952), and on Proverbs (Jerusalem, 1951). He corresponded on halakhic matters with Rabbi Solomon Abraham of Ozorkow and Rabbi Abraham Hayim Eliezer Waks of Kalish. One halakhic responsum appeared in the rabbinical periodical *Shaarei Torah* (Warsaw, 1933), addressed to Rabbi Joshua David Banin.

During the lifetime of Rabbi Judah Leib, Ger had grown great and powerful. It was not without reason that Rabbi Elimelekh Shapiro of Grodzisk called his illustrious contemporary, "King of Israel."

Rabbi Leibele Eger

In the nineteenth century, Hasidism captured many mitnagdic communities, but an even greater coup was the capture of notable mitnagdic halakhists. In fact, Rabbi Leibele Eger, the author of *Torat Emet*, actually became a hasidic rebbe. This spiritual and psychic transformation probably did much to demolish the "Iron Curtain" between *hasidim* and *mitnagdim*.

Antecedents

Rabbi Leibele's grandfather was Rabbi Akiva Eger of Poznan, author of *Hiddushei Rabbi Akiva Eger*. As a halakhic authority, he ranked second only to Rabbi Elijah Gaon of Vilna. He was also renowned outside the Jewish community. He even received a personal letter from King Frederick William III, thanking him for his services during the cholera epidemic of 1831. He published many works including novellae, responsa, and glosses on the *Mishnah*, the Talmud, and Maimonides' *Mishneh Torah*. Rabbi Leibele's father, Rabbi Solomon (1786–1852), was rabbi of Kalish in Russian Poland.

Rabbi Solomon succeeded his father as rabbi of Poznan. He organized the collections for *halukkah* Jewry (those who received charitable funds from abroad) in the Holy Land and wrote on talmudic and halakhic topics. In 1844, he urged Frederick William IV to help Jews found agricultural villages in the province of Posen, but the project was brought to an end by the political disturbances of 1848. He tried to enlist Rabbi Nathan Adler (1803–1890), Chief Rabbi of the British Empire from 1845, in his fight against the Reform movement. For thirty-five years, while he lived in Warsaw, Rabbi Solomon stayed in close touch with Rabbi Isaac Meir Alter, the author of *Hiddushei HaRim*, and with other hasidic leaders.

Rabbi Leibele was born in Warsaw in 1816 and was the youngest of five sons. Among his teachers was Rabbi Mordekhai Greenbaum, later rabbi in Neustadt. When his grandfather, Rabbi Akiva Eger, tested him, he had high praise for the tutor. "Your teacher," exclaimed the gratified grandfather, "is no ordinary teacher. He is a veritable *gaon* and I would gladly grant him a rabbinical diploma."[8] Rabbi Leibele joined the small circle of gifted young men who clustered around Rabbi Isaac Meir Alter. "The *mitnagdim* are being punished," jested Rabbi Isaac Meir, "their followers are rapidly converting to Hasidism." Rabbi Leibele also studied under his uncle, Rabbi Hayim Davidsohn, the rabbi of Warsaw. His father, Rabbi Solomon, wrote to him, "Drink in his words. Observe his actions. See how lovingly he greets the most humble of visitors. Learn from his friendliness and his love of humanity."[9]

Rabbi Leibele married Batsheva, daughter of Rabbi Azriel Meir Grundstein (d. 1840), father-in-law of Rabbi Akiva Eger. Rabbi Leibele left the communal *Beit HaMidrash* of Rabbi Grundstein for the *Beit HaMidrash* in Lublin, that had been formerly used by Rabbi Jacob Isaac Hurwitz, the Seer of Lublin. When Rabbi Leibele expressed the desire to stay for a time with Rabbi Menahem Mendel Morgenstern of Kotzk, the *rebbe* welcomed him. "It is worth walking hundreds of kilometers," said the *rebbe* of Kotzk, "to find a *hasid* like Rabbi Leibele."[10] His father-in-law was far from enthusiastic about his plans. However, Rabbi Leibele's wife adopted a different attitude. "Father," said Batsheva, "why do you not learn from the example of Jethro, the father-in-law of Moses, who left his wife and went into the wilderness? Do we read that Jethro sent messengers after him to fetch him back? Why not go to Kotzk yourself and see what is happening there?"[11]

With his wife's encouragement, Rabbi Leibele traveled to Kotzk. When he returned home, he told his father-in-law that he had learned three things. First, that a man is human. Second, that the Almighty created the world, and third, that the Almighty requires man to complete the task of Creation. Later on, Rabbi Leibele became a disciple of Rabbi Mordekhai Joseph Leiner of Izbica, whom he regarded as the true successor to Rabbi Jacob Isaac the *Hozeh* of Lublin. "When we hear Torah from Rabbi Leibele," remarked Rabbi Leiner, "it is as if we hear it at Sinai." He was highly venerated by his contemporaries. Said Rabbi Tzadok HaKohen of Lublin, "Had Rabbi Leibele lived in the time of the prophets, he would have been a prophet. In the time of the *tanna'im,* he would have been a *tanna,* in the days of the *amora'im,* he would have been an *amora.*"

Rabbi Leibele studied the works of the *Hozeh* of Lublin, *Divrei Emet, Zot Zikkaron,* and *Zikkaron Zot,* and was greatly influenced by them. "He never ceased to cherish these sacred words," testified his son, "and he regarded the *Hozeh* as his spiritual teacher."[12] Before delivering a discourse, Rabbi Leibele would open the book, and, if he had no time to study, would at least gaze upon it. He searched for the manuscripts of the *Hozeh* and, when he succeeded in finding them, he remarked, "A sacred light emanates from the writings. The printed words pale by comparison."

Rabbi Leibele as Rebbe

Rabbi Solomon died in 1852, and Rabbi Leibele at first refused to succeed his father as rabbi of Poznan. He could not tear himself away from Lublin, nor from his great disciple, Rabbi Tzadok HaKohen Rabinowicz of Lublin, who eventually persuaded him to become a *rebbe*. However, he did not deliver any discourses until after the death of Rabbi Menahem Mendel Morgenstern of Kotzk. Rabbi Leibele would prolong every service, even the liturgy of the Day of Atonement. The concluding prayer, *Neilah,* was rarely recited before midnight. "How can I let go?" he demanded, "of such a sacred day?" He prayed aloud, and his prayers were accompanied by bitter tears. He believed in elaborate preparations for prayer and for the performance of any *mitzvah.* "It would be inappropriate," he would say, "to welcome the prophet Elijah without due preparations."

The *rebbe* would frequently be invited to act as *mohel* and *sandak* and would carefully prepare for this role. By the time he had completed the morning service and his private devotions, it would be well past midday. Consequently, the delayed circumcision ceremonies aroused the ire of Rabbi Joshua Heschel Ashkenazi, who issued a ruling forbidding circumcisions to be performed after midday. "Whosoever contravenes this ruling is a transgressor," said Rabbi Joshua sternly.[13] This ruling caused heated controversy. Rabbi Leibele asked for the support of Rabbi Isaac Meir, who entreated Rabbi Ashkenazi to refrain from offending Rabbi Leibele. Rabbi Leibele also received strong backing from Rabbi Tzadok HaKohen, Rabbi Dov Berish Rapoport of Rava, and Rabbi Solomon Eibeschütz of Josefow. His own relatives, however, were slow to come to his assistance. Among them were Rabbi Samuel Birnbaum, son-in-law of Rabbi Akiva Eger and Rabbi Simon Sofer.

Rabbi Leibele died on the 22nd day of *Shevat* 1888, at the age of 72. His friend and colleague, Rabbi Jechiel Meir of Gostynin, died a day earlier on the 21st day of *Shevat.* Rabbi Israel Mordekhai wrote a eulogy under the title *Avel Gadol* (Warsaw, 1909). Two of Rabbi Leibele's manuscripts were published posthumously, *Torat Emet* on Genesis in 1899, and on Leviticus, Numbers, Deuteronomy, *Rosh Hashanah,* and *Yom Kippur* in 1890.

Chapter 18

Early Twentieth-Century Rebbes

At the end of the nineteenth century, there were six million Jews in Europe. In the Russian Empire, the Jewish population had increased from one million in 1800 to 5,189,000 in 1897. There were 811,000 Jews in Galicia, 266,000 in Rumania, 96,000 in Bukovina, and 851,000 in Hungary.

Yet the Jews, a literate and law-abiding community, were "second-class" citizens. There was a total of 140 statutes discriminating against the Jews in the twenty volumes of the Codes of Laws of the Russian Empire. The Jews were permitted to live only in an area that constituted no more than 4 percent of Russia's territory. The area became known as the Pale of Settlement. By 1880, 94 percent of the entire Jewish population of Russia was restricted to the Pale. Their predicament is graphically outlined in a memorandum of December 10, 1890, addressed to the Czar by the Lord Mayor of London:

> Pent up in narrow bounds within your Majesty's wide Empire, and even within those bounds, forced to reside chiefly in towns that reek and overflow with every form of poverty and wretchedness; forbidden all free movement, hedged in in every enterprise by restrictive laws; forbidden tenure of land or all concern in land, their means of livelihood have become so cramped as to render life for them well-nigh impossible.
>
> Nor are they cramped alone in space and action. The higher education is denied them, except in limits far below due

> proportion of their needs and aspirations. They must not freely exercise professions, like other subjects of your Majesty, nor may they gain promotion in the army, however great their merit and their valor.[1]

Emigration

The exodus from Eastern Europe of some two million Jews began in 1881 and continued with diminishing tempo until the outbreak of the First World War. In the years 1881–1890, Russian Jewish immigrants to the United States numbered 135,000. During the next decade the number doubled, averaging 30,000 a year.[2] Some rabbinical leaders did not encourage emigration. "It is proper for you to remain in your own land and walk in the ways of the Lord."[3] From London, Chief Rabbi Nathan Adler urged his Eastern European colleagues "to preach in the synagogues and houses of study to publicize the evil which is befalling our brethren who have come here, and to warn them not to come to the land of Britain, for such ascent is descent."[4]

Many hasidic rabbis agreed with him, and *hasidim* were not encouraged to uproot themselves from their familiar environment. Hence, although pogroms were a daily occurrence in the Czarist Empire, the proportion of emigrating *hasidim* was comparatively small. The cries of the victims of Kishinev and the shouts of their persecutors: "Kill the Jews!" "Burn their houses!" "Spare none!" echoed through a horrified but unhelpful world. Nevertheless, *hasidim* feared to expose their children to the spiritual dangers of the "Godless" countries even more than they feared the violence of the murderous mobs. America to them was not only a *goldeneh medinah* (golden country) but also a *frei land* ("free" country – loose, free in too many ways).

The *hasidim* endured the terror-raids in Russia, the Mendel Beilis murder trial, the World War, the Russian Revolution of 1917, the pogroms of Petlura, and the vicious onslaught of the Denikin, Czarist army, and the Black Hundreds. The situation continued to deteriorate, and was described in these words:

> Hundreds of thousands of Jews have been robbed of their last shirt; hundreds of thousands have been maltreated, wounded,

> humiliated; tens of thousands have been massacred. Thousands of Jewish women became the victims of the bestial instincts of savage hordes. Hundreds of thousands of Jewish women are haunted daily by one idea–that tomorrow they will no longer be able to hold their heads erect. The panic which seized on the Jewish population of these regions is without precedent in all history. . . . The Jewish masses in the Ukraine are on the verge of madness, and many have actually lost their reason. These unfortunate beings, having lost all that makes life worth living, their nearest, their homes, everything they had, all means of existence, mutilated physically and broken morally, how can they solve the problems of their existence? Where are they to find shelter? How can they save the children from dying of starvation and cold and all the accompanying miseries?[5]

The Makers of Miracles

Miracles did not cease with the end of the biblical period. Celebrated talmudists of the talmudic era, such as Honi Hame'aggel and Rabbi Haninah ben Dosa, were able to perform miracles, and this power was ascribed to a number of medieval rabbis as well. "Great is the power of the *tzaddik*," declares the Talmud, "for God decrees and the *tzaddik* annuls." The rabbis emphasize that man is surrounded at all times by miracles, many of which he is not even aware. Miracles were often worked by God through angels or through saintly men.

Hasidism has a great tradition of *baalei mofetim* (miracle workers). "In Mezhirech, the home of Rabbi Dov Baer, the *Maggid* of Mezhirech" testified Rabbi Shneur Zalman of Liady, "miracles were almost commonplace. They were bouncing off the tables and no one paid any attention." Rabbi Jacob Isaac Hurwitz, "Seer of Lublin" and Rabbi Elimelekh of Lyzhansk maintained the tradition of *mofetim* (miracles). It was said that the Seer of Lublin was endowed with the same *ru'ah Hakodesh* (Divine Spirit) as Samuel the Prophet, and that the only difference between them was that the Seer could not use the phrase, "Thus said the Lord." Among other notable *baalei mofetim* of Hasidism were Rabbi Solomon Zalman of Wielopole,

Rabbi Hayim of Wolbrom, Rabbi Joseph Barukh, "The Good Jew of Neustadt," Rabbi Israel Hofstein of Kozienice, and Rabbi Jehiel Meir of Moglienice.

The Dynasty of the "Saintly Grandfather"

Rabbi Jacob Aryeh Guterman, known as the *Sabba Kadisha* ("the saintly grandfather") founded a dynasty that produced three remarkable rabbis. He was born in 1792 in Warka, near Warsaw, and was a descendant of Rabbi Nathan Nata Spiro of Krakow, author of *Megalleh Amukkot* (Krakow, 1637). In 1810, Jacob Aryeh married Hayeh, daughter of Rabbi Berish of Richwal, a descendant of Rabbi Jacob Joshua ben Tzvi Hirsch (1680–1766), renowned for his work, *Penei Yehoshua,* novella on the Palestinian Talmud (Frankfurt, 1752). Rabbi Israel Hofstein, the *Maggid* of Kozienice, participated in the wedding festivities.

After his marriage, Rabbi Jacob Aryeh settled in Richwal, and for the next thirteen years, he spent every Passover in Kozienice. "Nowhere else in this world," he said, "can one hope to experience the kind of *sedarim* I enjoyed in Kozienice. Perhaps, in the world to come, it will be possible to repeat such experiences." He also visited the Holy Jew, Rabbi Jacob Isaac of Przysucha. He eventually became a tutor in the home of Rabbi Jacob Yekel, and he instructed Rabbi Hanokh Heinokh Hakohen Levin of Litomirsk, who later became the *rebbe* of Alexander.

The Influence of Przysucha

Rabbi Jacob Aryeh became rabbi in Richwal. To supplement his meager income, his wife sold merchandise in the neighboring villages. The *rebbe* refused to accept new garments presented to him by his *hasidim.* "Should I be ashamed of my poverty which is God's gift? Should I glory in new garments which are the gifts of flesh and blood?" Rabbi Jacob Aryeh became a disciple of Rabbi Simha Bunem Bunehardt of Przysucha, and there he met and befriended Rabbi Menahem Mendel Morgenstern of Kotzk.

Hasidim would say, "Rabbi Simha Bunem has three great

disciples. Rabbi Menahem Mendel of Kotzk burns up the whole world; Rabbi Isaac Kalishof Warka lights up the whole world. And when the third disciple, Rabbi Jacob Aryeh, walks about the *Beit HaMidrash* with his pipe in his mouth, all the angels in Heaven tremble before him." Miracles played no part in Przysucha. "Had I known that through miracles I could bring Jews back to God," said Rabbi Simha Bunem, "I would have planted the trees of Danzig in the streets of Przysucha." He set no great store in miracles and believed that it needed greater effort to be a good Jew. He believed that through the study of Talmud and *Tosafot,* the mind could be purified and ennobled.

A Miracle Worker against His Will

At the recommendation of Rabbi Isaac Meir Alter, Rabbi Jacob Aryeh became rabbi of Radzymin, a town in the Warsaw province inhabited in 1827 by 432 Jews (33 percent of the total population). By 1856, the Jewish community numbered 1,272. Only when Rabbi Isaac of Warka died did Rabbi Jacob Aryeh become rebbe. He was then 56 years old and, ironically, the disciple of Przysucha became known as a *baal mofet.*

Rabbi Simhah Bunem Kalish of Otwock, grandson of Rábbi Isaac of Warka, was 17 years old when he first visited the newly-appointed *rebbe* of Radzymin, who greeted him with these words, "I knew your grandfather very well. I knew your late father well too. Now tell me something about yourself, so that I may get to know you." "We read that Abraham the Patriarch dug wells," replied the youthful *rebbe.* "And we also read that Isaac dug wells. But the Torah does not tell us Jacob dug wells. It follows then that when the grandfather and the father do the groundwork, it is easier for the grandson to find water." The answer pleased the *rebbe* of Radzymin. "Peace be upon you, *rebbe* of Warka" he said with great cordiality. "You are very welcome."

Rabbi Jacob Aryeh did not hesitate to write stern letters to the great and wealthy Gentile squires, who refused to renew the leases of their hasidic tenant innkeepers. He warned them that such inhumane conduct might have dire consequences. When a childless couple came to him, the *rebbe* urged the would-be father to write a *Sefer Torah.* "By fulfilling the last *mitzvah* of the Torah, which is to write a *Sefer Torah,*" he explained, "you will be able to fulfill the very first *mitzvah* of the Torah, which is to have children."[7] The rebbe frequently visited Warsaw on communal matters and remained in contact with Rabbi Isaac Meir Alter. Every year before *Rosh Hashanah,* the *rebbe* of Ger would write to the *rebbe* of Radzymin asking to be remembered in his prayers.

Rabbi Jacob Aryeh met frequently with his friend and colleague Rabbi Menahem Mendel of Kotzk. "Why was man created?" Rabbi Mendel asked him. "To perfect his soul," replied Rabbi Jacob Aryeh, "to bring the earth closer to heaven." "Not so," replied Rabbi Mendel, "we learned in Przysucha that man was put on earth for one reason and one reason only, to raise the heavens."[8] His discourses were printed in *Derushim VeHiddushim,* published by the *Agudat HaRabbanim* (Warsaw, 1928). He gave *haskamot* to *Sefer Hinukh Beit Yehudah* by Rabbi Jacob Tzvi Yolles and to *Zot Zikkaron;* both printed in Warsaw in 1869. His work, *Divrei Aviv,* was printed by Rabbi Jehiel Meir in Warsaw in 1924, nearly fifty years after his death.

The *rebbe* once remarked to Rabbi Isaac Meir Alter, "I cannot understand how the Children of Israel could have sinned so grievously in the wilderness after they had experienced the Revelation on Mount Sinai." "Has it never occurred to you," replied the *rebbe* of Ger, "that even when our fathers sinned, they were more meritorious than we are?"

Ill health forced him to visit the spas of Carlsbad regularly. "Would that I could recover quickly," he wrote, "so that I would not have to waste so much time traveling to these foreign places." "It is fitting," he declared, "to give thanks to God when one crosses the ocean without mishap. It is customary to offer thanks upon recovery from illness. And we should be equally grateful when we are spared misfortune and ill health."[9]

His work, *Bikkurei Aviv* on *Midrash Rabba,* Genesis, Exodus, and Leviticus, was printed in Piotrokow in 1936. *Bikkurei Aviv* on the Torah was printed in London in 1948. The *rebbe* died on the first day of *Tammuz* 1874. He left three sons; Rabbi Israel, Rabbi Solomon Judah David (d. 1903), and Rabbi Abraham Hayim. Moving eulogies were delivered by Rabbi David Dov Meisels (printed in his *Hiddushei HaRid* on *Pesahim*) and by Rabbi Aaron Simhah Pilitzer of Gombion, whose discourse was printed in *Imrei Eish* (Warsaw, 1937).

Rabbi Tzvi Elimelekh of Dynow

The name by which Rabbi Tzvi Elimelekh Spira of Dynow became known was the *Benei Yissaskhar.* He is named for his great work, one of the classics of hasidic literature, that took its title from the verse, "And the sons of Issakhar were men that had understanding of the times" (Chronicles 2:33). This momentous commentary on the Torah was printed in 1850. Its author, Rabbi Tzvi Elimelekh of Dynow, was versed in both Talmud and *Kabbalah.* Each day before the morning service, he completed twenty-four *shiurim.* He was renowend as an *ohev Yisrael* (lover of Israel) and a *baal mofet* (miracle worker).

His parents had been bereaved of their children when young. Rabbi Elimelekh of Lyzhansk, the *No'am Elimelekh,* subsequently promised the mother that she would give birth to a boy who would live to be a "light to the world". Rabbi Tzvi Elimelekh, whose original surname was Lamzer but later changed to Spira, was born in 1777. He was the son of Pesah, a humble villager of Yavarnick, Galicia. His mother was the granddaughter of Rabbi Eleazar Lipman, father of Rabbi Elimelekh of Lyzhansk. When his uncle, Rabbi Elimelekh of Lyzhansk, heard that the infant had been named Tzvi, he remarked, "A deer (*tzvi*) is not a king (*melekh*), nevertheless greatness is destined for the lad."

Early Teachers

Rabbi Tzvi Elimelekh studied under Rabbi Leizer, a disciple of Rabbi Jacob Isaac Hurwitz, the Seer of Lublin. At the age of 16, he married the daughter of Samuel of Zitsch. When Rabbi Tzvi Elimelekh visited the Seer of Lublin, he called him "the *menorah* of the world." The Seer, in turn, called his young visitor "Mount Sinai." In Lublin, the Seer declared, "he who lives in the generation of the *Maggid* (of Kozienice) and is able to behold his holy countenance, yet does not do so, will not be worthy to welcome the Messiah." Hearing these pointed words, Rabbi Tzvi Elimelekh quickly made his way to Kozienice. He also visited Rabbi Moses Sofer of Przeworsk, author of *Or Penei Moshe* (Mezhirech, 1809), Rabbi Menahem Mendel of Rymanow, Rabbi Abraham Joshua Heschel of Opatow, and Rabbi Tzvi Hirsch of Zydaszow. When he visited the rebbe of Zydaszow, potatoes, a new vegetable imported from America, were placed before him. At first, Rabbi Tzvi Elimelekh declined to eat. The *rebbe* of Zydaszow persuaded him to partake of the vegetable, thereby enabling him to enjoy the abundance of the earth in a new form.

The Beginnings of a Career

Rabbi Tzvi Elimelekh began his rabbinical career by acting as *dayan* on the *beit din* of Rabbi Joshua of Dynow. He occupied rabbinical posts in Strzyzow, Ribitsch, Lancut, Halicz, Dubeck, and in Munkacs where he stayed for four years. In Munkacs, he introduced sixteen *takkanot* (enactments) that appeared in *Sefer Kehillot Yaakov* on *Berakhot* by Rabbi Jacob Tzvi Yolles, author of *Melo Haro'im* (Zolkiew, 1838). Rabbi Naftali of Ropczyce was displeased when his colleague became a *rebbe*. "Every leader," he said, "is allotted by Heaven a term of service lasting a certain number of years. Had he waited before commencing his rabbinate he would have lived much longer." However, total dedication and not longevity was the ambition of the *Benei Yissaskhar*. His comments on the verses Leviticus 1–2, "When any man of you bringeth an offering unto the Lord, ye shall bring your offering of the cattle, even of the herd or of your flock," reflect his beliefs. He explained that the words "of your" seem superfluous, but the implication is that if a man offers himself wholeheartedly as an offering unto the Lord, then he may bring cattle as a substitute. He spoke against unauthorized people officiating at weddings, against mixed dancing, and against the use of faulty scales.

He maintained that every Jew should study *Kabbalah*. "Through mysticism, the Jews will achieve redemption even before the appointed time and without suffering the 'Pangs of the Messiah'. No one is exempted from such study." In his attitude to study, he followed in the footsteps of Rabbi Tzvi Hirsch of Zydaszow.

The Many Works of Rabbi Tzvi Elimelekh

Apart from Rabbi Tzadok Hakohen Rabinowicz of Lublin, no other hasidic *rebbe* was so prolific a writer as Rabbi Tzvi Elimelekh.

He is the author of *Hasafot Martza* on *Sur Meira* of Rabbi Tzvi Hirsch of Zydaszow (Lvov, 1850) and *Regel Yesharah*, a *Kabbalist* version of the *Alef Bet* (Lvov, 1850). His work *Benei Yissaskhar* on Sabbath, *Rosh Hodesh*, and festivals was first printed in Zolkiew in 1850 and has since appeared in nineteen editions. *Agra Dekallah* on the Pentateuch and *midrashim* (Lvov, 1868), based on Sabbath discourses, went through six editions. *Maayan Gannim*, a commentary on *Or HaHayim* by Rabbi Joseph Yaavitz, first printed in Zolkiew in 1848, has been reprinted thirteen times. *Derekh Pikkudekha,* on the 613 Commandments (Lvov, 1851) has been reprinted eighteen times. Rabbi Tzvi Elimelekh also wrote *Berakhah Meshuleshet* on *Mishnah* and a number of tractates (Przemysl, 1897), *Veheyeh Berakhah* on *Mishnah Zera'im* and the tractate *Sabbath* (Przemysl, 1888). In all he was the author of twenty-nine works that were all printed posthumously. It is possible that only the work *Benei Yissaskhar* may have been printed in his lifetime, for on his tombstone one finds the words, "author of *Benei Yissaskhar.*"

His humility was proverbial, and he attributed his sayings to "scribes and books." A young *hasid* about to take leave of him asked him, "With what am I going home?" The rabbi assured him, "When you reach home, you will become aware of everything you have gained from your journey."

Religious Customs

The rebbe would kiss the *matzot, maror* (bitter herbs), and the four cups of wine during the *Seder*. He would recite *Sefirat Ha'omer* (counting of the *omer*) befor the *Seder*. He encouraged his sons to put on the *tefillin* of *Rabbenu Tam* immediately after becoming *bar mitzvah*. He would wear his *tefillin* while he acted as *sandak*. He himself began writing a *Sefer Torah* and had reached the section of *Mas'ei* (Numbers 33) when he died. He also wrote phylacteries for members of his family.

He maintained that there was no knowledge either in the realm of science or philosophy that could not be found in the Torah. He considered philosophic speculation a waste of time. By word and deed, he fought against *Haskalah*. His book *Maayan Gannim* is almost entirely devoted to this subject. "I am fully aware of the presumptuousness of the assimilationists. They respect neither the Prophets nor the *tannaim*. They are descended of the 'mixed multitude.'" He censured Moses Mendelssohn for "sinning and causing others to sin." He urged his followers not to acquire any heretical works, stating that in the house where heretical writings are to be found, it is forbidden to study the Torah. He did stress, however, the power of repentance. How can a man full of sin and transgression pray to God? He can because at the very moment of prayer, he is transformed into a new being and is worthy of praying.

He died on the 18th day of *Tevet* 1841, at the age of 58. He had four sons (Rabbi Eleazar, Rabbi David, Rabbi Meshullam Zusya, and Rabbi Samuel) and three daughters. His son Meshullam Zusya and his daughter Rebecca, predeceased him. The dynasty was maintained by Rabbi Eleazar (1808–1865), author of *Yodei Binah* on the Pentateuch (Przemysl, 1911), and Rabbi David (1802–1874), author of *Tzemah David* on the Torah (Przemysl, 1879). When Rabbi Tzvi Elimelekh died, the rebbe of Belz remarked, "a sincere, truly pious Jew par excellence, has departed from this earth."

Rabbi Israel Perlow, "The Child Rebbe" of Stolin

The story of *HaYenuka MiStolin* ("the Child Rebbe of Stolin"), was unique in the history of hasidic masters. The *Yenuka*, as he was called, was appointed *rebbe* by his father's *hasidim* at the tender age of four. *Hasidim* would travel long distances to the town of Stolin in the province of Pinsk, Belorussia to watch and admire this prodigy; watching, almost worshipping him as he grew from boyhood to manhood. People sought his blessings and advice, clothing his childlike utterances with profound meaning. Even the renowned mitnagdic scholar, Rabbi Isaac Elhanan Spector, one of the great halakhic authorities of the nineteenth century, addressed the little lad as "Gaon." "I met him when I visited Stolin," he reports, "and there is no doubt in my mind that he is a great scholar. He has the laws of the Torah at his fingertips."

Contrary to popular belief, a number of hasidic dynasties flourished in Lithuania, the fortress of the *mitnagdim* and home of Rabbi Elijah, Gaon of Vilna. The dynasty of Amdor (near Grodno) was established by Hayim Heikel. The Libeshei dynasty was founded by Rabbi Shemaryahu Weingarten; Berezna, by Rabbi

Jehiel Michael; Horodok, by Rabbi Wolf Ginsburg; and above all the dynasty of Karlin-Stolin was established by Rabbi Aaron the Great, a disciple of Rabbi Dov Baer of Mezhirech.

Rabbi Aaron of Karlin

Rabbi Aaron was highly venerated, and *hasidim* would say that "he was warmed by the fire of the Almighty which glowed in his heart." They would say that when he recited the "Song of Songs" on the eve of the Sabbath, he caused a great commotion among the Heavenly Host. The angels and *serafim* stopped singing in order to listen to Rabbi Aaron's enthralling chant. He advised his *hasidim* to spend one day each week alone, fasting, repenting, and studying Torah. He was the author of *Yah Ekhsof Noam Shabbat* ("Oh God! how I yearn for the delights of the Sabbath"). Rabbi Aaron died at the age of 36. His successor, Rabbi Solomon, died a martyr's death on the 22nd day of *Tammuz* 1792.

The *Yenuka*'s grandfather, Rabbi Aaron the Second, was Rebbe of Karlin-Stolin for nearly fifty years (1826–1872) and was the author of *Beit Aharon*, published in Brody in 1854. Joy was the keynote in Stolin during his "reign." "He who has not seen *Simhat Torah* in the court of Rabbi Aaron," *hasidim* used to say, "has never beheld a real celebration of *Simhat Torah*." Rabbi Aaron died in 1872, while his son, Rabbi Asher the Second (1827–1873), died only one year later in Drohobycz, Ukraine, where he was buried. Rabbi Asher's only son, born in *Kislev* 1868, was named Israel after Rabbi Israel Baal Shem Tov. After his father's death, his mother and the *hasidim* decided to "crown" him *rebbe*, appointing Rabbi Israel Benjamin Gloerman his guide and tutor. At his *bar mitzvah* in 1871, he took over the leadership of the *hasidim*. He married the daughter of Rabbi David Twersky, the grandfather of Rabbi Johanan of Rachmastrivka.

The Yenuka Comes of Age

Rabbi Israel was an outstanding leader who guided his *hasidim* during difficult and dangerous times: the pogroms of 1881, the Russo-Japanese War, the First World War, when nearly 300,000 Jews served in the Czarist armies, and the Russian Revolution. His knowledge of Russian and German helped him to intervene effectively with various government departments.

He was always on the move, visiting different towns from week to week so that he could keep in close touch with his scattered *hasidim*. He prayed aloud with contagious fervor, explaining in Yiddish, *As es brennt, shreit men* ("when one is on fire, one shouts"). Even *mitnagdim* sought his guidance. When he heard that an officer had arrived in Stolin with a troop of soldiers to organize a pogrom, he invited the officer to dinner and pleaded with him to cancel his evil designs. "Do not harm my children," the rebbe entreated him, "all the Jews of Stolin are my children." When a man asked Rabbi Israel which *yeshivah* he should attend, the rebbe replied, "If you want to study Hasidism, go to one of the *yeshivot* of Lubavitch. If you want to go to a mitnagdic *yeshivah*, go to the *yeshivah* of the *Hafetz Hayim* of Radin. But if you go to Radin, do not stop in Lida," (i.e., do not go to the *yeshivah* of Rabbi Isaac Jacob Reines (1839–1915), founder of the Mizrahi movement.)

Testament to His Sons

Rabbi Israel composed two wills, one addressed to his family and the other to his followers. Both were printed by A. Ben Ezra in *HaYenuka MiStolin* (New York, 1951). The *rebbe* instructed his family as follows:

> If my end comes while I am traveling, my body should not be carried to my home, unless the place is only a few hours distance from Mlynow (the burial place of Rabbi Aaron, the Second), Karlin (the burial place of Rabbi Aaron the Great and Rabbi Asher the First) or Drohobycz (the burial place of Rabbi Asher the Second). If it is the local custom to set up a tombstone, this should be done. No titles should be inscribed. Only my name and my father's name. . . . The main thing is the study of the Talmud, which makes all who know it conduct themselves better. I counsel my sons not to become involved in communal affairs or in any worldly matters. I urge them in particular to stay aloof from money matters and dealing with secular authorities. For, in the course of my long life, I have never seen anyone who emerged from all this unscathed and

unhumiliated, except in such matters as the study of the Talmud and the use of *mikveh*. The greatest principle of all is not to flatter anyone, for this sometimes leads to an unfortunate result. As our sages remarked, "Every flatterer eventually falls into the power of him who he flatters."[10]

A Supporter of Various Causes

In a special letter, dated the 12th of *Tammuz* 1921, Rabbi Israel exhorted his followers to guard against "dissension caused by flatterers and hypocrites for no flatterer shall come into the Lord's presence."[11] He urged his *hasidim* to form "one united band." At a time when Sarah Schenirer was in the process of establishing a *Beit Yaakov* school in Krakow, Rabbi Israel stressed the importance of religious education for girls. "They shall give good heed to the education of their daughters for on that depends the cornerstone of Judaism and the family, and they should endeavor to find them husbands soon after they reach marriageable age."

There were noted composers of music in the court of Rabbi Israel. The best known were Rabbi Jacob from Telekhan (a small town near Pinsk) and Rabbi Yossele Talner. Rabbi Israel was deeply involved in support of the *yishuv* and there are thirty-six extant letters written to his followers in the Holy Land. He had six sons and four daughters. Accompanied by two of his sons, Rabbi Asher and Rabbi Jacob Hayim, he journeyed to Berlin and then to Homburg, Germany, where he died on the second day of *Rosh Hashanah* 1921. He was buried in Frankfurt-on-Main. His mother, Devorah, died on the very same day.

Heirs of the Yenuka

Rabbi Israel was succeeded by his son Rabbi Abraham Elimelekh (d. 1942), son-in-law of Rabbi Mordekhai Joseph Twersky. According to the instructions in Rabbi Israel's will, a simple tombstone bears the inscription: "The *rebbe* of Stolin, Rabbi Israel, son of Rabbi Asher, who died on the second day of *Rosh Hashanah* 1921. May his soul be bound up in the bond of Eternal Life."

The *Yenuka* in adulthood more than fulfilled the hopes and aspirations of his youth. He became a father to his people, a wise and erudite counselor, a tower of strength to the community in an age fraught with physical peril and economic distress. He was unique even within *Hasidism*, a movement known for its innovations. It is interesting to note that the "Child *Rebbe*" phenomenon repeated itself recently in Stolin. Rabbi Yohanan Perlow died on the 21st of *Kislev* 1955. His sole survivor was his infant grandson Rabbi Barukh Jacob Meir, who was born in 1954. A sizeable number of Karlin *hasidim* pledged their allegiance to the second "*Yenuka*" and waited for him to grow in years and wisdom; a twentieth-century counterpart of the "Yenuka" of Stolin.

Chapter 19

Storm Clouds Gather

During the First World War, Poland became the principal battlefield of the Eastern campaigns. Six times between 1914 and 1917 Russian armies swept through Galicia and were beaten back by the Austrians. Each campaign brought death and desolation to the local population. Grand Duke Nicholas Nikolayevitch, commander-in-chief of the Russian army, found convenient scapegoats in the Jews. "The Jews are spies," and "The Jews are helping the Germans," were his slogans. Mass expulsions became the order of the day. Ironically, it was with relief that Polish Jewry greeted the German entry into Warsaw on August 5, 1915.

With the Bolshevik revolution and the establishment of the Union of Soviet Socialist Republics, the three million Jews in Russia obtained civil emancipation. But simultaneously, the authorities instituted drastic and devastating measures designed to extinguish every spark of Jewish religious life. Jewish schools, *hedarim* and *yeshivot* were made illegal. Synagogues were requisitioned and converted into workers' clubs. Yiddish was recognized, but *yiddishkeit* (Judaism) was outlawed. At that time, Rabbi Shalom Dov Baer (1860–1920), fifth rabbi of the dynasty of Lubavitch, remained in the Soviet Union and dedicated himself to the cause of *hinnukh* (education). He organized clandestine centers of religious instruction even in remote places and under the most undesirable conditions.

Circumventing the Authorities

Rabbi Joseph Isaac Schneersohn (1880–1950), son of Rabbi Shalom Dov Baer, was well qualified to continue his father's manifold tasks. With the help of Jacob and Eliezer Polikoff, he opened a spinning and weaving mill in Dubrovna that provided a livelihood for many Jewish workers. He even established a *yeshivah* in Bukhara as late as 1917. The authorities viewed with disapproval the educational and economic reforms of the sociologist rabbi, and he was imprisoned four times between 1902 and 1911. Nevertheless, when Rabbi Joseph Isaac succeeded his father in 1920, he intensified the campaign for Jewish education throughout Russia. Neither the menace of the *Cheka* (secret police) nor the machinations and the threats of the *Yevsektzia* (the Jewish section of the Russian Communist Party) could curb his activities. Forced to leave Rostow-on-Don, he lived for a while in Leningrad.

In 1927 he was arrested for the fifth time and thrown into the Spalierna Prison in Leningrad. Accused of "counterrevolutionary" activities, the sixth rabbi of Lubavitch was sentenced to death, a sentence later commuted to three years of banishment to Kostroma in the Urals. Through intense political pressure applied by President Herbert Hoover of the United States and Senator William E. Borath, he was released in 1928 and permitted to live in Malachovka (near Moscow). Eventually he settled in the Latvian capital of Riga.

Rabbi Schneersohn was tormented by the plight of his people in Russia, doomed to spiritual extinction. He traveled to Germany, France, the Holy Land, and the United States of America, where he was received by President Hoover in Washington. In 1934, the rabbi took up residence in Warsaw and established *yeshivot* in Warsaw and Otwock.

Poland between the Wars

Between the two World Wars, Poland was the greatest reservoir of European Jewry. The Treaty of Riga, signed in March 1921, placed the Western Ukraine and Belorussia under Polish sovereignty. It was a large country with a population of about twenty-seven million, of whom only about two-thirds were Poles. The rest of the population consisted of some four million Ukrainians, Germans, Belorussians, Lithuanians, and Tartars. Within the boundaries of the new Polish State were 2,500,000 of the 4,500,000 Jews who lived in the old Russian Empire. By 1939 there were 3,300,000 Jews in Poland, comprising 9.5 percent of the total population. The Jews were the second largest minority, and they made up one-third of the total urban population. Seventy-five percent of the Jews lived in the urban areas.

An Era of Discrimination and Suffering

Three hundred thousand Jews lived in Warsaw, 194,000 in Lodz, 55,000 in Vilna, 44,000 in Lublin, and 100,000 in Lvov. Despite the liberal Constitution and the Minority Rights clauses of the Treaty of Versailles, Poland's newly acquired independence brought neither social security nor economic freedom to the Jewish community. The ink of the Versailles Treaty was hardly dry when Jewish blood began to flow. Pogroms became an everyday occurrence, and Jewish life was soon the cheapest commodity in the country.

The much-vaunted tolerance of medieval Poland vanished beyond recall, as every class of Polish society embraced anti-Semitism, the convenient old-new creed. During the single month of November 1918, pogroms took place in no fewer than 110 different towns and villages. In that year, the United States sent a commission, headed by Henry M. Morgenthau (1856–1946), to study the situation. It was followed by a British Government mission in September 1919, consisting of Sir Stuart Montagu Samuel (1856–1926), President of the Board of Deputies of British Jews, and Captain Peter Wright. Samuel's plea that "a genuine and not a masked equality be accorded to the Jewish population of Poland" was, of course, ignored.[1] There were provocative municipal ordinances against ritual slaughter, a *numerus clausus* (a quota system for admittance into educational institutions), ghetto benches at the universities, and innumerable economic restrictions that almost annihilated Jewish commerce.

Leading Polish statesmen preached a virulent racialist policy that anticipated the Nazi platform. In 1926 Bogulaw Miedzinski, Deputy Speaker of the Polish Sejm, declared in the Diet, "Poland has room for 50,000 Jews. The remaining three million must leave

Poland."[2] The "Cold Pogrom" policy was officially endorsed by the State, which now took over and monopolized such key industries as salt, tobacco, alcohol, matches, and batteries. Inevitably, Jews, constituting a large percentage of those engaged in trade and commerce, suffered most from this totalitarian sequestration. "My Government considers that nobody in Poland should be injured," was the glib pronouncement of the Premier of Poland, General Slawoj Sladkowski (1885–1962), on June 4, 1936. "An honest host does not allow anyone to be hurt in his house. Economic warfare is, of course, permitted."[3]

The Polish masses were not content with economic boycott. Pogrom followed pogrom in sinister succession, occurring in Przytyk on March 9, 1936, in Minsk Mazowiecki, Brzesc (Brest-Litovsk) on May 13, 1937, and Czenstochowa on June 19, 1937. The Austrian Anschluss (March 12, 1938) gave Poland the opportunity to legislate for the denationalization of persons who had lived outside the country for more than five years. On October 28, 1938, over 15,000 Polish Jews were made homeless and stateless. Five thousand were kept virtual prisoners in a camp at Zbaszyn, a small Polish township where they had been driven across the frontier by the Germans.

The Agudah

More than a third of Polish Jews were *hasidim*, most of them associated with the *Agudah*, by then an intricately organized and widespread structure wielding tremendous power. The *Agudah* maintained its own schools, published a daily newspaper (*Dos Yiddishe Togblatt*), ran its own publishing house (*Yeshurun*), youth organizations (*Tze'irei Agudat Yisrael* and *Pirhei Agudah*), and even a women's division (*Bnot Agudat Yisrael*) that numbered 25,000 members by 1939. The *Poalei Agudat Yisrael* protected the interests of the working class and established, among other things, a fund to aid workers who were incapacitated by illness.

By 1936, the *Agudah* controlled 115 cooperatives with a total membership of 15,825. Striving to wrest communal leadership from the assimilationists, it provided candidates for both local and parliamentary elections. Between 1927 and 1937 the *Agudah* controlled

Polish Jewry, and 242 delegates represented Poland at the *Knessiah Gedolah* (*Agudah* World Conference) in 1929.

Agudists Rabbi Aaron Lewin (1879–1941) of Rzseszow (Reisa) and Rabbi Meir Shapira (1887–1934) were deputies in the Sejm, while Jacob Trockenheim and Asher Mendelsohn represented the *Agudah* in the Senate. Prominent *Agudah* leaders, all devoted *hasidim* of Ger, included Meshullam Kaminer (1861–1943), editor of the *Dos Yiddishe Togblatt*; Leib From (1908–1943), co-founder (with Judah Leib Orlean) of the *Poalei Agudat Yisrael*; Leib Mincberg (1887–1943), leader of the Jewish community of Lodz and member of the Sejm; Moses Deutscher (b. 1880), leader of Krakow Jewry; and Moses Lerner (1887–1943), Deputy Mayor of the Jewish community of Warsaw.

Rabbi Meir Jehiel Holstock of Ostrowiec

When Rabbi Dov Baer, the *Maggid* of Mezhirech, was 5 years old, the house in which he lived with his parents was destroyed by fire. Naturally, his mother was very upset. "Why are you so grieved?" the little lad asked his mother, "Rejoice that none of us are hurt." "I am not grieving over our possessions," replied his mother, "What really saddens me is the loss of our genealogical tree." "Do not worry," the future *rebbe* reassured her. "A new tree will start with me."

Rabbi Meir Jehiel founded an illustrious dynasty; and a large anthology of legends gathered around this frail figure, who fought so fiercely for his people on many fronts. He was born in 1857 in Sabin, a little village near Warsaw. His father, Abraham Isaac Holstock (or Halztick) was a baker. He was very pious and very poor. He journeyed regularly to Rabbi Meir Jehiel of Moglienice. His mother, Hannah Beila, was a devout follower of Rabbi Joshua Rabinowicz of Zelechow, another son of the Holy Jew, Rabbi Jacob Isaac of Przysucha. The family lived in one room, where they also prayed and baked bread. While he was baking, it was his father's custom to recite a number of Psalms such as Psalm 102, "A prayer of the afflicted when he is overwhelmed and poureth out his complaint before the Lord."

An Avid Student

Young Meir Jehiel would accompany his father on travels through the villages to sell bread. On festivals, father and son would visit Rabbi Hayim Elimelekh Shapiro of Grodzisk Mazowiecki, author of *Imrei Elimelekh* (Warsaw, 1876) and *Divrei Elimelekh* (Warsaw, 1890), who advised that the boy be entrusted to the care of the scholarly Rabbi Beril. "I am handing you a child," Rebbe Hayim Elimelekh Shapiro told the tutor. "Make him a great scholar." Several years later, Rabbi Beril told the rebbe of Grodzisk, "I have accomplished my task. I have made him into a scholar. Now it is your turn. Turn him into a *tzaddik*." When Meir Jehiel was 17 years old, he married the daughter of Rabbi Abraham of Warka and soon became known as the "Gaon of Warka." He lived a very ascetic life, spending the whole week in the *Beit Hamidrash* and returning to his family only on the Sabbath.

He studied the sixteenth-century moralistic work *Reishit Hokhmah* by Rabbi Elijah ben Moses de Vidas countless times and the *Moreh Nevukhim* ("A Guide to the Perplexed") by Maimonides.[4] His diligence was phenomenal. He could go through the entire Talmud between *Purim* and Passover. When he had reached the age of 25, he was offered the rabbinate of Skierniewice, a town in the Lodz province of Central Poland, which had a Jewish population of nearly 4,000 souls, on condition that he obtained *semikhah* (ordination) from Rabbi Joshua Trunk of Kutno. Consequently, he traveled to Kutno. "How far have you progressed in your studies?" asked Rabbi Joshua. "I can answer all the questions of the *Tosafot* in the tractate of *Yevamot*," replied the candidate. Rabbi Joshua readily granted him *semikhah* remarking, "Happy is the community that has you for rabbi."[5] Rabbi Meir Jehiel became acquainted with Rabbi Joshua's son-in-law, Rabbi Hayim Eleazar Waks, author of *Nefesh Hayah* (Piotrokow, 1876) who wrote in praise of Rabbi Meir Jehiel, "How can a mere fly comment on an eagle who flies through the skies?"

A Beloved Rabbi

His tenure as rabbi in Skierniewice lasted ten years. In 1888, he became rabbi in Ostrowiec, a town in the Kielce province of Poland, that had a Jewish population of 10,095 (51 percent of the total population) in 1921. Among the former rabbis of Ostrowiec were Rabbi Ezekiel Avigdor of the "Council of Four Lands" and Rabbi Eliezer ben Solomon Zalman Lipschutz. Rabbi Meir Jehiel was loved and revered by all sections of the community, and when Rabbi Elimelekh of Grodzisk died, Rabbi Meir Jehiel was appointed *rebbe*.

As a young man he had begun to indulge in very ascetic practices. He not only fasted from Sabbath to Sabbath, he even fasted on the Sabbath itself. It was said that only prior to the Day of Atonement would he eat a proper meal. As a result, his health was exceedingly precarious. Rabbi Abraham Mordekhai Alter of Ger was one of the many colleagues who begged him to forgo such hazardous extremes, but the *rebbe* refused to alter his life style.

The Beilis Trial and the Trials of the Jews

Despite his physical frailty, he was wholeheartedly involved in communal affairs. In 1911 the body of a non-Jewish boy was found in Kiev, and Menahem Mendel Beilis (1874–1934) was charged with ritual murder. The investigation lasted for two years and was accompanied by violent anti-Jewish propaganda in the Russian and Polish press and by the unavailing protests of Jews throughout the world. There was no substance to the accusation, which was based chiefly on the ranting allegations of Father Baranaitis, a Catholic clergyman from Turkestan. When the *rebbe* heard that the Poles of Ostrowiec were preparing a pogrom, he instructed the Jewish authorities to organize in self-defense. They armed themselves with axes and knives and stood on guard. As soon as the cowardly hoodlums appreciated that they were not dealing with defenseless victims but with armed resistance, they dispersed. The Kishinev disorders were not reenacted in Ostowiec.

During the First World War, a local Jewish teacher was accused of espionage. The *rebbe* pleaded so eloquently with the military authorities, that the man was released from jail. The resourceful *rebbe* devised measures that matched every situation.

A Legacy of Teachings and Inspiration

In 1921, his disciple, Rabbi Judah Joseph Leibush Rosenberg, published Rabbi Meir Jehiel's book entitled *Or Torah* on Genesis. The work was based on notes made by the rabbi's son, Rabbi Ezekiel (1887–1943), rabbi of Nasielsk, and by his son-in-law, Rabbi David of Gostynin. Rabbi Meir Jehiel was versed in *gematriah*, the method of exegesis based on the interpretation of a word or words according to the numerical value of its Hebrew letters. In biblical homiletics, he belonged to the school of Rabbi Jacob ben Asher. In his talmudic studies, he was a follower of Rabbi Jacob Pollak (1470–1541), the communal rabbi of Krakow, who was the father of *pilpul*.

Rabbi Meir Jehiel died the 20th of *Adar* 1928 and was succeeded by his son, Rabbi Ezekiel. He and his seven sons were murdered by the Nazis on the 10th day of *Tevet* 1943. Rabbi Reuven Mandelbaum has recently published a two-volume work, *Me'ir Einei Hakhamim*, containing many of the teachings of the *rebbe* of Ostrowiec, whose whole life was a lesson in the triumph of the mind over matter. He was so weak from years of fasting that he could barely walk. He was, however, strong enough to fight passionately for the community he loved so dearly. Under his inspired leadership, his people were ready and able to defend themselves. He was perhaps the most remarkable combination of mildness and militancy that Hasidism has ever known.

The Rebbe of Sokolow, Rabbi Isaac Zelig Morgenstern

Rabbi Isaac Zelig was heir to the great traditions of Rabbi Menahem Mendel of Kotzk. Nevertheless, he created his own niche in the history of Hasidism. Unlike Rabbi Menahem Mendel, who was concerned with the few and select and who stated "Would that I had but 200 Jews who had not bowed down to Baal," the *rebbe* of Sokolow was concerned with the masses.

He was a forceful speaker, and his discourses attracted large audiences. No great rabbinical assembly in Poland during the interwar years could take place without a speech delivered by the *rebbe* of Sokolow. He was community-minded, and never gave up until he achieved his purpose. He maintained that "if something is worthwhile, it should be done with enthusiasm." There were no half measures for him. Like his forebears, he was a perfectionist. He was the head of a *yeshivah*, a rabbi, a *rebbe*, an Agudist leader, and a prolific writer. He was, moreover, blessed with an incisive Yiddish and Hebrew style, whereby he could clothe his discourses with wit and humor.

A Child of Kotzk

Rabbi Isaac Zelig was born in Kotzk in 1864. He was the son of Rabbi Hayim Israel of Pulawy and a grandson of Rabbi David (d. 1873), whose discourses are to be found in *Likkutei Hadash, Meilot Hadashot*, and *Ahavat David.* Rabbi Isaac Zelig absorbed the sayings and aphorisms, the "Oral Law" of Rabbi Mendel, who had never published a book. Yet, his teachings left an indelible impression not only on the great courts of Ger and Alexander but also on all of Hasidism. Blessed with a phenomenal memory, Rabbi Isaac Zelig memorized the sayings of the old *hasidim* who had had the privilege of serving Rabbi Mendel of Kotzk.

At the age of 18, Rabbi Isaac Zelig married Hayah, daughter of Rabbi Mordekhai Schonfeld, a *hasid* of the *Sefat Emet* of Ger. In 1899, he became rabbi of Sokolow Podolski in the Warsaw province. In 1879, 4,430 Jews lived there, making up 55 percent of the total population. In the middle of the nineteenth century, Rabbi Elimelekh was rabbi of Sokolow. Sokolow was known as a city of controversy and dissension, and "rabbi baiting" was a popular pastime. As a result, few rabbis stayed there for any length of time. Rabbi Isaac Zelig was the exception. He lived there for forty years. He established a large *yeshivah* named *Beit Yisrael* (in memory of his father), and he himself gave regular discourses to the students.

When his father died in 1906, the *hasidim* divided their allegiance between his three sons, Rabbi Tzvi (1858–1920) of Lukowa, author of discourses on Torah and festivals entitled *Ateret Tzvi* (Warsaw, 1934); Rabbi Moses Mordekhai (1862–1929) of Pulawy, author of discourses on Genesis and Exodus known as *Midrash Moshe* (Warsaw, 1931) and Rabbi Isaac Zelig.

A Community Activist

The rebbe of Sokolow was no novice in communal affairs. In 1910, he had represented Polish Jewry at the Communal Conference in St. Petersburg. Among the other participants were Rabbi Joseph Isaac Schneersohn of Lubavitch and Rabbi Hayim Soloveichik (1826–1910) of Brest-Litovsk. The *Agudah* was founded in Poland in 1916 with the help of the German military rabbis, Rabbi Dr. Phinehas Kohn (later executive president of the World

Agudah Movement) and Dr. Emanuel Carlebach. At first the association was called *Shelumei Emunei Yisrael* ("wholly faithful Israelites," a reference to II Samuel 20:19), and the *rebbe* of Sokolow became one of its prominent leaders. In 1919, the *Agudah* participated in the Polish general election as an independent party, obtaining 92,293 votes and returning six deputies and two senators. At the third national conference of the party in October 1928, the name was changed to *Agudat Yisrael* (Union of Israel Party).

The *Agudah* established its own educational structure. Its success was due in no small measure to the *rebbe* of Sokolow who, with his oratory and publications, helped to consolidate the movement. The *rebbe* became one of the leaders of the *Agudat HaRabbanim* (Rabbinical Association) and traveled extensively on behalf of the movement.

In a discourse entitled *Elbono Shel Torah*, printed in 1920 (and reprinted in Tel Aviv in 1944), the *rebbe* urged the Orthodox Jews to rally to the banners of the *Agudah* in order to uphold the "honor of the Torah." He was the main speaker at the *Tzeirei Agudat Yisrael* foundation conference, held in Warsaw on the 15th of *Shevat* 1922. He addressed the Second *Knessiah*, which was held in Vienna in *Elul* 1929, urging the assembly to find means of "restoring the crown of the Torah to its former glory and arresting the stream of lawlessness in the Jewish scene."

A Visit to the Holy Land

Like his father Rabbi Israel, who authored *Shelom Yerushalayim* in 1886, the *rebbe* of Sokolow was deeply concerned with the state of the *yishuv*. In 1924 he visited the Holy Land with the *rebbe* of Ger and Rabbi Hirsch Heinokh Levin of Bendin. In the Holy Land he refused to accept *kvitlekh* saying, "Here everyone is a *rebbe*." He visited Jerusalem, Hebron, Tiberias, and Tel Aviv. On his return to Poland, he stayed in the home of his *hasid* Samuel Elijah Weller, where he urged Polish Jewry to "settle in the Holy Land for it is very good."

Like the *rebbe* of Radzin, the *rebbe* of Sokolow wrote prescriptions in Latin. He acquired his knowledge of medicine from his friend, Dr. Zalman Zygmunt Bichovsky of Warsaw.

The Eve of Destruction

In 1937–1938 the Jews in Poland suffered physical attacks. The peasants aimed at destroying Jewish sources of livelihood thereby ridding themselves of competitors. They wrecked shops, destroyed sewing machines, smashed the mirrors of Jewish barbers, and stole tools from Jewish workers. The *rebbe* urged the formation of self-defense units.

During the last ten years of his life, he suffered from ill health, and at the time of the outbreak of the Second World War, he was living in Otwock. The Germans entered the town on September 20, 1939, and immediately began terrorizing the Jews. On September 23, 1939 (the Day of Atonement), the Germans set the synagogue on fire. The *rebbe* celebrated *Sukkot* under the shadow of the Nazis. As he was sanctifying the Sabbath, the cup of wine fell from his hands. "They have killed my son," the brokenhearted father cried. His premonitions were true. His eldest son, Rabbi Mendel of Wengrow, had been killed by the Nazis on the Day of Atonement.

The *rebbe* died on the 3rd day of *Heshvan* 1940 at the age of 74. He was buried in Warsaw, near the grave of Rabbi Abraham Mordekhai Alter, son of the *Hiddushei HaRim*. The rebbe of Sokolow was succeeded by his son, Rabbi Benjamin Paltiel (b. 1895), who was married to the daughter of Rabbi Joseph of Amshinow, Deborah, and who also perished at Auschwitz in 1944. His daughter Beila married Rabbi Nahum Mordekhai Perlow, son of the Novominsker *Rebbe,* who was rebbe of Novominsk, in New York.

The *rebbe* of Sokolow wrote a number of articles for *Degel HaTorah* and *HaBe'er* as well as *haskamot* to the *Haggadah Tiferet Ish* by the rabbi of Novominsk, *Pardes Yosef* (Piotrokow-Lodz, 1931–1939) by Rabbi Joseph Patzenowsky, and *Gur Aryeh Yehudah* (Warsaw, 1928) by Moses Aryeh Judah Ziemba. All the manuscripts of the *rebbe* of Sokolow were destroyed in the Holocaust.

Rabbi Abraham Mordekhai Alter of Ger

The most powerful hasidic court in inter-war Poland was Ger. Rabbi Abraham Mordekhai Alter (1866–1948), rabbi of Ger, was the "Emperor of Hasidism," and Ger was the capital of his empire.

Among his followers were outstanding rabbinical scholars and leaders of Polish Jewry. The rabbi's influence was far-reaching. A word from him could decide a communal election, and any cause he favored was assured of success. When the rabbi of Ger came to a town, it was in the nature of a state visit, surrounded by pomp and ceremony.

Rabbi Abraham Mordekhai was born on 7th *Tevet*, 1866, and succeeded his father in 1905. Following the Kotzk tradition of spontaneity in prayer, many *hasidim* had been in the habit of bypassing the appointed hours and praying whenever and wherever the spirit moved them. The accession of Rabbi Abraham Mordekhai marked a return to meticulous observance of the *Shulhan Arukh* and emphasis on Torah study. On Friday evening and on the Sabbath between *Shaharit* and *Musaf*, time was set aside for study.

An Early Supporter of Agudah

Like his grandfather, Rabbi Abraham Mordekhai had a deep sense of communal responsibility. At the Bad-Homburg Conference in 1909, the *rebbe* helped pave the way for the founding of the *Agudah*. The *rebbe* of Ger attended the three Agudist Conferences (*Knessiah Gedolah*) of 1923, 1929, and 1937 at Vienna and Marienbad. The *rebbe* of Ger supported Orthodox publications, such as *Dos Yiddishe Togblatt*. He supported the *Beit Yaakov* movement. Under the influence of the *rebbe*, many *Hedarim* and *Talmud Torah* centers were combined into the *Horev* schools, and he supported the establishment of the *Metivta* in 1919, under Rabbi Meir Don Plotski, rabbi of Ostrowiec.

The *rebbe* supported the establishment of the *Yeshivat Hakhmei Lublin* and the *Daf Hayomi*. During the First World War, the German authorities sent Rabbi Phinehas Kohn (1867–1942), director of the *Agudat Yisrael* World Organization, and Rabbi Emanuel Carlebach (1874–1925) to Poland, where they established the Warsaw Orphanage under the aegis of the War Orphan's Fund of the *Agudah*. They tried to win over the Jewish population of Poland for the German cause. The rebbe of Ger was unconvinced. "I believe," he told the two rabbis, "that the Germans are descendants of the Amalekites."

Five Visits to the Land of Israel

"Just as a *hasid* must visit his *rebbe* from time to time," said the *rebbe*, "so I must visit the Land of Israel."[6] Embarking on his first visit in 1921, he left Ger on the day after *Purim* and traveled via Vienna and Trieste to Jaffa. The visit lasted twenty-eight days. Three years later, in *Shevat* 1924, the *rebbe* visited the Holy Land for the second time. This time he stayed six weeks and visited Hebron, Tel Aviv, Tiberias, and Safed. On his third trip in 1927 the *Rebbe* of Ger traveled to the Holy Land via Trieste and Alexandria. He was accompanied by his brother-in-law, Rabbi Hirsch Henokh Levin of Bendin, and his nephew, Rabbi Phinehas Levin. At the Cave of Makhpelah, the authorities were willing to allow the distinguished visitor to descend into the Cave (at that time the Jews were allowed no further than the first few steps) but the *rebbe* declined the concession. "All the children of Israel are the children of the King," commented the *rebbe*. "I do not desire any special privileges."

The *rebbe* of Ger's fourth journey took place in the winter of 1932, and this time he traveled an overland route through Vienna, Sofia, and Istanbul. This itinerary aroused the interest of hasidic Jewry. "I want to explore the different ways that lead to the Holy Land," he explained to his followers.[7] The *rebbe* was accompanied by his brother, Rabbi Menahem Mendel of Pabianice. After a stay of five weeks, the *rebbe* returned to Poland. On his return journey, there was a violent storm at sea. "This is because we are leaving the Holy Land," commented the *rebbe*.

When Hitler came to power in January 1933, the *rebbe* said: "For 150 years, our German brethren have not known the meaning of the word exile. Now they will probably find refuge in the Holy Land. I am afraid of one thing: they will take with them their assimilated customs and will adversely influence the vitality of the religious life."

His fifth pilgrimage, the last and longest, took place just before *Rosh Hashanah* 1935 and lasted eight months, until *Rosh Hodesh Iyyar* 1936. By then, the *rebbe* regarded himself as a resident of the Holy Land and no longer observed *Yom Tov Sheini*, (the second day of the festival celebrated in the Diaspora). He was reluctant to return home, but was counseled not to desert his "Great Multitude" in Poland.

In 1937, the third *Knessiah Gedolah* of the *Agudah* at Marienbad discussed the proposal of the Peel Commission (the Royal Commission set up by the British Government under Viscount Peel) that the Holy Land be partitioned into two sovereign states, one Jewish and the other Arab; with historic and strategic sites remaining under British jurisdiction. In forceful opposition, the rabbi of Ger quoted Joel 4:2, "I will gather all the nations, and I will bring them down into the valley of Jehoshophat: and I will enter into judgment with them there for My people and My heritage Israel whom they have scattered among the nations and divided My Land."[8]

A Love for Books

A dedicated bibliophile, the rabbi of Ger had a library of over 5,000 books, among them some early incunabula. He encouraged the publication of the unpublished manuscripts of Rabbi Menahem ben Solomon Meiri of Perpignan (1249–1346) on tractates *Sukkot* (Warsaw, 1910), *Berakhot* (1921), *Eruvin* (1913), *Pesahim* (Bilgoray, 1926); as well as *Eitz Hadaat* on Psalms by Rabbi Hayim Vital (Warsaw, 1926), and *Yakar Mipaz* on *Midrash Rabbah* by Rabbi Zusya of Plock, a disciple of Rabbi Simha Bunem of Przysucha, and *Zekhut Avot* by Rabbi Abraham ben Mordecai Galanti (d. 1588), printed in Bilgoray in 1919. The *rebbe* made extensive comments and glosses on *Otzar Hasefarim* (Vilna, 1880) compiled by Isaac Benjacob (1801–1863) which registered about 15,000 printed books and 3,000 manuscripts.

In 1907, Solomon Judah Friedlander (1860–1923), a native of Beshenkovichi, near Vitebsk, Belorussia and a student of the *yeshivah* of Volozhin, startled the literary Jewish world when he published *Seder Kodeshim* of the Jerusalem Talmud. He claimed that his work was based on a Spanish manuscript dated Barcelona 1212 that he had discovered in Turkey. He published *Zevahim* and *Arahim* in 1907, and *Hullin* and *Bekhorot* in 1909 with his commentary *Heshek Sholomo*. Friedlander asserted that he was of pure Sephardic descent (*sefaradi tahor*), from a well-known Algazi family and a native of Smyrna. Some of the leading scholars of the period, such as Rabbi Solomon Buber (1827–1906), editor of important works by medieval scholars; Dr. Solomon Schechter (1850–1915), discoverer of the Cairo *Genizah*; and Rabbi Shalom Mordekhai Schwadron of

Brzeziny accepted his word. Rabbi Abraham Mordekhai of Ger strongly supported Rabbi Meir Dan Plotzki, who in his book, *Shaale Shalom Yerushalayim* (1910), proved conclusively the fallaciousness of Friedlander's claims. His texts were literary forgeries. The *rebbe*'s views were endorsed by V. Aptowitzer, W. Bacher, and D. B. Ratner.

The rabbi was especially warm to young people. "In Ger there are 10,000 *hasidim* who eat on the Day of Atonement," was the startling statement that meant that 10,000 boys, too young to fast, were visiting Ger for the High Holy days.

Escape from Nazi-Occupied Poland

With the outbreak of the Second World War on September 1st, 1939, the fate of Eastern European Jewry was sealed. The *rebbe* urged his followers to subscribe generously to the Polish Air Defense Loan because he maintained, "the destiny of Jewry is bound up with the destiny of the Polish State." The *rebbe* moved to Warsaw, to the home of Rabbi Moses Rozenstock, and kept changing his place of residence to evade the Nazis, who spared no effort to locate the "Wonder Rabbi." An energetic committee in the United States managed to obtain an entry visa to the Holy Land for the *rebbe*. The rebbe, together with his wife Feige Mintze, his sons Rabbi Israel, Rabbi Simha Bunem, and Rabbi Phinehas Menahem, left Warsaw in *Adar* 1940 and arrived in the Holy Land after Passover.

The rabbi of Ger participated in a special Service of Intercession for Polish Jewry, held in the *Hurvah* Synagogue of Rabbi Judah Hahasid in Jerusalem on the 20th day of *Kislev* 1942. The *rebbe* died on the first day of the Festival of Pentecost 1948 at 4:30 P.M. Rabbi Dr. Isaac Herzog, then Chief Rabbi of the Holy Land, proclaimed in eulogy, "On *Shavuot* the Torah was given, and on *Shavuot* the Torah was taken away." As the Mount of Olives was then in Arab hands, the *rebbe* was buried, at the termination of the festival, in the courtyard of the *Sefat Emet Yeshivah* in Jerusalem.

Rabbi Alter Israel Simon Perlow of Novominsk

One of the most prominent *rebbes* in Poland during the inter-war years (1919–1939) was the *rebbe* of Novominsk, Rabbi Alter

Israel Simon Perlow (1875–1933), scion of the hasidic dynasties of Ostillo, Kaidanow, Chernobyl, Karlin, and Berdichev. His father, Rabbi Jacob (1847–1902), was the son of Rabbi Simon, who died at the age of 43. Rabbi Jacob was brought up in the home of Rabbi Solomon Hayim Perlow of Kaidanow (near Minsk, Russia) and married Hayah Havah Pearl, daughter of Rabbi Judah Leibush Liberson of Proskurow.

Rabbi Jacob Fulfills His Destiny

After fifteen childless years of marriage, the couple was blessed with a daughter, but Rabbi Jacob yearned for a son. "Go settle in Poland, for there you will establish a dynasty," counseled Rabbi Isaac ben Mordekhai (1789–1868) of Nesvizh. Rabbi Jacob followed this prophetic advice. He left Starosielce, White Russia; and, in 1872, set up his court in Minsk-Mazowiecki, a town in East Central Poland that had a Jewish population of 3,445. He was warmly welcomed by Rabbi Isaac Meir Alter of Ger.

Rabbi Jacob made many "converts" to Hasidism and soon won wide recognition. In 1896, he built a large *yeshivah*, one of the first hasidic *yeshivot* to be established in Poland, where hundreds of young men lived and learned. He also built a great synagogue that accommodated over a thousand worshippers. This was a showpiece court, complete with its own garden, orchards, stables, and horses. A tourist industry sprang up, and the municipality actually ran special trains to accommodate the considerable traffic of *hasidim* to and from Novominsk. He was the author of *Shufrah DeYaakov*, printed in Jerusalem in 1964.

Rabbi Alter Israel Simon and his twin sister Reizel (the mother of Professor Abraham Joshua Heschel) were born in Novominsk in 1875. In 1893, he married Feige Dinah, daughter of Rabbi Barukh Meir Twersky of Azarnitz, Russia, a seventh generation, direct descendant of Rabbi Israel Baal Shem Tov. After seven months in Azarnitz, Rabbi Perlow returned to Novominsk, where he headed his father's flourishing *yeshivah*. When his father died on the 23rd day of *Adar* I 1902, Rabbi Alter Israel Simon became *rebbe* of Novominsk.

The Upheaval of the First World War

The First World War brought many problems for the Jews. Casualties on the battlefield were not the only casualties suffered by the Jews. More heartrending were the sufferings of the civilian Jewish population in Polish territory, over which the tides of battle flowed back and forth. No sooner had war broken out than those Jews who lived near the battlefield were forced to evacuate their homes. Each side treated the Jews as enemies. Misery, death, and starvation overtook the Jewish population. In 1916, the *rebbe* left Novominsk and settled in Warsaw, which had a Jewish population of 300,000 and was then the home of fifty hasidic *rebbes*.

A New Center in Warsaw

Just as Galician *rebbes* found refuge in Vienna, so Polish *rebbes* settled in Warsaw. The home of Rabbi Alter Israel Simon at Francziskanska 10, quickly became one of the thriving centers of Hasidism. *Hasidim* of all "denominations" flocked to him. He knew the entire Mishnah by heart, and toward the end of his life he rehearsed twenty-one chapters daily. On the Sabbath he only spoke *Leshon Hakodesh* (Classical Hebrew). Crowds thronged to his famous Sabbath discourses that were remarkable for their length as well as their profundity. A typical *Shalosh Seudot* address would last nearly two hours. His eloquent addresses, his stirring prayers, his melodious voice, and his mature wisdom spread his fame far and wide. Once heard, the melodies of the *rebbe* of Novominsk were never forgotten. They were expressions of his soaring soul, revelations that awed and elevated his listeners. His prayers before the reader's desk on the High Holy days, particularly at *Neilah*, were highpoints in the lives of the *hasidim.* On *Kol Nidrei* night, he recited aloud the entire Book of Psalms.

Yet, even though it crippled the industrial life of the country, successive Polish governments adopted administrative measures specifically calculated to inhibit the Jews. Unemployment affected the Jews more than the non-Jews, for various forms of state welfare were barred to them. Thirty percent of Polish Jewry were in dire financial straits. In bitterness and despair, they turned to the *rebbe* for advice, and the Rabbi of Novominsk faithfully ministered to his people. Every day, twice a day, there were long lines of men and women who flocked to him for help, guidance, comfort, and inspiration. With infinite patience, he would listen and give practical counsel. At night, he would say to his family, "I cannot eat. I am sated with the sufferings and tribulations of the Children of Israel."

The *rebbe* of Novominsk was associated with the *Agudah* in Poland. The organization maintained its own schools, published daily newspapers, and had its own publishing house, youth organizations, and women's divisions. The *rebbe* participated in the many *Agudah* conventions held in Warsaw. He supported the daily newspaper (*Dos Yiddishe Togblatt*) and was active in the *Moetzet Gedolei HaTorah* (rabbinical council). Rabbi Abraham Mordekhai Alter, the *rebbe* of Ger, was a devoted friend who rarely passed through Warsaw without visiting him. "Go to the *rebbe* of Novominsk," the *rebbe* of Ger urged his followers.[9] He told Rabbi Jacob Rosenheim (1870–1965), the president of the *Agudah* from 1929 that "the ideal spiritual guide for the *Agudah* in Poland would be the *rebbe* of Novominsk, but he would not accept the position, since he is too preoccupied with prayer and learning."

Close Ties with Other Hasidic Leaders

The *rebbe* of Novominsk described as "my beloved brother," the *rebbe* of Alexander, the *Yismah Yisrael*, whom he would regularly meet in Kissingen, Germany. The rabbinate of Warsaw, Rabbi Ezekiel Michelson and Rabbi Joshua Gutschechter, frequently consulted him on religious matters, and Rabbi Gutschechter even gave him a *kvitl*. The *rebbe* of Novominsk advised the Jewish leaders to fight with every means for the survival of the Jews, by political means through the *Agudah* and by bringing their situation to the attention of the world through traditional *shtadlanut*. From his famous forefathers, the *rebbe* of Novominsk inherited a remarkable legacy; from Rabbi Solomon Hayim of Kaidanow, prayerfulness; from Rabbi Levi Isaac of Berdichev, love of humanity; from Rabbi Phinehas ben Abraham Shapiro of Korets (1726–1791), love of music; and from his father, diligence and a phenomenal memory.

He died on the 6th day of *Tevet* 1933, while studying *Mishnayot*.

His grave is in Warsaw. He left twelve children (four sons and eight daughters) and many volumes of writings on the Torah. Most of his manuscripts were lost in the Holocaust. *Tiferet Ish* on the Passover *haggadah* was printed in Warsaw in 1933, and *Tiferet Ish* on Torah was edited by his son, Rabbi Nahum Mordekhai Perlow, the late Novominsker *rebbe* of New York. It was printed in Jerusalem in 1969.

In an age of mounting persecution and in the gathering shadows of catastrophe, the *rebbe* of Novominsk managed miraculously to keep the spiritual flames of the *hasidim* burning brightly and bravely.

Alter Israel Simon's brother, Solomon Hayim Perlow (1860–1943), married the daughter of Rabbi Joshua Heschel of Bolechow. He was the author of a commentary on the prayer book (*Siddur Kehillat Shlomo*), published in 1907, and a 1,781-page anthology of hasidic commentary on the Psalms entitled *Mikdash Shlomo* (published in Bilgoray in 1937). Rifka Reizel, twin sister of the Novominsker *rebbe* married Rabbi Mordekhai Heschel (1866–1918), the rabbi of Pelcovizna and son of the rabbi of Medzibozh.

Activities of Other Rebbes in Inter-War Poland

The son of the *rebbe* of Radzyn, Rabbi Samuel Solomon (1908–1942) left Warsaw in 1928 and returned to Radzyn. With fatherly solicitude he cared for the young students in his charge, introducing many innovations into the somewhat stereotyped *yeshivah* routine. His students were spared the indignities of the rotation system, whereby they ate in a different household every day. In the *yeshivah* of Radzyn, named *Sod Yesharim* ("The Secret of the Upright"), over 200 students lived in comparative comfort.

The dynasty of Radzymin had been founded by the "miracle worker," Rabbi Aryeh Guterman (1792–1877), who played a significant role in Polish life. Guterman's wealthy grandson, Rabbi Aaron Menahem Mendel (1842–1934) owned twenty-one houses. Educator, organizer and social worker, he founded the *Shomer Shabbat* (Sabbath Observance) Society and *Tomkhei Assirim* (Prisoners' Aid Committee) and was president of the *Rabbi Meir Baal HaNes* Foundation, the organization that distributed the traditional charity boxes in the Diaspora to help raise funds for poor Jews in the Holy Land. In 1928 Rabbi Aaron Menahem Mendel journeyed there to settle a dispute over the distribution of these funds.

Lublin was also home to a number of famous hasidic rabbis such as Rabbi Solomon Eiger (d. 1914), son of Rabbi Abraham and author of *Shevet Yehudah* ("The Scepter of Judah"). Rabbi Abraham Heschel Rabinowicz lived at 30 Lubertowski Street, while at 27 Lubertowski Street lived Rabbi Moses Mordekhai Twersky (d. 1943), son of Rabbi Leib of Turisk, who had married a daughter of Rabbi Barukh Meir of Azarnits. After the Russian Revolution, Lublin became the center of the *Hasidim* of Bratslav, who gathered at *Yeshivat Hakhmei Lublin* of Rabbi Meir Shapiro. "I am a *rebbe* without *hasidim.* You are *hasidim* without a *rebbe.* Let us, therefore, join forces," he facetiously suggested.

Chapter 20

Torah Study

Although Poland was the home of Torah study, it was not at first the home of hasidic *yeshivot.* During the nineteenth century, mitnagdic Lithuania had the monopoly, and the "voice of the Torah went forth out of Mir and the word of the Lord from Slobodka." Hasidic *bahurim* (young men) studied in the *shtiblekh* and the *Battei Midrashim* (houses of study) of the *rebbes.* In the inter-war years, however, Polish *rebbe* began to establish their own *yeshivot,* and their young followers were spared the difficult choice between inadequate study in the warm and familiar atmosphere of the *shtibl,* and a thorough talmudic grounding in the alien setting of a mitnagdic *yeshivah,* such as Mir, Baranowicze, Radin, or Ponovezh in Lithuania.

During his residence in Otwock (1927–1929), Rabbi Joseph Isaac Schneerson founded a number of *Tomkhei Temimim* (supporters of the Godly) *yeshivot.* Meanwhile, Rabbi Solomon Henokh Hakohen Rabinowicz (b. 1882) of Radomsk, son of Rabbi Ezekiel, author of *Knesset Yehezkel* ("Gathering of Ezekiel"), was establishing the *Keter Torah* (crown of the Torah) *yeshivot,* and soon there were thirty-six branches in Poland and Galicia. Although many rabbis followed the *rebbe* of Radomsk, he regarded himself as a *hasid* of Chortkow. The rabbi of Radomsk was a man of substance who owned a glass factory as well as houses in Sosnowiec, Berlin, and Warsaw. He had one of the finest libraries in Poland and was the author of *Tiferet Shlomo* ("The Glory of Solomon"), homilies on the Pentateuch and the Festivals.

The Yeshivot *of Radomsk*

The successor-designate of the rabbi of Radomsk was his first cousin and son-in-law, Moses David Hakohen Rabinowicz (b. 1906), a disciple of Rabbi Dov Berish Weidenfeld of Trzebinin and the author of *Zivhei Kohen* ("The Sacrifices of the Priest"). He lectured three times daily to 150 students in the *Kibbutz Gavohah* ("Academy for Higher Study") in Sosnowiec. Under his direction, the *yeshivot* of Radomsk established high standards, particularly among the famous *Keter Torah* colleges of Lodz, Bendin, Radomsk, Piotrokow, and Czenstochowa. The rabbi himself supplied half the expenses of the *yeshivot*, and the remainder was subscribed by his *hasidim*. No provision was made, however, for the Rabbinical Diploma, because emphasis was on study for the sake of study and not for certification. *Gemara* (Talmud) and *Tosafot* (critical notes on the Talmud by medieval French and German scholars) were the main subjects of the concentrated curriculum. Under the influence of Rabbi Israel Meir Kahan, the *Hafetz Hayim*, particular attention was paid to *Kodashim* (the Fifth Order of the *Mishnah* dealing with Temple rituals). Students and teachers were not necessarily *hasidim* of Radomsk. The principal of the *yeshivah* of Radomsk in Sosnowiec was Joseph Lask, a *hasid* of Ger.

Rabbi Meir Judah Shapiro

"Nowadays, *yeshivah* students should not live in shacks and eat like beggars," declared Rabbi Meir Shapiro. "I will build a palace for them."[1]

Rabbi Meir Judah Shapiro was a colorful personality. Born in Siebenbuergen, Romania, near Czernowitz, on the 7th of *Adar* 1887, he was the son of Rabbi Samson. He traced his ancestry to Rabbi Phinehas ben Abraham Korets (1726–1792), author of *Midrash Pinhot* and *Minhat Shai*. At the age of 9, Rabbi Meir was known as a prodigy, the "*illui* of Shatz." An outstanding student, young Meir knew the Code *Yoreh Deah* and its commentaries by heart. Rabbi Shalom Hakohen Schwadron, author of *Daat Torah* said, "I have seen Rabbi Meir uprooting mountains and pulverizing them to tiny fragments in his discussion on *halakhah*. I apply to him the benediction: 'Blessed be he who is the creator of lights,' " a word play on the name "Meir," which means light in Hebrew.

He was ordained by Rabbi Isaac Shmelkes of Brody, Rabbi Samuel Isaac Schor, and Rabbi Meir Arik. Rabbi Meir married the daughter of the wealthy Jacob David Reitman, of Tarnopol, Galicia. At the age of 23, he published his first work, *Imrei Daat* on Torah, but the work was destroyed in a fire at the bindery of Tarnopol in 1914.

In 1910, he became rabbi in Glina, where he spent ten years and where he founded his first *yeshivah.* He subsequently became rabbi in Sanok (1920–1923) and later in Piotrokow (1924–1930). When asked why he changed rabbinical positions so frequently, he replied, "Only a nail with a head can be easily removed from one place and put into another." He was an excellent educator, deeply concerned with the spiritual welfare of young people. A member of the Central Council of the Rabbinical Association, he served as a member of the Polish Parliament (Sejm) from 1922 to 1928. In 1922, he was elected president of the *Agudah* in Poland.

At a rabbinical conference held in Warsaw on the 23rd of *Tevet* 1922, Rabbi Meir stressed that "by merely passing resolutions we have achieved nothing. We must not be satisfied with publicizing our resolutions and restrictions. . . . We make an impression on the lowest strata of the people and convince them . . . awaken them and teach them."

The Daf Yomi

Rabbi Shapiro was an innovator. Among his far-reaching innovations was the *Daf Yomi,* which he proposed at the first *Knessiah* on the 3rd of *Elul* 1923 in Vienna. This was a simple scheme that achieved universal acceptance. It requires the study each day of one page of the Talmud. The same page is studied everywhere so that in seven years the entire Babylonian Talmud would be covered in a cycle of studies that would unite the scattered Jewry of the world in intellectual and historic bonds. "If every Jew everywhere was to study the same page of the Talmud on the same day," said Rabbi Meir, "there could be no greater expression of Divine unity between the Book (the Torah) and the people of the Book."[2]

The *Daf Yomi* (daily page) caught the imagination of both scholar and layman and was inaugurated on *Rosh Hashanah* 1924.

On that day Rabbi Abraham Mordekhai Alter of Ger told his followers, "From now on I am going to study a page of the Talmud each day," and many followed his example. Rabbi Israel Meir Kahan (1835–1933), the *Hafetz Hayim,* bestowed on Rabbi Meir the title, *Baal HaDaf Yomi*. The first *siyyum* of the entire Talmud was celebrated on the 15th of *Shevat* 1931.

The Yeshivat Hakhmei Lublin

Rabbi Shapiro's second major achievement was the establishment of *Yeshivat Hakhmei Lublin.* At that time, *yeshivah* students in Poland and Lithuania lived a spartan life. Few Yeshivot had dormitories, or even kitchens. Spiritual food was offered in great abundance, but little provision was made for physical welfare. To keep body and soul together, a *yeshivah* student often "ate days," meaning that each day he would eat his dinner in a different home. Many students had difficulty finding lodgings. In Warsaw it was not uncommon for *yeshivah* students to serve as night watchmen in shops and factories. "We should be grateful for the existence of thieves," jested Rabbi Shapiro. "Were it not for them, shopkeepers would not employ watchmen, and if watchmen were not needed, where would *yeshivah* students find accommodation?"

A man of action, Rabbi Shapiro translated his dream into reality. In Lublin, onetime seat of the medieval "Council of Four Lands" and former home of Rabbi Solomon ben Jehiel Luria, Rabbi Jacob Pollak, and Rabbi Jacob Isaac, the Seer of Lublin, Rabbi Shapiro erected his "palace." The foundation stone was laid on *Lag B'Omer* 1924, in the presence of the rabbi of Ger and his own rebbe, Rabbi Israel Friedmann of Chortkov. The site, at Lubertovska 37, was donated by Samuel Eihenbaum. Aware that poverty-stricken Polish Jewry was incapable of financing such a costly enterprise, he set out for the United States on the 10th of *Elul* 1927. There, in the course of thirteen months, he delivered 242 discourses and collected $53,000. He also visited England, France, Germany, and Switzerland.

The new *yeshivah* building was consecrated on the 29th day of *Sivan* 1930 at an impressive ceremony attended by the *rebbe* of Ger and Chortkov and some 5,000 people. Over the entrance of the *yeshivah* were engraved the words of Psalms 34:12, *lekha banim, shimu li, yirat Hashem alamedkhem* ("Come ye children, hearken unto me.

I will teach you the fear of the Lord.") The *yeshivah* in Lublin was one of the finest pre-war buildings in Poland. It was six stories high with 120 rooms, a large auditorium, stately lecture halls, and a library of over 40,000 books. There was even a replica of the Temple, designed by Henokh Weintrop, to aid students in their study of *Kodashim* (The Fifth Order of the *Mishnah* that deals with the law of ritual slaughtering, sacrifices, and other subjects connected with Temple ritual).

The *yeshivah* opened with 120 students. Only the most promising were admitted. They were required to know 200 pages of the Talmud by heart. The *yeshivah* reflected the founder's concern for the comfort and well-being of the students. It had its own bakery and its own laundry. Once, when asked where he intended to find 500 rabbinical positions for the 500 students of the *yeshivah*, Rabbi Shapiro replied, "Only two of them will become rabbis, the other 498 will be lay people (*baalei battim*) capable of appreciating a rabbi."

In 1933 Rabbi Shapiro accepted an invitation to become rabbi of Lodz, the community undertaking to pay off the *yeshivah's* debt of 50,000 zlotys. The energetic rabbi had never enjoyed the best of health. On Monday, the 3rd day of *Heshvan* 1934, he suddenly became very ill. He took leave of his students and drank a *lehayim* (a toast to life) with them. He had insured his life for 50,000 zlotys. "It seems," he mused, "that the only thing that will relieve the *yeshivah* of its financial troubles is my death."[3] His dying words were, "only with joy." He died on Friday the 7th of *Heshvan* 1934. Among those who delivered eulogies was Rabbi Menahem Ziemba of Warsaw. The Memorial Prayer was recited by Cantor Yankele Hass. Although the Nazis completely destroyed the Jewish cemetery in Lublin, by some miracle, the tomb of Rabbi Meir remained untouched. On the 26th of *Elul* 1958, on his 25th *Yahrzeit*, his remains were reinterred on Har Hamenuhot in Jerusalem. He was the author of *Or Hameir*, printed in Piotrokow in 1926.

In the *Deutsche Jugend-zeitung* (February, 1940) we read:

> It was a matter of special pride to us, to destroy this Talmudic Academy, known as the greatest in Poland. We threw out of the building the large Talmudic library and brought it to the marketplace. There, we kindled a fire under the books. The conflagration lasted twenty hours. The Jews of Lublin stood around weeping bitterly. Their outcries rose above our own

voices. We summoned a military band, and the triumphant cries of the soldier drowned out the noise of the wailing Jews.[4]

The *Yeshivah* building has survived. It now houses the Lublin Medical College. The Hebrew words have been replaced by the words "Collegium Maius."

The Rabbi of Alexander

The rabbi of Alexander also attracted a vast multitude. Rabbi Isaac Menahem Mendel Danziger (1880–1942) stood at the helm for eighteen years, founding *yeshivot* both at Alexander and at Lodz. Like his father, Samuel Tzvi (d. 1924), author of *Tiferet Shmuel* ("The Glory of Samuel"), he stressed Torah, *tefillah* (prayer), and service to fellow men. Just as Warsaw was the stronghold of Ger, so Lodz, "the Manchester of Poland," was the capital of Alexander *hasidim*, and Lodz alone had no fewer than thirty-five Alexander *shtiblekh*. There were few towns in Poland that did not have such a *shtibl*.

Considerable rivalry existed between the followers of Ger and Alexander. Ger represented the power of the *Agudah*, and Belz supported the *Mahzikei HaDat*, while the rabbis of Alexander stood aloof from political parties. Alexander was the third force in hasidic Poland. Alexander, however, took no organized part in civic or national elections, leaving its followers free to follow their own political beliefs. Many were closely associated with the work of *Mizrahi*.

Hasidism Enters Warsaw

Paradoxically, although more than one-third of Warsaw's Jewish population were *hasidim*, the principal rabbis of the city were *mitnagdim*; among them were Rabbis Solomon Lipshitz, Hayim Davidsohn, Dov Berush Meisels, and Abraham Weinberg. Until the First World War, there were no hasidic rabbis at all in Warsaw, for the *rebbes* generally avoided the big cities. They preferred remote hamlets, where they could sequester themselves with their *hasidim*.

The First World War, however, brought a number of rabbis to Warsaw, and soon the capital of Poland became the home of over fifty *tzaddikim*.

Rabbi Bentzion Halberstam

The fourth day of *Av* is a tragic day for the *hasidim* of Bobow, for it is the anniversary of the brutal murder of the second rebbe of Bobow, son of the dynasty's founder. Rabbi Bentzion Halberstam was arrested by the Nazis together with his faithful disciple Avigdor Briner, his youngest son, Rabbi Moses Aaron, and his three sons-in-law. They were rabbi Ezekiel Shragai Halberstam (son of Rabbi Isaac Isaiah of Shtechow); Rabbi Moses Stempel, son of Rabbi Feivish Stempel (1880–1944), who was an elected member of the Polish Parliament from 1922–1927, and who, together with Dr. Raphael Landau, controlled the Jewish community of Krakow; and Rabbi Solomon Rubin (son of Rabbi Moses Rubin). Rabbi Bentzion's last wish was granted. He was allowed to don his Sabbath garments before they were taken to the outskirts of Lvov, compelled to dig their own graves, and brutally slain. Another son, Rabbi Hayim Joshua, was sent to Siberia, where he died in prison.

The dynasty of Bobow (Bobowa), a town in Western Galicia, was founded by Rabbi Solomon (1847–1906), a grandson of Rabbi Hayim Halberstam of Sanz. It was expanded and developed by his son, Rabbi Bentzion, who was born in 1874 in Bikovsk, where his father was rabbi. At Bentzion's *bar mitzvah*, in the home of his grandfather, Rabbi Joshua Rosenfeld of Kaminka (who died on the 17th of *Heshvan* 1887), Rabbi Bentzion inspired the gathering, not only with his learned discourses, but also with his melodies. Rabbi Bentzion first lived in Vishnitz, near Krakow, where his father served as rabbi for three years, and then settled in Bobow in 1893. He married Haya Freidel (1882–1974), a daughter of Rabbi Shalom Eliezer Halberstam (1863–1944), who was murdered in Auschwitz. When his father, Rabbi Solomon, died on the 1st of *Tammuz* 1906, his only son Rabbi Bentzion succeeded him.

The Importance of Song

A melodious singer as well as a noted scholar, Rabbi Bentzion combined the erudition of Sanz with the music of Ropczyce. He maintained that "Hasidism without a melody was like a body without a soul." "Serve the Lord with joy," was the vibrant theme that surged through Bobow. Simple folk melodies became vehicles for awesome concepts. When he heard Rabbi Bentzion sing the elegy, "By the rivers of Babylon," the famous cantor, Yossele Rosenblatt (1882–1935) exclaimed, "Without a Holy Spirit (*Ruah Hakodesh*), it is impossible to compose such a melody."

Rabbi Bentzion adopted the musical concepts of Rabbi Naftali Tzvi Horowitz of Ropczyce and Rabbi Eliezer of Dzikow. He was blessed with a melodious voice and was renowned for his musical creativity. Naturally, he had received no formal grounding even in the rudiments of music theory, yet there was music in his veins. *Hasidim* flocked to listen to the compositions of this untutored genius. His father, Rabbi Solomon, loved to listen to his prayers. "If a Jew can pray like this before his Maker, we cannot stop him," he said. "He literally pours out his soul before the Creator."

Soon after he became *rebbe*, Rabbi Bentzion established a *yeshivah* in Bobow. During the First World War (1914–1918), he lived in Vienna, then the home of Rabbi Abraham Jacob Friedmann of Sadgora. For a short time too, Rabbi Bentzion lived in Marienbad. In 1919, he returned to Krakow and then to Bobow, where he established the *yeshivah Eitz Hayim* in memory of Rabbi Hayim of Sanz, the *Divrei Hayim*. He established a network of forty-six such *yeshivot* throughout Galicia. A special organization called *Tomkhei Oraita* ("supporters of learning") cared for the material needs of the students.

Rabbi Bentzion was one of the first hasidic rabbis to pay special attention to the young, whom he treated with tenderness and consideration. He urged his followers to live in harmony and to "avoid controversy and dissension so that love and friendship prevail among you." He stressed that the *hasidim* should refrain from talking during prayers and during *Keriat HaTorah* (Reading of the Law). He advised them to avail themselves of the best medical treatment for "an experienced physician is to be preferred." The rabbi participated in communal affairs, often intervening successfully with the government departments.

Fighting Anti-Semitic Legislation

On February 7, 1936, a bill of so-called "humane slaughter" was introduced in the Polish Sejm by Deputy Janina Prystor, wife of the Senate Speaker and former Prime Minister of Poland, requiring among other things, that animals be stunned before they are slaughtered, a measure designed to outlaw *shehitah*. The Prystor Bill, a near replica of an earlier Nazi-sponsored, Bavarian anti-*shehitah* bill, was adopted almost unanimously. The Rabbi of Bobow participated at a meeting held in Warsaw of 300 rabbis at which a "Fortnight Without Meat" was proclaimed. From March 14 to March 30, Jews were required to refrain from all meat (except poultry, which was not affected by the bill) even on the Sabbath and to observe a day of fasting. Yielding to pressure by the Jewish community, the Government permitted *shehitah* for a limited quantity of meat "for groups in the population whose religion requires a special method of slaughtering."[5]

Helping Jewish Refugees

On October 28, 1938, over 15,000 Polish Jews residing in Germany, some of whom had spent most of their lives in that country, were roused from their beds by the Nazis and driven across the frontier into Poland. Among them were old people, invalids, and infants. The train stopped four miles from the Polish frontier, and the passengers were ordered to leave the carriages. Five-thousand Jews were kept virtual prisoners in a camp at Zbanszyn, a small Polish township, where they lived under the most pitiful conditions, suffering fever and pestilence. The rebbe of Bobow wholeheartedly supported the organization of relief measures. "We must be mindful of the plight of those of our brethren who have been expelled from their native soil," the rebbe wrote. "The rich should give more, and the poor should not give less. Let everyone contribute according to his ability." Polish Jewry rose heroically to the occasion and raised thirty-two million zlotys out of their own depleted resources.[6]

Living By Law, Service and Deeds of Kindness

The *rebbe* based his lifestyle on Torah, *avodah* (ritual service), and practice of charity. He established and maintained *yeshivot* to counteract the secular spirit of the inter-war years and was also concerned with the physical welfare of the student. He knew each of them, and each had access to him. He urged them not to be ascetic, for asceticism weakens the body and enables the evil powers to dominate. He forbade the reading of secular or heretical literature. He himself burned a carton of "missionary" books received by post from England.

His charity was legendary. No one ever left his house empty-handed. He would pay the medical bills of his indigent *hasidim* and would arrange marriages for his students. He was particularly concerned with the plight of orphans. When Rabbi Solomon Leib of Linsk, an orphaned scholar in Bobow, was about to be married, the rabbi himself sent for Mendel the tailor and selected the materials for the groom's garments. Similarly, his wife Hayah Freidel, took the bride to Tarnow and bought her a trousseau. At the wedding, the rebbe rejoiced as if his only child was getting married. Death held no terror for him. "How can we hide from the pangs of the Messiah?" he asked. The rabbi's commentary on the Pentateuch, *Kedushat Tziyon*, was printed in New York in 1967 by his son. The second part was published in 1978.

The rebbe has no tombstone. His grave is not known, but he lives in the dynamic work of his son Rabbi Solomon, who revived the spirit of Bobow in New York and, in 1958, laid the foundation of Kiryat Bobow at Bat Yam, Israel. "In my eye I can already envisage Kiryat Bobow as a traditional city," said Rabbi Joseph Kahaneman, *Rosh Yeshivah* of the Yeshivah of Ponovezh in Bnei Berak. London also boasts a spacious Bobow *yeshivah*, due to the efforts of Rabbi Leibish Stempel. Out of the ashes, Bobow lives again.

Rabbi Samuel Engel of Radomyshl

Hasidim were often accused by *mitnagdim* of disparaging scholarship, but the accusation was unfounded. While Hasidism certainly reached out to the unlettered masses, it also attempted to bring them closer to a Torah-centered life. It never lost sight of the fact that only through study could this ideal be fully realized. Rabbi Dov Baer, the *Maggid* of Mezhirech and Rabbi Shneur Zalman of Liady were among the great talmudists of their generation. In the nineteenth and twentieth centuries many *hasidim* in Poland, Galicia, and Hungary were acknowledged experts of the Torah. Outstanding scholars included the Holy Jew of Przysucha, Rabbi Menahem Mendel

Morgenstern of Kotzk, Rabbi Isaac Meir Alter of Ger, Rabbi Abraham Bornstein of Sochaczew, and Rabbi Tzvi Hirsch Spira of Munkacs, the *Pit'hei Teshuvah.*

One of the greatest hasidic scholars of the inter-war years was Rabbi Samuel Engel of Radomyshl. He was a shy and reticent man who shunned the public eye. Yet halakhic questions were addressed to him from all over the world, and his decisions were accepted without question. His scholarship was immense, and his ability to marshal arguments was masterly. He was deeply concerned with the plight of the *agunah* (a woman whose husband was believed dead but whose death could not be proved), one of the most difficult problems in rabbinic jurisprudence. This problem was compounded by the mass exodus of Eastern European Jews in the years following 1881, the casualties suffered during the First World War, and the postwar pogroms. Rabbi Joel Serkes once declared that "to endeavor to alleviate the lot of the *agunah* is as meritorious as rebuilding one of the desolations of Jerusalem." Rabbi Samuel was always mindful of this comment. He generally adopted the "lenient approach," and, consequently, hundreds of women were spared lives of loneliness and unassuaged grief. His rulings were invariably upheld by his contemporaries, in fact, according to Rabbi Joseph of Rymanow, "the rulings of the *Maharash* (Rabbi Samuel) were accepted by the Heavenly Court."

The Illui *of Tarnow*

Rabbi Samuel was born on *Rosh Hodesh Iyyar* 1858, in Tarnow, Galicia. His father, Zeev Wolf, was related to Rabbi Joseph ben Judah Engel (1859–1920); author of 100 works on *halakhah, aggadah,* and *Kabbalah.* Zeev Wolf died when Samuel was only 6 years old. His mother, Esther, took the child to Rabbi Hayim Halberstam, the *Divrei Hayim,* rebbe of Sanz. The rebbe said to him, "I will give you three pieces of advice. First, do not study the vernacular; I know you are blessed with a good mind but the study of the vernacular muddles the mind. Second, always pray from a *siddur* (rather than repeat prayers by heart), and third, always listen to your mother. King Solomon was deemed worthy of kingship because he had hearkened to his mother's counsel."

As a youth, Rabbi Samuel showed considerable intellectual

ability, and the zeal for study that characterized him throughout his life. By the age of 14, he was already renowned as the "*illui* of Tarnow," for he knew by heart the commentaries of *Havvat Daat* by Rabbi Jacob Lirmatowski and the *Peri Megadim* by Rabbi Joseph ben Meir Teumim. He was blessed with a phenomenal memory. Like the *tanna* Rabbi Eleazar ben Hyrcanus, he was "a cemented cistern that loses not a drop." His contemporaries were lavish in their praise. Rabbi Dov Berish Katz Rapoport, author of *Derekh HaMelekh* on Maimonides (Lvov, 1892), remarked, "I have discussed the concept of usury with many scholars but none of them showed Rabbi Samuel's grasp of the subject."

At the age of 16, he married the daughter of Rabbi Isaac of Bilgoray and remained in the home of his father-in-law for twelve happy years, studying eighteen hours a day. To everything he did he brought great energy, and in his intensive study he seemed to find rest and refreshment. The rabbi of Gorlice, Rabbi Barukh Halberstam, described the ardent young scholar as "a cupboard full of books." "Unique in his generation," was the comment of Rabbi Eleazar Shapiro, the *Minhat Eleazar*. "Only two people grasped my discourse," said Rabbi Hayim Halberstam, "one was the rabbi of Bergsasz (author of *Kol Aryeh*) and the other was Rabbi Samuel of Bilgoray."

In 1878, at the age of 20, Rabbi Samuel became rabbi in Bilgoray and received his rabbinical diploma from Rabbi Shneur Zalman Ashkenazi, author of *Torat Hessed* (Warsaw, 1883).

After a peaceful seven years in Bilgoray, he was forced to flee in order to escape the wrath of the Russian authorities who were suspicious of his Austrian citizenship. He stayed in Rudnick for nearly two years, with Rabbi Barukh of Gorlice with whom he studied *Kabbalah*. It was at the suggestion of Rabbi Barukh that Rabbi Samuel became the head of the *beit din* of Duklo. In 1886, he became rabbi of Radomysl, where he stayed until the outbreak of the First World War. Then he found refuge in Waitzen. In 1917, he settled in Kosice, Hungary (later part of Czechoslovakia), where, as *Av Beit Din*, he spent eighteen years. When Rabbi Issahar Dov Rokeach of Belz visited the town, he paid Rabbi Samuel a courtesy visit. He walked up the stairs to his home. "To visit Rabbi Samuel," said the *rebbe* of Belz, "even self-sacrifice is warranted." Rabbi Samuel was friendly with the *rebbes* of Chortkov and Vishnitz, who sent their sons to receive rabbinical diplomas from him.

While he was lenient in interpreting the laws that applied to the hapless *agunah*, he did not compromise when it came to Sabbath and the laws of family purity. "When Sabbath violations are widespread," he wrote to Rabbi David Tzvi Zehman of Duklo, "one cannot adopt permissive views." On laws of *Mikvaot* he totally endorsed the views of the Rabbi Hayim Halberstam of Sanz. He set high standards for the community's *shohetim*, and he urged them to spend their spare time studying and doing charity. He did not favor the idea of combining the duties of a *shohet* with that of a *hazzan*. Each day, before reciting the prayers, he would recite eighteen chapters of Psalms. He would then study the *Rav*'s *Shulhan Arukh*, which he regarded as an indispensable guide to the intricate laws of Passover. He would study the *No'am Elimelekh, Benei Yissaskhar*, and *Tiferet Shlomo* daily. Not a day would pass without his mentioning the name of the *Divrei Hayim* and his descendants.

Although he was not a flamboyant orator, his powers of persuasion were considerable. He was tireless and single-minded in pursuing the goals to which he was committed. His humility was proverbial. He even refused to wear rabbinic garb. Throughout his life, this man of peace never involved himself in controversies or dissension. Shortly before his demise, he was invited to become rabbi of Tarnow, his native town, but due to ill health and advancing years he decided not to accept the offer. He died on the eve of Shabbat *KiTissa*, the 19th of *Adar* 1935. His third wife, Sprinze, daughter of Rabbi Abraham Hurwitz, died two months later.

The *Maharash* was a prolific writer. In Jaroslav in the year 1905, he published the first part of a work consisting of ninety-nine responsa. Part 2, containing another seventy-two responsa, appeared in 1908. Part 3, with 124 responsa, was printed in 1925, and Part 4, with 104 responsa, in 1929. In 1936, his son-in-law, Rabbi David Halpern, published Part 5, with 110 responsa and in 1938, Part 6, with 130 responsa. His erudite grandson, Rabbi Elhanan Halpern of London, resumed publication of the literary legacy of his grandfather, and he printed *Shem Shmuel* in 1941, Part 7 of the responsa in 1957, and Part 8 in 1958. Rabbi Halpern also printed *Siftei Maharash* on Torah and *Hiddushei Maharash* on *Kiddushin* (1966), as well as a complete edition of all Rabbi Samuel's work printed in Jerusalem in 1981.

Rabbi Samuel was survived by two sons, Rabbi Hayim and Rabbi Tzvi, and by five daughters. Rabbi Hayim succeeded his father as rabbi of Radomysl, and Rabbi Tzvi perished in the Holocaust. It was not without reason that the Zieshonover Rabbi called Rabbi Samuel "the *Noda BeYehudah* of our times." Rabbi Samuel perhaps did not have a definitive answer for every question, but in the thousands of responsa produced by this noble prince of the Torah, many Jews found and are still finding direction and inspiration.

Chapter 21

Pillars of Eastern Europe

There were sizeable hasidic groups outside Poland. Rabbi Moses Teitelbaum, the "*Yismah Moshe,*" was a man of many talents: hasidic *rebbe,* halakhic scholar, *yeshivah* principal, and codifier of considerable authority. Indeed it was Rabbi Moses Teitelbaum who brought Hungarian Jewry into the hasidic world.

Born in Przemysl, Galicia, in 1759, the son of Rabbi Tzvi Hirsch of Zbarow, he traced his ancestry to Rabbi Moses Isserles (1525-1572), the *Rema,* and Rabbi Abraham Joshua Jacob Heschel (d. 1664), who headed *yeshivot* in Lublin and Krakow after the Chmielnicki massacres. Rabbi Heschel was the author of *Toledot Aharon* (Lublin, 1682) and *Hiddushei Halakhah* (Offenbach, 1723). Rabbi Moses studied under his uncle, Rabbi Joseph of Kalbaszow and Rabbi Aryeh Leib Halevi, author of *Derishat Ari* on *Even Ezer* (Lvov, 1804).

Rabbi Moses married Hayeh Sarah, daughter of the wine merchant Rabbi Nisan of Przemysl. "Three young men seek your hand in marriage," the father informed his daughter. "One is poor but a scholar; another is rich and has a smattering of scholarship; the third is exceedingly wealthy but exceedingly ignorant." "What makes a man wealthy?" replied the daughter, "if not knowledge of the Law of God?"[1]

Hasidic Influences on Rabbi Moses

After his marriage, Rabbi Moses returned to Strzyzow where he resided for three years. At the age of 17, he was reputed to know

800 pages of the Talmud by heart. In 1788, his father-in-law died, and Rabbi Moses became rabbi in Sieniawa, Galicia. Rabbi Moses succeeded Rabbi Barukh Teumim Frankel, who became rabbi in Leipnik. Rabbi Moses' only daughter, Miriam Hannah, married Rabbi Aryeh Leibish Lipschitz, author of *Aryeh Devei Ila'i* and five tractates and responsa *Ateret Zekenim* on Talmud (Przemysl, 1874). He was also a follower of Rabbi Jacob Isaac, the Seer of Lublin. It was due to the influence of his son-in-law that Rabbi Moses visited the Seer. In fact, he visited the Seer three times. Rabbi Moses also visited Rabbi Israel, the *Maggid* of Kozienice, Rabbi Menahem Mendel of Rymanow, and Rabbi Abraham Joshua Heschel of Opatow, the *Ohev Yisrael*.

Beliefs and Dreams

When Rabbi Moses became rabbi in Ujhely (Satorjhely), a city in East Hungary, it was one of the main Jewish settlements in Hungary, and Jews had lived there since 1771.

Rabbi Moses was punctilious in observing the prescribed hours of prayer as laid down in the *Shulhan Arukh*. He was a mystic, to whom religious secrets were revealed in dreams. Once, in a dream, he was taken to the Garden of Eden, where he saw *tannaim* studying the Talmud. "Is this, then, all there is in Paradise?" the rabbi exclaimed in astonishment. He was told, "You are wrong in believing that the *tannaim* are in Paradise. Paradise is in the *tannaim*." It was also revealed to him in a dream, that the reason Rabbi Isaac Luria lived for only thirty-four years was because the wicked Balaam also lived to the same age, and Rabbi Isaac Luria was destined to atone for the evil wrought by Balaam.

Rabbi Moses lived in daily expectation of the coming of the Messiah. Each night before he went to sleep, he would prepare his Sabbath clothes and remind the beadle to wake him the moment the Messiah arrived. Whenever the rabbi heard a noise, he would ask, "Has he come?"

Like Rabbi Levi Isaac of Berdichev, Rabbi Moses would hold "public dialogues" with the Almighty. On the eve of the Day of Atonement in his eighty-second year, he is said to have exclaimed, "Master of the Universe. Had I known in my youth that I would grow old before the coming of the Messiah, I would not have been able to survive all these years. I would have died in anguish. Only faith and hope have kept me alive to this day."[2]

Rabbi Moses lived in humble quarters and refused to let his *hasidim* provide him with a more suitable home. "Why should I build a house here in the land of the Gentiles? Surely the Messiah will come soon, and I will return to the land of my forefathers." Once he remarked, "I cannot understand why the *tzaddikim*, in the world of Eternity, are not trying to hasten the coming of the Messiah. They should turn heaven and earth upside down. Perhaps, when they enter the Garden of Eden, they become oblivious to what happens to mortal man."[3]

On another occasion, he cried out, "Lord of the Universe, grant my request and let the Messiah come. I am not concerned for my own welfare. I care only for sufferings of the *Shekhinah*, the Divine Presence, grieving over the grief of your children." *Hasidim* attributed to Rabbi Moses the soul of Jeremiah, the prophet who lamented the destruction of Jerusalem. Rabbi Moses distributed *Kamaot* (amulets) to petitioners who requested them, and even scholars sought his blessings. When his son was sick, Rabbi Moses Sofer (1762–1839), famous for his seven-volume responsa *Hatam Sofer*, entreated Rabbi Moses to pray for a quick and complete recovery. Even Gentiles sought the Rabbi's blessings. The mother of Louis Kossuth (1802–1894), who later headed the struggle for Hungarian independence from Austria, came to the *rebbe* when her child was ill.

Religious Customs and Practice

Rabbi Moses made thirteen *Takkanot* (enactments). He opposed mixed dancing and forbade Jews to hire gentiles to work for them on the Sabbath. Every Sabbath from *Rosh Hodesh Elul* to *Hoshana Rabba*, he delivered a discourse in the synagogue. He wore a *shtreimel* (fur hat) even on weekdays. He would rise at 5:00 A.M. and rarely completed the morning service before 2:00 or 3:00 P.M. The evening service would take place when it was almost midnight. He fasted on the Fast of the First Born (the eve of Passover) and would not take advantage of the *siyyum* in order to forgo the fast. Although he stressed the need for humility, he insisted that men should also glory in being a "creation of God."

His wife died on the eve of *Rosh Hodesh Nisan* 1840. Rabbi

Moses died on Sabbath, the 28th of *Tammuz* 1841. He asked the leaders of the community to appoint as his successor his son, Rabbi Eleazar Nisan (1786–1855). Twenty-five years after his death, his grandson Rabbi Jekutiel Judah published his responsa *Heishiv Moshe* (Lvov, 1866). Rabbi Moses was also the author of *Yismah Moshe* (Lvov, 1849–1861), discourses on the Torah, on Prophets (Marmaros Sighet, 1906), and *Tefillah LeMoshe*, commentary on Psalms (Krakow, 1880). It was the *Yismah Moshe*, as Rabbi Moses was called, who caused Hasidism to flourish in Hungary. He founded the great hasidic dynasties of Sighet and Satmar.

The Spread of Hasidism to Hungary

There are indications of the presence of Jewish communities in Hungary as early as the ninth century. Under the Ottoman regime Jews enjoyed a large measure of civic equality and religious liberty, although they were subject to heavy taxes. The Turkish rule ended with the Peace of Carlowitz in 1699, finally ending the Muslim attempt to conquer Europe. Hungary became the possession of the Hapsburgs, and a new era began for the Jews.

The influx of Austrian and German Jews was followed by the settlement of Moravian and Bohemian Jews. Jews distinguished themselves in the economic recovery of Hungary, particularly during the reign of Emperor Joseph II. The more enlightened Judaic regulations (1782) gave the Jews permission to settle in all cities of the Empire, and the rights to establish schools, lease lands, and engage in all trades and professions. The Jewish badge was abolished, but Jews were required to adopt German names.

Rabbi Eizig of Kallo

According to tradition, Rabbi Israel Baal Shem Tov visited Hungary in 1746, and Rabbi Levi Isaac of Berdichev lived in Crolly for a time. Rabbi Aaron of Zhitomir spent three years in Hungary, but the founder of Hasidism in Hungary was Rabbi Eizig Isaac Taub, rabbi of Nagykallo (Kallo). The "Kalever Rebbe," as he was popularly known, was born in Szerencz (Zempen county, northeastern Hungary) in 1751. It was said that two of his ancestors,

Ezekiel and Eizig, had fled from Spain after the expulsion of the Jews in 1492. Eizig's father, Ezekiel, leased land in Szerencz from Count Almassy.

Eizig, the elder of his two sons, was a frail child. Like Moses and King David, Eizig was a shepherd. While feeding his flock, he would say, "Master of the Universe, I wish to emulate your attributes and have compassion for every creature." He was blessed with a melodious voice and fervently believed in the words of Rabbi Johanan, "If one reads the Scriptures without a melody or repeats the *Mishnah* without a tune, of him Scripture says, 'Wherefore I gave them also statutes that were not good' " (Ezekiel 20:25).

At first, he studied under a tutor, Rabbi Isaac of Przeworsk. Later he became a disciple of Rabbi Shmelke Horowitz of Nikolsburg (1726–1778). Returning home, he became the teacher of the children of Jacob Fisch, the head of the Jewish community of Nagykallo. Some years later he became the rabbi of Nagykallo. He married Feige, the daughter of Ansil Kohn of Tarezak.

The Shepherd's Song

Some hasidic sources state that it was Rabbi Aryeh Leib Sarah's (1730–1791) who discovered Rabbi Eizig. Leib Sarah's was the itinerant *tzaddik* who wandered through the countryside always seeking new adherents. He heard the young shepherd Eizig singing, "*Shekhinah, Shekhinah,* how far away you are; *galut, galut* how long you are. But if the *galut* were not so long, we could be together." After listening for a while, Rabbi Leib Sarah's asked the boy who taught him the song: "Why, all the herdsmen here sing these words," came the reply. "Do they really use these words?" insisted the rabbi. "No," explained the lad. "Instead of *Shekhinah,* they say 'beloved.' " Rabbi Leib Sarah's asked Eizig's parents for permission to take the boy to Rabbi Shmelke, and the little shepherd's melody became popular with many *tzaddikim*. Rabbi Hayim Halberstam of Sanz, the *Divrei Hayim,* hummed it every Friday night before reciting *Kiddush*.

Rabbi Eizig was also believed to have been a disciple of Rabbi Elimelekh of Lyzhansk. Like Rabbi Aryeh Leib Sarah's, Rabbi Eizig was always ready to help the poor and the needy, and he followed the precepts of Hasidism as taught by Rabbi Shmelke and Rabbi

Elimelekh. But his songs and his stories are unique, and they have been lovingly preserved. His song, "The Cock is Crowing Already" (*Szol A Kakas Mar*) became popular throughout the country.

The cock is crowing already
It will be dawn already,
In the green forest, in the open field
A bird is walking.
But what a bird
But what a bird,
Legs yellow and wings blue
It's waiting for me there.
Wait, my rose, wait
Just you always wait,
If God willed me for you
I shall be yours.
But when will it be already?
Yiboneh hamikdosh ir Zion temalleh
(When the Temple will be rebuilt and Zion will be repopulated)[4]

His melodies express the grief of the *Shekhinah* in exile and the yearnings of the House of Israel for redemption.

He was venerated by his *hasidim* and highly regarded by the *Hatam Sofer*, Rabbi Moses Sofer (Schreiber), and by Rabbi Hayim Tirer of Czernowitz. Rabbi Eizig was tireless in mustering support for the poor in the Holy Land. He was president of the *Kollel Eretz Yisrael*, and he undertook the task of transmitting to the Holy Land the money collected by Rabbi Moses Teitelbaum.

Before his death, the *rebbe* sent for the *Hevrah Kaddisha* and instructed them, "Do not inscribe words of praise upon my tombstone. I have never liked flattery. The marble slab should only tell the onlooker that I was a simple and honest Jew who studied the law and taught the people with truth and love." In the year 1821, on the 7th day of *Adar* II, Rabbi Eizig died. He had been rabbi of Szaboloz county for forty years. The brief inscription on his tombstone conforms to his last wishes. It read: "He could study and was an honest Jew."[5] All male children born to his *hasidim* in the year following his death were named after him.

For nearly twenty years afterward, the position of rabbi in Nagykallo remained vacant. His tomb became a much frequented place of pilgrimage especially on *Lag B'Omer*. His son, Rabbi Moses

Hayim (d. 27th of *Tammuz* 1831) of Radzol succeed him as *rebbe*. Rabbi Eizig was justly known as the "Saintly Rabbi of Kallo" or the "Singing Tzaddik."

The Dynasty of Munkacs

Munkacs was the home of Rabbi Solomon Spira, the founder of the dynasty of Munkacs in Carpathian Russia, who left an imprint on Hasidism and *halakhah*. He had an extraordinary and many-sided personality. Zest and vitality, courage and enthusiasm flowed from him. Rabbi Solomon was born on the Sabbath, the seventh day of *Hanukkah* 1832, in Lancut. His father, Rabbi Elazar of Lancut, author of *Yodei Binah* on Torah (Przemysl, 1911), was the son of Rabbi Tzvi Elimelekh of Dynow, the *Benei Yissaskhar*. When his father accepted the position as rabbi of Lancut, Rabbi Solomon succeeded him as rabbi of Strzyzow where he spent twenty-two years. Even-tempered and on good terms with all, he could administer a well-deserved rebuke without creating resentment. His lively personality filled his followers with vigor and warmth. In 1880 he became rabbi in Munkacs (Mukacevo) the town where his grandfather, the *Benei Yissaskhar* had been rabbi. After the death of Rabbi Moses Teitelbaum, Rabbi Solomon took a leading role in supervising and maintaining the orthodox and traditional trends of Jewish education in Hungary. Whatever he took up, he carried through with untiring thoroughness. He was utterly fearless in argument, for his position was always based on full knowledge of the facts and strong personal conviction.

Rabbi Solomon–A Great Collector of Books

He was a great bibliophile and diligently sought early Hebrew printed books. This tradition of book collecting was continued by his descendants. On one occasion, a number of precious manuscripts were stolen from his library. The rebbe was terribly distressed. He did not give any discourses on the following Sabbath. "It seems," he told his *hasidim*, "that my Torah is not desired by Heaven." On the following day, one of his *hasidim*, Moses Joseph Lefkowitz, came and told him the good tidings that a fisherman had found the stolen manuscripts by the river. The rebbe was overjoyed, and he omitted saying *Tahanun* (prayer of supplication) on that day, regarding it as a semi-festive day.

He died on the 21st day of *Sivan* 1883. Prior to his death, he washed his hands and said, "I feel like a *kohen* prior to his *Avodah* (ritual service) in the *Beit Hamikdash*." He was survived by two sons, Rabbi Moses Leib of Strzyzow (1850–1917) and Rabbi Tzvi Hirsch (1845–1914). Under his older son, Munkacs became a great center of Hasidism. Tzvi Hirsch was a disciple of Rabbi Hayim Halberstam of Sanz and of Rabbi Ezekiel of Sianawa. Tzvi Hirsch was one of the greatest halakhic luminaries of Hasidism. He wrote a monumental work, *Darkei Teshuvah* ("Ways of Repentance") on *Yoreh De'ah*. Among his other noted works were *Tzvi Tiferet* and *Be'er Lehai Ro'i* ("The Well of the Living One Who Seeth Me") on the *Zohar*. He played a prominent part as a rabbi and *rosh yeshivah* (dean of *yeshivah*) and was the uncompromising spokesman of the *hasidim* in Hungary and Galicia. No problem defied his analysis. His masterly responsa reflected Jewish life in all its ramifications. The greatest talmudic authorities enthusiastically welcomed his works. He died on the 15th day of *Tishri* in the year 1914.

The Minhat Eleazar

His son Hayim Eliezer (1868–1937) was an outstanding scholar. Among Hayim Eleazar's works were responsa, *Minhat Eleazar* ("The Offering of Eleazar"), in four parts. He was a great opponent of both political Zionism and the *Agudat Yisrael*. Few escaped his censure. In the parliamentary election of 1935, he made the following appeal to his followers:

> I am writing to you concerning the elections for Parliament, a subject on which no Jew may remain silent, though many say, either out of ignorance or a desire to deceive, that the voting has nothing to do with the question of Jewish religion. In view of this it is my duty to proclaim that according to our Holy Law it is forbidden to offer the slightest assistance to the Zionist heretics and free thinkers, much less to vote for their candidate, who is a traitor to our Torah and seducer of our young Jewish children in his Hebrew secondary school, that

> source of heresy and disobedience to our God, Messiah, Torah and the Holy Faith which we have inherited from our rabbis and forefathers. Every Jew must do this to oppose this danger. Furthermore, every Jew, young or old, who voices an opinion in favor of the Zionist list for Parliament, is sinning gravely by abetting the criminals, of the likes of such our Torah says "Cursed be he who does not keep the words of this law."[6]

He was embroiled in a bitter controversy with Rabbi Issahar Dov Rokeah of Belz. Their animosity was more a result of differences in temperament than of the conflicting religious opinions held by the two rivals. This was a clash of two forceful personalities. They were both difficult and dogmatic, and neither was of a conciliatory disposition.

Vishnitz

Influential, too, was the dynasty of Vishnitz, which was founded by the Kabbalist Jacob Kopul (d. 1787) of Kolomyja, in Galicia. His son Rabbi Menahem Mendel (1768–1826) settled in Kosov, not far from Stanislaw, near the Hungarian border. The *rebbe*, like the Besht, lived by three principles: love of God, love of Israel, and love of the Torah. He maintained that his three-fold ideal could be achieved through music. The traditions of Rabbi Menahem Mendel were continued by his son Rabbi Hayim (1795–1854). Rabbi Hayim's youngest son, Rabbi Menahem Mendel (1830–1885), settled in Vishnitz (which then belonged to Austria) and married Miriam, the daughter of Rabbi Israel Friedman, founder of the Ruzhin-Sadgora dynasty. Modeling himself after his father-in-law, Rabbi Menahem Mendel built a palatial residence with a large *Beit HaMidrash* surrounded by gardens and orchards. He employed a man whose sole duty was to distribute money anonymously to charitable causes. Such vast sums were involved that his son-in-law Rabbi Nahum of Stefanesti remarked, "If the rabbi of Vishnitz had kept for himself all the money he has given to charity, he would have been richer than Rothschild." Rabbi Menahem Mendel's son, Rabbi Barukh (1845–1893), also made his home in Vishnitz, where he published his father's writings and works on the Pentateuch entitled *Imrei Barukh* (Kolomyya, 1912). He died at the age of 48, leaving twelve children. The most outstanding of Rabbi Barukh's progeny was Rabbi Israel (1860–1933), known among the *Hasidim* as *Ohev Yisrael* ("Lover of Israel"). He succeeded his father as rabbi of Vishnitz when he was 33 and was particularly interested in education, setting up a Talmud Torah and a *yeshivah Beit Yisrael* ("The House of Israel"). With the outbreak of World War I, he found refuge in Grosswardein (Nagyvarad) in Transylvania. A staunch supporter of the *Agudah*, Rabbi Israel often urged his followers to vote for the "right candidate" at elections. Many *tzaddikim* were among his disciples and from these distinguished followers he refused to accept money. "A coachman does not charge a fellow coachman," he said with a smile. Rabbi Israel's discourses are to be found in *Ahavat Yisrael* (Grosswardein, 1943). Fourteen years after Rabbi Israel's death, he was reburied in Bnei Berak on the Fast of Esther, 1949. His son welcomed the coffin with the Vishnitz melody *"Shalom Aleichem"* ("Welcome ye Ministering Angels"). Three of Rabbi Israel's five sons settled in the Holy Land.

Spinka

Rabbi Isaac Eizig Weiss (1875–1944) of Spinka, son of Rabbi Joseph Meir, a disciple of Rabbi Sholem of Belz, had thousands of followers throughout Hungary. In Unterland, the lower part of Hungary, and in Marmaros there were large groups of *hasidim*. A hasidic Jew even became the vice-president of the Central Orthodox Bureau.[7]

Vienna–Refuge for Hasidism's Leaders

During the First World War, between 200,000 and 300,000 Jews found refuge in Austria, 77,000 of them in Vienna.[8] Prominent among them was Rabbi Israel Friedmann (1858–1933) of Husyatin, author of *Tiferet Yisrael* ("The Glory of Israel"). He advocated the establishment of *Torah Melakhah* schools, where study of the Torah could be combined with craft-training. His son, Nahum Mordekhai (d. 1946), wielded great influence from his home in Heinestrasse, Vienna. The other hasidic rabbis who lived in Vienna were Rabbi Abraham Jacob Friedmann of Sadgora (1887–1961), Rabbi Mordekhai Sholem Friedmann of Boyan, Rabbi Mordekhai Shragai

Freedmann of Husyatin, Rabbi Mordekhai Shalom Joseph Freedmann of Sadgora-Przemysl and Rabbi Isaac Meir Heschel of Kopyczynce (1864–1933). His son Abraham Joshua Heschel remained in Vienna until 1933. There, together with Akiva Schreiber, he founded the *Shomer Shabbat* organization to stimulate Sabbath observance. The Ninth and the Second Districts of the capital of Austria resounded with the songs and discourses of the *hasidim.*[9]

Chapter 22

In the Shadow of Death

With the outbreak of the Second World War on September 1, 1939, the fate of Eastern European Jewry was sealed. The Jewish leaders called upon the community to "defeat the intentions of Hitler to make Poland a country of slaves." The rabbis of Sochaszew, Alexander, and Ger urged their *hasidim* to subscribe generously to the Polish Air Defense Loan. "The fate of Jewry," wrote the rebbe of Ger, "is bound up with the fate of the State." Physically as well as financially, Polish Jews, including the *hasidim*, played an active role in defense measures. Old and young, some of them with dangling *peiot* (earlocks) and long *kapotes*, dug trenches, even on the Sabbath, in view of the imminence of war. However, the partially mobilized Polish army was no match for the superior armaments of the enemy. Against the Nazi blitzkrieg and the Russian invasion, Polish resistance was quashed in a month. The Jews were helpless as systematic persecution began in the towns and the villages, the first steps towards the Nazi objective of genocide.

The Ghetto in Warsaw

The population of Warsaw multiplied rapidly as Jews were transferred from provincial towns and as refugees flowed in from outlying areas. In the six years between 1939 and 1945, the culture of millennia perished in a bloodbath such as the world has never seen. Poland became a central cemetery for the great Jewish communities of Europe. By the time a ghetto was established on October 16, 1940, there were, in that confined area, between 450,000 and 500,000 Jews. The three years of agony that followed actually brought a revival of Hasidism. Many Polish hasidic rabbis had found refuge in Warsaw, and even *maskilim* would come to them for comfort and inspiration.

In the valley of the shadow of death, they sang their melodies and served their Maker as best they could. There was not enough food for *shirayim*, but nothing could extinguish the indomitable optimism of Hasidism.

Chaim A. Kaplin, in his *Scroll of Agony*, records:

> Even though we are now undergoing terrible tribulation, and the sun has grown dark for us at noon, we have not lost our hope that a ray of light will surely come. Our existence as a people will not be destroyed. Individuals will be destroyed, but the Jewish community will live on. . . . *Hasidim* were even dancing, as is their pious custom. Someone told me that on the night of the holidays (*Sukkot*), he met a large group of zealous *hasidim* on Mila Street, and they sang festive songs in chorus and in public, followed by a large crowd of curious people and sightseers. Joy and revelry in poverty-stricken Mila Street. When they sang, they reached such a state of ecstasy that they could not stop until some heretic approached them shouting: "Jews, to safeguard your life is a positive biblical command; it is a time of danger for us. Stop this." Only then did they become quiet. Some of them replied in their ecstasy, "We are not afraid of the murderer."[1]

In the Judenrat, the Jewish Community Council (at 26 Grzybowska Street) set up by the Nazis under the chairmanship of Adam Chernikov, hasidic leaders were represented. Among them were Isaac Meir Levin (b. 1894), president of the *Agudah* in Poland (later Minister of Social Welfare in Israel, 1949–1952); Dov Shapira, Simon Stockmaker, and Eizig Ackerman. These overburdened men did their utmost to lighten the yoke of their brothers. By a decree of the chairman of the Council of January 20, 1941, the Sabbath was recognized as an official day of rest. A public soup kitchen for students was opened in the *Beit Yaakov* school on Nalewki Street. To the end, Meshullam Kaminer worked on a traditional Yiddish translation of the Bible, and Alexander Zusya Friedmann (b. 1897) organized an underground network of schools and study courses for young and old, so that the "Torah should not be forgotten in Israel."

On July 22, 1942, on the eve of the Fast of *Av*, deportations began, and the daily number of Jews transported from the ghetto to Treblinka reached 10,000 by October 1942. Within fifty-five days, 350,000 Jews had been deported to such demoniac death factories as Treblinka, Majdanek, Oswiecim (Auschwitz), Sobibor, Chelmno, and a dozen other infamous destinations. In the Schultz shoemaking factory at 44-46 Novolipki Street, the hasidic manager, Abraham Handel (later in Tel Aviv), sheltered many rabbis. Among the illustrious employees were Sholom Rabinowicz, son of Rabbi Hayim Meir of Neustadt; Moses Betzalel Alter, son of Judah Leib; Abraham Alter, rabbi of Pabianice; David Halberstam, rabbi of Sosnowiec; Rabbi Kalonymus Shapira of Piaseczno, author of *Hovot Hatalmidim* ("The Duties of the Disciples"); Alexander Zusya Friedmann, and Rabbi Joseph Perlow of Novominsk.

A survivor has drawn a vivid picture of this strange workshop:

> Here you see sitting at the wood blocks mending shoes (the work mostly consisted of pulling out nails with pliers) the Koziglower Rabbi, Aryeh Frumer, the former *rosh yeshivah* (dean) of *Yeshivat Hakhmei Lublin*. . . . From time to time he addresses a word to the rabbi of Piaseczno. . . . *Gemarot* (talmudical passages) and biblical texts are quoted, and the names of Maimonides and Rabbi Jacob ben Asher are mentioned, and who now cares about the S.S. men, about the Volksdeutsch supervisor, or about hunger and misery and persecution and the fear of death! Now they are soaring in higher regions. They are not in the shop at 46 Novolipki Street, where they were sitting, but in the lofty halls.[2]

Such hasidic leaders as Rabbi Moses David Rabinowicz, son-in-law of the rabbi of Radomsk, worked for a time for the *Hesed Shel Emet* Burial Society. Others were active in *Toz* (the Society for the Protection of Health among the Jews) or the *Judenrat,* which employed 5,000 people. The rabbis of Ger, Bobow, Lubavitch, and a few others, narrowly escaped the Holocaust. However, most of the hasidic rabbis in Poland, a total of well over 200, perished with their families and followers in the action that began on July 22, 1942, on the eve of *Tisha B'Av*. The Jewish historian Emanuel Ringelblum records, "Most of the rabbis were shot during the raids. The long beards and the sidelocks aroused the hatred of the Germans, and many a rabbi paid with his life for his great courage in sticking to his beard and sidelocks."[3]

The Heroic Deaths of the Rabbis

They died the death of martyrs under circumstances recalling only too closely Jewish heroism in the days of the Maccabees. Rabbi Ezekiel Halevy Halstock, son of the Rabbi of Ostrowiec, died together with his seven sons proclaiming the Jewish declaration of faith, "Hear O Israel, the Lord our God, the Lord is One." In Treblinka the rabbi of Alexander perished, as did Isaac Menahem Mendel Danziger and his seven sons-in-law; Rabbi Moses Betzalel, brother of the rabbi of Ger; Rabbi Hayim Jerahmiel Taub, the rabbi of Zwolen, and the Rabbi of Grodzisk. Rabbi Israel Shapira also met his Maker there in 1942, uttering the words of *Ani Maamin* ("I believe with a perfect faith in the coming of the Messiah").

Rabbi Benjamin Paltiel Morgenstern (b. 1895) of Sokolow, as well as Rabbi Isaac Weiss of Spinka (d. 1944) and Menahem Mendel Hager were murdered in Auschwitz. Every crematorium had its hasidic victims. Rabbi Elimelekh Aryeh Hakohen Rabinowicz, brother of the rabbi of Radomsk, died in Mauthausen. Rabbi Moses of Boyan (b. 1891), the spiritual head of the *Yeshivat Hakhmei Lublin*, died in 1943 at Belzec.

Moses Mordekhai Twersky

Another martyr was Rabbi Moses Mordekhai Twersky who was born in Turisk in 1877. It was there that he married Malka, daughter of Rabbi Barukh Meir Perlow of Azarnitz, Podolia, a descendant of Rabbi Aaron of Chernobyl. Thus he became the brother-in-law of Rabbi Alter Israel Simon Perlow, the *rebbe* of Novominsk. In 1918, Rabbi Moses Mordekhai settled in Lublin, where the Jewish population numbered 30,000 – some 30 percent of the town's population. His lifestyle was austere. He would rise at 2:30 A.M. and recite the entire *Sefer Tehillim* (The Book of Psalms), which he knew by heart. He would then repeat from memory the substance of the *kvitlekh* (petitions) that he had received from his *hasidim* the previous day, invoking the help of the Almighty on their behalf. After a brief rest, he would go to the *mikveh* and then to the *Beit HaMidrash* where he would conclude his morning prayers by 9:30 A.M. He would then drink two glasses of milk after which he would don *Tefillin Rabbenu Tam.* At 12:30 he ate a light lunch, his only meal of the day. The menu invariably consisted of a small roll and a quarter of a chicken, half of which was distributed to the *hasidim* as *shirayim.* After 4:00 P.M. he made himself available to all who came to unburden their hearts.

The lengthy discourses he delivered on Sabbath and festivals were filled with *Ahavat Yisrael.* On the last day of Passover, he would deliver five discourses on the Passover *haggadah.* On *Sukkot* he devoted four hours to the ritual waving of the *Arba'ah Minim.* On *Simhat Torah* the *rebbe* carried a small *Sefer Torah* while making the prescribed seven circuits as the *hasidim* watched intently. Every day he spent hours in private prayer but rarely officiated at the reader's desk. His Friday night melody of *Shalom Aleikhem* was renowned. Mothers would bring their young children to the *rebbe* so that he would place his hands on their heads and bless them individually.

An active president of the *Shomrei Shabbat Ve'haDat* Society, the *rebbe* succeeded in persuading many firms to close on Sabbath. In 1925 he gave support to the hasidic delegation led by Rabbi Aaron Kirshenbaum, Alexander Hasid, and his own son, Rabbi Abraham Isaac, to travel to the Holy Land in order to establish *Nahlat Lublin.* Subsequently, 7000 dunams were purchased in Hadera. During that time, the *rebbe* was closely linked with Rabbi Meir Shapiro, *rosh yeshivah* of *Yeshivat Hakhmei Lublin* (1925–1933). In 1931 he encouraged his son Rabbi Abraham Isaac to undertake a fund-raising mission to France and England on behalf of *Yeshivat Hakhmei Lublin.* Periodically, the *rebbe* would travel to different localities to meet his *hasidim.* However, he rarely visited Warsaw, since he did not wish to infringe on the territory of his brother, Rabbi Nahum (1875–1943), who lived on Mila Street and was known as the Trisker Rebbe.

The Fate of Rabbi Moses Mordekhai

Even the horrors of the Nazi occupation that destroyed Polish Jewry did not weaken the *rebbe*'s firm belief that justice would ultimately prevail. In one of his discourses during the war, he dealt with the matter of *eglah arufah*. In the event of an unsolved murder, there is a ritual ceremony in which the neck of a heifer is broken to atone for the land and the guilty person involved in the deed. It is significant the *rebbe* stressed that the section concerning *eglah arufah* (Deuteronomy 21: 1–9) is sandwiched in between two sections each of which begins with the identical words "When thou goest forth to battle against thine enemies." The moral is that even in times of war, when murder is so commonplace, when human life is cheap and of no account, we still should not become callous and come to disregard the shedding of innocent blood.

To escape arrest, the *rebbe* moved into the house of his follower Isaac Gitlis. His son Rabbi Abraham Isaac in London, and his *hasidim*, together with Dr. Schwartz, director of the Joint Distribution Committee in Europe, made valiant efforts to rescue him. Rabbi Abraham Isaac cleared the way for the *rebbe*'s departure by depositing $3,000 in a Swiss Bank, intended as a bribe for the Gestapo General. The rescue plan was all set but for one thing: the Swiss Government barred the entry of any refugees. Through the efforts of the *rebbe*'s son-in-law, Rabbi Menahem Tzvi Eichenstein of St. Louis, an American visa was dispatched to Switzerland. When the Gestapo came to Lublin, the *rebbe* refused to leave, handing them instead a letter intended for his son Rabbi Abraham Isaac. "What is the captain's duty when his ship capsizes? Should he desert the boat?" he wrote to his son. "I live in the midst of my people, and I cannot desert them." Together with his wife and daughter Gittel, the *rebbe* perished on the 8th of *Iyyar* 1942 in the Kemnita Forest near Lublin.

Meeting Death with Heroism and Dignity

In Lvov, on that fateful Friday, *Rosh Hodesh Av* 1941, Rabbi Bentzion Halberstam (b. 1884) shared the fate of many of his followers. Many of the sages, fragile and aged, utterly defenseless, met their heavily armed assailants with death-defying valor. Rabbi Solomon Henokh Rabinowicz of Radomsk resisted the deportation. "I know you have come to kill me," he told the Nazis. "I am ready to die. But I will die here in my own home. I will not enter your gas wagons." On a Sabbath day in 1942, he was shot in his house at 30

Novolipki Street, together with his son-in-law, and was buried in the sepulcher of the rabbi of Novominsk.

The rabbi of Radzyn, Samuel Solomon, urged his *hasidim* in the ghetto of Wlodawa (near Lublin) to fight back, to escape to the forests, and to join the partisans. He vehemently denounced the Jewish collaborators, stating that "Whoever treads the thresholds of the *Judenrat* (the Jewish Council appointed by the Nazis) will forfeit both worlds, for they are aiding the Nazis in their extermination of the Jews." The poet Isaac Katznelson (1866–1944) wrote "The Song concerning the Radzyner" in tribute to the *rebbe*.

Partisans and Martyrs

Rabbi Isaac, Rabbi Abraham, and Rabbi Berl, brothers of the Radoszycer *rebbe*, Rabbi Kalmish Finkler; the Rovner *rebbe*, Aaron Patshenik (b. 1899), son of Rabbi "Itzikel," the Brezener *rebbe*, joined the partisans. Among the heroines was Perele Perlow, wife of the Kaidanover *rebbe* and daughter of the Biala *rebbe*, Jerahmiel Tzvi of Siedlice. With her husband she escaped from Baranowicze to Vilna, and there she established a synagogue and a religious institute for women. From the valiant Kaidanover rebbetzin, the women and girls of the ghetto drew comfort and strength in those black hours.

The Indestructible Soul of Polish Jewry

With dignity and with faith, the *hasidim* went to their deaths. Hillel ben Aaron Eliezer Zeitlin (1872–1943), kabbalist, philosopher, and journalist, exercised tremendous influence over the Jewish intelligentsia. Born in Kormo, in White Russia, he settled in Homel in the early 1890s. An ardent Zionist, he supported the Jewish Territorial Organization (which aimed at finding a suitable site, not necessarily in Palestine, for Jewish settlement on an autonomous basis). For a time he lived in Vilna, then this "Litvak from the land of the Litvaks" ("Lithuanian from the land of Lithuania"), made his home in Warsaw. At ease in Hebrew and in Yiddish, he wrote many monographs that were both learned and lucid. The subjects of his controversial articles in the Yiddish paper, *Der Moment*, ranged from the *Tanya* of Rabbi Shneur Zalman of Liady to the stories of Rabbi Nahman of Bratslav, from the Sejm elections to anti-Semitism.

An impassioned writer who preached religion, a one-man party with a highly individualistic philosophy, Zeitlin was regarded as a heretic by the ultra-Orthodox and a hypocrite by the *maskilim*. Yet to his home at 60 Zyska Street, Warsaw, flocked *hasidim*, *mitnagdim*, writers, politicians, Agudists, Bundists, and Zionists to listen and to learn from this modern "prophet." He was no demagogue. He spoke quietly with eyes closed, apparently oblivious to the people around him. Yet every public appearance brought eager crowds to hear him.

On the road to Treblinka, Hillel Zeitlin heard the footsteps of the Messiah. He went to meet him on the eve of *Rosh Hashanah*, 1943, wearing *tallit* and *tefillin* and reciting passages from the *Zohar*, engaging on the fringes of earthly hell in mystical, esoteric speculation. This personified, was the indestructible soul of Polish Jewry.

Survivors relate how the frail young Rabbi Joseph Perlow of Novominsk (then 30 years old) wandered around Bergen-Belsen comforting the sick and suffering prisoners. He was so fragile in physique that even the Nazis exempted him from forced labor. Yet, he was so indomitable in spirit that he regularly gave away his own meager allocation of food. He died at Bergen-Belsen on April 16, 1945, the morning after its liberation by the British Second Army under General Sir Miles Dempsey. Courage was not the exclusive prerogative of the young. The 82-year-old rabbi of Warsaw, Isaac Meir Kanal, deliberately provoked a Nazi by snatching his revolver and was shot immediately. But he attained his goal, which was, records an eyewitness, "to be buried according to the Jewish ritual."[4] Rabbi Heinokh Levin of Bendin offered his portion in the world to come for a glass of water, so that he could recite his last prayers in a state of purity.

Rabbi Menahem Ziemba

The *hasid* Menahem Ziemba played a key role in the last days of the Warsaw Ghetto. Menahem was born in 1883 in Praga, a suburb of Warsaw. His father, Eleazar Lippa, died when the boy was barely 9 years old, and he was brought up by his grandfather

Rabbi Abraham. An ailing child, Menahem possessed a phenomenal memory and a most incisive mind. At the age of 18, he married Mindele, daughter of Hayim Isaiah Zederbaum, a wealthy iron merchant. Relieved of financial worries, the young husband could now dedicate twenty hours a day to his studies. For five or six hours each day he shared his talmudical "discoveries" with a small group of students. He maintained that the master should not prepare his lectures in advance, since it was more profitable for the students to participate in the preparations.

The death of his father-in-law compelled Rabbi Menahem to attend to business, but even ironmongery did not distract him from his studies. Moreover, he did not study in a vacuum, but kept in touch with the intellectual giants of the era. The talmudist, Rabbi Meir Simha Hakohen of Dvinsk referred to him as a "beautiful vessel." In 1919, Rabbi Menahem Ziemba published his work *Zera Avraham* ("The Seed of Abraham"), and two years later he published *Totza'ot Hayim* ("Offspring of Life"), a compendium on the "Thirty-Nine Categories of Labor" prohibited on the Sabbath. For his work on Maimonides, *Mahazeh LaMelekh* ("Visions of the King") a novella on *Yad Ha-Hazakah*, he was awarded a literary prize by the Warsaw municipality.

In 1930 he contributed to the periodical *Degel HaTorah* ("The Banner of the Torah"), edited by Rabbi Menahem Kasher, director of the *Metivta Yeshivah* in Warsaw. When Rabbi Kasher left for the United States, Rabbi Ziemba published the last two issues himself. Every Sabbath evening he delivered a midrashic discourse, and every day, from noon until 2:00 P.M. he gave a *shiur* (discourse) to selected young men. He received many "calls" to distant pulpits. When Rabbi Joseph Hayim Sonnenfeld died, Rabbi Moses Blau was deputed to offer Rabbi Ziemba a rabbinical post in Jerusalem, but Rabbi Ziemba refused to leave his beloved Warsaw. To the end, he remained a devoted disciple of Ger, and the rabbi of Ger loved him dearly. "Come, let us ask our Menahem," he would say.

Rabbi Ziemba was the author of twenty published works. Among unpublished manuscripts destroyed in the Holocaust were a four-volume set of responsa, a 2,000–page commentary on the Palestinian Talmud, *Menahem Yerushalayim* ("Comforter of Jerusalem"), and a work on Maimonides. When he lost his 18-year-old son Judah, he wrote *Gur Aryeh Yehudah* ("Judah is a Lion's Whelp") in memoriam. In 1935 Rabbi Ziemba was elected to the

Vaad Harabbanim in Warsaw, where he worked closely with Rabbis Jacob Meir Biderman and Abraham Weinberg.

An Impassioned Plea

During the Nazi occupation, Rabbi Ziemba, together with David Shapira and Simon Stockmaker of the Rabbinical Council, were the spokesmen of traditional Judaism in the ghetto. At the memorable Council of War on January 14, 1943, Rabbi Ziemba spoke out with characteristic fire:

> Of necessity we must resist the enemy on all fronts. . . . We shall no longer obey his orders. Henceforth we must refuse to wend our way to the *Umschlagplatz*, which is but a blind and a snare, a veritable stepping stone on the road to mass annihilation. . . . Had we lived up to our so-called status of "a people endowed with wisdom and understanding" we would have discerned the enemy's plot to destroy us as a whole, root and branch, and would have put into operation all media of information in order to arouse the conscience of the world. As it is now, we have no choice but to resist. We are prohibited by Jewish law from betraying others, nor may we deliver ourselves into the hands of the archenemy. . . . Our much vaunted prudence–not to be identified with a genuine wisdom and true understanding–blurred our vision and turned out to be more devastating than folly and stupidity. To paraphrase the words of our sages, Korah of old accentuated his innate aptitude for provisions to such an extent that it blurred his vision, and in the end it was his folly that brought his ultimate doom. At the present, however, when we are faced by an arch foe, whose unparalleled ruthlessness and total barbarism knows no bounds, *halakhah* demands that we fight and resist to the very end with unequaled determination and valor, for the sake of the Sanctification of the Divine Name.[5]

Rabbi Ziemba was murdered while crossing Kupiecka Street on the third day of *Hol Hamoed* Passover 1943, during the uprising he had called for so passionately. The revolt of the Warsaw Ghetto began on the first night of Passover, April 19, and continued until May 16, 1943. Soon the streets of Warsaw: Novolipki, Nalewski,

Francieczkanska, Mila and Muranowski, once citadels of Hasidism, were piles of rubble, nearly a square mile in area. The loss suffered during the war by the Jews of Poland, who numbered 3,300,000 in August 1939, was reckoned at between 2,350,000 and 3,000,000 persons. As the Holocaust raged, the lights of Hasidism were dimmed, and a deathly pall descended. Sages by the score perished with the Holy Scrolls in their hands and holy words on their lips. The Jewish quarters of Warsaw, Lodz, Lublin, Otwock, Ger, and Alexander, once citadels of piety and learning, were dust and ashes, physical symbols of the almost total destruction of Hasidism in Eastern Europe.

Chapter 23

The Hasidic Way of Life

Hasidism is one of the "martyr movements" of history. Like adherents to new religious sects throughout the ages, *hasidim* were at first persecuted, their principles distorted, and their practices maligned. Learned talmudists put aside the calm deliberation that cloaked their every utterance, precipitously condemning the movement and excommunicating its followers. In one instance, the protagonists of *Jüdische Wissenschaft* ("Science of Judaism") sided with Hasidism's bitter opponents, the *mitnagdim*, and were equally irrational in their condemnation. Anti-hasidic texts abounded. Joseph Perl wrote *Megalleh Temirin* ("Revealer of Secrets") and *Bohein Tzaddik* ("The Test of the Righteous"), and he had a number of followers. Israel Lobel wrote *Taavat Tzaddikim* ("The Lust of the Righteous") and *Sefer Havikku'ah* ("The Book of Debates"). David Markov produced *Zemir Aritzim Veharbot Tzurim* ("The Discomfiture of the Wicked"), and *Shever Poshim* ("Destruction of the Sinners").

Ignorance and Derision

In his memoirs, Solomon Maimon writes, "the Besht (he calls him Joel instead of Israel) became very celebrated on account of some lucky cures that he affected by means of medical knowledge and his conjuring tricks, and he gave out that this was done not by natural means but solely through *Kabbalah* and the use of sacred names. In this way, he played a very successful game in Poland." He accused the *Maggid* of "indulging in vulgar jokes." He disparaged the hasidic leaders further: "It was an accepted fact," he wrote, "that the *tzaddik* has to be enthusiastic in prayer, had to have ecstatic dreams and visions. How can a clever plotter appeared inspired? Alcohol . . . now had to take the place of the inspired demon. To predict the future was a more difficult task, yet it had to be accomplished; his reputation depended on it. Among his intimates were expert spies, worthy of serving the secret police. They discovered many secrets and told them to their leader, thus he was enabled to assume an appearance of omniscience."[1]

"They could not understand," comments Dr. Shalom Spiegel, "the awkward simplicity, the crude depth of the clumsy attempt to stammer the ineffable. They saw merely the repellent exterior, and, because they rejected the irrational and unaesthetic, they viewed the entire hasidic movement as an aberration and a snare, a quackery, or at least, self-delusion."[2]

The Beginning of Understanding

By the second half of the nineteenth century, a number of *maskilim*, gifted with deeper insight, began to express different sentiments. The German social philosopher and precursor of Zionism, Moses Hess (1812–1875), rather grudgingly gives Hasidism its due in *Rome and Jerusalem*, published in 1862.

> Although the *hasidim* are without a social organization, they live in socialistic fashion. The house of the rich man is always open to the poor, and the latter is as much at home there as he is at his own home. They seem to have taken as their motto the saying in *Avot*, "He who says what is mine is thine, is a saint". . . . A sect that practices such self-abnegation and whose members are capable of such religious enthusiasm, must have for its foundation something more than mere crudeness and ignorance.

The essayist Eliezer Tzvi Zweifel (1815–1888) wrote about the movement in a more positive vein. In *Shalom Al Yisrael* ("Peace on

Israel"), he defends the life and works of the Besht and demonstrates that Hasidism is deeply rooted in mysticism.

The historian Heinrich Graetz (1817–1891) illuminates many an obscure period in Jewish history, but plainly he himself was groping in the dark when he dealt with the movement that was making such headway in his own lifetime. According to him, "the new sect, a daughter of darkness, was born in gloom, and even today proceeds stealthily on its mysterious way . . . ugly as the name, Besht was the form of the founder of the order that he called into existence."[3] Showing an astonishing disregard for historical accuracy, he castigates Dov Baer, the *Maggid* of Mezhirech. So the master historian showed himself remarkably inept in his interpretation of this signal contribution to Jewish life and thought.

Dubnow's Assessment

Not until the end of the nineteenth and the beginning of the twentieth century did Hasidism really receive a realistic evaluation. In his *History of the Jews in Russia and Poland*, Simon Dubnow (1860–1941) was able to paint a more objective picture based on a non-hostile study of the facts. This is how he describes a journey through Poland: "The train has taken me through Zloczow, Zbarazh, and other historical places in hasidic history. In the forests that we passed I saw a vision, the Besht, as he was praying amidst nature and gathering medical herbs, or the shades of Michal of Zloczow, Wolf of Zbarazh, and others."[3]

In his *History of Hasidism*, the only work he wrote in Hebrew, Dubnow attempts an assessment. In his preface to the Yiddish edition he writes: "I had to gather the building material all by myself, digging for sand and clay, making the bricks, and then erecting the building according to a definite architectural plan. I used the entire hasidic literature, both learned and legendary material, and I attempted to find some system in the maze of the various hasidic currents and tried to reveal the kernel of truth present in the native folktales."[4] Yet he lists only 194 works in his hasidic bibliography, insisting that the creative period of Hasidism ended in 1815. Despite this objectivity, he asserts that "the Besht began by dabbling in magic."[5] In the eyes of Moritz Steinschneider (1816–1907), father of "Jewish bibliography," Hasidism was a "malady of Judaism."[6]

A New Perspective

But the time came for the historians and writers to enter the "*Pardes*," the garden of Hasidism, and they assigned the movement an honorable position in the chronicles of religious revivals.

To Samuel Abba Horodetzky (1871–1957) in his work *HaHasidut VehaHasidim*, a collection of essays covering the movement from the Besht to Rabbi Israel of Ruzhin, Hasidism is a revolt against the severe legalism of the rabbinate. "Legal and practical Judaism is hemmed in within the 'four ells of the halakhah.' This is the God of Rabbi Akiva, who derived numerous laws from every letter and iota of the Torah," writes Horodetzky. "He is the God of Maimonides, of Joseph Karo, of Isserles, and the God of the Gaon of Vilna. It is the *Kabbalah* that supplied Judaism with poetic feeling and complete devotion to God."

Isaac Leib Peretz (1852–1915) popularized Hasidism in the first decade of the twentieth century, and the Yiddish novelist and playwright Sholem Asch (1880–1957), in his novel *Der Thillim Yid* ("Salvation"), gives a glowing account of Hasidism. Micah Joseph Berdichevsky (1865–1921), Gershom (Gerhard) Scholem (b. 1897), Hillel Zeitlin (1872–1943), and Eliezer Steinmann (b. 1892) made notable contributions, and Hasidism was now seen from a startling new perspective.

"We must admit," writes *Ahad Haam* (pseudonym of Asher Ginsberg, 1856–1927), "that if we want to find original Hebrew literature today we must turn to the literature of Hasidism; there rather than in the literature of the *Haskalah* one occasionally encounters (in addition to much that is purely fanciful) true profundity of thought which bears the mark of the original Jewish genius."[7] The philosopher Martin Buber (1878–1965), who had grown up in the home of his grandfather Solomon Buber (1827–1906), researched in depth the form and content of Hasidism and found it surprisingly relevant to our time. He spent the summer months of his youth in the towns of Sadgora and Chortkov, citadels of Hasidism. It was Buber who brought Hasidism to the attention of the world at large. For Buber, religion was a dialogue between God and man, and in Hasidism the dialogue was particularly meaningful. He found truth and beauty in the stories, and his *Tales of Rabbi Nahman, The Legends of the Baal Shem*, and the *Tales of the Hasidim* brought the essence of Hasidism home to millions. It was "*Kabbalah* transformed into

Ethos." "The hasidic movement," writes Buber, in his work *The Origin and Meaning of Hasidism,* "takes over from the *Kabbalah* only what it needs for the theological foundation of an enthusiastic but not over-exalted life in responsibility–responsibility of a single individual for the piece of the world entrusted to him." All Buber's philosophical writings are permeated with the traditions of Hasidism.

Hasidism–A Common Fellowship

In Hasidism there was no chasm between theory and practice. The life of the *hasid* was regarded as the best exposition of Hasidism, for the Besht was a revivalist rather than a revolutionary. His objective was to revitalize the Jewish religion and the Jewish people, to make the "crooked straight and the rough places smooth." Unlike the Essenes, the *hasidim* did not believe in asceticism or in detachment from the turmoil of the material world.

The hasidic sky was composed of many planets, each set in its appointed place, each revolving in its own orbit and each contributing to the brilliant light that floodlit the Jewish world. Upon the foundations laid by the Besht, many superstructures were erected. There were marked differences in the philosophies of Ruzhin and Kotzk, Sochaczew and Sadgora, Ger and Lubavitch, yet all were united in common fellowship.

Under the wings of the Besht, all could find shelter–the scholar and the unlearned alike. But though Hasidism uplifts the poor, it neither glorifies poverty nor denigrates wealth. It simply eliminates the barriers between man and man, and between man and his Maker. Much is expected of the *hasid*. He is required to fulfill himself, to perfect himself, as his own personal contribution to the redemption of the world. Hasidism recognizes no aristocracy, neither the aristocracy of wealth nor the aristocracy of learning. All are children of the living God. All men are equal, and no man is more equal than his neighbor. Hasidism translates the concept, "All Israel is united in fellowship" into every phase of human relations. "Let no man think himself better than his neighbor," said the Besht, "for each serves God according to the understanding which God gave him."

The Definition of the Word

How does one define a *hasid*? Hasidism has no "articles of faith," nor does it demand adherence to a formal code. A *hasid* is known, not by the beliefs he holds, but by the life he leads. Faith in the *tzaddik*, joy, humility, devotion (*kavanah*), and enthusiasm (*hitlahavut*) are signposts along the hasidic pathway. Hasidism attaches importance to every word, to every thought, and to every act, for every Jew is a coworker with the Almighty in the renewal of creation.

In the Bible, *hasid* connotes a man of piety, and the term is even applied to the Deity. "The Lord is righteous in all His ways and gracious (*hasid*) in all His works," sings the Psalmist (Psalms 145:17). "Let the saints (*hasidim*) exult in glory; let them sing for joy upon their beds. Let the high praises of God be in their mouth, and a two-edged sword in their hands" (Psalms 149:5).

The epithet *hasid* is frequently used in this sense in rabbinic literature. According to Hillel, "an ignorant man cannot be a *hasid*" (Avot 2:6). Rabbi Jose Hakohen is termed a *hasid* (Avot 2:11), because he obeyed the spirit, rather than merely the letter of the law. "The former *hasidim*," says the *Mishnah*, "would spend a long time meditating before prayer."[8] "A foolish *hasid*," says the Talmud, "is one who sees a woman drowning in the river and says: 'I am forbidden to look at a woman, so how can I save her?' "[9]

There are references in the Talmud and in the Books of the Maccabees to the second-century B.C.E. sect of the "Hasideans" (from the Greek transliteration of the Hebrew *hasidim*). These valiant defenders of the Law fought Antiochus IV "Epiphanes" (reigned 175–163 B.C.E.), at first refusing to defend themselves on the Sabbath. Later they allied themselves with the Hasmoneans, and then they merged with either the Pharisees or the Essenes. In the thirteenth century, the *hasidei Ashkenaz* ("the pious men of Germany") produced such personalities as Judah ben Samuel Hehasid of Regensburg (d. 1217) and his disciple Eleazar ben Judah of Worms.[10] During the eighteenth century a number of small groups arose who were also known as *hasidim*.

The Tzaddik

The concept of the *tzaddik* did not originate with the Besht. Noah is termed "a man righteous (*tzaddik*) and whole-hearted in his generation" (Genesis 6:9). "The *tzaddik*," says the prophet Habbakuk (2:4), "shall live by his faith." The Book of Psalms lists the attributes of the *tzaddik*, and the Book of Job depicts his sufferings. "Great is the power of the *tzaddik*," says the Talmud,"for God decrees and the *tzaddik* annuls."[11]

Developing this concept even further, Hasidism produced a type of leader unique in the Jewish religious hierarchy. The *tzaddik* is teacher, counselor, and confessor, to whom the *hasid* could unburden his heart. He is a friend in this world and an advocate in the world to come, giving life new meaning, new color, and new hope. He is not an official of the *Kehillah*. He is neither elected nor appointed by the community. Unlike the rabbi (*rav*), he requires no ordination, and unlike the priest (*kohen*), his office is not necessarily hereditary.

The *tzaddik* was not self-sufficient. He looked to his followers for inspiration, just as they looked to him for guidance. Although he reached for the skies, he was mindful of his earthly commitments. "The *tzaddik*," writes Buber, "lifts up the holy sparks from the depth of earthliness and removes the stains from the souls of men."[12] According to the Besht, the *tzaddik* is the messenger of the *Shekhinah*. "The will of the *tzaddik*," declared the *Maggid*, "reflects the will of God."[13]

"A helper is needed," says Buber,[14] "a helper for both body and soul, for both earthly and heavenly matters. This helper is called a *tzaddik*. He can heal both the ailing body and the ailing soul, for he knows how one is bound up with the other, and the knowledge gives him the power to influence both. It is he who can teach you to conduct your affairs so that your soul remain free, and he can teach you to strengthen your soul to keep you steadfast beneath the blows of destiny."

Heavy are the burdens of the *tzaddik*. "His heart," declared the *Maggid*, "is flooded with the lifeblood of others and weighed down with the sorrows of his people." The *Maggid* viewed his great influence with sadness. "For what sin," he sighed, "have I become renowned?," for renown brings the *tzaddik* even weightier responsibilities. When the time came, runs the legend, for the appearance on earth of Rabbi Levi Isaac of Berdichev, Satan writhed in anguish, lest the sage redeem the House of Israel. But Satan's fears were allayed. He was told that Levi Isaac would become a *rebbe* and would be so enmeshed in communal matters that Satan would still have ample scope for his activities. Yet the hasidic leaders were not without misgivings about the "cult of the *tzaddik*," as detractors called it. "I can foresee," prophesied the Besht, "that before the advent of the Messiah, rabbis will sprout forth like the grass of the field, delaying the redemption, because the conflicting loyalties of their followers will divide the community and bring about causeless strife."

Heirs to the Title

There was no clear-cut rule regarding succession. Dov Baer of Mezhirech succeeded the Besht. Tzvi Hirsch of Rymanow (d. 1846), a tailor's apprentice, succeeded his master, Rabbi Menahem Mendel. As a rule, however, son followed father, and thus the dynasties were perpetuated. Inevitably, quarrels occasionally broke out between the followers of different *rebbes* and, to the amusement of *mitnagdim* and *maskilim* alike, these controversies sometimes degenerated into unseemly squabbles.

Poverty and Wealth

The lifestyles of the *tzaddikim* varied considerably. The Besht could not sleep unless all the money in his house had been distributed among the poor. Similarly, many of the great rabbis endured abject poverty, refusing to accept the "gifts of flesh and blood." On the other hand, there were *tzaddikim*, like the rabbis of Ruzhin and Sadgora, who lived in luxury with servants to tend their palatial residences and fine horses in their stables. It is said that Rabbi David Talna (Talnoye) sat on a golden throne, inscribed with the words "David, King of Israel." Rabbi Abraham of Turisk possessed a rare *menorah*, wrought in gold and silver, over which skilled craftsmen had worked for many years.

Great Scholars among Hasidism's Leaders

Hasidim are often accused of disparaging study, but such an accusation is without foundation. Rabbi Dov Baer and Rabbi Shneur Zalman were among the greatest talmudists of their generation, and in the nineteenth and twentieth centuries many hasidic rabbis in Poland, Galicia, and Hungary were acknowledged "Princes of the Torah." Rabbi Jacob Isaac (The Holy Jew), Rabbi Mendel of Kotzk, Rabbi Isaac Meir of Ger, Rabbi Abraham of Sochaczew, Rabbi Jechiel Meir Halevy, Rabbi Menahem Mendel of Lubavitch, Rabbi Tzadok Kohen of Lublin, and Rabbi Tzvi Hirsch Spira of Munkacs, were outstanding scholars.

Hasidism and Miracles

Miracles did not cease with the end of the biblical era. Such celebrated sages of the talmudic era as Honi Hame'aggel and Hanina ben Dosa were said to perform miracles, and this power was ascribed to a number of medieval rabbis. However, the wonder-working aspect of Hasidism was invariably overemphasized. Many hasidic leaders did not believe in miracles, and this sizeable and significant category included the rabbis of Przysucha, Kotzk, Izbica, and Lubavitch. On the other hand, *hasidim* firmly believed that the Besht, the Seer of Lublin, Rabbi Jacob Aryeh of Radzymin, and Rabbi Hayim Meir Jehiel of Moglienice were indeed miracle workers, and a wealth of legends was woven around their supernatural activities.

Customs and Practices

Rabbi Issakhar Baer of Rodoszyce (b. 1843) was known as a *Baal Mofet,* "A Miracle Worker," and his fame spread far and wide. He would give petitioners *kamaot* (amulets). The rebbe stressed that it was essential for a *hasid,* even if he had attained perfection, to visit his rebbe regularly. He was vehemently opposed to delaying the services beyond the hours prescribed by the *Shulhan Arukh,* as was the custom in the courts of Przysucha, Kotzk, and Alexander. He was equally opposed to the omission of *piyyutim* and *Tahanun.* He would remain awake throughout each Friday night in prayer and study. "All the *hasidim* are exhausted," he explained. "They have worked very hard all week, and on Friday night they sleep soundly. So who will keep watch over the House of Israel, and who will devote this sacred night to the study of the Torah?"

On Friday night, before the recitation of the *Kiddush,* the rebbe would immerse himself in the *mikveh*. During the Festival of Tabernacles, he would set aside seven chairs in his *Sukkah* for the *Ushpizin* (the seven guests, Abraham, Isaac, Jacob, Joseph, Moses, Aaron, and David, who, according to tradition, participate in the festive meals of *Sukkot*). The *rebbe* would leave his home on *Rosh Hodesh Elul* and spend the entire High Holy Day period, right through *Simhat Torah*, in the *Beit Hamidrash*. He would light *Hanukkah* candles in the morning before the service throughout the Festival of *Hanukkah*.

The rebbe died on the 18th of *Sivan* 1842 at the age of 79. When the "Seraph" of Moglienice, Rabbi Hayim Meir, visited the grave of Rabbi Issakhar Baer, he took off his shoes because he asserted, "This place is holy." The *rebbe* left two sons, Rabbi Israel Isaac Brun and Rabbi Meir, and three daughters (Rebecca, Pearl, and Miriam). Two months before the outbreak of World War II, on the 18th of *Sivan* 1939, the anniversary of the *rebbe*'s *Yahrzeit*, his *Beit HaMidrash* in Radoszyce was completely destroyed by fire. Ironically, what would have been considered a tragic accident under ordinary circumstances, actually saved the sanctuary of the *rebbe* from desecration by the Nazi hoodlums.

Hasidic Customs Initiated by the Besht

It is known that the Besht distributed *kamaot* (amulets), and two scribes were kept busy writing them. Amulets were popular in ancient times and are referred to in the *Mishnah* and *Tosefta*.[15] The amulet was simply a strip of parchment about two by ten inches in size, inscribed with one or two verses from the Bible. For the most part, the successors of the Besht discontinued this practice.

Dear to the Besht was the custom of observing *Tikkun Hatzot* (midnight service) that had been practiced by the sixteenth-century Kabbalists. Apart from Elimelekh of Lyzhansk and Aaron of Karlin, few *tzaddikim* recited these mournful elegies over the destruction of the Temple.

A Visit to the Rebbe

"It is a man's duty," says the Talmud, "to pay his respects to his teacher on festivals, on New Moons, and on the Sabbath."[16] A visit to the *rebbe* was a major event in the life of the *hasid.* "Those who travel to the *rebbe,*" says Rabbi Nahman of Bratslav, "are recompensed. Although they may not receive Torah from him, they are nevertheless rewarded for their efforts." According to Rabbi Uri of Strelisk, a *hasid* is obliged to travel to the *rebbe,* even though he must forego a certain amount of Torah study and prayer in order to make the journey."[17]

"Court" affairs were governed by the *gabbai,* who acted as liaison between the rabbi and his followers. Usually, each visitor presented a *kvitel* (petition). Ordinarily, the petitions were related to basic human needs: recovery from sickness, longing for a child, the need for finding a suitable mate for one's children, or the difficulty of earning a livelihood. The *hasid* wrote his name and the name of his mother on the petition. Accompanying the *kvitel* was a *pidyon* (redemption money), the amount varying according to one's finances. It was usual to give a sum corresponding to the numerical value (eighteen) of the Hebrew word *hai* (life). *Hasidim* would even place *kvitlekh* at the graves of their *rebbes.*

The hasidic leaders would ceremoniously *fihr tish* (conduct a table), and the *hasidim* would share a symbolic meal with their *rebbe.* The master would utter *divrei torah* (Words of Torah) and the *hasidim* would sing joyous melodies in fiery fellowship. Watching the *rebbe* was as important as listening to him. Every gesture was observed and analyzed. It was the *hasid*'s privilege to share *shirayim* (remnants) of the rabbi's food. The rabbi would merely taste a dish and then pass it down the table, a custom that can be traced back to antiquity. "He who leaves no bread on the table (at the end of a meal) will never see a sign of blessing," warns the Talmud.[18] The Palestinian Talmud records that Rabbi Johanan bar Napaha would gather up the morsels left over from the previous night's meal and eat them, saying "Let my portion be among those who were here (in the synagogue) yesterday."[19]

Hasidism developed the idea further, maintaining that the *tzaddik* sanctified the food, setting free the imprisoned *nitzotzot* (sparks) and restoring them to their source.

Sabbath at the Rebbe's Court

It was a special privilege for a *hasid* to spend the Sabbath with his *rebbe.* In preparation, he would visit the *mikveh* (ritual bath). The *tzaddik* would wear his finest garments, usually a *kapote* of silk or velvet. Many *tzaddikim* would don a *tallit* during the Evening Service that ushered in the Sabbath. Some would utter a benediction over spices before the *Kiddush* on Friday night, because the Talmud relates that on the eve of Sabbath before sunset, Rabbi Simon bar Yohai and his son saw an old man bearing two bundles of myrtle. "What are these for?" they asked him. "They are in honor of the Sabbath," he replied.[20]

In Lurian style, the *hasidim* would set twelve twisted loaves on the table at every Sabbath meal, a visual reminder of the "twelve cakes" that were set out in the Sanctuary (Leviticus 24:4). During the Reading of the Law, the most important *mitzvah*, apart from the *kohen* and *levi* portions, was *shishi* (the sixth portion) that corresponded to the *Kabbalistic* symbol *yesod*. The *tzaddik*, the foundation (*yesod*) of the world, was customarily honored with *shishi*.

Shalosh Seudot, the third Sabbath meal, was the highlight of the day. The menu rarely consisted of more than fish and bread, but the sparse meal was supplemented by spiritual fare. In the gathering dusk, the rabbi spoke in illuminating phrases, and the *hasidim* sang such mystical melodies as *Atkinu Se'udata* or Luria's *Benei Hekhala*. Together they swayed and danced in an ecstasy that transcended the barriers of time and place. After *Havdalah*, many rabbis chanted the prayer poem of Rabbi Levi Isaac of Berdichev, *Gott fun Avraham* ("God of Abraham"). Both the *rebbe* and his *hasidim* were reluctant to let the honored guest (the Sabbath) depart and prolonged the day as much as possible. At the conclusion of the Sabbath they celebrated the *Melaveh Malkah* ("Accompanying the Sabbath Queen"), chanting hymns and relating hasidic tales.

The Shtibl

The hasidic center was the *shtibl*, the Yiddish word for the little room, that served as both place of worship and house of study. Hasidic rabbis would establish branches, *shtiblekh*, in the various towns wherein their followers worshipped. In Poland, most towns had several such *shtiblekh*, probably a Gerer, an Alexander, and a Belzer *shtibl*. Here the *hasidim* would commune with God as well as with each other, discussing the depth of the rabbi's discourses and the manifold facets of his personality.

The *Shivhei HaBesht,* an anthology of legends concerning the Baal Shem Tov, was published in Kapust in 1815. Many treasuries of hasidic fables followed. It was believed that relating stories of *tzaddikim* was equivalent to reciting prayers.

Prayer

Prayer was the pivotal point. *Kavanah* (devotion) and *hitlahavut* (fervor) were essential, and the intimate atmosphere of the *shtibl* encouraged uninhibited outpourings of the soul. The Besht and Rabbi Levi Isaac of Berdichev worshipped with blazing intensity. For Rabbi Uri of Strelisk, known as the "Seraph," prayer was so devastating an experience, that he regularly took the precaution of preparing his "Last Will and Testament" before attending the synagogue. The Besht attributed his powers to the intensity of his prayers rather than to the extent of his studies. *Hasidim* believed that prayer could achieve the impossible, and could even change the order of nature.

They tied a *gartel* (belt, girdle) around their waists to make a division between the heart and the genitals and found a reference to this ritual in the Book of Isaiah (11:5) "And righteousness shall be the girdle of his loins and faithfulness the girdle of his reins."

Yet, *tzaddikim* like the rabbis of Ruzhin and Sadgora were seemingly calm and dispassionate when they stood in prayer. "There are *tzaddikim,*" it was said, "who serve God with all their limbs, and there are *tzaddikim* who fear God so much that they are too terrified to move as much as a muscle during the service." Rabbi Nahum of Chernobyl advocated this latter mode of prayer. "We behold many people engaged in study and prayer," he stated, "they raise their voices . . . they clap their hands, they jump to their feet. Many ignorant people imagine that this constitutes prayer. The truth is not so. It is fitting that a man should pray in awe and dread."

Total involvement generally characterized hasidic worship, for the Psalmist says (35:10): "All my bones shall say, Lord, who is like unto Thee." Inevitably their opponents mocked these manifestations: "They (the *hasidim*) rise to offer prayers of thanksgiving and praise, intermingled with songs and whistles, twisting their lips and twinkling their eyes, frisking and whooping."

The *hasidim* adopted the Lurian liturgy, *Nusah Ari.* Rabbi Dov

Baer favored the Lurian liturgy, and he was supported by many authorities.[21] In his prayer book published in Shklow in 1803, Rabbi Shneur Zalman made substantial changes in the liturgy, and *Habad hasidim* use this text. The *hasidim* generally omitted *piyyutim* (liturgical poems), but recited special introductions to various prayers, composed by rabbis like Elimelekh of Lyzhansk.

"Permissible pleasures" were not scorned. At a *siyyum* (completion of the study of a tractate of the Talmud), on the anniversary of the *tzaddik*'s death, on *Purim* and *Simhat Torah*, at weddings, and similar festivities, *hasidim* would drink spirits in careful measure, and wish each other *lehayim* (to life), and thus "banish grief from the heart."

Asked why the *hasidim* drank whisky after the service, whereas the *mitnagdim* usually studied a chapter of the *Mishnah*, Rabbi Israel of Ruzhin replied: "The *mitnagdim* pray frigidly, without enthusiasm or emotion. They appear almost lifeless. After their prayers, they study the *Mishnah*, an appropriate subject when one mourns the dead. But the prayers of the *hasidim* are alive, and living people need a drink." The *hasidim* called this *tikkun*, (repair), for by creating harmony in this way, they were smoothing out some of the disharmonies in the cosmos.

Gemilut Hasadim

Of the three pillars on which the world is based, Torah, Divine Service, and practice of charity, Rabbi Meir of Przemyshlany maintained that the most important one is the practice of charity (*gemilut hasadim*). The wealthy Jew should regard his wealth as a loan from the Almighty and not as his possession. Rabbi Simha Bunem explained why we do not utter a blessing before giving charity. If a man were to make preparations prior to fulfilling this *mitzvah* by ablution or by reciting the formula "For the Sake of the Sanctification," the poor man would surely die of hunger in the meanwhile.

Education

Hasidim followed the established educational patterns. At a very early age sons were sent to the *heder*. Secular subjects had no place in the curriculum, and Hebrew grammar and the study of the Bible were neglected. "Verily, grammar is useful," admits Rabbi Menahem Mendel of Vitebsk. "I know that our great ones studied it, but what can we do, now that the godless have taken possession of it?" At first the *hasidim* did not send their sons to the *yeshivot,* and the young men would study in the *Beit HaMidrash*. But, by the twentieth century, *hasidim* had established their own *yeshivot,* such as the *metivta,* set up in 1919 under Rabbi Meir Don Plotski, rabbi of Ostrowiec. Hasidic youngsters, reluctant to travel to far-off institutions, converged on this local fountainhead of scholarship. Candidates had to be over 13 years of age and able to master unaided one page of the Talmud and *Tosafot* (commentaries compiled in the twelfth and thirteen centuries). Unlike other *yeshivot,* which concentrated wholly on talmudical studies, the *metivta* devoted two hours a day to Polish language, mathematics, and history. This revolutionary departure did not go unchallenged. Rabbi Hayim Eliezer Shapira of Munkacs termed it "heresy."

In the inter-war years, many hasidic *yeshivot* sprang up, and today they flourish in Israel, England, and the United States.

Dress and Customs

Hasidim still wear the distinctive attire favored by their ancestors. Proudly they wear the *kapote,* the *yarmulka* (skull cap), the *shtreimel* (fur hat), and the *gartel* (girdle). They button their coats from right to left. Any innovation in dress is regarded as *hukkat hagoy* (imitating the Gentiles). Even wearing a collar and tie was regarded by some *hasidim* as the beginning of heresy. Like the Kabbalists, they do not countenance the trimming (even with scissors) of beard and sidelocks.

Many rituals distinguish *hasidim* from their fellow Jews. Some *hasidim* don two pairs of *tefillin* each morning, because Rabbenu Tam disagreed with Rashi as to the order of the texts on the four parchments, and so two versions of *tefillin* are available. To satisfy both celebrated authorities, devout *hasidim* use both. On *Hol Hamoed,* however, they do not put on *tefillin* at all. On Passover they eat only *matzah shemurah,* (unleavened bread made from flour that had been supervised from the moment the wheat was harvested). Mendel of Kotzk would drink five cups of wine at the *seder* celebration instead of the customary four. Special verses are recited before the sounding of the *shofar* on the New Year, and the *shofar* is sounded when the congregation recites the silent *Musaf Amidah. Hasidim* have *hakkafot* (processional circuits around the *almeimar* with Scrolls of the Law) on *Shemini Atzeret* as well as on *Simhat Torah.* Eventually the *mitnagdim* joined forces with the *hasidim* in the strenuous and ceaseless battle against *Haskalah.* The warning of the *mitnaged,* Rabbi Moses Sofer (1763–1839) of Pressburg, "Touch not the works of Dessau (Mendelssohn)," was echoed by all hasidic leaders. A refusal to compromise ensured the continuance of traditional Judaism and kept the flames burning in the darkest days.

Chapter 24

A Renaissance of Joy and Song

Music and dance have always been important in Judaism. When Elisha wished to prophesy, he demanded, "Now bring me a minstrel" (II Kings 3:15). Half of the 150 Psalms in the Book of Psalms were designed to be sung with instrumental accompaniment, and the Temple musicians were organized into twenty-four guilds according to the instruments they played. The Bible records the victory dances with which Miriam and the Israelite maidens celebrated the defeat of Pharaoh's host. David and Saul returning from battle were met with "timbrels and joy" (I Samuel 18:6), and David danced in holy ecstasy before the Ark of the Lord (II Samuel 6:14–16).

Dances figure in the rituals of the Temple. The Talmud describes the picturesque torch dances in which the leading citizens participated. "Whosoever has not witnessed the joy of the Festival of Water Drawing"[1] (during *Sukkot*), comment the sages, "has seen no joy in his life."

Music in Worship throughout Jewish History

With the destruction of the Temple, instrumental music was no longer used to accompany the liturgy, although the tradition of singing the Psalms and some of the prayers was transferred to the synagogue. By the ninth century, the musical accents, called in Hebrew *taamim* (literally, tastes) or *neginot* (notes), were generally accepted. Cantillation of the Torah and *haftorah* was now according to marks placed above and below the Hebrew text. It was held that the Torah and the Books of the Prophets must be chanted according to their appointed melodies, because these melodies were handed down to Moses on Mount Sinai.[2]

During the Middle Ages, the Jews paid little attention to music, having other matters on their minds. "The exile," laments the sixteenth-century scholar Leon of Modena, "dispersion over the face of the globe, the incredible persecution that has afflicted us, all these have inevitably caused us to neglect the arts and the sciences. . . . Therefore we have today been obliged to borrow the music of our neighbors and to adapt our religious chants from it." By the sixteenth century, the *baal tefillah* (master of prayer) had been replaced by a cantor, sometimes accompanied by a choir. Salomon Rossi of Venice (1587–1628) officiated in Ferrara with a choir of eight voices. But it was not until the nineteenth century that *hazzanut*, the art of "liturgical singing," was really developed to its fullest.

Hasidism and Music

Hasidism brought about a veritable renaissance of Jewish music. For the Masters of Mysticism, melody was rich with mystical meaning, and the *Zohar* often elaborates on this theme. "In the highest heavens," says the *Zohar,* "there is a certain Temple with gates that can be opened only by the power of song." The *Zohar* explains that all creation sings glorious songs of praise to the Creator. All the prophets, save only Moses, "father of the prophets," used melody to heighten their receptiveness to Divine inspiration.[3]

The Kabbalists of Safed, among them Isaac Luria, Solomon Alkabetz, and Israel Najara, created many notable melodies that have echoed through the ages, that throb with faith, joy, yearning, and hope. They fervently believed that only when they were joyous, did the Divine Presence dwell among them.

"Serve the Lord with joy," was the vibrant theme that surged through Hasidism. "No child can be born except through joy. By the same token," reasoned the Besht, "if a man wishes his prayers to bear fruit, he must offer them with joy."[4] The most important aspect of fulfilling a *mitzvah* (good deed) is the joyfulness with which it is carried out. The Divine Presence is the antithesis of melancholy.

Sadness emanates from the *kelipot* (shells of sin), but the Godhead radiates joy. The path to the Realm of Repentance passes first through the Sphere of Song. The Besht applied the verse, "Thou shalt be altogether joyful" (Deuteronomy 17:15), to man's approach to everyday life, while the Torah applies it to the Festival of Tabernacles. He believed that there could be no absolute evil, because in "every occurrence there was an element of good, in every judgment there was mercy. . . ."

"A poor man," the Besht related, "once came before his king with weeping and bitter lamentation. Out of compassion the king gave him a few coins. Then another petitioner came in. He, too, was in great need. However, he smiled cheerfully and made his requests in a pleasant, merry manner. The king's mood brightened, and he gladly presented the second petitioner with lavish gifts." Echoes are found in hasidic melodies of military marches and of Russian, Polish, Viennese, Moldavian, Walachian, and Rumanian tunes. It is the singer who refines the song. "Even in the songs of the non-Jew," maintained the Besht, "there are sparks of the Divine."

Hasidism and Dance

The dance, too, was revived by the *hasidim.* It was no longer confined to the *mitzvah tanz,* "the handkerchief dance," performed at weddings by close kinfolk of the bride and groom. It became a form of self-expression and "sacred service" complementary to the song. Among the *hasidim,* the dance reached the highest level of religious enthusiasm, even to the point of self-oblivion. Hands as well as feet were caught up in the passion of the dance. This was no social pastime, no mere "poetry in motion," no auto-intoxication. This was religious ecstasy that lifted the participants out of themselves and out of their surroundings into the highest heavens. The *hasid* danced on festivals, on the Sabbath, on the anniversaries of the *tzaddik*'s death. And the dance itself was a prayer, a mystical experience, a passionate outpouring of love for the Creator and His works.

"My dancing," remarked Rabbi Leib, son of Rabbi Abraham "the Angel," "was more important to God than all my prayers." When Rabbi Levi Isaac danced on *Simhat Torah,* "all the upper worlds were hushed into silence, and even the ministering angels held their breath and stopped their daily songs of praise before the Holy One,

Blessed be He, and never was there in Heaven such a great spiritual delight."[5] The rabbi of Shpola composed many *niggunim*. One of them is a dialogue in which the Almighty inquires of His children: "Where have you been? Why have you forsaken Me? Dear children, please return home. I feel forlorn without you." Each verse is sung in Hebrew, in Yiddish, and in Russian.

The Role of the Cantor

In the Middle Ages, cantors were criticized from all sides. They were censured for prolonging the service unduly and for mispronouncing the text. Rabbi Jacob Joseph of Polonnoye tabulates many of their alleged offenses:[6]

> Our souls are sick with listening to *hazzanim*, for in every fine and pious community the plague has spread. They sin and cause others to sin. When they prolong their melodies without end, the people gossip in the synagogue, interrupting the silence of prayer at times when it is forbidden to interrupt. . . . How has he the shamelessness to stand up as the advocate, the messenger of the congregation, the intermediary between Israel and our Father in Heaven, before the great and awful King, the root and source of all worlds?

Yet the cantor's role was all-important. Rabbi Phinehas of Korets said of the *Maharil*, Rabbi Jacob b. Moses Halevi Mölin (1360–1427), that he reached spiritual heights because he was a *sheli'ah tzibbur* (a congregational reader) and sang well. "The *hasidim* narrowed the gulf between reader and congregation, for all worshippers were urged to participate." Sincerity and spontaneity were of more consequence than mere harmony. "All the worlds," writes the *Maggid*, "are nourished by the songs of Israel, the sacred songs to God: and even as in days of old, when the Holy Temple stood, the songs of the Levites in their sacred service of worship would ascend upwards, and the worlds were stimulated and nourished by them, so God today should be worshipped in joy, in song and in lyrical praise."[7]

The synagogal melodies were dear to the Besht, and he loved to officiate at the reader's desk. It was his custom to read the *Musaf* (the additional service) on the New Year, and on the Day of Atonement he would recite *Neilah* (the concluding service). The *Maggid* himself did not act as reader for his *hasidim*. His reader was Rabbi Judah Leib Kohen, author of a Torah commentary, *Or Haganuz* ("Hidden Light"). The *Maggid* did, however, compose a number of melodies.

Hasidic Songs

Hasidic music was unique in many ways. Songs were handed down from father to son. Often simple folk melodies became vehicles for awesome concepts.

Prayers and *zemirot* (Sabbath melodies) were, of course, composed in Hebrew. But many of the hasidic lyricists gave expression to their hopes and longings in Yiddish.

Every dynasty had its own favorite tunes, and they became almost "signature tunes." From the melody that a *hasid* hummed, it was often possible to identify the school to which he belonged. "Every Israelite has a portion in the world to come, and the main delight in the world to come will be derived from melody," declared the poet of Hasidism, Nahman of Bratslav. "The only way to detach oneself from the world and to approach the Almighty is through song and praise." He maintained that "through songs calamities can be averted. Music emanates from the prophetic spirit and has the power to elevate and inspire."[8] Rabbi Nahman interpreted the words of Jacob to his sons in Genesis 43:11, "Take of the choice fruits of the land (*zimrat ha'aretz*) in your vessels and carry down to the man a present," to mean "take of the songs of the land," since the word *zimrat* (fruit) can also be read as *zemirat* (song).

"Every branch of wisdom in the world has its own specific melody," Rabbi Nahman explained in his characteristically cryptic manner, "and it is from that melody that wisdom itself is derived. Even Epicurean philosophy has tunes of its own. Moreover, all learning has a melody in accordance with its nature and rank: the loftier the learning, the more sublime is the tune pertaining to it, and thus it ascends even higher and higher until it reaches the primal point of creation which is the beginning of the Divine emanation." To Nahman, everything was a song. "Winter is like conception, like birth. In the winter all vegetation is dead, when summer comes all awakes to life,[9]" "and when a man prays in the field, all nature aids him and adds power to his prayers." Rabbi Nathan, his disciple, confessed that when he heard Rabbi Nahman singing he felt compensated for all his suffering. Rabbi Nahman held, moreover, that "the root of all blessings is to be attained only through dances." Hence, *hasidim* used to say, "Whosoever has not seen the Rabbi of Bratslav dancing, has not seen true goodness."

Music and Habad

Habad also established its own musical traditions. The founder of the dynasty, Shneur Zalman, himself a gifted singer, believed that only step-by-step could one ascend to the highest of spiritual heights. There are certain stages: *hishtapkhut hanefesh* ("outpouring of the soul"), *hitorerut* ("spiritual awakening"), and *hitpaalut* ("ecstasy"). At each stage music could help. The first rabbi of Lubavitch composed what became known as the Rabbi's Song (*der rebbe's niggun*). This is the anthem of *Habad* chanted only on special festival occasions, such as on the 19th of *Kislev* (the day when Shneur Zalman was released from prison). This pensive song consists of four bars that correspond to the four *Kabbalistic* regions: *beri'ah* ("creation of the plant world"), *yetzirah* ("living beings"), *asiyah* ("making or creating of man") and *atzilut* ("emanations").

In many cases words were superfluous. Shneur Zalman once said to one of his followers, "I realize that you have not quite grasped the import of my discourse. So I will sing you a song." Shneur Zalman sang, and the *hasid* listened. "Now I understand what you wish to teach," responded the *hasid* with warmth and intelligence. "I feel an intense longing to be united with the Lord."[10]

Similarly, *hasidim* relate that Rabbi Shneur Zalman once visited Shklow, a city renowned for its scholars and militant *mitnagdim*. There the *rebbe* met a rather hostile group, and to conventional queries, he could only return conventional answers. So he raised his voice in song. So moved were his listeners, that it seemed to them that their questions were answered, and their problems were solved.

The orchestra and choir of Rabbi Dov Baer, son of Rabbi Shneur Zalman, won great renown, and his court was the training ground of many famous *hazzanim*. In his "Tract on Ecstasy," (*Kuntress Hahitpaalut*), Dov Baer explains:

> First, it is necessary to understand the nature of the ecstasy produced by melody. This is in the category of spontaneous ecstasy only produced involuntarily, without one's desiring it, and without any effort of will. This is an ecstasy that is felt, and yet the one who experiences it is himself not aware of it, because it does not result from an intention of the self to produce ecstasy, but is produced automatically and comes of its own accord without it being known to him.[11]

The Value of Music for Other Hasidic Dynasties

Although all *hasidim* agreed on the importance of melody, in the nineteenth century there were marked differences in attitude. The melody and dance of the Karliner *hasidim* were on the same level as study and meditation. The Seer of Lublin would sing some of the prayers and would listen with great pleasure to the mellifluous tones of his reader, Rabbi Feivish, for "when Rabbi Feivish sings, 'All of them are beloved, pure and mighty', [a quote from the morning service]; the Holy One Blessed be He says to His Heavenly host, 'Let us go down and contemplate the virtues of mortal man and you will be abashed.' "

The Seer employed a "court jester" or *badhan*, Mordekhai Rakover, who with extemporized quips and rhyming jests, merrily lampooned the guests at weddings and other festivities. The phrase *Le'El asher shavat mikol hamaasim* ("To the God who rested from all His works"), was set by the Seer to a melody that he had heard in the "Heavenly spheres." In Przysucha, Kotzk, and Ger, however, music played a subsidiary role, and the emphasis was on study. Nevertheless, Rabbi Isaac Meir of Ger remarked, "Were I blessed with a sweet and beautiful voice, I would sing a new hymn for You every day. For as the world is created anew every day, new songs are created with it." Different types of melody were favored by various groups of *hasidim*, for there was nothing stereotyped or regimented about hasidic life. Some liked sentimental lyrics, while others preferred exuberant, rollicking rhythms.

A number of cantors resided at the court of Rabbi Hayim of Sanz, and outstanding among them was Rabbi Abush Meir. Rabbi Hayim had no ear for "modern" *hazzanim*. "Their melodies do not come," he said, "from the Temple of music but from the notes themselves." The rabbi of Belz attached great religious significance to the dance. "I cannot tell you the reason for dancing on *Simhat Torah*," he said, "but I can tell you that all the prayers that did not ascend to God during the whole of the year will ascend to him on this day through these dances."

The Songs of Modzitz

Both Kuzmir (Kazimierz) and Modzitz occupy high places in the history of hasidic musicology. What *Habad* did for the philosophy of Hasidism, Modzitz did for its music. The founder of the dynasty was Rabbi Ezekiel of Kuzmir (1806–1856). He was born in Plonsk, the son of Tzvi Hirsch, one of the disciples of the Besht. His father was probably murdered by the Cossacks. Ezekiel lived for a while in Warka and visited a number of hasidic leaders. The Seer said of him, "His face resembles the face of Abraham our Father." Rabbi Ezekiel became the patron of hasidic music in Poland. Like his master, the Seer, Rabbi Ezekiel employed a *badhan* and a choir. Commenting on the verse of Deuteronomy 22:4, "Thou shalt surely help to lift him up again," which refers to an animal that has fallen by the wayside, Rabbi Ezekiel explained that a man was duty-bound to help the singer by joining in the song. He would say, "I do not feel any delight in the Sabbath unless it brings forth a new melody." He died in 1856 at the age of 50. His commentary on the Pentateuch, *Nehmad MiZahav* ("More Precious Than Gold"), contains many references to song and dance.

Rabbi Ezekiel left four sons. One of them, Rabbi David Tzvi of Neustadt, founder of the Yablona dynasty, followed the traditions of Kotzk and paid little attention to music. The family tradition was maintained by Rabbi Samuel Elijah of Zwolen (1818–1888), who was gifted with a fine voice as well as a fine mind. "The law of God is perfect," he declared, "therefore melody, too, must be perfect. Great responsibilities rest upon the singer. He has to prepare and purify himself most carefully. Nor should he deviate one iota from the song, lest he transgress the precept, 'Thou shalt not add unto the word which I command you, neither shall ye diminish from it' " (Deuteronomy 4:2).

All five sons of Rabbi Samuel Elijah were music lovers. The eldest, Rabbi Moses Aaron (1837–1918), succeeded his father, but made his home in Novy Dvor. Another son, Rabbi Hayim Jerahmiel Taub, studied under Rabbi Joab-Joshua Weingarten of Kinsk, and eventually settled in Warsaw at 16 Pavia Street. He composed many subtle melodies. His father, Samuel Elijah, was his musical mentor, and the son would lead the prayers during the High Holidays. Samuel Elijah remarked that he was sustained throughout the year by the pleasure he had derived from his son's prayers on the Days of Awe. The inspired cantor rarely concluded *Musaf* (the additional service) before 5:30 P.M., for he was apt to lose all sense of time when he sang before his Heavenly Father.

Rabbi Jacob Taub of Radom, second son of Rabbi Samuel Elijah, was a gifted musician, and his father-in-law, Rabbi Leib Epstein of Ozarow (d. 1914), also took great delight in music. Both enjoyed officiating as cantors for the congregation.

Rabbi Israel of Modzitz

The baton of Rabbi Ezekiel fell to Rabbi Israel of Modzitz. Born in Racionz, he showed early signs of musical talent. At the age of 14, he married the daughter of one of the most outstanding *baalei tefillah* (cantors) of Poland, Hayim Saul Freedman of Ozarow. For thirteen years, the young husband lived with his parents-in-law, devoting himself exclusively to intensive study. He was influenced by the work *Menatze'ah Beneginut* (Vilna, 1884) of Tzvi Nisan Golomb.

In his work *Divrei Yisrael* ("Words of Israel"), Rabbi Israel devotes a lengthy excursus to music. "They say," he writes, "that the Temple of Song stands next to the Temple of Repentance, but I maintain that the Temple of Song is the Temple of Repentance." Moreover, he claimed, "Whenever I hear a Jew singing, I can ascertain whether he is wise or foolish and how much he fears God." He likened the seven tones of the scale to the seven spheres in the kabbalistic theory of creation and to the seven days of the week. "There are two phrases in our liturgy, 'Lord of Wonders, who chooses song and Psalm,' and 'King of the Universe, who hast chosen us from all the nations and hast given us Thy law'. I do not know which phrase is of greater significance." He maintained that "a person should be attuned to the songs in his own heart."

His father died on the 26th of *Iyyar* 1888, and Rabbi Israel settled in Demblin, known by the *hasidim* as Modzitz, where a large house had been acquired for him. His court became a center for melody. His first composition was an arrangement of a verse from Psalms 114, "When Israel went forth from Egypt." If a morning passed without bringing forth a new melody, he would sigh, "I have lost a morning." In addition to being a very prolific composer, he enjoyed the role of *sheliah tzibbur* and delighted his listeners with his innovative renditions. For every festival he produced an appropriate musical celebration. When his wife once complained that the preparations for the wedding of one of their children were incomplete, he assured her that his preparations were complete.

The Modzitzer melodies captivated the hasidic world. The rebbe himself did not read music, and his melodies were not written down. Nonetheless, literally by word of mouth, they were carried far and wide. He composed melodies for prayer and Sabbath songs. Some of his melodies were without words, others are taken from the Sabbath eve *zemirot* and from the liturgy. The highlight of his week was *shalosh se'udot*. He composed melodies for *Benei Hekhalah, Yedid Nefesh* and *Mizmor LeDavid. Mitnagdim* and even Gentiles would crowd outside the *Beit HaMidrash*, enthralled by the melodies of the untutored genius.

Out of Pain, Song

The rabbi would receive *hasidim* late at night, and audiences would continue until 3:00 A.M. In 1913, he fell dangerously ill. "Through the merit of your songs by which you have redeemed thousands of Jewish souls," Rabbi Menahem Kalish of Amshinow assured him, "the Almighty will grant you a speedy recovery." That same year, one of his legs was amputated in Berlin. Pain did not extinguish the fiery spirit of this charismatic personality. He refused the use of anesthetic and, on the operating table, he composed a soaring song, *Ezkerah Elokim Ve'ehemayah* ("When I think thereon, O God, I must mourn" (Psalm 77:4), consisting of thirty-two different movements. This song, which takes one and a half hours to recite, became a classic with the *hasidim* of Modzitz.

The doctors marveled at the composure of their venerable patient. "In the next room," remarked Professor James Adolf Israel (1843–1926), "lies a cabinet minister who moans and complains all the time. I said to him, 'you ought to be ashamed of yourself, I have here an aged rabbi, and whenever he is in pain, he sings'." In 1914, at the outbreak of the First World War, the rebbe settled in Warsaw. He composed *Mizmor LeDavid*, which he called "The War and Peace Melody."

He died on the 12th of *Kislev* 1921. His sepulcher (*ohel*) is one of the few that survived intact in the vandalized Warsaw cemetery. Rabbi Israel was the author of *Divrei Yisrael* (Lublin, 1901–1904; Warsaw, 1912, 1930; and New York, 1937), *Haggadah Shel Pesah* (Warsaw, 1928), and *Tiferet Yisrael* (Warsaw, 1936–1938, New York, 1941, 1947). "The rabbi of Modzitz," said the rebbe of Ostrowiec, "has bequeathed to the world a precious treasure–his immortal melodies."

The Successor of Rabbi Israel

Next in the line of the Modzitzer melody makers was Rabbi Israel's son, Rabbi Saul Jedidiah Eliezer Taub, who was born in 1887 at Ozarow. He was rabbi in Rakow from 1918 to 1922, and in 1929 he settled in Otwock, near Warsaw. Rabbi Taub received no formal grounding in the rudiments of musical theory, yet there was music in his veins. *Maskilim*, as well as *hasidim*, cantors from all over Poland, music-lovers Jewish and Gentile, flocked to Otwock to listen to the compositions of this untutored genius. What other rabbis achieved through scholarship, Rabbi Taub achieved through music, drawing many to Hasidism. More than a thousand people sat at his table every Sabbath at *Shalosh Se'udot* to hear his Torah discourses and his melodies. He is said to have composed more than 700 of them.

When the Second World War broke out, he was among the 1,100 Polish refugees who fled to Vilna. He narrowly escaped the Holocaust, journeying via Siberia and Japan to the United States. He arrived in New York in 1940, where he published the third part of his father's commentary on Leviticus, *Divrei Yisrael*. Rabbi Taub could not resist the call of the Holy Land, which he had visited in 1925, 1935, and 1938. He settled there in 1947, but he was not destined to live there for very long. He died on November 29, 1947, on the day the United Nations passed a resolution prescribing the partition of Palestine into an Arab State and a Jewish State and the internationalization of Jerusalem. He was the last person to be buried on the Mount of Olives in 1947.

Songs in Adversity

The dynasty of Bobow (Bobowa), founded by Rabbi Shlomoh Halberstam and today headed by Rabbi Solomon Halberstam of New York, is renowned for its musical creativity. The composition of hasidic melodies was not confined to Poland. The melodies of Vishnitz, a dynasty established by Rabbi Kopel Hasid and his son Rabbi Menahem Mendel Hager in Kosov, near Stanislaw, echoed through Hungary, Rumania, and Czechoslovakia.

Even in the valley of the shadow of death, even as they trod the fearsome paths that led to the crematoria, where a multitude of *hasidim* perished, even there, song sustained them. It was then that Rabbi Azriel Pastag, a *hasid* of Rabbi Taub, composed a triumphant melody that was a passionate affirmation of undying faith. "I believe," he sang, and hundreds of thousands sang with him, "with perfect faith in the coming of the Messiah, and though he tarry, yet will I wait daily for his coming." This was the faith for which the *hasidim* lived, and this was the faith for which they gave their lives in sanctification of God's Name.

Today's Heritage of Song

Echoes of hasidic music are still heard today. The most prominent of the nineteenth and twentieth-century *hazzanim*, such as David Brod Shtresliker (1883–1948), Nisan Spivak, or Nissi Belzer (1824–1906), Jacob Margowski (known as Zeidel Rovner), and a host of others, were all brought up in hasidic homes. Hasidic music has influenced synagogal music, and the songs and dances of modern Israel are greatly indebted to Hasidism. The steady output of long-playing albums of hasidic song and dance is audible evidence of the timelessness of hasidic melodies that poignantly express the strivings of the Jewish soul.

Chapter 25

Lady Rabbis and Rabbinic Daughters

Popular misconception puts the hasidic woman in her place—the kitchen and the nursery—assigning to her the sole function of producing and serving an ever-increasing family. This is a falsification of the facts. The fact is that the *hasidah*, as she was called, occupied an honored position in the hasidic world.[1] Often it was the wife who converted the husband, for Hasidism attracted women, and they reacted to the basic principles of the movement with sensitivity and appreciation. They read hasidic anecdotes (printed in Yiddish) as avidly as their twentieth-century counterparts devour romantic novels.

The Besht's Attitude toward Women

The Besht never forgot the devotion of his own wife, Hannah. Despite her brother's opposition, Hannah had married Israel when the hidden Master appeared to be a poor, ignorant peasant, and their abiding love had weathered many hardships. Israel loved her deeply, and after she died he did not remarry. "Heaven has departed with her," he grieved, "I thought that a storm would sweep me up to Heaven like the prophet Elijah, but now that I am only half a body, that is no longer possible." In his Last Will and Testament, *Tzavaat HaRibash*, he urged *hasidim* to honor their wives.

The Besht adored his only daughter Udel, who accompanied him on many of his journeys. To her he applied the verse in

Deuteronomy 33:2, "At his right hand was a fiery Law unto them," for the first letters of the Hebrew words *eish dat lamo* (a fiery law unto them) make up the name Udel.[2]

When the Besht visited Satanow, he perceived a great spiritual light and found that this radiance emanated from a woman. "Shame on you!" he rebuked the leaders of the community, "through a woman have I seen the light."[3] He believed that women's prayers were particularly efficacious. The Besht liked to tell how a certain community had once proclaimed a public fast in order to ward off some imminent disaster. The whole community, men and women, young and old, assembled in the synagogue. Weeping before the Ark and trembling with terror, the rabbi prayed for many hours. Yet neither the piety of the rabbi nor the prayers of the elders could force open the Gates of Heaven. They opened at the cry from the heart of a simple woman, a humble mother in Israel. "Master of the Universe! Thou art a merciful Father and Thou hast many children," she pleaded. "I am a mother of five children, and when but one child suffers I cry out, and my heart goes out to it. Surely, Thou art more compassionate than I am. Even if Thy heart were made of stone, it should melt at the agonizing cry of Thy children. O, God, listen to them and save them."

When one of his followers, Jonah Spradlaver, complained to the Besht of his wife Yente's strange behavior, the Master reassured him. "She has seeing eyes and hearing ears," he enigmatically announced, bestowing upon her the title "prophetess." Yet husbands were not always gratified by the spiritual prowess of their wives.

Tales of Kindness toward Women

Hasidic writers tried increasingly to raise the prestige of women in Jewish life. It is said that the wife of one of his opponents met Rabbi Levi Isaac of Berdichev in the street and poured a pail of water over his head. Rabbi Levi Isaac went to the synagogue and prayed, "O Lord, God of Israel, do not punish the good woman. She must have done this at her husband's command, and she is therefore to be commended as a loyal wife."

To lighten the burden of the widow was a major *mitzvah,* and in such situations hasidic rabbis did not stand on their dignity. Rabbi

Hayim Halberstam was once walking through the marketplace, where he noticed a widow behind her fruit stall bitterly bewailing the lack of customers. Without further ado, Rabbi Hayim took her place at the stand and shouted: "Buy fine apples, a gulden a dozen." The news that the *tzaddik* had turned salesman spread through the market, and people rushed to buy from the holy man. The poor widow made a fine profit that day.

Great Hasidic Women

Not since the biblical days that had brought forth the "Four Matriarchs" and the "Seven Prophetesses" (*Megillah* 14a), has Jewry produced women as outstanding as those who emerged in the heyday of Hasidism. Rabbi Leib Sarah's (1710–1791) was, however, the only hasidic personality whose name was always associated with that of his mother. He is also the subject of more stories than any other *tzaddik* save the Besht, for he traveled ceaselessly, rescuing and redeeming fellow Jews. His mother, Sarah, had been a woman of rare beauty, who had married an elderly scholar in order to escape the unwelcome attentions of the local squire's son. Presumably, she was rewarded for this act with the birth of her illustrious son, and the way in which her name is eternally linked with his.

Feige, daughter of Udel, was said to be endowed with "divine spirit," that her son Rabbi Nahman of Bratslav seemed to inherit. Like the daughters of Rashi, Merish, daughter of Rabbi Elimelekh of Lyzhansk, was renowned for her scholarship. *Hasidim* would go to hear her learned discourses and to receive her blessings. Freida, eldest daughter of Rabbi Shneur Zalman, was honored by *Habad hasidim.* She collected her father's aphorisms and wrote a number of remarkable manuscripts on a variety of subjects.

Distinguished for Brilliance, Knowledge and Charity

Even the study of *Kabbalah* did not satisfy the spiritual aspirations of certain hasidic women. Perele, eldest daughter of Rabbi Israel of Kozienice and wife of Rabbi Ezra Zelig Shapira, Rabbi of Magnuszew (d. 1849), wore *tzitzit* (ritual fringes), fasted on Mondays and Thursdays, and received petitions from her followers. She lived a life of poverty, promptly distributing among the needy all the money that she received from the *hasidim*. "The *Shekhinah* rests upon her," acknowledged Rabbi Elimelekh of Lyzhansk, and her own father urged his *hasidim* to visit her.

Rachel, daughter of Rabbi Abraham Joshua Heschel of Opatow (1745–1825), was equally renowned. Her father, an ardent believer in her powers, declared, "She has a holy spark." She accompanied him on many journeys, and he consulted her constantly. Most of the *hasidim* of Opatow (Apta) paid court to the daughter as well as to the father, for they believed that she, too, could accomplish great things.

Rebecca, wife of Rabbi Simha Bunem, was known for her hospitality and her kindliness. Her home in Przysucha was a second home to all her husband's disciples, and many of them later became leading lights of Hasidism. After the death of her husband and her son, she devoted herself to charitable causes. Traveling from place to place, she held out a helping hand to all who were in need. Often she appealed to her husband's disciples, and her appeals were always heeded. The "miracles" wrought by Rebecca were acts of lovingkindness.

Wives and Daughters

The adage "like mother, like daughter" certainly applied to the wife and daughter of the rabbi of Belz. Malka's daughter, Eidele, married Rabbi Isaac Rubin of Sokolow (d. 1876), a son of Rabbi Asher of Ropczyce. Interestingly enough, Rabbi Isaac had been reluctant to become a *rebbe*, whereas his wife was suited for the role. She delivered discourses, distributed *shirayim*, and generally conducted herself like a *rebbe*. "All Eidele needs is a rabbi's hat," remarked her father, fondly.

Similarly, Sarah, daughter of Rabbi Joshua Heschel Teumim Frankel, made a name for herself among the *hasidim*. She was born in 1838 in Tarnopol. Her father died when she was only 3 months old, and she was brought up by Rabbi Josele, the "good Jew" of Neustadt, who later married her off to his grandson, Rabbi Hayim Samuel Horowitz Sternfeld. When her husband died in 1916, Sarah more or less took his place. A system of regular contributions was instituted to support her, and this money she distributed among the poor. Her sayings were wise and her parables so apt, that even rabbis sought her counsel and her blessings. She fasted regularly, and asceticism was her way of life. Yet it proved to be no barrier to longevity. She died in 1937 at the age of ninety-nine.

In the same way, "Malkale the Triskerin," as she was called, daughter of Rabbi Abraham of Turisk (1806–1889), conducted *tish* (public meals), distributed *shirayim* and received petitions twice daily from *hasidim*. She insisted, moreover, on being present when *hasidim* visited her father, the *Maggid*.

Another celebrated woman of rabbinic learning and piety was Hannah Havah, daughter of Rabbi Mordekhai Twersky (1770–1837) of Chernobyl, who, according to her father's testimony, was endowed "with the Holy Spirit from the womb and from birth." He deemed her equal in piety to his sons, "the eight candles of the *menorah*." Her aphorisms and parables spread her fame throughout Poland. She dealt tenderly and tirelessly with the women who flocked to her for guidance. She emphasized the importance of correct and careful education and urged her followers to be charitable in every way.

The Maid of Ludmir

The most famous of all hasidic women was Hannah Rachel (1805–1892), only child of Monesh Werbemacher, who became known as the "Maid of Ludmir" (Vladmir Volynski). The limited education that was then provided for girls did not satisfy little Hannah Rachel. She studied the *midrash*, the *aggadah*, and many books of *musar*. She was betrothed at an early age, but the betrothal brought her little happiness. A warmhearted and affectionate child, she was forced to live a lonely and friendless existence. There was no one to share her thoughts. Sometimes surges of exultation lifted her spirit, but more often she fell prey to moods of prolonged melancholy. Then she would find comfort only at the grave of her mother, where she poured out all her longings and inner desires. On one of her regular visits to the cemetery, she fell asleep at the graveside. When she awoke, it was midnight. The weird shapes and shadows looming large in the deserted "House of Life," filled her with terror. Half-dazed, she began to run and stumbled into a half-filled grave. This shock disrupted her already fragile constitution. She became very ill, and for a while she hovered between life and death. When she finally recovered, she startled her father with this announcement: "I have just returned from the Heavenly Court, where I received a new and sublime soul." Indeed, the new Hannah Rachel was different. She donned *tzitzit*, wrapped herself in a *tallit* and, like Michal, daughter of King Saul, she put on *tefillin.*[4] When her father died, she recited *Kaddish* for him. Inevitably, the betrothal was annulled.

Financially well provided for by her father, the learned lady spent her time in secluded meditation. A synagogue was built with an adjoining apartment for her. Every Sabbath at *shalosh se'udot*, the door of her room would be opened. Heard but not seen, the Maid of Ludmir would deliver erudite discourses to which men of piety and learning listened eagerly and appreciatively, for scholars and rabbis were among the numerous *hasidim* of the Maid of Ludmir. Finally, at the age of 40, she succumbed to the persuasive tongue of Rabbi Mordekhai of Chernobyl and agreed to wed the talmudic scholar whom the rabbi of Chernobyl warmly recommended. However, her influence waned after the marriage, and she emigrated to the Holy Land.

The Maid and the Messiah

Legend has it that in the Holy Land the Maid entered into a mystical partnership with a *Kabbalist*, and both resolved to hasten the coming of the Messiah. After prolonged and elaborate preparations, a time and place were set for the enactment of the great drama. The Maid of Ludmir arrived punctually at the appointed site, a cave outside Jerusalem, and waited anxiously but in vain. The *Kabbalist* collaborator had been inexplicably detained by a venerable sage, the ubiquitous prophet Elijah in disguise, whose role it was to prevent the hatching of the apocalyptic plot. The Messianic era was not due yet and could not be precipitated.

The Unsung Heroines

The women on the hasidic "roll of honor" who were "rabbis" and "wonder workers," students of *Kabbalah*, and talmudists, were, of course, exceptions. The majority of hasidic women were themselves unlettered, yet they were often largely responsible for the erudition of their husbands and sons. Often they maintained and sustained the family, relieving their husbands of material cares, so that they could devote themselves exclusively to matters of the mind and the soul. The lives of these wives were difficult and often dangerous. Feige, wife of Rabbi Isaac Meir of Ger, was a vendor of cloth. Yokheved, wife of Rabbi Judah Leib of Ger, became a sugar merchant. The wife of Rabbi Jacob of Radzymin turned traveling peddler, wandering from village to village with her wares. Perele, wife of Rabbi Nathan David of Szydlowiec, supervised an estate, and Hannah Deborah, wife of Rabbi Tzadok Hakohen of Lublin, dealt in clothes.

Tamarel Bergson

An important role was played by Tamarel Bergson, wife of Baer Smulevitch and ancestress of the French philospher, Henri Bergson. What Beatrice de Luna, known as Gracia Mendes (1510–1569), did for the Sephardim in the sixteenth century, Tamarel did for the *hasidim* 300 years later. She employed a number of young men who later became *rebbes.* She herself was a devoted *hasidah* of Rabbi Isaac of Warka, Rabbi Mendel of Kotzk, and Rabbi Isaac Meir of Ger. Her generosity was proverbial, and she helped countless *hasidim* to extricate themselves from material misfortunes.

Liberal Access to Books

The *hasidim* were unyielding in their opposition to *Haskalah.* No secular subject was allowed to penetrate the walls of the *yeshivah.* No *yeshivah* student dared to openly read the works of Judah Leib Gordon (1830–1892) or Shalom Jacob Abramowitsch (1836–1917). *Ahavat Tzion* ("The Love of Zion") and *Ayit Tzavua* ("the Painted Hawk") by Abraham Mapu (1808–1867) could be perused only in secret. But the hasidic fathers were more lenient with their daughters, who read whatever they wished, but were denied any formal education. Though Glückel of Hameln writes in her memoirs of *heder* education for girls,[5] this was certainly not the norm. For the most part, the intellectual thirst of the women in Eastern Europe was confined to the *Tzenah Ure'enah* ("Go Forth and See") by Jacob ben Isaac Ashkenazi of Janow. This book was a sixteenth-century Yiddish version of the Pentateuch interlaced with tales, interpretive comment, and romantic fiction.

Formal Education for Women

By the beginning of the twentieth century, however, the mood had changed. Many hasidic parents now encouraged their daughters to study, and gloried in the not inconsiderable intellectual attainments of these eager and perceptive young women. In small Polish towns, private tutors were in great demand, and music, Polish, and French were favorite subjects. In the larger towns, many girls attended such Jewish schools as the *Tarbut* (under the auspices of the Zionists) and *Zisho* (the Central Yiddish School Organization). Paradoxically, the daughters of hasidic families were often forbidden to enroll at *Tarbut* or *Zisho* institutions, but they were permitted to attend the Gentile *gymnasium*. Some even completed the curriculum of "eight classes" and graduated.

A secular education was of more than academic use to these women. Often they, as breadwinners, needed to deal intelligently with the non-Jewish world. Yet many fathers came to regret the liberalism that had allowed them to expose their young daughters to the new horizons that opened for them in the *gymnasia*. The *Tzenah Ure'enah* was discarded in favor of the epic *Pan Tadeusz* by the Polish poet Adam Mickiewicz (1798–1855). Matchmakers and parentally arranged marriages were no longer accepted with docility. Many now regarded the *yeshivah bahur* (student) as unworldly and parochial. New knowledge gave them new ideas. Often newly emancipated young women fled from fatherly reproofs with husbands of their own choosing.

The Beit Yaakov *Movement*

Certainly, it was not easy for an educated girl to find fulfillment in her own home, for the menfolk lived in a world of their own. Sarah Schenirer, founder of the *Beit Yaakov* Schools, described the scene:

> And as we pass through the *Elul* days, the trains which run to the little *shtetlekh* (towns), where the rebbes live, are crowded. Thousands of *hasidim* are on their way to them to spend the *Yamim Nora'im* ("Solemn Holy Days") with the *rebbe*. Every day sees new crowds of old men and young men in the hasidic garb, eager to secure a place on the train, eager to spend the holiest days in the year in the atmosphere of their *rebbe*, to be able to extract from it as much holiness as possible. Fathers and sons travel, and those who can afford it make this journey several times a year. Thus they are drawn to Ger, to Belz, to Alexander, to Bobow, to all those places that had been made citadels of concerted religious life, dominated by the leading figure of a *rebbe*'s personality.
>
> And we stay at home, the wives, the daughters, and the little ones. We have an empty *yom tov*. It is bare of Jewish intellectual content. The women have never learned anything about the spiritual meaning of our festivals. The mother goes to the synagogue, but the services echo faintly into the fenced and boarded-off galleries where the women sit out of sight. There is much crying by the elderly women. The young girls look at them as though they belonged to a different century. Youth and the desire to live a full life shoot up violently in the strong-willed young personalities. Outside the *shul* the young girls stand chattering; they walk away from the *shul* where their mothers pour out their vague and heavy feelings. They leave behind them the wailing of the older generation and follow the urge for freedom and self-expression. Further and further away from *shul* they go, further away to the dancing, tempting light of a fleeting joy.[6]

Sarah's father was a merchant and a *hasid* of Belz. During the First World War, she lived in Vienna and was influenced by Rabbi Dr. Flesch. "I listened intently to Dr. Flesch's inspiring sermon," Sarah recalled. "The rabbi painted a vivid picture of Judith, the heroine of Jewish history. He held her image up as an example to the girls and women of our day and urged them to walk in the footsteps of the illustrious women of ancient times. . . . I said to myself: 'How I wish that the women of Krakow might know who we are and who our ancestors were.' "[7]

The first *Beit Yaakov* school for girls was founded in Krakow under the guidance of Sarah Schenirer in 1917. The name *Beit Yaakov* alludes to the verse, "O house of Jacob (*Beit Yaakov*) come ye and let us walk in the light of the Lord" (Isaiah 2:5). Under Schenirer, propagandist and pedagogue, the movement flourished, and by 1924 there were nineteen schools with 2,000 students. In 1937–1938 there were in Poland 248 *Beit Yaakov* Schools with an enrollment of 35,585 students. The *Beit Yaakov* Schools were acknowledged by the *Knessiah Gedolah* (The Great Assembly), of the *Agudah* to be "the best solution for the education of girls." The *Keren HaTorah* (the special *Agudah* fund established by German-Jewish Orthodoxy for Torah institutions) gave financial support. Moral support came from the rabbi of Belz and Rabbi Israel Kahan (1835–1933), author of *Hafetz Hayim* ("Desiring Life").

The Success of the Movement

The curriculum of the *Beit Yaakov* schools was heavily weighted in favor of Judaic studies. Each student was obliged to learn fifty Psalms by heart and to become thoroughly acquainted with Jewish law and liturgy, but secular subjects were also studied. To meet the ever-increasing demand for instructors, the *Beit Yaakov* Teachers' Seminary was built in Krakow in 1931 at a cost of $60,000. *Beit Yaakov* graduates formed an association, and many became the backbone of the *Agudah* women's movement known as *Bnot Agudat Yisrael* and *Neshei Agudat Yisrael* that numbered 20,000 in 1937.

Typical of the approving attitude of the hasidic *rebbes* was the stand taken by Abraham Mordekhai Alter, the rabbi of Ger. "It is a sacred duty to work nowadays for the *Beit Yaakov* movement," he wrote. "The future mothers of Israel are being educated in the true traditional spirit of the Torah and are receiving a sound all-round schooling."

Openly and appreciatively, hasidic writers and *rebbes* acknowledge the vital role of women in Jewish life. It did not matter that they had neither the time nor the opportunity for esoteric study or spiritual achievements. No wonder women responded with such instant warmth to Hasidism. Its appeal was emotional, its tenets deeply rooted in reality. In Hasidism the mundane day-to-day routine acquired a new dimension and a new nobility.

Chapter 26

"If I Forget Thee, O Jerusalem"

"If I forget thee, O Jerusalem, let my right hand forget her cunning," wept the Jews by the alien waters of Babylon, "let my tongue cleave to the roof of my mouth, if I remember thee not" (Psalms 137:5–6). Throughout their long and bitter exile, they kept alive the memory of their ancient homeland, and for the kabbalists it was particularly precious. "Happy is he who is fortunate enough to dwell in the Holy Land," says the *Zohar,* "He causes the dew to fall upon the earth."[1]

The Besht set out for the Holy Land three times, on one occasion reaching as far as Istanbul, but each time "Heaven held him back,"[2] for the fusion of the holy man and the Holy Land would precipitate the coming of the Messiah. In vain, the Besht yearned to fulfill the *mitzvah* of living in the Land of Israel and of planting the seeds of Hasidism in the hallowed soil. Although the Master was not destined to accomplish this task himself, his aims were achieved through his pupils and associates.

In 1746 Rabbi Abraham Gershon Kutower, the brother-in-law of the Besht, a learned talmudist and kabbalist, emigrated to Israel. Rabbi Jonathan Eibeschütz spoke of Rabbi Gershon with the utmost reverence.[3] At first, Rabbi Gershon had not recognized the hidden greatness of his sister's husband, but later he became a devoted follower of the Besht. Rabbi Gershon arrived in Jerusalem on the eve of New Year and was warmly welcomed by both the Sephardim and the Ashkenazim. He settled first in Hebron and later in Jerusalem. The Besht often wrote to him and occasionally sent funds.

In one letter the Besht counsels, "Let the words of *musar* (ethics), which I have spoken to you always be in your mind."[4] For the Besht, distance was no obstacle. "One Friday night, during the service," said the Besht, "I searched for Rabbi Gershon throughout Palestine and could not find him anywhere. But the next morning I found him." Rabbi Gershon explained that he had spent that particular Sabbath at Acre, worshipping on Friday night in a synagogue that was technically outside the boundary of Israel. "Pray for me," the Besht wrote to his brother-in-law, "Pray that I may be worthy to join the inheritance of the Lord, for the Almighty knows that I have not given up hope of going to the Land of Israel."[5]

The adoption by the *hasidim* of the *Nusah Ari* ("the Lurian liturgy") forged another link with the Holy Land. But many *hasidim* yearned for a more personal attachment and sought to settle there.

Like the second-century *tanna*, Nahum Ish Gamzu, Rabbi Nahman of Horodenka accepted every misfortune with the words *gam zu letovah* ("this, too, is for the best"), for his faith was as "strong as a pillar of iron."[6] He accompanied the Besht on many travels. "I have afflicted my soul, and I have immersed myself in ritual baths, but I could not rid myself of alien thoughts until I became attached to the Besht." Together with Rabbi Menahem Mendel of Przemyslany (d. 1772), Nahman set out for the Holy Land. The voyage was difficult and dangerous. When the ship tossed on the stormy seas, Rabbi Nahman exclaimed, "Lord of the Universe, if it has been decreed by Thy Heavenly Court that we should perish, this Holy Congregation, jointly with the *Shekhinah*, declare that we decline to accept the decree. We demand its prompt annulment." The passengers landed safely on the 12th of *Tishri* 1764. Rabbi Nahman and Rabbi Menahem Mendel lived in Tiberias and Safed.

The Arduous Journey

"*Eretz Yisrael* is an exalted land," wrote Rabbi Jacob Joseph of Polonnoye, "and the Holy One, Blessed be He, hath given it to Israel as a perpetual gift. It is reserved exclusively and entirely for them."[7] Rabbi Jacob Joseph made careful preparations for his pilgrimage, and the Besht gave him a letter to deliver personally to his brother-in-law. However, for reasons unknown to us, the journey was never made, and the letter was never delivered. Later Rabbi Jacob Joseph published it in his book *Porat Yosef* under the heading: "This is the epistle that the Besht gave me to hand to Rabbi Gershon."

According to Rabbi Phinehas of Korets, it was unnatural for a man not to yearn for the Holy Land. Commenting on Moses's prayer, "Let me go over, I pray Thee, and see the good Land" (Deuteronomy 3:25), Rabbi Phinehas commented, "Moses said to God, 'I do not wish to be as the ten spies who brought back an unfavorable and gloomy report. I wish to see only the 'good of *Eretz Yisrael*.' "[8] In 1790, Rabbi Phinehas left Ostrog for Israel, but he died in mid-journey at Shepetovka in 1790 or 1791.

In 1777, 300 *hasidim* left Galati in Rumania under the leadership of Rabbi Menahem Mendel of Vitebsk (1730–1788), Rabbi Abraham Hakohen of Kalisk (Kalishki), and Rabbi Israel Plotzker. Five months later, after many hardships, they reached their destination. "At last the day has come for which we have waited with such impatience," wrote one of the leaders, "How happy we are in the Holy Land, the delight of our hearts, the joy of our thoughts is the land which is sanctified by different types of sanctity."[9]

Conditions of Poverty and Support from Abroad

Although the *hasidim* were received with great friendliness by the Jewish communities, the arrival of so large a group of newcomers created economic problems. Their funds soon petered out, and they naturally had no means of earning a living. "Even a man with the heart of a lion melts when he beholds infants begging for bread." So Rabbi Menahem Mendel enlisted the support of his followers in Russia. He sent Rabbi Israel of Plotzk to raise funds for the *halukkah* (literally, division), as the collections made abroad for the support of the *yishuv* (settlement) in the Holy Land came to be known. Rabbi Israel was the forerunner of many *meshullahim* or *shaddarim* (emissaries), who repeatedly visited hasidic centers in Eastern Europe for this purpose.

"It is your responsibility," writes Rabbi Israel to the heads of the Jewish community in Russia, "to build up the House of our God, and it is incumbent upon Jewry to support the settlement in the Holy Land . . . Hasten to perform this great *mitzvah* and to sustain the Children of Israel, feeding the hungry and clothing the naked, in order that they, who live on the holy soil, may pray for the scattered community of Israel in exile." His appeal was not unheeded. With the help of Rabbi Shneur Zalman, a fund (*maamadot*) was set up, and considerable sums were collected. Rabbi Israel, however, did not return to the Holy Land. As he was passing Pastow, the burial place of Rabbi Abraham, "the Angel," he seemed to hear a summons. "Abraham is calling me," he said. "He wants me to be buried by his side." Abraham's request was granted.

Thwarted Pilgrimages

When Rabbi Hayim of Krasny (d. 1793), son-in-law of Rabbi Ze'ev Wolf of Zhitomir (d. 1800), was shipwrecked en route, he regarded the incident as a mark of Divine displeasure and forbade the inscription of titles on his tombstone because "I have not been deemed worthy of visiting *Eretz Yisrael*."

Although Rabbi Schneur Zalman, founder of *Habad*, could not abandon his followers, he actively helped to support the *yishuv*. He arranged for systematic collections and regularly dispatched funds. Similarly, Rabbi Israel of Kozienice actively encouraged fund-raising for this pious endeavor.

The Prayers of Nahman of Bratslav

Not since Judah Halevi (c. 1075–1141), that "fiery pillar of sweet song," to whom Jerusalem was the "city of the world," had Zion had as lyrical a lover as the poet of Hasidism, Rabbi Nahman of Bratslav. The emotions that Judah Halevi expressed in his "Song of Zion," Rabbi Nahman voiced in the pithy aphorisms for which he was renowned. Like Judah Halevi, he traveled widely throughout the Holy Land but, unlike the poet, he did not visit Jerusalem. He described in minute detail his visits to Elijah's Cave on Mount Carmel, to the tomb of Rabbi Simon ben Yohai at Meron, and to the grave of his grandfather, Rabbi Nahman of Horodenka.

When he returned to his home, he composed many prayers. Among them were these words of supplication:

> O Lord God, who is merciful and gracious, slow to anger and abundant in truth and mercy. In Thy great mercy make me and the Children of Israel worthy that our hearts may yearn

for the Land of Israel, the foundation of our Holy Faith, the land which the Lord has chosen for His people . . . Grant me the strength and resolution that I should fulfill this craving of my heart . . . Thou alone knowest how great is my need of the land because of the distraction, confusion, and imperfection that beset my life and remove me far from thee.[10]

The Bond Between the Holy Land and Hasidim

Although relatively few of the great hasidic masters were actually able to make the journey to the Holy Land, most of them made the journey in spirit, for they stressed again and again the mystic significance of Zion. Rabbi Levi Isaac of Berdichev loved the Land of Israel as dearly as he loved the People of Israel. "When the Jews dwell there securely in the Land of Israel," he declared, "then the country is inhabited. But when the Israelites are in exile, then the country is regarded as a wilderness, even though it may be inhabited by other nations. The land of Israel belongs to the people of Israel. And only they can possess it."

Prophetically, Rabbi Solomon of Lutsk, disciple of the *Maggid* of Mezhirech, linked the future of the land with the revival of Hebrew as a living language. In his *Divrat Shlomo* ("Words of Solomon"), printed in 1859, he writes, "It is essential that the people living there should use the Holy Tongue, the language in which the Universe was created. If they do not speak the Holy Tongue, then the land does not really belong to them, and they can easily be banished."[11]

Throughout the nineteenth century, the links between Hasidism and *Eretz Yisrael* were maintained, and a steady stream of pious pioneers exchanged comfortable homes for the rigors of a spartan existence. When Jacob Samson, the rabbi of Shepetovka, visited his friend Benjamin Wolf of Zbarzh[12] (d. 1822) in Tiberias, he saw the rabbi's wife laboring over the wash-tub. "Rabbi, this linen is not mine!" she exclaimed, "I am washing it for others, and I am not being paid for the task. But I feel no regrets. No sacrifice is too great for the privilege of living here."[13]

Hastening the Messiah's Coming

The Seer of Lublin urged Jews to refuse to accept the prevailing conditions. He urged them to repossess the land of their forefathers.

Only then would there be hope for Israel's redemption. Rabbi Simha Bunem compared the love of Israel for the Land of Israel with the love of a bride for her bridegroom. With the coming of the Messiah, the "marriage" would be consummated. The first visit to the Holy Land of Sir Moses Montefiore fired the imagination of the *hasidim*. Rabbi Simha Bunem reputedly asked why Montefiore had not attempted to purchase the Holy Land from the Turks. He was asked, "What use is the purchase of this territory before the arrival of the Messiah?" "When the land passes out of the hands of the Arabs into Jewish hands," replied Rabbi Simha Bunem, "the Messiah will come immediately."[14]

Rabbi David of Lelov, disciple of the Yehudi, urged his eldest son Moses (1778–1850) to visit the Holy Land and there to hasten the redemption. Moses' father-in-law, the Yehudi, also encouraged the young man to undertake the journey. The father bequeathed property to his sons Avigdor and Nehemiah but left nothing to Moses because "a house is ready for you in Jerusalem, the Holy City." In 1843, Moses sought to fulfill his father's wish. "When with the help of the Almighty, I will arrive safely in the Holy Land, I will go directly to the Western Wall in Jerusalem," promised Moses. "There will I lift up my voice like a trumpet and I will bring the Messiah."

Personal and pecuniary problems, however, stood in his way. His wife, Rebecca Rachel, opposed the journey, and none of her husband's colleagues could move her. Summoned to a special gathering to discuss the matter, she stood in the doorway and cried, "Have respect for the daughter of the Holy Jew." Rabbi Moses traveled throughout Poland with his disciples and with Rabbi Solomon of Radomsko to raise money for the trip. He left Rumania in 1850 with his children, ten disciples, and two attendants. His wife remained behind. He celebrated the High Holidays on the high seas and a *sukkah* (booth) was erected on the boat.

The voyage took two months. When he finally arrived in Jerusalem, he was exhausted and in rapidly failing health. Since he no longer had the strength to walk to the Western Wall, he begged his sons to carry him there. "I must be at the Western Wall this very day," he told them. On the way, Arabs attacked the little group, and Rabbi Moses did not reach the Wall. He died seventy-two days after arriving in the Holy Land. Yet his last wish was fulfilled, and he was buried near the grave of the prophet Zechariah in Jerusalem.[15]

Through the strenuous endeavors of Rabbi Isaac Meir of Ger, 40,000 rubles were raised for the *yishuv* between 1838 and 1840. During the Polish Rebellion in 1863, Rabbi Isaac Meir commented, "We see how the Poles are sacrificing themselves to liberate their country from the hands of the foreigners. What are we doing to regain our land?" He had a grave foreboding about the future of the Jews in Europe.

A Renewed Love of Zion

The publication, in 1862, of *Derishat Tziyon* ("Quest of Zion") by Rabbi Tzvi Hirsch Kalischer (1795–1874) gave impetus to the *Hibbat Tziyon* ("Lovers of Zion") movement. Under the leadership of Leon Pinsker (1831–1891), Moses Leib Lilienblum (1843–1910), and Judah Leo Levanda, *Hibbat Tziyon* societies were formed in Russia, Austria, and Germany. With the help of Baron de Rothschild (1854–1934) of Paris, several settlements were established in the Holy Land.

As a rule, *hasidim* did not join the *Hibbat Tziyon* movement, but there were such notable exceptions as Elijah Guttmacher (1796–1875) of Gratz. Rabbi Hayim of Pulawy (1870–1906), a grandson of Rabbi Mendel of Kotzk, formed *Agudat Ha'elef* ("The Group of the Thousand"), aimed at settling a thousand *hasidim* in the Holy Land. In collaboration with Rabbi Isaac Jacob Reines (1839–1915) and Rabbi Samuel Mohilewer (1824–1898), Rabbi Hayim wrote a booklet, *Shelom Yerushalayim* ("Peace of Jerusalem"), that demonstrated that every Jew was duty bound to participate in the rebuilding of the Holy Land.

Fulfillment of Mitzvot

In a letter to Rabbi Hayim, Rabbi Judah Leib of Ger writes, "Certainly he upon whom the fear of Heaven rests takes it upon himself to fulfill the Commandments of tithes and *maaser* for he, who knows that members of his family will not object to them, need not be afraid. It will be reckoned as a *mitzvah*. Although the *aliyah* is not considered for its own sake, nevertheless, we can say that eventually it will turn out to be for its own sake."[16] Like Rabbi Hayim Eleazar Waks of Kalish, Rabbi Judah Leib urged that *hasidim* import Palestinian *etrogim*.

Reaction to Zionism

While the Jewish world at large was growing increasingly enthusiastic over the possible restoration of the Jewish home through political means, *hasidim* did not generally share this enthusiasm. For the battle still raged between Hasidism and *Haskalah*. The *hasidim* associated *Haskalah* with assimilation and even apostasy, and many of the *maskilim* carried the flag of Zionism. Moreover, repossession of the promised land at this stage was regarded as tantamount to interference with the Divine order of things.

Dr. Theodor Herzl (1860–1904), father of political Zionism, was anxious to enlist the support of the *hasidim*. In his diary, under May 8, 1896, he recorded, "The *hasid* Aaron Marcus (1843–1916) of Podgorze (Galicia) again writes me a very fine letter, in which he holds out the possibility that the three million *hasidim* of Poland will join my movement. I answer that the participation of the Orthodox will be welcome, but that no theocracy will be created."[17]

Three years later, Herzl pleaded passionately for the cooperation of Rabbi Judah Leib of Ger and wrote to him:

> In the name of thousands of Jews whose existence, threatened by hostile neighbors, grows daily more difficult; in the name of the starving multitudes who engage in all kinds of occupations to feed their children; in the name of the thousands of refugees who flee from Russia, Rumania, and Galicia, to America, Africa, and Australia, where the danger of assimilation awaits them; and finally in the name of God and the Torah, we urge the honorable rabbi to tell us openly the sins which we have committed by espousing Zionism.[18]

The Zionist leader kept in touch with Rabbi Judah Menahem Halevi of Przemysl (1862–1920), rabbi of Botosani, Rumania, "who offered to negotiate with the wonder rabbi, Moses Friedmann of Chortkow. I sent a letter in which I invited Friedmann to send me his son."[19] Herzl met the rabbi's son, and Aaron Marcus joined them in trying to persuade the *rebbe* to call a conference of rabbis to promote the aims of Zionism. In Herzl's entry under November 10, 1897, he writes, "A man from Jerusalem named Bak came to see me. He is traveling round Europe in order to found an agrarian bank for Palestine–a vest pocket Jewish company, evidently his vest pocket. He claims to be under the patronage of the Galician wonder rabbi, Friedmann."[20] Herzl also met another hasidic rabbi. "One of the most curious figures I have just encountered," writes Herzl, "is the Rymanower *Rebbe* Horowitz, son-in-law of the wonder rabbi there. He came to me, accompanied by his secretary."[21]

Sacred Duties

Rabbi Abraham of Sochaczew urged Jews to settle in the Holy Land providing they could, for this is the fulfillment of a *mitzvah* that is equal to the sum of all the *mitzvot*. Moreover, there is no limit to the reward of those who participate to redeem the land.[22] To Rabbi Israel of Pulawy he wrote, "I have examined the contents of your little book, and I have derived much pleasure from it, for with sweet and pleasant phrases it fills the heart with love of the Holy Land . . . It is proper to purchase an estate in *Eretz Yisrael* . . . I, too, want to do this."[23] In 1898, he sent his son and his son-in-law to purchase land from the Turkish overlords, but the transaction was not completed.

Fund-raising alone did not satisfy the rabbis of the dynasty of Warka (founded by Rabbi Isaac of Warka). Rabbi Simha Bunem Kalish, son of Rabbi Isaac, took his wife and five children to the Holy Land in the winter of 1887. Like all Russian tourists, he had a thirty-day permit. When it expired, he was arrested and imprisoned for five days until the community secured his release. He was permitted to stay for three months and then had to return home. Twenty years later, in 1906, he came back to Jerusalem and there he remained. He died in 1907 and was buried in Tiberias next to Menahem Mendel of Vitebsk.

For Rabbi Meir Jehiel of Ostrowiec, the poor of the Holy Land took precedence over the poor in his hometown, and he diligently collected monies for them. He used to say, "I am from the Land of Israel, but we were exiled because of our sins and now I live in Ostrowiec. Similarly, whenever a Jew is asked: 'Where do you come from?' he should reply, 'I come from the Holy Land, but now I live temporarily in exile.' "

Without exception, hasidic rabbis agreed that it was a sacred and important task to support the poor of the Holy Land. Rabbi Israel of Ruzhin became a Turkish citizen, and on his passport were the words "a native of Jerusalem." In 1843, Nisan Bak of Jerusalem told him that the Czar of Russia was planning to buy a site near the Western Wall to erect a monastery. Quickly, the rabbi raised the money that enabled Bak to acquire that strategic piece of land. According to legend, when the Czar heard that he had been outmaneuvered by the rabbi of Ruzhin, he exclaimed: "That Jew always blocks my path." A beautiful synagogue, named alternately *Tiferet Yisrael* or *Beit Haknesset Nisan Bak* was built and opened in 1873 and served as a rallying center for the *hasidim* of Ruzhin.

Rabbi Israel was not impressed with the events of 1848, *Annus Mirabilis* (the National Revolutions of 1848–1850). "There will come a time," he ominously predicted, "when the nations will drive us out of their lands. How shameful that after our too long drawn-out exile, the redemption should take place under such circumstances."[24]

A century before the Balfour Declaration, the rabbi of Ruzhin foretold, "As in the time of Ezra, a government will again arise that will permit the Jews to return to the land of their fathers." He was worldly enough to realize that a country cannot be built up by the settlement of a few celebrities. "If I go to Israel," he said, "they will ask me why I did not bring my people with me? What answer can I give them?"

Rabbi Israel's son, Rabbi Abraham Jacob Friedmann of Sadgora, wrote to Sir Moses Montefiore asking him to persuade the Czar to allow collections for the Holy Land "without fear or dread."[25]

Chapter 27

The Return to Zion

"The land of Israel for the people of Israel founded on the Torah." This was the platform of the *Mizrahi* (lit. *merkaz ruhani*, "spiritual center"), an organization set up in 1902 in Vilna by Rabbi Jacob Isaac Reines of Lida. By 1937, the *Mizrahi* had branches in most Polish towns and operated a network of schools, youth groups, and related organizations. But few *hasidim* were involved with the *Mizrahi*, and the urgent need for "solutions to contemporary problems in the spirit of the Torah" led to the Katowiece Conference and the birth of the *Agudat Yisrael* ("Union of Israel") in 1912. Within a decade the *Agudah* had become the political arm of the *hasidim*.

Assembled at Katowiece, in Upper Silesia , on May 27, 1912, were over 200 communal leaders, laymen and rabbis, *mitnagdim*, and *hasidim*, brought there by a wide diversity of motives. Jacob Rosenheim (1870–1965), vice-president of *Die Freie Vereinigung für die Interessen des Orthodoxen Judentums* ("Free Association for the Interests of Orthodox Judaism"), founded by Rabbi Samson Raphael Hirsch in 1855, yearned to unite the unorganized Orthodox masses of Eastern Europe. Others, like Rabbi Abraham Mordekhai Alter of Ger, felt that only a Torah-entrenched citadel could hold back the tidal waves of assimilation, the anti-religious ideology of the secularists, and the nationalism of the Zionists.

Although Rosenheim, the movement's founder and lifelong guide, maintained that this was not going to be "an organization like other organizations," the *Agudah* ultimately adopted the whole familiar complex of institutional accouterments: constitution, general council, executive committee, acting committee, a rabbinical council–*Moetzet Gedolei HaTorah*) with an executive of eleven members, and even a press bureau.

The Agudah *against Zionism*

Soon there were sizeable *Agudah* groups in Budapest, Amsterdam, and Vienna. Nominally its headquarters remained in Frankfurt until 1935, but its heart and soul were lodged in hasidic Poland. During the interwar years, nearly one-third of Polish Jewry, most of them *hasidim*, were associated with the *Agudah*. Moreover, in an intricate and often devious manner, the *Agudah* did play party politics. Isaac Breuer (1883–1946), one of the founders, believed that "political Zionism seeks to exchange the *galut* of Israel for the *galut* of the nations," a belief that colored the *Agudah* attitude. Admittedly anti-Zionist, the *Agudah*, in poignant paradox, was also passionately pro-Zion. Its program stated: "It shall be the purpose of *Agudat Yisrael* to resolve all Jewish problems in the spirit of the Torah, both in *galut* and in *Eretz Yisrael* . . . The colonization of the Holy Land, in the spirit of the Torah, shall be directed toward creating a source of spirituality for the Jewish people." It established a *Keren Hayishuv* (Settlement Fund) and a *Keren Eretz Yisrael* (Palestine Fund), to establish training camps in Poland and to acquire territory in the Holy Land. The Jewish Agency for Palestine agreed to issue 6 to 7 percent of its immigration certificates to *Agudah* members. However, for most Agudists, love of Zion remained a purely spiritual passion, and only a few translated the ancient yearning into reality.

Between the two World Wars, most of the hasidic rabbis were associated with the work of the *Agudah*. Their attitude to Zionism was negative, and they did not cooperate with the Jewish Agency, believing that "to restore Palestine without a firm religious basis would be to establish the very worst possible form of darkness."

The Effect of the Balfour Declaration

The Balfour Declaration issued in November, 1917 by Mr. A. J. (later Lord) Balfour, the Foreign Secretary of Great Britain, to Lord

Rothschild regarding the "establishment in Palestine of a national home for Jewish people" and the promise of the British Government "to use their best endeavors to facilitate the achievement of this object" spurred many *hasidim* to action. In Austria, even before the end of the First World War, a number of hasidic rabbis had already established a society, *Yishuv Eretz Yisrael*, under the leadership of Rabbi Hayim Meir Jehiel Shapira (1863–1924) of Drohobycz. Their manifesto, printed in the Hebrew periodical *Hatzefirah* ("The Dawn") in 1918, urged Orthodox Jews to help rebuild the Holy Land. "Our program is the program of Ezra and Nehemiah, to establish settlements in the Holy Land in the spirit of the Torah." Among the signatories was Shalom Hayim Friedmann of Sadgora. Rabbi Shapira even participated in the Twelfth Zionist Congress at Carlsbad in 1921. Eventually *Yishuv Eretz Yisrael* merged with the *Mizrahi*.

It was Isaac Gerstenkorn, a *hasid* of the rabbi of Skierniewice who in 1924, founded the townlet of Bnei Berak on the borders of Ramat Gan, a garden suburb of Tel Aviv. Various districts sprang up and Bnei Berak became a thriving Torah center.

Hasidim *Settle the Land*

The first major attempt by *hasidim* to establish an agricultural settlement was made in 1925 by Rabbi Ezekiel of Yablona, a descendant of Rabbi Taub of Kazimierz. "I would rather be a laborer in the Land of Israel," his father Rabbi Jacob had remarked, "than a rebbe in the Diaspora." Together with Rabbi Isaiah (d. 1967), son of Rabbi Elimelekh Shapira of Grodzisk (d. 1945), and Rabbi Eliezer of Kozienice, the rabbi of Yablona formed a society called *Nahlat Yaakov* ("Inheritance of Jacob") "to enable everyone to buy land by spreading the payments over five years." Later *Nahlat Yaakov* merged with a similar association, *Avodat Yisrael* ("Service of Israel"), founded by the *rebbe* of Kozienice.

Toward the end of 1925, the Yablona Rabbi and twelve of his followers established Kfar Hasidim ("the village of the Hasidim") on the banks of the River Kishon.

With astonishment and approval, Dr. Chaim Weizmann (1873–1952) describes in his autobiography an encounter with these unusual pioneers:

> On the way to Nahalal we passed a hill crowned with a newly erected barracks, around which clustered a number of people who looked like recently arrived refugees. They made a striking group. We discovered that they were *hasidim* who, led by their rabbi (the rabbi of Yablona), had landed in Palestine only a few days before. Many of them had since then been compelled to sleep in the open, which, in spite of the light rains still to be expected in April, they were finding a wonderful experience. Balfour (Lord Arthur James Balfour, 1848–1930), alighted from the car and went into the barracks to receive the blessings of the rabbi. I told him that if he would come again in a year or two he would find quite a different picture; he would find these people established on their own land, content, and looking like peasants descended from generations of peasants.[1]

The Jewish National Fund allotted them 6,000 dunams near Nahalal, and soon there were 110 families living there. Their industry and courage "aroused general admiration and served to bridge the wide gap that existed between their outlook and that of the workers."[2]

The Incident of the Screen

In 1928 a hasidic rabbi inadvertently caused an unpleasant incident in Jerusalem. During a visit earlier that year, Rabbi Aaron Menahem Mendel Guterman, the rabbi of Radzymin, had set a simple canvas screen at the Western Wall to separate men and women worshippers. The Muslim authorities complained that this violated the rules regulating Jewish access to the site. The British police inspector, Douglas Duff, on duty there, instructed the man in charge of arrangements for the High Holy Day Services to remove the screen, and he agreed to do so. Next morning, however, the screen was still in place. While the congregation was in the midst of solemn Day of Atonement ritual, police moved in to remove the offending screen. Enraged at this desecration of the holy day, the worshippers attempted to stop the police, and a number of Jews were injured in the ensuing turmoil.

The affair became a cause célèbre, and the subject of a British

White Paper. An international commission, appointed in 1930 by the League of Nations, barred benches, chairs, and screens from the Wall.

Rabbi Israel Alter of Ger in Eretz Yisrael

Rabbi Mordekhai Alter was succeeded by his son, Rabbi Israel, who was born in Ger on 24th of *Tishri* 1895 (October 13) and was named after the father of the *Hiddushei HaRim*, who was rabbi of Ger. His mother was Haya Rada Yehudit. When he was 15 years old, Rabbi Joseph Rozin (1858–1936) the Gaon of Ragochow, author of *Tzofenat Pane'ah*, remarked, "This young man already knows *Shas* (Talmud)." At the age of 15, on the fourth day of Nisan 1910, he married Hayeh Sarah, daughter of Rabbi Jacob Meir Biderman (son-in-law of the *Sefat Emet*).

During World War I, Rabbi Israel lived in Warsaw at *Twarda* 29. When his father returned to Ger after the war, Rabbi Israel remained in Warsaw, where he prayed in a *shtibl* in the home of Rabbi Leibel Schochet. His daughter Rebecca Yohebed was born in 1917 and his son Yehudah Aryeh in 1921. His wife and his two children perished during the war. In *Iyyar* 1940 Rabbi Israel managed to escape from Poland, together with his father, and reached the Holy Land. There in 1948 he married Perl, daughter of Rabbi David Weidenfeld and sister-in-law of Rabbi Abraham Weinberg of Slonim, who lived in Tel Aviv. They had no children. In accordance with the Last Will and Testament of Rabbi Abraham Mordekhai, Rabbi Israel, the third son, succeeded his father as rebbe of Ger on *Shavuot* 1948.

It was said of Rabbi Israel, that although time was precious to him he had time for everybody. Twice daily he would receive people in private audience. He was able to grasp the most complicated problem with almost lightning speed. People of all shades of religious observance sought his advice on a wide range of matters. His home, on Rehov Malkhei Yisrael in Jerusalem, and his heart were open to everyone in need. His discourses were of rare brevity, seldom lasting more than a few moments. Their brevity did not diminish their depth, and there was originality in every one. He took an active interest in the work of the *Agudah*, which he touchingly called "the *Agudat Yisrael* of my father," and was one of the prominent leaders of the *Moetzet Gedolei HaTorah*.

The Activities of Rabbi Israel of Ger

He expanded *Yeshivat Sefat Emet* in Jerusalem and encouraged the building of the vast *Yeshivat Hiddushei HaRim* in Tel Aviv and other educational institutions, such as the *Kollel HaTorah Lehora'ah* in Bnei Berak. He was one of the staunchest supporters and founders of *Hinukh Atzmai* (Orthodox educational establishments of the *Agudah*). He wholeheartedly supported his cousin, Rabbi Phinehas Levin, the leader of the *Beit Yaakov* movement in Israel and aided the new hasidic settlement at Hatzor in the Galilee. When an American Orthodox leader asked the *rebbe*, "What do you say to the current situation?" the *rebbe* replied "I recite Psalms." Time was very precious to him. His clocks and watches were meticulously synchronized. *Farbrengt nisht die zeit* (do not waste time) was one of his favorite expressions. He was never even one minute late for prayers.

A Sabbath Visit to the Gerer Beit Hamidrash

The writer visited Rabbi Israel one Friday evening in December 1971. Inside the spacious, modern *Beit HaMidrash*, there were nearly 400 *hasidim*. Some were studying the Talmud, others were discussing the weekly portion of the law or the *Sefat Emet*. At about 10:00 P.M., four hours after the beginning of the Sabbath, a small side door suddenly opened and Rabbi Israel entered. Instantly the atmosphere changed, and a hushed silence enveloped the entire gathering. The *hasidim* rose to greet him and made a path for him through their midst. Briskly, he strode to the center table, *hasidim* on both sides forming a cordon. He looked at them, and they looked at him. No words were spoken. To be near him was in itself an experience, and to catch his eye was an honor.

By a sign known only to the initiated, he indicated those who were to join him at the table; a selection process called *homot* ("the ceremony of the walls") by the followers of Ger. The rabbi and some forty selected followers took their seats. The young *hasidim*, known in Poland as the "Cossacks of Ger," pushed forward. The others leaned over one another and stood on tiptoe to observe every feature of their revered leader. After singing one or two melodies, the rabbi commented briefly on the weekly Portion of the Law. A rather retiring man, he was very sparing with words and scorned rhetoric.

He spoke quickly and quietly, yet the ideas were almost telepathically transmitted from *hasid* to *hasid*. I could not hear his words as I was at the far side of the *Beit Hamidrash*, but a young *hasid* near me courteously and clearly repeated the discourse as though he heard every word.

Commenting on the verse, "And they told him all the words of Joseph" (Genesis 45:27), the *Midrash* states that Joseph identified himself by reminding his father that the last subject they had studied together was the section on the heifer (Deuteronomy 21:1–9). The heifer is killed in expiation of an unsolved murder, symbolizing that the community is not responsible for a crime perpetrated in its midst. Similarly, the brothers of Joseph could not be blamed for selling him, because the act was predestined by Providence.

After the discourse, the *gabbai*, Hanina Schiff, announced the names and places of origin of the *hasidim* who were supplying wine for the congregation that evening. "Moshe Hayim David of Lodz gives wine," he cried. "Aaron Shohet of Bnei Berak," "Moshe Keshenover," "Samuel Yitzhok of Sokolow." As they were named, the *hasidim* rose and the *rebbe* wished them *lehayim*. After partaking of the wine and fruit (*peirot*) that had been brought in, the *rebbe* gave *shirayim* to his *hasidim*. Sabbath melodies were chanted by Jacob Kaminer, Leibel Goldknoff, and Hayim Moshe Knoff. With the recitation of Grace After Meals, the *tish* came to an end, and the *rebbe* disappeared as abruptly as he had come.

Until his later years, the *rebbe* would take long early morning walks through Jerusalem, and early risers in far-flung suburbs would often greet him striding along, swinging his stick, his young aides panting to keep up. The *rebbe* died on Sunday the 2nd of *Adar* 1977 (February 20) and was buried the same day on the Mount of Olives in *Helkat Poilin*, and over 100,000 mourners attended the funeral. *Kaddish* was recited by his brothers Rabbi Simha Bunem and by Rabbi Phinehas Menahem. "A great spiritual light of the nation of Israel has been extinguished . . . the teacher of tens of thousand of *hasidim*, the Ark of the Lord, father of Polish Hasidism, the glory of the People and the Torah," eulogized the Ashkenazi Chief Rabbi of Israel, Rabbi Shlomo Goren.

The rebbe's daughter, Rebecca Yokheved, had married Rabbi Aaron Rapoport (son of Rabbi Israel Joseph of Bilitz) on 4th *Nisan* 1938, and the *rebbe*'s only son Rabbi Aryeh Leib perished in the Holocaust. He was succeeded by his brother Rabbi Simha Bunem, who had married Ita, daughter of Rabbi Nehemiah. Simha Bunem has one daughter, Rebecca, and a son Rabbi Jacob Aryeh who lives in Bnei Berak. Ger controls nineteen Torah institutions that include ten *kollelim.* in Jerusalem, Haifa, Ashdod, Tel Aviv, Bnei Berak, and Hatzor in the Galilee. There are six *yeshivot* and three *Talmud Torahs.*

Hasidic Rebbes of Jerusalem

Relatively few hasidic rabbis reside in Jerusalem. The Holy City paradoxically enough, has never been the home of many hasidic rabbis. Among the few who lived there was the Sochaczewer *Rebbe,* Hanokh Heinokh Bornstein (d. 1966), who arrived there in 1923 and set up a number of *shtiblekh.* The Hungarian rabbi, Joseph Meir Kahana of Spinka (b. 1910) who headed the *yeshivah Imrei Yosef* ("Words of Joseph") in Jerusalem, and Rabbi Meir Kalish of Amshinow, also resided there.

In his *Beit Hamidrash* in Rehov Yosef ben Mattitiahu, Rabbi Jehiel Joshua Rabinowicz (b. 1895) carried on the traditions of Biala and Przysucha. After living in Siedlice until the outbreak of the war, he eluded the Nazis by fleeing to Siberia. After long and arduous wanderings, he arrived in Israel in 1947. After a brief stay in Tel Aviv, he settled in Jerusalem. Devout and unworldly, Rabbi Jehiel Joshua was known as a "miracle worker" and a "great servant of the Lord." He reprinted some of the hasidic writings of his grandfather, Rabbi Isaac Jacob of Biala, and has established a *yeshivah, Or Kedoshim* ("Light of the Holy Ones") in Bnei Berak. He died on the 21st of *Shevat* 1982, and is survived by four sons who all became rebbes: in Lugano, Jerusalem, and Bnei Berak.

Jerusalem is the home of Rabbi Abraham Isaac Kahn (b. 1910) the *Toledot Aharon.* The founder of the dynasty was his father-in-law, Rabbi Aaron Roth (1894–1947), who rejected easy answers and tried to solve problems in depth. Rabbi Aaron came to Jerusalem some fifty years ago from Satmar in Rumania. With no rabbinic lineage of his own, he created a hasidic community. After spending several years in Jerusalem, he returned to Satmar and established a hasidic group in Bergeszaz, near the Czech border. In 1939, he returned to Jerusalem where he established the *Shomrei Emunim* Synagogue in Me'ah She'arim. Rabbi Aaron died at the age of 52, in 1947. There was a powerful struggle between his only son, Rabbi

Abraham Hayim Roth, and his son-in-law, Rabbi Abraham Isaac Kahn, a student of Satmar. Kahn created an independent community. He is an extremist, closely associated with *Edah Haredit.* Apart from Ger, no other rabbi in Jerusalem attracts so many followers. He has already raised a generation of diligent and zealous disciples.

The rebbe insists that his followers wear the golden striped kaftan worn by the *haredi* community of the old *yishuv* in Jerusalem. Weekdays they wear a kaftan with blue and gold stripes. He has a large synagogue, a *yeshivah* with about 200 students, a *Talmud Torah* for about 300 youngsters and a *kollel* for married students. The community abides by a book of regulations that lays down strict rules of behavior and dress. Members are forbidden to live outside Jerusalem or even leave the city for more than three days without permission. Once a year, all members gather in the synagogue to formally sign adherence to the sect's regulations. These *hasidim* are known for their militancy. They have been involved in numerous recent skirmishes in Jerusalem including the smashing of cars on Sabbath, the burning of garbage bins, and a raid on an apartment of student revelers.

The dynasty of Slonim was represented by Rabbi Abraham Weinberg (1890–1981). His father, Rabbi Noah, was a grandson of the *Yesod HaAvodah* who settled in Tiberias. He was one of the leaders of the *Agudah* and an active member of the *Mo'etzet Gedolei HaTorah.* In his Last Will and Testament, he appointed his son-in-law, Rabbi Shalom Noah Brazovsky, as his successor.

A neighbor of the *rebbe* of Amshinow in the Bayit Vegan neighborhood of Jerusalem was Rabbi Johanan Twersky (d. 1982) the Rachmastrivka Rebbe. A scion of Chernobyl, he was the son of Rabbi David with whom he left Russia a half-century ago. During his father's lifetime, he studied in the *Sefat Emet yeshivah,* and on the death of his father he assumed the mantle of leadership. He set up a *yeshivah,* a *kollel,* and a *yeshivah ketannah* on Rehov David Yellin, Jerusalem.

Belz in the State of Israel

Number 63 Rehov Ahad Ha'am in Tel Aviv, was the residence of Rabbi Aaron Rokeah (1886–1957) of Belz. For four perilous years (1940–1944) the rebbe had lived precariously in Nazi Europe, moving from Przemysl to Vishnitz, to Krakow, and to Budapest.

He even changed his name, first to Singer then to Twersky in order to confuse the Germans who pursued him so relentlessly. After a brief stay in Haifa, he settled in Tel Aviv with his brother, formerly Rabbi of Bilgoray, and his beadle, David Shapira. From Antwerp, from Manchester, from New York, and from Lugano, *hasidim* would travel to see him. He impressed all sections of the *yishuv* with his great attachment to the Land, and his personal example stimulated a wave of hasidic immigrants from many countries.

The *rebbe* divided his time between Tel Aviv and Jerusalem, where he spent the summer months. The Jordanians once complained to the U.N. Armistice Commission about heavy military traffic on Israeli territory. It transpired that the alleged military convoy consisted of an escort of 234 civilian vehicles filled with *hasidim* of the rabbi of Belz accompanying him to Jerusalem.

During the Sinai Campaign (October 28 to November 3, 1956), the rabbi fasted for three days spent in a marathon prayer for an Israeli victory. He spent all his time alone in his room appealing to the Creator on behalf of the "Israeli army fighting against seven armies." When he finally emerged, he declared, "My sons, we have won with the help of the Almighty." He died on the 21st of *Av* 1957 and, after an interregnum of nine years, was succeeded by Rabbi Issahar Dov (Beril) Rokeah (b. 1948), his brother's son. The youthful rebbe's marriage in 1966 to Sarah, daughter of Rabbi Moses Hager of Shikkun Vishnitz, was the most publicized and picturesque Jewish wedding of the year, attended by thousands of *hasidim* from all over the world. The young *rebbe* Issahar Dov made his home in Jerusalem, where there is a large modern Belzer *yeshivah*. His former residence in Tel Aviv has been converted into a *yeshivah*.

Modzitz occupied a high place in the history of hasidic musicology. One of the great melody makers was Rabbi Saul Jedidiah Eleazar Taub. Narrowly escaping Nazi clutches, he settled in Tel Aviv in 1947. He was the last person to be buried on the Mount of Olives before it was taken over by the Jordanians. He was succeeded by his son Samuel Elijah (1905–1984). Born in Lublin, he received *semikhah* from Rabbi Solomon David Kahana, Rabbi Tzvi Ezekiel Michelson, and Rabbi Isaiah Gutschechter. When he was 30 years old, he went with his father to visit the Holy Land for the first time. It was then that he decided to remain. His prayers were unique especially during the month of *Tishri* when he officiated at the reader's desk, and he composed twelve new melodies every year. He was succeeded by his only son Rabbi Israel Dan who was born in Warsaw on the 9th of *Tevet* 1928.

One of the first *rebbes* of the House of Ruzhin to settle in Tel Aviv was Rabbi Israel of Husyatin (1858–1949). It was a matter of great pride to him that his ninetieth birthday (16 *Kislev*) coincided with (November 29, 1947) the United Nations passing the Partition Resolution. His son-in-law, Rabbi Jacob Friedmann (1878–1953) succeeded him. Before he died on the 18th of *Heshvan* 1953 he said, "I am not concerned with my own pain. The main thing is that it should be well with my people." He was buried next to his father-in-law.

In the north of Tel Aviv, above the newly built and handsomely appointed synagogue was the home of Rabbi Mordekhai (Motel) Shalom Joseph Friedmann (1897–*Nisan* 1979) of Sadgora-Pzemysl. He was the possessor of a valuable library of 15,000 volumes. In 1939, the rabbi settled in Tel Aviv. He was active in the *Agudah*. Yet, despite his identification with the *Agudah*, he disliked political machinations. Unlike many of his rabbinical colleagues, he celebrated *Yom Haatzma'ut*, Israel's Independence Day, each year. He was succeeded by his son, Rabbi Abraham Jacob. Born on the 5th of *Elul* 1928 in Vienna, he lived for a time in the United States. In 1953 he married the daughter of Rabbi Joseph Feldman, and ever since he succeeded his father as *rebbe* he has expanded hasidic educational establishments. He has a *Talmud Torah* in Bnei Berak for 350 pupils, a *yeshivah* for young boys for ninety students between the ages of 13–17, a *yeshivah gedolah* for the age group of 17–23. He also controls a *kollel* in Jerusalem and a *Talmud Torah.*

Rabbi Isaac Freidmann of Bohush was born in Spikow in Russia in 1903, the son of Rabbi Shalom Joseph Friedmann, a descendant of Ruzhin. During World War II, his home in the capital of Rumania was a haven for refugees, and the rabbi saved many lives. In 1959, he moved to Tel Aviv. He is the people's *rebbe* rather than the scholars' *rebbe*. "My name is Friedmann," he points out, "a man of peace." The rabbi maintains a small *kollel* of six students. On the Sabbath, he sings a number of wordless melodies that according to tradition were sung in the Temple in Jerusalem.

The most prolific of the contemporary hasidic rabbis was Rabbi Moses Jehiel Epstein (1890–1971) of Ozarow, Poland. After twenty-five years in New York, he settled in Tel Aviv in 1953. The last eighteen years of his life were devoted to his great works, *Eish Dat* (eleven volumes) and *Be'er Moshe* (seven volumes), a total of over 10,000 printed pages. He died on *Rosh Hodesh Shevat* 1971. His grandson Rabbi Tanhum Becker succeeded him.

Hasidic Leaders in Bnei Berak

The greatest concentration of *hasidim* in the Holy Land is to be found in Bnei Berak. The rebbe of Alexander was Rabbi Judah Moses Danziger (1893–1973). He was the son-in-law of Betzalel Hayim, son of Rabbi Jehiel of Alexander. He was succeeded by his only son, Abraham Menahem.

The dynasty of Nadvorna was represented in Bnei Berak by Rabbi Hayim Mordekhai Rosenbaum (1904–1978). He was succeeded by his son, Issakhar Baer. In 1976 Rabbi Abraham Hayim Roth, the *Shomrei Emunim Rebbe* moved to Bnei Berak. He founded a *Talmud Torah* that now enrolls hundreds of children. He organized *kollelim* for youngsters as well as evening *kollelim*. A *hevrah tehillim* for children on Sabbath, and a *Beit HaMidrash* where working people ensure that the voice of the Torah is heard all day and every day.

Twentieth - Century Ascetic

Although Hasidism is generally opposed to ascetism, there have been ascetics among the *tzaddikim*. A present–day example was Rabbi Moses Mordekhai Biderman of Lelov. He was born in 1904 in Jerusalem and lived for two decades in Tel Aviv before he finally made his home in Bnei Berak. A descendant of the Holy Jew, he followed the Przysucha custom of praying late in the day. The Morning Service was rarely finished before the evening. He died in 1987.

The songs of Kalev are now to be found in Bnei Berak, the home of Rabbi Menahem Mendel Taub. After seventeen years in the United States, the rabbi settled first in *Rishon Letzion*, where he established Kiryat Kalev, and then moved to Bnei Berak. The rabbi has also launched a number of educational projects. From time to time he and his entourage leave Bnei Berak and spend the Sabbath in different parts of Israel. He is a spell-binding storyteller, a man of great charm and phenomenal energy.

Spinka was represented in Bnei Berak by Rabbi Jacob Joseph, son of Rabbi Israel Hayim the eldest son of Rabbi Isaac Eizig. He was born in 1915 in Spinka. After the war, he lived in Crown Heights, New York, and in 1955 he settled in Bnei Berak. On Friday night he did not deliver discourses. Instead, the *rebbe* told tales of the *tzaddikim*. The rabbi was very selective in his choice of students. He also maintains a *yeshivah* in Jerusalem, where he died on the 14th of *Nisan* 1988.

In Bnei Berak lived another Spinka *Rebbe,* Rabbi Nahman Kahane (1904–1976). During World War II, he lived in different Rumanian ghettoes and afterwards became rabbi at Cluj (Klausenburg). He sent his four children as illegal immigrants to the Holy Land, where he joined them in 1950. On Friday night, the rabbi gave three discourses, two before the meal and one after it. He was succeeded by his son Rabbi Moses Eliakim Beriah.

Habad in Israel

Notable among the hasidic settlements is Kfar Habad, located five miles from Tel Aviv and established in 1949 by the rabbi of Lubavitch, Joseph Isaac Schneersohn (1880–1950) for the survivors of the death camps. Lubavitch has a long history of active affiliation with the Land of Israel. In 1823, Dov Baer had established a colony in Hebron. In 1840, Rabbi Menahem Mendel, the *Tzemah Tzedek*, sent over 15,000 rubles to found synagogues in Jerusalem, Safed, and Tiberias, and organized collections to support indigent Lubavitch settlers. His son, Shneur Zalman, kept in close touch with Menahem Mendel Ussishkin (1863–1941), the Zionist, who, in 1882, founded Bilu (an acronym for: *Beit Yaakov Lekhu Venelkhah,* "O House of Jacob, come ye and let us go," [Isaiah 2:5]), the first modern Zionist pioneering movement, and strongly supported *aliyah.*[3]

Rabbi Joseph Isaac Schneersohn visited the Holy Land for seventeen days in *Av* 1929, meeting the religious leaders: Rabbis Sonnenfeld, Kook, and Meir, and the Chief Justice of the High Court, Mr. Gad Frumkin. It was his wish that a hasidic settlement be established in the Holy Land and many years later this wish was fulfilled.

In Kfar Habad, on the ruins of a former Arab village, Safariya, there are now nearly 500 families, most of them engaged in farming. In the Kfar Habad *Talmud Torah* (established in 1954) the timetable is evenly divided between talmudic and secular studies. The pride of the settlement is *Yeshivah Tomhei Temimim* where 300 students between the ages of 17 and 22 are enrolled. Attached to the *yeshivah* is a *kollel* for advanced students of Rabbinics. Kfar Habad also offers vocational training which makes it a rarity among yeshivot, both mitnagdic and hasidic, where the ideal is the study of the Torah for its own sake. With the help of the Joint (American Jewish Joint Distribution Committee) and Ort (Organization for Rehabilitation through Training), Kfar Habad has set up a printing press. There is also an agricultural school, carpentry, locksmith, and tool shops, and facilities for training in electronics and motor mechanics.

On 2 *Iyyar* 1955, five students and a teacher were reciting the Evening Service when they were murdered by Arab terrorists. The rabbi exhorted the inhabitants not to panic, and a special institute called *Yad Hahamishah* ("Memorial of the Five") School of Printing and Graphic Arts was set up in their memory. To strengthen the village, Georgian families were encouraged to settle there, and a piece of the Soviet Union has now been transplanted to Kfar Habad.

The *Rebbe* of Lubavitch, Rabbi Menahem Mendel, is anxious to expand his activities in Israel. A second Habad village has been established near the first one. The cornerstone was laid in March 1969, on the rabbi's 67th birthday, and the new village will eventually accommodate 5,000 people.

After Kfar Habad, the largest Habad settlement is Nahalat Har Habad, near Kiryat Malachi, which was established in1969 and where there are now over 500 families. It has an industrial school, a diamond polishing factory, and even a *kollel*, established in 1969.

Educational Lubavitch establishments in Israel include *Yeshivah Torah Emet* in Me'ah She'arim, Jerusalem, as well as small branches in various other regions. There are twenty *Ohole Yoseph Yitzhak* schools and kindergartens in Israel.

The *Zeirei Agudat Habad* ("Young Habad") is charged with many activist missions designed to bring Judaism to Jews. They blow the *shofar* on the New Year for patients in hospitals, and have for many years carried out "Operation *Tefillin*." Thousands of visitors to the Western Wall are urged to put on phylacteries.

Kiryat Vishnitz

Kiryat Vishnitz (near Bnei Berak) is the 130 dunam settlement established by the Rumanian rabbi Hayim Meir Jehiel Hager. He was born on 14 *Kislev* 1888, in Vishnitz and was ordained by Rabbi Shalom Mordekhai of Brezany and Rabbi Benjamin Aryeh Weiss of Czernowitz. At 17, he married his cousin Margalit, daughter of Rabbi Mordekai Zeev of Rachmastrivka. In 1940, the *yeshivah* at Vishnitz was closed and in the same year the Russians occupied Bukovina.

Miraculously, the rabbi's family survived the Holocaust. When transports to Auschwitz began, the rabbi escaped with only his *tallit* and *tefillin*. For a time, he chopped wood in a labor camp and eventually he made his way to Budapest. After the war, he settled in Tel Aviv where he had so many followers that a hall had to be rented to accommodate them on the High Holy Days. After three years, he was ready to found his own settlement. Acquiring a site in Bnei Berak, he established the first hasidic settlement since the establishment of the State of Israel.

The foundation stone was laid at the site of an abandoned orange grove near Zichron Meir on 2nd *Sivan* 1950. The settlement grew rapidly and problems were resolved with dispatch and ingenuity. By 1973, it housed over 350 families, a population of nearly 3,000. The street names tell the story of the dynasty of Kosov and Vishnitz: *Rehov Torat Hayim, Rehov Imrei Barukh, Rehov Ahavat Shalom, Rehov Tzemah Tzeddek*. Predictably, the chief building is the magnificent *yeshivah Beit Yisrael V'Dameshek Eliezer,* modeled after the far-famed *yeshivah* that had been destroyed in Bukovina.

The *kiryah* is virtually self-sufficient, particularly with regard to its educational facilities. It is also well equipped with social welfare organizations. *Beit Shalom* houses 100 elderly people. The *Gemilat Hesed* fund grants interest-free loans to the needy. *Ezrat Nashim* provides financial aid for indigent students; the *Bikkur Holim* ("Society for Visiting the Sick") takes care of the ailing. The settlement has its own diamond factory, bakery, and printing press. It has its own generator. The *kiryah* is proud of its high birthrate and is known as "the university for child bearing." The average family has six or seven children and ten or twelve is not unusual. Contrary to popular misconception, the *hasidim* do not avoid military service and many members of the *kiryah* are on the army military reserve list. The rabbi encouraged them to participate in the Six Day War, which he called "the beginning of the Redemption." Rabbi Hayim Meir died on 9th *Nisan* 1972. He was succeeded by his son Rabbi Moses Yehoshua Hager (b. 1916).

Ramat Vishnitz

On the heights of Mount Carmel, overlooking the blue waters of the Mediterranean, stands *Ramat Vishnitz,* a hasidic center established by Rabbi Barukh Hager, the fourth son of Rabbi Israel. He founded his settlement on the 3rd *Tammuz* 1954. It has a large synagogue, *Mekor Barukh,* which seats 500 people. There is a *Talmud Torah* for 120 children, an elementary school recognized by the Ministry of Education, a home for elderly people, and many social welfare organizations. The rabbi was pleased with the progress of the settlement. "Red Haifa is getting whiter and whiter," he remarked, meaning of course, that the Labor-controlled teeming city was becoming more and more observant. He died on 2 *Heshvan* 1963, and is survived by three sons and a daughter.

An interesting and fairly recent development is the hasidic *aliyah* from the United States. One of the leaders of this Exodus from the New World was Rabbi Jekutiel Judah (b. 1904), son of Rabbi Tzvi Halberstam, rabbi of Klausenburg. Rabbi Judah's wife and ten of his children were murdered by the Nazis, and an eleventh child died of typhus. Such tragedy would have broken a lesser man and caused him to lose faith, but Rabbi Jekutiel Judah emerged with a fiery determination to rebuild a hasidic community that had been completely destroyed.

In order to mobilize the conscience of Jewry, the rabbi traveled to the United States. In 1947, he settled in the Williamsburg section of Brooklyn, founding *Yeshivah Sheerith HaPletah.* Even though Rabbi Jekutiel Judah was establishing his roots in the United States, his heart was in Israel. He constantly spoke of the miracles of its rebirth and counseled many of his followers to settle there.

In 1953, he acquired 300 dunams of land near Netanyah, and the foundation stone was laid on March 4, 1956. A year later, the rabbi arrived in Israel with a Scroll of the Law and a nucleus of fifty American immigrants. He remained in the forefront of negotiations with architects, building contractors, and engineers, and was involved in every detail of the development. Its most impressive building is "The Great Synagogue." The centerpiece of this synagogue is a 300-year-old Italian Ark constructed of beautiful red-veined wood and ornately covered. Diverse Torah institutions cater for every age. The most interesting building in the *kiryah* is probably the Laniado Hospital, the first religious hospital to be built for eighty years. The American Government contributed $400,000 toward the project. The hospital is under the supervision of the Israel Minister of Health but has an international Board of Directors drawn from Europe, Canada, the United States and Israel.

The rabbi's efforts are not confined exclusively to his *hasidim.* He is particularly concerned with the status of Israel's Yemenite and North African citizens and becomes incensed when he hears of discrimination or intolerance toward them.

Encouraged by the success of the *kiryah,* the Rebbe established a *shikkun* of fifty dunams to the northwest of Jerusalem, near *Shikkun Habad* at Tel Arza. Among the Sanz institutions in Bnei Berak are a *kollel* for fifty students, a school for girls, a kindergarten, and a commercial center. Small Sanz groups flourish in Petah Tikvah, in Tiberias (Kiryat Shmuel) and in Safed, and a large tract of land has been established in Be-ersheba for a new Kiryat Sanz.

Rabbi Halberstam does not believe in courting publicity. He shuns every artifice and gimmick that might in any way color the facts of what he is trying to accomplish. Action, not words, seems to be his favorite maxim and his ambition is nothing less than to establish Torah institutions in every town in Israel. Rabbi Halberstam now resides in New York but maintains a close link with his *kiryah.*

Bobower and Satmarer Communities

The Rabbi of Bobow, Bentzion Halberstam, was killed in Lvov in 1941. His son, Rabbi Solomon Halberstam, found refuge in the United States. In December 1959, he founded the small town of Bobow near Bat Yam and also established a *yeshivah, Bnei Tziyon,* near Jerusalem.

In March 1963, Rabbi Hannaniah Yom Tov Lippe Teitelbaum

(1906–1966) of Sasow, a descendant of the *Yismah Moshe*, founder of Hasidism in Hungary, set up a settlement near Ramat Gan called Kiryat Yismah Moshe. He married the daughter of his uncle, Rabbi Joel Teitelbaum of Satmar, uniting two distinguished dynasties. Even the rabbi of Satmar (who made his home in New York) and whose opposition to political Zionism was virulent, developed a settlement called Kiryat Yoel in Bnei Berak.

Today, Israel is a thriving center of hasidic publishing and many of the hasidic classics have been reprinted; indeed, in all more than 600 volumes have appeared in the last twenty five years. The noted writers and historians who have written about Hasidism in the last three decades include Shmuel Yosef Agnon (1888–1970), the son of a *hasid* of Chortkow and the Nobel laureate in Literature for 1964. He settled in Germany at the outbreak of World War I, returning to the Holy Land in 1924. Agnon's literary work reflects Jewish tradition and Jewish folklore. *Sippurim Shel Tzaddikim* (1931) and *Days of Awe* are rooted in childhood reminiscence of his native hasidic Galicia.

The passionate love of the *hasidim* for the Holy Land today finds creative and tangible expression. The largest concentration of *hasidim* is to be found in the United States, but Israel has the second largest group, numbering well over fifty thousand. Jerusalem, Tel Aviv, and Bnei Berak are the contemporary counterparts of Ger, Satmar, and Belz. In no other country are there so many prolific writers on the history of Hasidism, and literally hundreds of volumes have been brought out in the last decades.

Now that the reestablished Jewish State is a miraculous fait accompli, many *hasidim* are among its staunchest supporters, working as well as praying for its welfare and security.

Chapter 28

Defenders of the Faith

Out of the ashes, phoenixlike, a new Hasidism has arisen. Pietists in long, silken *kapotes* and streaming side-curls add color and character to Jewish life in London, New York, and Jerusalem. Proudly they identify themselves as *hasidim* of Ger, Belz, Bobow, Lubavitch, and Satmar, euphonious names that linger lovingly upon their lips. These are the contemporary Defenders of the Faith, who have replanted the traditions of their fathers in lands of freedom.

Hasidism in Great Britain

Over 120,000 Russian and Polish Jews settled in England between 1870 and the beginning of the First World War. By 1914, London had a Jewish population of some 150,000. Of these about two-thirds were immigrants from Eastern Europe who had settled there during the last two decades. Among them were a small number of *hasidim* worshipping in the countless *hevrot* (societies) they had formed in the East End of London. In 1887, these small congregations were welded by Mr. Samuel Montagu, M.P. (first Lord Swaythling, 1832–1911) into the Federation of Synagogues. Among the houses of worship were the *Jerusalem Shul* in Union Street and the *Hevrat Agudat Ahim Nusah Ari* at 58 Hanbury Street, which later moved to 18 New Court, Fashion Street.

In the Anglo-Jewish press, Hasidism was misunderstood and misrepresented.[1] The first sympathetic interpretation of Hasidism in England was made by Solomon Schechter (1850–1915). On November 13, 1887, he delivered a lecture to the Jews' College Literary Society that stressed the simple grandeur and nobility of hasidic teaching. This actually represented a change of heart on Schechter's part, for Schechter (whose background was hasidic) had been sharply satirical on the subject in an earlier work, *Letters by Hasidim.*"[2]

Israel Zangwill (1864–1918) followed in Schechter's footsteps. In his *Children of the Ghetto* published in 1892, Zangwill writes:

> In the eighteenth century, Israel Baal Shem, the Master of the Name, retired to the mountains to meditate on philosophical truths. He arrived at a creed of cheerful and even stoical acceptance of the Cosmos in all its aspects and a conviction that the incense of an enjoyed pipe was grateful to the Creator. But it is the inevitable misfortune of religious founders to work apocryphal miracles and to raise up an army of disciples who squeeze the teaching of their master into their own mental moulds and are ready to die for the resultant distortion . . . The Baal Shem was succeeded by an army of thaumaturgists, and the wonder-working rabbis who are in touch with all the spirits of the air enjoy the revenue of princes and the reverence of Popes.[3]

Six years later, in his book *The Dreamers of the Ghetto,* Zangwill includes Israel Baal Shem among those Jews who were saturated with the idealistic spirit of the race and who rebelled against the drab existence of their people. "The Baal Shem came," says Zangwill, "to teach man the true life and the true worship . . .[4] and though his spirit ascended to the celestial spheres and held converse with the holy ones, this did not puff him up with vanity."[5]

Dzikower Hasidim *in London*

A number of *hasidim* participated in the formation in 1890 of the *Mahzikei Shomrei Shabbat* which later became known as the *Mahzikei Ha-Dat,* the Spitalfields Great Synagogue, one of the spiritual fortresses of Anglo-Jewry. In 1896, the Austrian *hasidim* established a Dzikower *shtibl* at 37 Fieldgate Street, in the heart of the

East End of London. On March 14, 1908 they even enacted their own bye-laws (*takkanot*),[6] which consisted of seventeen articles. The annual general meeting of members was to be held during the month of *Tishri*. The Executive consisted of a president (first *gabbai*), vice-president (second gabbai), six members of the committee, one treasurer, two trustees, a secretary, and a collector. Every Sabbath and festival a prayer was offered in honor of Rabbi Alter Ezekiel Eli Horowitz and Rabbi Joshua Horowitz, the rebbes of Dzikow. Annually, on the 11th day of *Iyyar*, the *hasidim* commemorated the *Yahrzeit* of Rabbi Naftali of Ropczyce. On May 14, 1914, larger premises were opened at 30 Dunk Street. Among its leaders were Naftali Gerstler, Nahman Israel, Moses Israel, and Aaron Feigenbaum.

Represented Dynasties in London

In 1900, the *hasidim* of Ruzhin set up a center at 13 Buxton Street. Eight years earlier, a shtibl, *Kehal Hasidim* was founded, first at 18a Old Montagu Street and later in Black Lion Yard, to cater to *hasidim* on a "non-sectarian basis." On November 6, 1892, it became affiliated to the Federation of Synagogues.[7] Among prominent members were Asher Weingarten, David Frost (1872–1938), Abraham Phinehas Landau, Barukh Wolkowitch (1833–1953), and Hanina Bluzenstein.[8]

Meanwhile, a number of *hasidim* were making names for themselves. For instance, Moses Avigdor Chaikin (1852–1928) wrote *Sefer Kelalei Haposkim* ("Rules of the Codifiers"). For thirty years (1890–1920), this fervent *hasid* of Habad served Anglo-Jewry as Minister in Sheffield, as Chief Minister of the Federation of Synagogues and as a member of the London *Beit Din*.[9] "His was the joyousness of the true *hasid*," declared Chief Rabbi J. H. Hertz, "the optimism, the charity in judgment, the obstinate refusal to despair of his fellow mortals and their destiny, which made him a friend to all, beloved of all, loving God and loving all God's children."[10]

The Influx after World War I

Belgian fugitives from the First World War founded in North-east London such *shtiblekh as the Schiff Beit Hamidrash* (founded by

Moses Samuel Schiff), and *Selig Shemayah's Shul* and, in 1916, the Galician-born Judah (Leibish) Rickel (d. 1929) opened a *shtibl* for his countrymen. Among the worshippers there were Hayim David Orlinsky (d. 1941), Hayim Stark (d. 1952), Hayim Rothenberg (1878–1941), and Judah Waller (1871–1953), a devoted *hasid* of Bobow.

Among the early pioneers of Hasidism were Rabbi Meshullam Zusya Golditch (1876–1940), father of Dayan I. Golditch (d. 1987) of Manchester and popularly known as "Reb Zusya," and Rabbi Alter Noah (Kohen-Tzedek) Kaizer (1850–1920), father of the Yiddish writer A. M. Kaizer (1896–1967). Rabbi Noah Kaizer was born in Neshitz, Ukraine, and ministered in a rabbinical capacity to a number of communities in Russia, Austria, and Rumania before emigrating to the Holy Land. He came to England in 1895, where he published a seventy-page kabbalistic treatise *Netivot Hen* ("The Paths of Grace")[11] as well as other works.[12] While in England, he studied old Hebrew kabbalistic manuscripts at Oxford and Cambridge.[13]

The 1920s brought more hasidic rabbis to London. In 1923 Rabbi Jacob Arye Twersky of Turisk, son of Mordekhai Zusya, rabbi of Jassy, Rumania, opened a *Beit Midrash* in Sidney Square. A scion of Ruzhin, his home became a haven of refuge, offering hospitality to many people from the Continent of Europe.

Rabbi Jacob Arye was born in Turisk in 1895. From 1917 to 1920 he lived in Odessa and Kamenetz-Podolsk. He came to London and was soon joined by his wife and children. In 1965, he settled in Bnei Berak where he established a *Beit Midrash* and lived a comparatively retired life. He died on 21st *Tishri* 1979 and was buried on the Mount of Olives. His *Beit Midrash* in Bnei Berak is maintained by his son Isaac.

Rabbi Hanokh Heinokh, son of Dov Rubin of Sasow, was born in Sasow, near Lvov in 1889. He was the son of Rabbi Eliezer, author of *Zikhron Eliezer.* He was a descendant of Rabbi Hanokh Heinokh Dov of Olesk, the author of the classical works, *Lev Same'ah* on Genesis (Przemysl, 1895), *Lev Same'ah Hahadash* (Arad, 1936) on the Passover *haggadah* and on the prayer book. In 1925, the 34-year-old *rebbe,* his wife, and three young children came to England and established a *Beit Midrash* at 14 Fordham Street in the East End of London. Although he was very shy, he radiated such genuine warmth and kindliness that he attracted followers from all over London. He was a *baal tzedakah* who never rejected an appeal for help. He supported many worthy causes generously and anonymously. He died at the age of 40 on the 13th of *Tammuz* 1929. An *ohel* was erected over his grave in London that is still visited by many *hasidim*, who pray at the graveside of the compassionate rebbe who had passed away at such an untimely age. He was succeeded by his son, Simha, who maintains and even enhances the great traditions of *tzedakah* and *gemilut hasadim*, qualities that are part of the rich legacy of Sasow.

Rabbi Israel Aryeh Margulies

Rabbi Israel Aryeh Margulies was born in Przemyshlany in 1893. He received *semikhah* from Rabbi Menahem Monish Babad, rabbi of Tarnopol and from Rabbi Abraham Menahem Halevi Steinberg of Brody. In 1927, Rabbi Israel Aryeh came to England with his wife and young children. He established a *Beit Hamidrash* at 45 Umberston Street. He attracted many followers, drawn by his melodious voice and warm personality. In 1932, he moved to more spacious accommodations to 14–16 Vallance Road, East London and later to Minister Road, Cricklewood. On *Simhat Torah* all roads led to Minister Road. Congregants of all "denominations" from the United Synagogues, from the Federation Synagogues, and from other *shtiblekh* made a point of celebrating *Simhat Torah* with the rebbe.

The *rebbe* was deeply interested in education. After intensive activity, the Northwest London Jewish Day School was opened. The *rebbe* insisted on setting and maintaining high standards in both secular and religious studies. He applied himself diligently to collecting the funds that enabled the school to expand in new premises. He died on the 24th day of *Tevet* 1955. No one succeeded him.

The Shatzer Rebbe

The scholarly Rabbi Shalom (1878-1958), son of Rabbi Mordecai Joseph Moskovitz of Shatz, established his court at 67 Chicksand Street. In 1897, he married his cousin, the daughter of Rabbi Meir Moskovitz. He was rabbi in Shatz for sixteen years and for seven years he lived in Cologne, Germany, where he established a *shtibl.* He was keenly interested in astrology and botany. He visited the Sternwarte Planetarium in Munich frequently and on one occasion, he drew the attention of the curator to errors in the description of the animals. He strongly opposed the conscription of women in the State of Israel. He was against television, terming that medium an "abomination." In his will, he writes:

> It is known that I have always tried to help people to repent. Whoever is in need of any kind of *yeshuah* (help) or a *refuah* (speedy recovery from illness), he should visit my grave–if possible on Friday before noon. He should light a candle and make his request. Then I shall certainly intercede with my saintly forefathers that they should awaken God's mercy for a *yeshuah* or a *refuah.*
>
> But there is a definite condition attached–that the person concerned must promise me to better his way of Yiddishkeit in at least one point. For example–he whose business operates on Shabbat must promise to keep it closed. He who shaved his beard with a razor blade should now shave in a way that is permitted. A woman who did not keep, God forbid, the law of *niddah* and *tevilah* must promise me that from now on she will observe these laws properly. A woman who did not cover her hair must promise from now on to wear a *sheitel* (wig). A *ben Torah* who does not learn must promise that from now on he will learn every day–particularly *Gemara*–and so on. Each person shall promise to better his ways in at least one point. Then, with the Almighty's help, I shall try to awaken God's mercy.
>
> But this must be clearly known to all those who come to my grave and make such a promise, that they are bound to keep their word and not try to deceive me, God forbid. For then I shall be very angry. Because unfortunately there is already so much deceit in this world–but not in the world to come, which is the world of truth.

The Rabbi of Kielce

Rabbi Hayim Judah Schonfeld (1892–1967) of Kielce established his *Beit Hamidrash Kol Yaakov* first at 17 Fenton Street and then in Golders Green. A gentle and kindly sage, he devoted his life to *Taharat Hamishpahah* (Jewish family purity). He was a most loveable, easygoing, and approachable man, but on the subject of *Taharat Hamishpahah*, he was implacable. His zeal knew no bounds. Publicly and privately, he incessantly harangued the establishment, directing appeals to Chief Rabbi Joseph Herman Hertz (1872–1946) and all the *dayanim* of the London *Beit Din*.

He was born in Wloclawek, Poland. His father was a descendant of Rabbi Betzalel ben Abraham Ahkenazi, author of *Shitah Mekubbetzet*. In 1917, he married Malka Hannah, daughter of Rabbi Elimelekh Jacob Isaac, Rabbi of Suchednew who was a descendant of the Holy Jew of Przysucha. Like the rabbi of Turisk, the Kielcer Rebbe also settled in the Holy Land where he died.

Another scholarly rabbi of retiring disposition was Rabbi Jacob Joseph Spira (d. 1946), a descendant of Dynow and Ropczyce. He was the author of a number of works.[14]

Prominent among these early hasidic pioneers was Rabbi Nathan David Rabinowicz of Biala, youthful descendant of traditions centuries old. The founder of the Biala dynasty was Rabbi Jacob Isaac (1847–1905), the son of Rabbi Nathan David of Szydlowiec (1814–1866), in turn a direct descendant of Rabbi Yaakov Yitzhok, the "Holy Jew" of Przysucha. Following the teachings of Przysucha, the *Rebbe* of Biala discouraged protestations of piety. He maintained that sincerity was measured by service, charity, and lovingkindness. The four sons of the *Rebbe* of Biala established their own courts at Parszew, Siedlice, Miedzyrzec Podalski, and Lublin.

Isaac Jacob was born in Szydlowiec on Sabbath the 14th of *Tevet*. Interestingly enough, it was on the 14th of *Tevet* that the medieval scholar, poet, and grammarian Rabbi Abraham ben Meir Ibn Ezra (1092–1177) completed his work *Iggeret HaShabbat* ("The Letter on the Sabbath"), first printed in Luria's *Shulhan Arukh* in 1610 and later in *Mivhar Amarim* (Livorno, 1840). This is significant because this *mitzvah* more than any other absorbed the heart and soul of the Biala *Rebbe*. There is hardly a discourse wherein he does not touch upon some aspect of the seventh day.

The *Divrei Binah* (as the *rebbe* was called) named his first book *Yishrei Lev* ("Upright of Heart") an acrostic of his father-in-law's name, "for most of my wisdom I have derived from him," he wrote. After thirty years as *rebbe*, the rebbe of Ostrow died on the 28th of *Nisan* 1873, and the *Divrei Binah* was barely 26 years old when he succeeded his father-in-law. He moved to Biala Podolsk, a town in the province of Lublin. The *rebbe* was widely known for his open heart and his open house. A special kitchen at his court provided meals for visiting *hasidim* and for poor townfolk. As a practical demonstration of his wish that the poor be treated as members of his household, the *rebbe* himself regularly sampled the dishes to make sure they were up to standard. He vehemently opposed the activities of the *maskilim* whom he described as "little foxes destroying the vineyard of the Lord." He stressed the importance of unity, using a verse in Exodus (25:20) to illustrate his point. "And the Cherubs shall spread their wings on high screening the Ark-Cover with their wings, as they face each other." He maintained that "As long as men can face each other openly, in friendship and brotherhood, then all is not lost. It is never too late for an individual to seek redemption." Just as there are specialists in medicine, so the *tzaddik* specializes in helping sinners to repent.

The *rebbe* left an Ethical Will that bears eloquent witness to the writer's humility and kindliness. He implored his children to cast aside jealousy and enmity and to love each other. The pragmatic father advised his sons to settle in different localities should they decide to take up the rabbinate, thereby lessening the likelihood of fraternal friction. He also requested that notification of his death be conveyed by his *hasidim* through prayer to his father (whose grave was in Szydlowiec), his father-in-law (whose grave was in Warsaw), and the Yehudi (in Przysucha) so that his ancestors might intercede for him in the Heavenly Court. "I would urge you to announce, by means of posters and through the newspapers, that I ask forgiveness of those who pressed gifts into my reluctant hands. They regarded me as a *tzaddik* but verily I was unworthy." He died in Warsaw on the 23rd of *Adar* 1905. No *ohel* was erected over his grave but according to his wishes, a space of four cubits was marked off around his tomb, the site purchased in perpetuity. However, a Warsaw *Beit Din* later ruled that his children could be buried in this reserved plot.

The *rebbe* had three daughters, Matale, Hannah, and Rachel Gitel and four sons who branched off and established their own dynasties. The eldest son, Rabbi Nathan David of Parczew (1866–1930) married Leah Rezel, daughter of Rabbi Jehiel Jacob of Kozienice. The second son, Rabbi Meir Solomon Judah (1868–1942) settled first in Miedzyrzecz and then in Warsaw. The third son, Rabbi Abraham Joshua Heschel (1875–1933) made it his life's work to publish his father's writings. It was he who edited *Yishrei Lev* on Sabbath (Lublin, 1906), *Divrei Binah* ("Words of Understanding"), commentaries on the Torah (Lublin, 1909, 1913; Piotrokow, 1929), and on the *Haggadah*, and Ethics of the Fathers. He made his home in Lublin and was himself the author of *Yeshuot Avraham*, a commentary on Genesis (Lublin, 1934). The fourth son, Rabbi Jerahmiel Tzvi (1880–1906) married Havah, daughter of Rabbi Judah Aryeh Leib Epstein of Ozarow (d. 1903), author of *Birkat Tov*, a commentary on the Torah. Rabbi Jerahmiel Tzvi lived in Siedlice, and was one of the most remarkable of the hasidic *rebbes*. He excelled as reader of the congregation. Once, when he was ill, his anxious mother urged his father to dissuade Rabbi Jerahmiel Tzvi from officiating at the reader's desk, but the father refused to interfere. "The entire Heavenly Court waits to hear the prayers of my son. How dare I stop him?" He was appointed rebbe at the age of 26, but died barely six months after assuming the title. His wife Havah and six small children survived him.

Settlement in London

The eldest and most illustrious of these orphaned children was Nathan David who was born in Ozarow on the 11th of *Iyyar* 1900. By the age of 6 the child prodigy already knew the Torah by heart and was being acclaimed as *gadol beyisrael* (A great one in Israel). He studied at the *yeshivot* of Ozarow and Radzymin. At the age of 18, on the 15th of Kislev 1918, he married Szaindla Brakhah, the eldest and favorite daughter of Rabbi Alter Israel Simon Perlow of Novominsk. Rabbi Nathan David obtained *semikhah* from Rabbi Jehiel Meir Halevy Halstock of Ostrowiec, and Rabbi Tzvi Ezekiel Michelson of the Warsaw *Beit Din*.

On December 18, 1927, he arrived in London. His *Shtiblekh*, first at 6 Osborn Place off Brick Lane, and from 1932 at 10 St Mark's Rise, Dalston, attracted people from all walks of life and of all ages. He brought with him a fire that was foreign to the Jews of London's East End. There were those who had known his grandfathers, Rabbi Isaac Jacob of Biala and Rabbi Leibish Epstein of Ozarow in the old country, and there were others for whom this was their first introduction to Hasidism. They came to see him *fihr tish* (conduct the table) and to hear him expound Torah at *Shalosh Se'udot* and *Melave Malkah.*

His preaching and his teachings were marked by passionate intensity. When he officiated at *Ne'ilah,* his voice shook with tears of anguish as he wrestled in prayer for his people. His discourses were delivered with warmth and vehemence. His life was Torah and, as he wandered through its fathomless profundities, he found challenge and fulfillment. But at the same time he was keenly interested in ordinary issues, and students enjoyed debating with him and sharpening their young minds against the whetstone of his fiery intellect. They found him approachable, empathic, and perceptive, equally able to communicate with the old-time *hasidim* and their semi-alienated children.

A Sympathetic Ear and Voice

Londoners who had never heard of Hasidism found a friend in the *rebbe* of Biala, for he genuinely loved people, and his approach was positive. Like Rabbi Levi Isaac of Berdichev, he looked for man's good points rather than for his failings. Often he would quote the verse, "For the House of Israel is the vineyard of the Lord of Hosts" (Isaiah 5:7), adding, "who am I that I should disparage or condemn that which belongs to the Almighty Himself?"[15] No one was thrust out of the field. Not with "fire and brimstone" but with love were people brought back to their Father in Heaven. The *rebbe* was, at one and the same time, a mystic and a man of the world, paradoxically blending asceticism with worldliness, rigid, uncompromising piety with tolerance and humanity.

There were no visiting hours at the *rebbe's* house. All day long his door was open. All were free to consult him and most left his presence comforted. He was always ready to minister to the spiritual and even material needs of the congregation. No form of recreation, no personal ambition, no desire for temporal honor or social distinction ever distracted this saintly scholar from the austere and devout life. He was an ascetic, and in his secluded life he reached an unparalleled degree of spiritual perfection.

He was always *besimhah* (happy). When life was a struggle and at times tempestuous, he remained serene, maintaining, in the darkest days of the war, that all would be well and that justice would triumph. There was no "iron curtain" between him and his followers but a touching, intimate, and unique relationship between the *tzaddik* and the *hasid*. To his *hasidim* he was a father and a friend who never failed them.

A Will in the Biala Tradition

The Biala Rebbe's literary output was considerable, and he wrote incisive commentaries on the Torah, the *Pirkei Avot* (Ethics of the Fathers), and the *Zohar*. In his Last Will and Testament he stated that "my manuscripts have not so far been revised. I therefore instruct my son to burn them immediately after my burial."[16] A small slim volume, *The Ethical Will*, written in the face of death and in the darkening shadow of illness, reveals his true greatness. It is a remarkable document, a loving and luminous message to his children, his wife, and his closely knit *hasidim*. I do not think that there is anything in contemporary rabbinic writing to compare with this remarkable document.

With fatherly exhortations, he urged his followers to live in fraternal harmony and to keep faith with the Almighty. He bequeathed to his wife a loving legacy, "an equal share of all the Torah that I have learned and all precepts, however few, which I have performed."[17] He died on the eve of *Rosh Hodesh Hesvan* (29th of *Tishri*) 1947, at the age of 47. He was interred at the *Adat Yisrael* cemetery, at Enfield, according to directions noted in his will. "A space of four cubits should be left around my grave, in which no one should be buried nor should an *ohel* be erected there." In this respect, he followed the tradition of his grandfather, Rabbi Isaac Jacob of Biala, who was buried in Warsaw and left similar instructions.

The late *Dayan,* H.M. Lazarus wrote regarding the document, "On reading through the will, I was moved to tears. They were not tears of sorrow; but of an overwhelming sense of veneration for the meek, saintly friend who, on his impending departure, wrote a fatherly message of sweet counsel and directions to all those he loved."

Hasidic Congregations in London

In the Northwest London suburbs there was a small group of *hasidim* under Rabbi Berish Finkelstein (1890–1977), a *hasid* of

Radzyn. In the Golders Green area, there are hasidic congregations: *Beit Shmuel* under the guidance of Rabbi Elhanan Halpern and a *kollel* and synagogue *Beit Yissakhar Dov* under Rabbi Gershon Hager, son of the late Rabbi Berish Hager (d. 1968). The largest hasidic concentration is to be found in North London. Over 7,000 *hasidim* live in the Stamford Hill area, centering on Cazenove Road. The numerous *Shtiblekh* include Belzer, Bobower, Gerer, and Satmarer.

Hasidic Institutions in London

In 1973 the *hasidim* of Belz acquired a house in Leweston Place to serve as a *heder*. Imposing premises became available on Clapton Common, set on over an acre of land. There the community of Belz found a worthy home, capable of housing its manifold activities. It has a *Beit Hamidrash* that is open to the public from early morning till late at night. A *Talmud Torah* with almost 300 children on the roll, a *yeshivah ketanah*, a *kollel Avreikhim,* where young, newly married men are given every encouragement to continue their studies, and a girls' school with 200 pupils. The community has even appointed its own *dayan*, Rabbi Joseph Dov Babad. This Belzer community is not free from dispute. There are *hasidim* who oppose the leadership of Rabbi Issakhar Dov and who regard him as too controversial a leader.

The dynasty of Bobow also established roots in London. It started in a small building in Darenth Road, North London, and has recently acquired a spacious complex in Egerton Road. In addition to the *Beit Hamidrash* and *yeshivah,* Bobow has a modern *mikveh* and *Talmud Torah* which has grown to accommodate one hundred children. In 1984, the *rebbe* inducted his son-in-law Rabbi Benzion Blum as *Dayan* of the community.

There are many *Batei Midrash, Talmudei Torah,* and *yeshivot* representing a colorful variety of different hasidic dynasties. Most of the hasidic synagogues are affiliated with the Union of Orthodox Hebrew Congregations, set up in 1928 by Rabbi Victor Schonfeld (1880–1930) and enlarged by his son, the late Rabbi Dr. Solomon Schonfeld. Today *hasidim* and *mitnagdim* have transcended their one-time rivalries and cooperate harmoniously in Union activities relating to *shehitah,* rabbinate, *mikvaot, hevrah kaddisha*, and *kashrut.* The *hasidim* operate their own educational network, the *Yesodei Hatorah* schools (established in October 1942 by Wolf Schiff,

Getzel Berger, and Phinehas Landau), the *Metivta* Talmudical College, and a *Beit Yaakov* Seminary for girls.

Lubavitch did not arrive in London until 1959, but instantly made its presence felt. A synagogue center has been built (at a cost of $120,000) in Stamford Hill, and primary and grammar schools have been set up by dynamic young emissaries of Rabbi Schneerson, the current Lubavitcher Rebbe, in New York. Thus Lubavitch helps fill the vacuum left by the departure to Israel of such men as the Rabbi of Turisk.

Outside London

There are also small hasidic groups in Manchester, among them the *Kehal Hasidim* Synagogue founded in 1902 in Red Bank. A *Nusah Ari shtibl* was established in Glasgow by Simon Felstein; in 1914 it became known as *Beit Yaakov* Synagogue, and in 1938 it was amalgamated with the *Po'alei Tzedek* Synagogue. Their spiritual leaders were S. D. Morgenstern, J. D. Luria (d. 1957), and J. D. Siroka. In 1897, a *Hasidishe* Synagogue was established in Leeds, and there is a *Nusah Ari* Synagogue in Liverpool.

Chapter 29

The New World

From 1881 to 1925, over 2.5 million Jews immigrated to the United States of America. The overwhelming number were of East European origin: 1,190,590 from Russia, 281,150 from Austria-Hungary, and 95,534 from Rumania.[1] A number of *hasidim* arrived in New York with the wave of immigration from Eastern Europe in the nineteenth century. They established their own *shtiblekh*. One of the earliest hasidic pioneers was Rabbi Eliezer Hayim Rabinowicz of Skole, who arrived in New York in 1895 but returned to Poland after a short time. He was followed by Rabbi David Mordekhai Twersky (d. 1956) of Talnoye who established the *Kehal Hasidim* congregation in New York in 1913, and by Rabbi Barukh Joseph Zak (d. 1949), the Kobriner Rebbe who came in 1917.

Among the *rebbes* who settled in New York in the 1920s was Rabbi Abraham Joshua Heschel Rabinowicz (1860–1938), the rebbe of Monastrysche, one of the founders in 1928 of the Union of Grand Rabbis of the United States and Canada. Other pioneers were Rabbi Isaac Hurwitz of Melitz, Rabbi Mordekhai Solomon Freidmann of Boyan (d. 1971), and Rabbi Judah Aryeh Perlow (1887–1961), a brother of rabbi A. Y. S. Perlow of Novominsk who arrived in New York in 1925. Rabbi Perlow was the author of *Lev Aryeh* ("The Heart of a Lion"), published in 1939, and of *Kol Yehudah* ("The Voice of Judah"). His home on South Ninth Street in Williamsburg, Brooklyn, became one of the first outposts of Hasidism.

The dynasty of Novominsk was represented by Rabbi Nahum Mordekai Perlow (1896–9th *Elul* 1976).[2] A dedicated scholar and an active member of the *Agudah,* Rabbi Nahum led a life of study and service to his *hasidim* in the tradition of his great father, Rabbi Alter Yisroel Shimon of Novominsk. Rabbi Nahum Mordekai was succeeded by his son Rabbi Jacob, the author of *Adath Yaakov* (Jerusalem, 1983), a novella on the Talmud.

Another hasidic pioneer was Rabbi Jacob (d. 1946), son of Rabbi Israel of Stolin (d. 1921) who arrived in New York in 1923. He ministered to the four Stolin *shtiblekh* in New York and one in Detroit. The majority of the *hasidim* came from Poland, Galicia, and Russia. A Hungarian *rebbe,* Rabbi Phinehas Shalom Rothenberg (d. 1968) of Kosow, arrived in 1926.

Before the Second World War, and during the war, *rebbes* who found refuge in New York included Rabbi Abraham Joshua Heschel (d. 1967) of Kopycznice and Rabbi Saul Taub of Modzitz who settled in Brooklyn.

The Hasidic Influx after World War II

It was not until after the end of the Second World War that the *hasidim* really began to exert an influence on the Jewish community. Williamsburg became the center of the Hungarian *hasidim,*[3] while others settled in Crown Heights. As these neighborhoods underwent population shifts, many *hasidim* moved to Boro Park and Flatbush. As estimated 250 hasidic *shtiblekh* now exist in Boro Park. In all, there are from 65,000 to 75,000 *hasidim* in New York. A number of *rebbes* left New York City and founded their own hasidic communities in other parts of New York State.

The Satmarer Rebbe

Perhaps no hasidic rabbi of the twentieth century has inspired as much veneration and as much antagonism as Rabbi Joel Teitelbaum of Satmar. His charismatic personality communicated hope for thousands of his followers. Rabbi Joel was a direct descendant of Rabbi Moses Teitelbaum, author of *Yismah Moshe.* Rabbi Joel was born in Sighet, Hungary on January 13, 1887 (18th *Tevet*). His father, Rabbi Hannaniah Yom Tov Lippe was the author of *Kedushat Yom Tov.* His mother, Hannah, was the daughter of Rabbi

Joel Ashkenazi, rabbi of Zloszow and author of responsa *Mari Ashkenazi.*

Young Joel studied with his father and with a private tutor, Jacob Hirsch Turner. He was ordained by Rabbi Moses ben Aaron Greenwald and in 1904, married Havah, daughter of Rabbi Abraham Hayim Horowitz, rabbi of Plantshow in Galicia. He accepted a rabbinic post in Yenice, and in 1911 he moved to Orshowa. Thirteen years later, he became rabbi in Korolleh Carei or Nagy Karoly in Transylvania. In 1932, he visited the Holy Land. In 1934, he became rabbi of Satmar in Rumania, and for the next five years the rabbi devoted himself single-mindedly to transforming Satmar into a stronghold of Orthodoxy.

Public Works and Private Tragedies

His keen mind enabled him to go straight to the root of any problem. After the Sabbath morning service, he would visit stores that were open for business, pleading with the owners to close for the day, and his passionate concern persuaded many to comply. Nearly 300 students were enrolled in his *yeshivah.* Mindful of the material needs of his charges, he established a *beit tavshil,* (soup kitchen) popularly known as "Minza," to provide hot midday meals. In addition, each student received one kilo of bread every morning. The *Tomkhei Tal* (Supporters of the Poor) Committee was set up to supervise these important activities. Great emphasis was placed on *taharat hamishpahah* (family purity), and the *mikveh* at Satmar was constructed according to his detailed specifications.

Rabbi Joel's personal life was beset with tragedy. Of his three daughters, two died before World War II while the third, Hayeh Rachel, died after the war in New York. His wife died in Satmar in 1936. Two years later, he married Feige Rachel, daughter of the *rebbe* of Czenstochowa, a descendant of Sanz and Kozienice.

Escape from the Nazis

During the Second World War, Rabbi Joel, his wife, and his beadle, Joseph Ashkenazi, escaped to Klausenburg in a Red Cross Ambulance. On May 3, 1944, they were arrested and taken to the ghetto of Klausenburg and then to Bergen-Belsen, where they remained until December of that year. One potato a day was their only source of sustenance. Through the intervention of Dr. Rudolf Kasztner, the rebbe was among the 1,684 people who were permitted to leave for a neutral country. The train, known as "Noah's Ark," reached the Swiss border on December 7, 1944, (21st of *Kislev*), a day celebrated by Satmar *hasidim* as a day of deliverance.

For several months the *rebbe* stayed in Geneva, in the home of a *hasid*, Moses Gross. Through the efforts of Chief Rabbi Isaac Herzog, the rebbe was allowed to enter the Holy Land. He arrived in 1945 and shortly afterwards established a *yeshivah Yitev Lev DeSatmar*. However, he decided to immigrate to the United States and made his home at 554 Bedford Avenue in the Williamsburg section of New York, where many hasidic refugees had settled.

The Satmar Community in Williamsburg

The Satmar community *Kehal Yitev Lev DeSatmar* flourished[4] and became a self-sufficient and cohesive entity, a testimony to Rabbi Joel's remarkable flair for organization. By the 1980s, over 30,000 *hasidim* were living in the area, in renovated tenements along Lee and Division Avenues, and many of these deeply committed Jews were *hasidim* of Satmar. Satmar issues a weekly newspaper (*Der Yid*). It has its own welfare network including a holiday fund for orphaned children, insurance and pension plans, an emergency ambulance service, a burial society, and five large synagogues. It operates its own butcher shops and supervises the production of a variety of processed foods. It maintains *mikvaot,* a *shatnes* laboratory, a kindergarten, *Beit Rachel* schools for girls, and bakeries where *matzot* are baked by hand on the eve of Passover.

The *yeshivah* building, near the old Brooklyn Navy Yard, was acquired by the late real estate magnate, Getzel Berger of London, and is one of the largest *yeshivot* in the world. The Satmar community is responsible for the education of some 4,000 children in fifteen schools. To become a member of this elite community, a man must undertake to observe the Sabbath and to bring up his children according to Orthodox tradition. A committee of three interviews and investigates every applicant.

Scholar and Gentleman

Rabbi Joel was the head of the Central Rabbinical Congress of Rabbis of the United States and Canada. He was the author of the polemical works *VeYoel Moshe* (New York, 1959), *Kuntress Al Hage'ullah Ve'al Temurah* (New York, 1962), and *Divrei Yoel,* a seven-volume commentary on the Torah and responsa published posthumously. Rabbi Joel was one of the most outstanding hasidic leaders of this generation. Rabbis and *rebbes* gathered around his Sabbath table. It was not unusual for over one-hundred people to seek his counsel in the course of a single day.

He had a complex personality, uncompromising in the realm of religion yet kindly and considerate, generous to a fault, and endowed with a keen sense of humor. Many Satmar *hasidim* owed their financial success to monetary gifts from the *rebbe,* whose acts of kindness were always imaginative and always discreet. His services were remarkable experiences. At one time, in his active days, he used to officiate at the Sabbath morning services, and on *Shabbat Rosh Hodesh.* In 1968, after he suffered a stroke, he lived either in Belle Harbor, Long Island, or in Monroe, New York in semi–isolation. Population shifts caused many *hasidim* to abandon Williamsburg. In 1962, Satmar tried to establish a colony in the Mount Olive township in New Jersey but was unable to receive a zoning permit. However, in 1976 Kiryat Yoel, a village of 340 acres, was set up near Monroe, in Orange County, New York.

Harsh Anti-Israel Stance

The years did not diminish Rabbi Joel's implacable antagonism to the "secular State of Israel." He claimed that Jewish destiny was to pray for the coming of the Messiah who would bring redemption and the restoration of the Jewish homeland.[5] In his opinion, political activism was not the right way. "If I am left with only one *minyan* of adherents," he declared, "I will not refrain from expressing my beliefs." Satmar *hasidim* have demonstrated in public against the State of Israel, even picketing the United Nations Building in New York carrying anti-Israel placards.[6] He regarded the State of Israel as a pure embodiment of a secular ideal and opposed mass *aliyah* to Israel.

After the death of Rabbi Selig Reuben Bengis (1864–1953), Rabbi Joel became the spiritual head of the *Edah Haharedit* that encompasses the extremist *Neturei Karta* (literally, "the Guardians of the City"). Still, Rabbi Joel's opposition to the State of Israel was not incompatible with commitment to the Land of Israel, which he visited in 1952, 1955, and 1959. He founded two settlements there, in Bnei Berak and in Jerusalem.

The Death of a Giant

In 1968, Vice-President of the United States Hubert Humphrey called upon the *rebbe* to discuss the tension that prevailed between black militants and the Jewish community. The *rebbe* died on Sunday (the 26th of *Av*) August 19, 1979 at Mount Sinai Hospital, New York. Over 100,000 people attended his funeral in Monroe, where he was buried in a privately consecrated cemetery. *Kaddish* was recited by his nephew and successor Rabbi Moses Teitelbaum of Sighet.

"The Rabbi of Satmar and I differ on many issues," commented Rabbi Aaron Kotler. "I do not have the same approach – either in Torah Study nor in political matters. But I must say that he is a giant in Torah and a giant in *midot* (ethical qualities)."

A Wedding in the Family

On December 4, 1984 more than 10,000 *hasidim* attended the wedding of Menahem Mendel Teitelbaum, grandson of the *rebbe* to Brukhah Sima Meisels. The wedding took place at the Nassau Coliseum, Uniondale, Long Island. A fleet of fifty chartered buses carried the celebrants from their villages in the Orange and Rockland counties of New York, and the Williamsburg section of Brooklyn. It was a great clan gathering with guests flying in from Israel, England, and Latin America. The feast cost more than $250,000 and was paid for by the wealthy members of the community. This was a twelve-hour wedding of weddings and it was a joyful assertion of the sect's vitality, unity, and identity.

New Hasidic Communities

The district wherein most of the *hasidim* live is undergoing radical population changes, and the result has been some interesting experiments in hasidic living. In 1963, a group of *hasidim* set up a community in Rockland County, about forty miles from Times Square. Similarly, New Square, named after Skvira in the Ukraine, was established in Spring Valley, thirty miles from New York, by Rabbi Jacob Joseph Twersky (1900–1968) of Skvira. The *hasidim* inhabit modern Cape Cod cottages scattered over 130 acres of grassy wooded slope in Spring Valley. They are mostly artisans and diamond merchants who commute daily to New York.

The son-in-law of the rabbi of Skvira, Rabbi Mordekhai (Mottele) Hager of Vishnitz, principal of *Yeshivah Ahavat Yisrael*, leads thirty families in a self-contained community in Monsey. Irvington is home to the *hasidim* of Rabbi Raphael Blum of Kashau, while Rabbi Jekutiel Judah Hallberstam of Klausenberg resides in Union City, New Jersey. The borough of Queens has never been the breeding ground of Hasidism. However, there are a few rebbes living in Rego Park. Rabbi S. S. Rubin of Sulitza, a scion of Ropzcye and Zydaszow, resides in Far Rockaway. Staten Island has become the home of Rabbi Isaacson, a grandson of the rebbe of Nadvorna.

Lubavitch

While *hasidim* of Satmar and Skvira deliberately live in virtual isolation, Lubavitch has developed a comparatively cosmic orientation. Rabbi Joseph Isaac Schneersohn, sixth rebbe of Lubavitch, arrived in New York on March 19, 1940, and devoted the last decade of his life to setting up a framework for Jewish religious education. He founded the Central *Yeshivah Tomkhei Temimim* schools with branches in the United States and Canada. He set up *Mahneh Yisrael* ("The Camp of Israel") to strengthen Orthodoxy, and *Merkaz Leinyanei Hinukh*, the central organization for Jewish education (established in 1947). He established girls' schools under the names *Beit Sarah* ("House of Sarah") and *Beit Rivkah* ("House of Rebecca"), in Canada, the Holy Land, France, and Morocco. He founded the *Kehot* Publication Society that publishes (in English, French, Russian, Spanish, Yiddish, and Hebrew) texts on *Habad* philosophy and a vast assortment of other material, ranging from elementary guide books on Jewish religion to books on hasidic philosophy.

After the war, Rabbi Joseph Isaac established *Ezrat Pleitim Vesiduram*, with an office in Paris administered by Rabbi Benjamin Gorodezki, for the relief and rehabilitation of refugees. To thousands of persons physically and spiritually displaced, he brought material assistance and a message of hope.

Lubavitch Today

The present rabbi of Lubavitch, Rabbi Menahem Mendel Schneerson, a central figure in the world of Torah and Hasidism, is the seventh generation in direct male descent from Rabbi Shneur Zalman of Liady. He was born on the 11th day of *Nisan* 1902 in Yekaterinoslav (now Dnepropetrovsk), in South Russia. His father, Rabbi Levi Isaac, was rabbi of Yekaterinoslav and his mother was the daughter of Rabbi Meir Solomon Yanovsky, rabbi of Nikolayev. In 1929 he married Hava Moussia, the daughter of Rabbi Joseph Isaac Schneersohn. In 1936 he studied philosophy at the Sorbonne in Paris and graduated with a degree in electrical engineering. In 1944, his father-in-law appointed him to head the *Kehot* Publishing House, and in 1946 he was appointed head of the *Merkaz Leinyanei Hinukh*. After the death of his father-in-law on January 28, 1950 (the 10th of *Shevat*), Rabbi Menahem Mendel was appointed his successor. The *rebbe* has not visited Israel, and he denies the validity of scientific theories of the eternity of the world.

The term *ufaratzta*, found in Genesis 28:14 ("And thou shalt spread"), is the theme of a melody popular with Lubavitcher *hasidim*, and it is also the motto of the present rabbi. He has expanded the already far-reaching and manifold activities of the movement.[7] To give one instance, he has reached out to North Africa, and now *Habad* brings the hasidic teachings to the Sephardim of Casablanca, Marrekesh, Sefrou, and Meknes. A network of sixty-seven *Ohalei Yosef Yitzhak* Lubavitch institutions, evening classes, girls' schools, and a teachers' seminary have been established to provide for many pupils throughout the world.

Lubavitch disciples have organized a "Peace Corps," student evangelists who bring Judaism to Jews in many far-flung places in the United States and abroad. A total of 35,000 children are enrolled in the Lubavitch schools in the United States, North Africa, Argentina, Denmark, Brazil, Italy, and Canada. Rabbi Shemariah Gurary, brother-in-law of the rabbi, is the director of the United Lubavitch *Yeshivot*, with fifteen branches throughout the U.S.A., where many youngsters receive a Torah education.

His followers are obliged to devote themselves to "spreading the fountains outside" by demonstrating to their fellow Jews the *mitzvot* of donning phylacteries, kindling the Sabbath lights, pronouncing the benediction of the *lulav*, sounding the *shofar*, and eating *matzah shemurah*. These activities are organized as a military operation with a fleet of vehicles that are known as "*mitzvah* tanks." From *Merkaz Leinyanei Hinukh* there emerges streams of books, pamphlets, and journals designed for all age groups, in Hebrew, Yiddish, English, French, Russian, Arabic, German, and Turkish.

From his residence at 770 Eastern Parkway in Brooklyn, New York, the rabbi directs his far-reaching spiritual empire. From the day he became *rebbe* until he suffered a heart attack a few years ago, the rebbe would receive visitors on Sundays. Even now, the *rebbe* spends the entire day supervising *Habad* activities. On his way to the Camp David talks in 1978, Israeli Prime Minister Menahem Begin visited the rebbe to ask for his blessing. There are now Lubavitch centers in sixteen cities in California. There are about eighty Lubavitch centers throughout the United States.

Other Centers in Brooklyn

Another celebrated *rebbe* is Rabbi Spira, a descendant of Rabbi Elimelekh Shapira of Dynow, author of *Benei Yissaskhar* ("Children of Issahar"). Rabbi Spira, the Bluzhever *rebbe,* survived the Nazi Holocaust. His life and the lives of 200 other camp inmates were saved at the eleventh hour by the arrival of the American liberation forces. At its head was a tank driven by a young Jewish soldier, Phinehas Kohn of Pittsburgh.

The Miracle of Bobow

Rabbi Solomon Halberstam, the present *Rebbe* of Bobow, was born on 1 *Kislev* 1907, in Bobow. At the age of 18, Rabbi Solomon married his cousin, the daughter of Rabbi Hayim Jacob Teitelbaum. After the German invasion of Russia, Rabbi Solomon was confined to the labor camp at Bochnia, near Krakow. His wife and two children were taken to Auschwitz. The rabbi and his mother escaped first to Grosswardein and from there to Rumania. After the war, he made his way to Italy and eventually settled in New York, first in Manhattan then in Crown Heights and subsequently in Boro Park, Brooklyn. In 1947, he married his second wife, Freda, the daughter of Rabbi Rubin by whom he has had five daughters and one son.

The *Rebbe* founded a network of educational establishments. The list of his institutions is most impressive. A large *yeshivah* in Boro Park, a magnificent fifty classrooms girls' school the Miriam Locker School-*Bnot Tziyyon*, a *Talmud Torah* with almost 1,000 children and a large *kollel*. The *rebbe* also set up a computer studies career development center for young men. The Bobow holiday camp gives many children the opportunity of spending the summer vacation in a traditional atmosphere.

The *rebbe* does not hesitate to break new ground. He introduced a scheme whereby courses leading to jobs in industry are taught in his *yeshivah* trade school. At one time he planned to build a twenty-million dollar housing project for 200 families at Parsons Boulevard, in Long Island, and the foundation stone was laid on June 27, 1965. Because of the opposition of local residents, however, the plan was abandoned.

Until recently, a prominent part of New York hasidic life was played by Rabbi Abraham Joshua Heschel, *rebbe* of Kopycznce (1888–1967), an active member of the *Agudah* and a strong supporter of the *Hinukh Atzma'i* (the *Agudah*'s educational network in Israel). The *rebbe* made ten visits to the Holy Land. "To love a great *talmid hakham* is easy," he once remarked, "but to love the ordinary man, the one who is even difficult at times, is true *ahavat Yisrael* (love of Israel)."

Boro Park

There are over 200 synagogues and Jewish institutions in Boro Park, which lies in the middle of several well-known Brooklyn communities including Bensonhurst, Bay Bridge, and Flatbush.

Half of the synagogues are hasidic. The *hasidim* of Ger have established three large *shtiblekh* and a *yeshivah Yagdil Torah* for elementary-school-age children and a *mesivta,* named after the late rebbe of Ger. The *Beit Jacob* schools of Boro Park are some of the largest in the world.

The Rebbe of Boston

A leading hasidic *rebbe* was Rabbi Moses Halevi. He was born in the Holy Land in 1909 and came to America with his mother in his childhood to join his father, Rabbi Phinehas David Horowitz who lived in Boston. Rabbi Moses studied in Europe under Rabbi Asher Lemel Spitzer in Kirchdorf and under Rabbi Moses Kliers in Tiberias. Rabbi Moses married the daughter of Rabbi Hayim Abraham Eichenstein of Zydaszow. In 1941, he moved to Williamsburg and was known as the "Bostoner *Rebbe.*" He was intensively involved in the strengthening of the foundations of Torah life, particularly in the area of *glatt kosher* meat provisions. Besides his efforts in the development of the Torah institutions *yeshivat Darkei Noam* and *Beit Hamidrash Netzah Yisroel,* the rebbe was a staunch supporter of the *Agudah* and was a member of the presidium. He died on 13 *Sivan* 1985, and was succeeded by his son Rabbi Hayim.

Voshnitz–Monsey

Just thirty miles from Manhattan, in the Spring Valley, New York area, is the small hasidic settlement of Monsey established in 1964 by Rabbi Moses Hager of Vishnitz. The *Shikkun* is steadily growing. Nearly 200 students study at the *yeshivah,* 60 men at the *kollel,* and 200 girls at *Bnot Vishnitz.* There are even students from the Holy Land, England, and Uruguay.

Other Centers in the United States

There are also hasidic rabbis in Chicago, Philadelphia, and Boston, as well as other American cities. Rabbi Jacob Israel

Twersky (1899–1973), a descendant of a long line of hasidic *rebbes*, lived in Milwaukee, Wisconsin. He was born in Hornistopel, near Kiev, and emigrated to the United States in 1927. After serving congregations in New York, he settled in Milwaukee, where in 1939 he founded the congregation *Beit Yehudah*. Of his five sons, only one of them–Rabbi Michael–succeeded as *rebbe*.

Rabbi Eliezer Zuya Portugal, the *rebbe* of Skulen who died in New York on 29th *Elul* 1982, was a colorful personality. For many years he served as rabbi in Skulen, Rumania and then in Czernowitz. Despite all the personal dangers he faced, he continued his outstanding religious activities especially among the thousands of orphans left as a result of the war. Twice he was imprisoned by the Communist authorities in Rumania for his educational activities. He settled in New York in 1960. Parallel to his relief activities is his widespread work for Torah especially among the youth. He set up some fifty *hinukh* institutions in the Holy Land under the name *Hesed LeAvraham*. They included boarding schools for boys and girls, *Talmud Torah* for evening study, and Torah clubs for children. Until his final years, when he was blind and very frail, he personally administered his institutions.

Ten percent of American *yeshivot* in the New World are hasidic, and 8.1 percent of the Jewish children in New York attend hasidic school.[8] There are between 40–50,000 *hasidim* in New York City.

Hasidism in the Western World

In Montreal, there is a *metivta* founded by the rabbi of Klausenburg under the direction of Rabbi Samuel Undsorfer (a former *rosh yeshivah* in England), as well as *yeshivot* under the auspices of Lubavitch and Satmar and a large Lubavitch day school. Toronto, too, has a *Yesodei Hatorah* School. There are also hasidic groups in the suburb of St. Kilda in Melbourne.

One-eighth of Antwerp's Jewish community is hasidic. Their spiritual leader was Rabbi Moses Isaac Gerwirczman (1882–1976), popularly known as "Reb Itzikel." He was a descendant of Rabbi Elimelekh of Lyshansk and was known as "miracle worker." He was the most venerated *tzaddik* of post-war Europe. He died on the Day of Atonement 1976[9] and was succeeded by his son-in-law Rabbi Eleazar.

Conclusion

The second half of the twentieth century has seen a diminution of Hasidism. There are probably no more than 200,000 *hasidim* throughout the world, but the movement's significance cannot be estimated on a numerical basis. Today Hasidism is receiving the careful attention of writers and thinkers of many denominations. In the wake of Martin Buber, a neo-mysticism and neo-Hasidism is evolving. Although he has introduced new elements into Hasidism and evolved a theory of Hasidism that the Besht might not instantly recognize, Buber is largely responsible for the new interest in this remarkable revival movement. He wrote the following:

> The flowering period of the hasidic movement lasted five generations. The *tzaddikim* of these five generations offered us a number of religious personalities of a vitality, a spiritual strength, a manifold originality such as have never, to my knowledge, appeared together in so short a time span in the history of religion. But the most important thing about these *tzaddikim* is that each of them was surrounded by a community which lived a brotherly life, and who could live in this way because there was a leading person in their midst who brought each one nearer to the other by bringing them all nearer to that in which they believed. In a century which was, apart from this, not very productive religiously, obscure Polish and Ukranian Jewry produced the greatest phenomenon we know in the history of the spirit . . . a society which lives by its faith.[10]

Hasidism is many things to many people. It is Judaism at its finest, most lively, and creative form. Hasidism is the struggle for social justice; concern for the poor and the underprivileged; spiritual democratization, and the hallowing of the everyday.

Hasidism brought new hope and new happiness to hundreds of thousands in the darkest days of Jewish history. It brushed away the cobwebs and revitalized Judaism not by introducing revolutionary doctrines, but simply by leading the people back to the principles preached by the great prophets and teachers of Israel.

Today Hasidism exerts a discernible influence on Israeli writers.[11] Its inspiration can be detected in the poetry of Nobel Prize winner Nelly Sachs, the stories of Samuel Joseph Agnon–another Nobel Prize winner–the novels of Isaac Bashevis Singer and Eli Wiesel, and the writings of the philospher, the late Abraham Joshua Heschel, even as it can be seen in the works of their predecessors, Isaac Leib Peretz, Sholem Asch, and Franz Kafka. Our super-sophisticated and over-organized society may well recall with nostalgia the soaring ecstasy of Hasidism and the radiance that illuminated the Jewish world for 200 years. And, recalling this, they may realize that Hasidism has a relevant and immediate message for this generation and the next.

Footnotes

Chapter 1

1. Mark Wichnitzer, *A History of Jewish Crafts and Guilds*, New York, 1965, p. 209; Isaac Lewin, "The Protection of Jewish Religious Rights by Royal Edicts in Ancient Poland," *Quarterly Bulletin of the Polish Institute of Arts and Sciences in America*, April 1943.
2. Moses Isserles, *Responsa*, nos. 63 and 64, Amsterdam, 1711.
3. Even Metzulah, *A Chronicle of the Massacres in 1648*, Venice, 1562.
4. Simon M. Dubnow, *Pinkas Medinat Lita The Minutes of the Lithuanian Council of Provinces*, Berlin, 1925; Israel Halpern, *Pinkas Vaad Arba Aratzot* (Acta Congressus Judaeorum Regni Polaniae, 1580–1764), Jerusalem, 1945; "The Council of Four Lands and the Hebrew Book," in *Kiryat Sefer* IX, Jerusalem, October 1932–1933, pp. 367–394; Bernard Weinryb, *Texts and Studies in the Communal History of Polish Jewry*, New York, 1950, p. 14.
5. Dubnow, *History of the Jews in Russia and Poland,* vol. I, p. 112.
6. Ibid., pp. 116–118.
7. Meyer S. Lew, *The Jews of Poland*, London, 1944, pp. 90–92.
8. Dubnow, op. cit., pp. 156–157.
9. Ibid., pp. 166–167.
10. L. Wolf, *Menasseh Ben Israel's Mission to Oliver Cromwell,* London, 1901, p. 87.
11. Israel Halpern, "Al Sakkanat Gerush Liklal Yisrael BePolin VeLita BeMahatzit HaSheniah Shel Me'ah HaShevaEsrai" (Threatened Expulsion of Polish and Lithuanian Jewry in the Latter Half of the Seventeenth Century), *Zion* XVII, Jerusalem, 1952, pp. 65–74.
12. Majer Balaban, *Die Judenstadt von Lublin*, Berlin, 1919, pp. 50, 106.

13. Dubnow, op. cit., p. 179.
14. Raphael Mahler, *A History of Modern Jewry,* London, 1971, p. 301.

Chapter 2

1. G. Scholem, *Major Trends in Jewish Mysticism*, London, 1955, p. 301.
2. Ecclesiasticus 21.
3. *Bavli, Hagigah*, 11b.
4. Ibid., 14b.
5. *Bavli, Sanhedrin*, 65b, 67b.
6. *Yerushalmi, Sanhedrin,* VII.
7. *Tractate Eikhalot,* II, ed. Jellinek, *Beit Hamidrash*, Leipzig, 1853, pp. 40–47.
8. *Shem Olam*, Vienna, 1891, p. 11.
9. Moritz Güdermann, *Geschichte des Erziehungwesens und der Kultur der abendländischen Juden während des Mittelalters und der neuen Zeit*, Vienna, 1880–1888, Heb. trans., part 1, p. 141; Simon G. Kramer, *God and Man in the Sefer Hasidim*, New York, 1966.
10. *Zohar*, 11, 149b, 152a.
11. S. A. Horodezky, *Hatekuphah*, XXII, Warsaw, 1926, p. 30.
12. *The Life of Gluckel of Hamelin*, ed. Beth Zion Abrahams, London, 1962, pp. 45–46.
13. *Maayan Ganim*, quoted by Dubnow, op. cit., p. 134.
14. *Autobiography of Solomon Maimon*, London, 1954, p. 43.
15. Dubnow, *Nationalism and History*, "Essay on old and new Judaism" ed. Koppel S. Pinson, Philadelphia, 1958, pp. 4–5.
16. Israel Abrahams, *Jewish Life in the Middle Ages*, London, 1932, p. 187.
17. *Toledot, Vayeshev*, Lvov, 1863.
18. Maimon, op. cit., pp. 31–32.
19. *Ben Porat Yosef, Tzav*, ed. Lvov.
20. Isserles, op. cit., no. 7.

Chapter 3

1. According to a Lubavitch tradition the date of birth was 18th *Elul.*
2. *Shivhei HaBesht*, p. 13.
3. L. Abrahams, *Midrash Ribash Tov,* Kecskemet, 1927, p. 45.
4. *Shivhei HaBesht,* p. 41.
5. Ibid., pp. 44–45.
6. Jonathan Eibeschütz, *Luhot Edut,* Altona, 1755, p. 57; A. J. Heschel, "Rabbi Gershon Kutover," in *The Hebrew Union College Annual,* XXIII, Cincinnati, 1950–1951, p. 18.

7. *Shivhei HaBesht,* 2, 4; Heschel, op. cit., p. 24.
8. *Maggid Devarav LeYaakov*, ed. Solomon of Lutzk, Korets, 1781.
9. Martin Buber, *Mamrei*, London, 1946, p. 106.
10. *Toledot*, 174b, 58c, 86d.
11. *Tzavaat HaRibash* (Testament of the Besht), Warsaw, 1913, p. 9.
12. *Toledot*, 59b.
13. Martin Buber, *Tales of the Hasidim*, vol. 1, p. 5.
14. Mishnah, *Ethics of the Fathers,* VI:1.
15. Lubavitch gives the date as 18th *Sivan*.

Chapter 4

1. Maimon, op. cit., pp. 173–174.
2. Ibid., pp. 175–176.
3. *Shivhei HaBesht*, p. 64; Dresner, op. cit., p. 50.
4. Preface to *Toledot*.
5. Dresner, op. cit., p. 251.
6. *Toledot, Bo.*
7. *Ben Porat Yosef, Vayehi.*
8. Jacob Joseph, *Toledot*, 85b.
9. *Tosefta to Midrash Phinehas*, Bilgoray, 1929, p. 21; A. J. Heschel, "Rabbi Phinehas Koritzer," in *Yivo Bletter, Journal of the Yiddish Scientific Institute*, vol. XXXIII, pp. 1–48.
10. Heschel, op. cit., pp. 44–45.
11. "Rabbi Isaac of Drohobycz," in Abraham J. Heschel, *The Circle of the Baal Shem Tov,* ed. Samuel H. Dresner, The University of Chicago Press, Chicago and London, 1985, pp. 152–153.
12. Moses Hayim Kleinman, *Zikaron Larishonim*, Piotrokow, 1882, p. 137.
13. Isaac, J. J. Safrin, *Netiv Mitzvotekhah Shevil ha-Yiyhud*, Jerusalem, 1947, paragraph 4.
14. Kamelhar, *Dor Deah*, Bilgoray, 1933, 1.28.
15. R. Isaac Yehiel Safrin of Komarno, *Zohar Hai*, Lvov, 1875–81; Exodus p. 7d.

Chapter 5

1. Israel Berger, *Esser Orot*, Piotrokow, 1907, p. 55; David Shapiro, "Levi Yitzhak of Berdichev," *Men of the Spirit*, ed. Leo Jung, Kymson Publishing Company, New York, 1964, pp. 403–415.
2. Samuel H. Dresner, *Levi Yitzhak of Berdichev*, Hartmore House, New York, 1974, p. 65; A. Waldman, *Shem HaGedolim HeHadash*, Jerusalem, 1965, p. 88.

3. Hayim Lieberman, *Yivo Bletter*, New York, 1937, vol. III, pp. 92–93; M. Wilensky, *HaHasidim Umitnaggdim*, Mosad Bialik, Jerusalem, 1970, vol. 1, p. 116.
4. Dresner, op. cit., p. 103.
5. Ibid., p. 68.
6. Ibid., p. 135.
7. Ibid., p. 82.
8. A. Kahana, *Sefer HaHasidut*, p. 258.
9. I. Berger, op. cit., p. 48.
10. Dresner, op. cit., pp. 108–109.
11. Ibid.
12. M. Buber, *Tales of the Hasidim–Early Masters*, Thames & Hudson, London, 1956, p. 212.
13. S. Kaminer, *Shnei HaMorot*, Kishenev, 1896, p. 96.
14. Dresner, op. cit., p. 94.
15. Buber, op. cit., p. 219.
16. *Kedushat Levi*, Slavuta, 1798, p. 9.

Chapter 6

1. Barukh of Shklow, in his introduction to the Hebrew translation of *Euclid's Geometry*, The Hague, 1820.
2. Samuel Joseph Finn, *Kiryah Ne'emanah*, Vilna, 1871.
3. Abraham Katzenellenbogen, *Hesped Al Hagra*, Vilna, 1871.
4. Jonathan Eibeschütz, op. cit., p. 71.
5. Rabbi Hayim of Volozhin, in *Hut Hameshulash*, no. 9; in Louis Ginzberg, *Students, Scholars and Saints*, Philadelphia, 1943, p. 140.
6. Israel Cohen, *Vilna*, Philadelphia, 1943, p. 225.
7. Maimon, op. cit., p. 172.
8. Dubnow, *Toledot HaHasidut*, p. 112.
9. Commentary on Proverbs 24:31 and 25:4; Ginzberg, op. cit., p. 140.
10. *Tzavaat HaRibash*, p. 23.
11. *Toledot*, 105b.
12. Hielman, *Beit Rabbi*, Part 1, Chapter 12.
13. Dubnow, *Geschichte des Chasidismus*, Berlin, 1931, vol. 1, pp. 181–182.
14. Cohen, op. cit., pp. 235–237.
15. Ibid., p. 237.
16. Dubnow, *Toledot*, p. 121.
17. Ibid.
18. Hielman, op. cit., p. 40; Teitelbaum, *Harav MeLiady*, pp. 218–221.
19. Maimon, op. cit., p. 240.
20. *Psalms* 109:126; *Berakhot* 54a; Cohen, op. cit., p. 240.

21. Ibid., Dubnow, op. cit., pp. 141ff.
22. Jacob Marcus, *The Jew in the Medieval World,* Cincinnati, 1938, pp. 276–278.
23. Cohen, op. cit., p. 244.
24. Joshua Heshel Levin, *Aliyot Eliyahu*, Stettin, 1856, p. 74.
25. Dubnow, *History*. Vol. 1, pp. 375–376.
26. Israel Klausner, *Vilna Betekufat HaGaon,* Jerusalem, 1942, pp. 20–45.
27. W. Z. Rabinowitsch, *Lithuanian Hasidim,* p. 46; Dubnow, *Yevreyskaya Starina*. Vol. III, St. Petersburg, 1910, p. 84ff.; J. Hessen, *Yevreyi v Rosiyi*, St. Petersburg, 1906, p. 142ff.

Chapter 7

1. Eliezer Steinmann, *Be'er HaHasidut, Habad.* Vol. 1, p. 231.
2. Ibid.
3. Horodezky, *Leaders of Hasidism,* p. 49.
4. Teitelbaum, op. cit., pp. 48–49.
5. Ibid., p. 147.
6. Hilman, *Igrot Baal HaTanya*, p. 238.
7. In Yiddish by Uriel Zimmer, New York, 1958; in English by Raphael Ben Zion, Los Angeles, 1945; and by Nisan Mindel, *Likkutei Amarim*, New York, 1962.
8. N. Mindel, *Tanya*, p. 18.
9. Ibid., p. 31, note 17.
10. *Tanya*, Chapter 13; Louis Jacobs, *Tract on Ecstasy*, London, 1963; bibliography of *Habad* is given by A. M. Habermann, in *Jubilee Volume for Zalman Shocken*, Jerusalem, 1952, pp. 293–370.

Chapter 8

1. Buber, *Tales of Rabbi Nahman,* trans. Maurice Freidman, New York, 1956, pp. 24–25.
2. *Shivhei Moharan*, Lvov, 1874, p. 49.
3. Louis Newman, *The Hasidic Anthology*, New York, 1944, p. 299.
4. Z. M. Rabinowicz, "Yahas HaKabbalah VehaHasidut el HaRambam," in *Moses ben Maimon,* ed. J. L. Fishman, Jerusalem, 1935, pp. 279–287.
5. *Shivhei*, p. 164.
6. Horodezky, *HaHasidut*, 11, p. 40.
7. *Kitvei Rabbi Nahman*, ed. Steinmann, Tel Aviv, 1951, p. 305.

8. *Likkutei Moharan*, Ostrog, 1821, 2, 5.
9. *Shivhei*, 9b.
10. *Sefer Hamidot*, Lvov, 1872.
11. *Sihot Vesippurim Moharan*, Jerusalem, 1910, 23, 24.
12. *Likkutei Tefillot*, Zolkiew, 1872.
13. *Likkutei Moharan Tanina*, Mogilev, 1811, 2, 8.
14. Abraham B. Gottlober, *Haboker*, Warsaw, 1876, VI, p. 75.
15. Horodezky, *HaHasidut*, III, p. 29.
16. Nathan of Nemirov, *Hayei Moharan*, Lvov, 1872, 8, 9, 12, 18.
17. Ibid.
18. Jacob S. Minkin, *The Romance of Hasidism*, New York, 1955, pp. 263–264.
19. Martin Buber, op. cit., p. 43.
20. Meyer Levin, *The Golden Mountain*, New York, 1951, p. XIII.
21. Horodezky, op. cit., Berlin, 1922; D. Kahana, op. cit., Warsaw, 1923; Steinmann, op. cit., Tel Aviv, 1951.
22. *The Tales of Rabbi Nachman,* New York, 1956, in the Foreword.
23. New York, 1932.

Chapter 9

1. *Menorat Zahav*, Warsaw, 1902, p. 7; Bezalel Landau, *Rabbi Elimelekh of Lyzhansk*, Jerusalem, 1963, p. 196; *Sefer Tiferet Ha'Ahim*, Warsaw, 1924.
2. Bavli, *Sanhedrin*, 37b.
3. A. S. B. Michelson, *Ohel Elimelekh*, Przemysl, 1910, p. 177.
4. Eliezer Zeev Shtik, *Sihot Yekarim*, Satmar, p. 1b.
5. Menahem Mendel Bedek, *Yalkut Menahem*, Vilna, 1903, p. 16.
6. *Ohel Elimelekh*, no. 192.
7. Dov Ehrman, *Devarim Arevim*, Munkacs, 1903, p. 17b.
8. Rabbi Henokh Wagshal, quoted by Landau, op. cit., p. 320, 326, note 1.

Chapter 10

1. Mahler gives the number as 750,000, *Yidn in Amoliken Poylen in Likht Fun Tzeferen*, Warsaw, 1938, pp. 30–37. Thaddeuz Czascki gives the number as 900,000, *Presprawa O Zydaichi i Kaitaitch*, Krakow, 1810, p. 117.
2. Dubow, *History*. Vol. 1, p. 277.
3. Cecil Roth, *History of the Great Synagogue*, London, 1950, p. 108.

4. Rabbi Joshua of Ostrow, *Toledot Adam,* Josefow, 1874; in *Rumzei Hanukkah;* see Buber, *Tales of the Hasidim,* London, 1956, p. 287.
5. *Avodat Yisrael,* Josefow, 1842; *Parshat Vayishlah, Avot* II:2, IV:9.
6. Printed by his grandson, Josefow, 1842.
7. *Beit Yisrael,* Warsaw, 1876.
8. Anna Potocka "Pamietniki" S 35; Leone Dembowski "Pamietnik" *Atheneum* (1882): 3.2; Rabinowitz, *HaMaggid MiKozienice.*
9. *The Cambridge History of Poland 1697–1935,* Cambridge, 1951, p. 210.
10. Rabinowitz, op. cit., p. 59, notes 47–51.
11. Moses Menahem Walden, *Nifla'ot Harabbi,* Warsaw, 1911.
12. Israel Berger, *Esser Orot,* p. 44b.
13. Walden, op. cit., p. 290.
14. A. Marcus, *Der Chassidismus,* Heb. trans., Tel Aviv, p. 114.
15. Isaac Eisig of Komarna, *Heikhal Haberakhah,* Lvov, 1872, p. 276b.
16. Berger, op. cit., 84, 96.
17. A. I. Bromberg, *ha-Hozeh Milublin,* Jerusalem, 1962, pp. 118–119.

Chapter 11

1. *Yoreh De'ah,* ccxlii, 15.
2. Bavli, *Megillah,* 13a.
3. *Likkutei Ramal,* Piotrokow, 1910.
4. Rashi and Rabbenu Tam differed as to the order of the texts of the four paragraphs in the Bible (Exodus 13:l; Exodus 13:ll; Deuteronomy 6:4–9; Deuteronomy 11:13–21). Some pious Jews put on two pairs of *tefillin* according to the two versions. H. M. Rabinowicz, *Rabbi Jacob Isaac Przysucha,* Piotrokow, 1932.
5. Rabinowicz, op. cit., p. 108.
6. Not in 1815 as in *Nifla'ot HaYehudi,* p. 16, or Marcus, op. cit., p. 16.
7. Joseph Levinstein, Piotrokow, 1909, *Torat HaYehudi,* Bilgoray, 1911; Aryeh Mordecai Rabinowicz, *Keter HaYehudi,* Jerusalem, 1929; Moses Joshua Leib Taub, *Kitvei Kodesh;* Warsaw, 1926.
8. Rabbi Nathan Nato of Korbiel, *Rish'pei Esh HaShalom,* Piotrokow, 1907, p. 49.
9. *Eretz Tzvi,* Warsaw, 1874; H. M. Rabinowicz, *Rabbi Simha Bunem of Przysuche,* Tel Aviv, 1944, p. 10.
10. Samuel Shinover, *Ramatayim Tzofim,* Warsaw, 1881, p. 178.
11. J. Levinstein, *Si'ah Sarfei Kodesh,* Lodz, 1928, vol. III, p. 14.
12. Shinover, op. cit., p. 163.
13. J. Shipper, *Zydzi . . . w dobie powstania Listopadowego,* Warsaw, 1923, quoted by Rabinowicz, op. cit., p. 36.
14. Y. D. Kamelhaer, *Dor De'ah,* New York, 1952, p. 278.

15. Rabbi Samuel of Sochaczew, *Shem Mishmuel*, Piotrokow, 1927, *Toledot.*
16. J. Levinstein, *Simhat Yisrael*, Piotrokow, 1910, p. 56.
17. Ibid., p. 27.
18. Shlomoh Tal, *Rabbi Naftali Tzvi of Ropczyce*, Mosad Harav Kook, Jerusalem, 1983.
19. *Zera Koddesh, V'Ethchanan*, p. 110a; S. Tal, op. cit., p. 61.
20. Ibid., p. 103.
21. Ibid., p. 104.
22. Ibid., p. 36.
23. Yitzchak Alfasi, *Harav M'apta*, Mechon Sifsei Tzaddikim, Jerusalem, 1981, p. 32.
24. Ibid., pp. 71–80.
25. Ibid., p. 42.
26. Ibid., p. 48.

Chapter 12

1. Joseph Fox, *Rabbi Menahem Mendel of Kotzk*, Jerusalem, 1967; Meir Urein, *Sneh Bo'er Be'Kotzk*, Jerusalem, 1962; *Kotzker Mayses: 50 Wunderlekhe Mayses*, ed. Luzer Bergman, Warsaw, 1924; P. Z. Glikman, *Der Kotzker Rebbe Admor Reb Menachem Mendel*, Piotrokow, 1938–1939.
2. Joseph Fox, *Rabbi Menahem Mendel of Kotzk* (Heb.), Mosad Harav Kook, Jerusalem, 1967, p. 64.
3. Yitzchak Alfasi, *Gur*, Tel Aviv, 1954, p. 64.

Chapter 13

1. A. I. Bromberg, *Rabbi Israel Friedmann of Ruzhin*, Jerusalem, 1955, p. 93.
2. Ibid., p. 170.
3. Ibid., pp. 155–159.
4. For the dynasty of Belz, see M. E. Gutmann, *Migibore Hahasidut*, Tel Aviv, 1952; A. I. Bromberg, *Belz*, Jerusalem, 1955; Marcus, op. cit., pp. 224–226.
5. Jiri Langer, *Nine Gates*, James Clarke, London, 1961, p. 7, trans. from the Czech by Stephen Jolly.

Chapter 14

1. P. Wright, *Report By Sir Stuart Samuel on His Mission to Poland*, London, 1920, p. 35, Comd. 674.

2. Arthur Green, *Menahem Nahum of Chernobyl*, Paulist Press, New York, 1982, p. 23.
3. Op. cit., p. 34.
4. Ibid., p. 32.
5. Ibid., p. 38.
6. Abraham Abele, *Beit Avraham*, Sudylkow, 1837; L. Jacobs, *Tract of Ecstasy*, London, 1963, p. 24.
7. L. Jacobs, *Seeker of Unity*, London, 1966. Nothing, however, is known about the third son of Schneur Zalman, and the silence has given rise to many rumors; *Beit Rabbi*, part 1, p. 113.
8. Paragraph 16.
9. L. Greenberg, *The Jews in Russia*. Vol. 1, p. 44.
10. *Outlines of the Social and Communal Life of Chabad-Lubavitch*, New York, 1953, p. 19; Hielman, *Beit Rabbi*, part II, p. 5, note 1.
11. J. Lestschinsky, *Schriften fuer Ekonomic un Statistic, I,* Berlin, 1921, pp. 30–32.
12. Dubnow, op. cit., vol. 2., p. 18.
13. Greenberg, op. cit., p. 33.
14. Joseph I. Schneerson, *The Tzemah Tzedek and the Haskalah Movement*, New York, 1962.
15. Lucy S. Dawidowicz, *The Golden Tradition,* pp. 197–198.
16. Gutmann, *Rabbi Dov Milieowe,* Tel Aviv, 1952; Joshua Racker, *Der Sandzer Tzaddik*, New York, 1961; A. I. Bromberg, *Rabbi Hayim Halberstam of Sanz*, Jerusalem, 1949.
17. Lyck, ed. Eliezer Lipman Zilbermann, 1869, no. 27, reprinted in *Yalkut HaRoim, Odessa*, 1869, pp. 5–9.
18. A. I. Bromberg, *Rabbi Hayim Halberstam of Zanz,* p. 38.
19. Ibid., p. 24.
20. Ibid., p. 125.
21. Horodetsky, op. cit., vol., 3, pp. 135–136.
22. Bromberg, op. cit., p. 112.

Chapter 15

1. Yehudah Leib Levine, *Admorei M'Izbice*, Jerusalem, pp. 11–53; Sh. Z. Shragai, "Hasidut Habesht Befisat Izbice-Radzyn," in *Sefer HaBesht*, ed. Maimon, pp. 153ff.
2. Ibid., pp. 54–65.
3. Ibid., pp. 66–104.
4. Ibid., p. 75.
5. A. I. Bromberg, *HaYehudi HaTov Migostin*, Jerusalem, 1956, p. 30.
6. Ibid., p. 36.

7. Ibid., p. 89.
8. Ibid., p. 88.
9. A. I. Bromberg, *Migdolei HaHasidut*. Vol. 3, Jerusalem, 1956, p. 6.
10. Ibid., p. 42.
11. Ibid., p. 45.
12. A. I. Bromberg, *Migdolei HaHasidut, Rabbi Avrohom Bornstein*. Vol. 5, Jerusalem, 1955, p. 38.
13. Ibid., p. 160.
14. Ibid., p. 158.
15. A. I. Bromberg, *Migdolei HaHasidut, Rabbi Zadok HaKohen*. Vol. 7, Jerusalem, 1950, pp. 26–32.
16. Ibid., p. 94, see Samuel Unger, *Toledoth HaKohen Milublin*, Jerusalem, 1966, p. 31.

Chapter 16

1. A. I. Bromberg, *R. Hanokh Heinokh HaKohen Levin of Alexander*, Jerusalem, 1958, p. 18.
2. Ibid., p. 92.
3. Ibid., p. 94.
4. A. I. Bromberg, *Admorei Alexander*, Jerusalem, 1954, p. 18.
5. Ibid., p. 19.
6. Ibid., p. 26.
7. Ibid., p. 34.
8. Ibid., p. 34.
9. Ibid., pp. 60–61.
10. Ibid., p. 71.
11. Ibid., p. 113.

Chapter 17

1. *Encyclopaedia Shel Galuyot*, Warsaw, II, pp. 200–227.
2. L. Loewe, *Diaries of Sir Moses and Lady Montefiore*, London, 1890, vol. 1, pp. 354–355.
3. Lucian Wolf, *Sir Moses Montefiore*, London, 1884, p. 152.
4. Loewe, op. cit., vol. 1., p. 383.
5. A. I. Bromberg, *Sefat Emet*, Jerusalem, 1956, p. 19.
6. Ibid., p. 110.
7. Ibid., pp. 108–109.
8. A. I. Bromberg, *Mishpachat Eiger*, Jerusalem, 1958, p. 91.

9. Ibid., p. 92.
10. Ibid., p. 98.
11. Ibid., pp. 99–100.
12. Ibid., p. 110.
13. Ibid, pp. 121–123.

Chapter 18

1. I. Elbogen, *A Century of Jewish Life,* Philadelphia, 1945, p. 217.
2. Joseph Samuel, *Jewish Immigrants to the United States from 1881–1910,* New York, 1914, p. 93.
3. Israel Meir Kahan, *Nidhei Yisrael,* Warsaw, 1894; quoted by Lloyd P. Gartner, in *The Jewish Immigrant in England, 1870–1914,* London, 1960, p. 30.
4. *Hameilitz* (December 30, 1888), xxviii, p. 387, Gartner, op. cit., p. 24.
5. Elbogen, op. cit., pp. 499–500.
6. A. I. Bromberg, *HaHadmorim L'Beith Radzyn,* Jerusalem, 1968, p. 37.
7. Ibid., p. 58.
8. Ibid., p. 73.
9. Ibid., p. 65.
10. W. Z. Rabinowitsch, *Lithuanian Hasidism*, London, 1970, pp. 103–104.
11. Ibid., pp. 105–106.

Chapter 19

1. Sir Stuart Samuel, *Report by Sir Stuart Samuel on his Mission to Poland* (Comd. 674, Miscellaneous, no. 10), London, 1920, p. 15.
2. Simon Segal, *The New Poland and the Jews*, New York, 1938, p. 88.
3. Ibid., pp. 85–86.
4. Issar Frankel, *Rabbi Meir Yehiel of Ostrowiec*, Tel Aviv, 1953, p. 17.
5. Ibid., p. 19.
6. A. I. Bromberg, *Rabbi Avrohom Mordecai Alter of Ger*, Jerusalem, 1966, p. 111.
7. Ibid., p. 144.
8. Ibid., p. 146.
9. A. I. Bromberg, *Admorei Novominsk,* Jerusalem, 1960, p. 154.

Chapter 20

1. Aaron Sorsky, *Rabbi Meir Shapiro*, Tel Aviv, n.d., p. 38.
2. Ibid., p. 36.

3. Ibid., p. 56.
4. Isaac Lewin, *Israel of Tomorrow*, New York, 1946, ed. Leo Jung, pp. 389–397.
5. On the problem of Shechita in Poland see Moses Moskowitz, "Anti-Shechitah Legislation," in *Contemporary Jewish Record*, vol. 2, no. 3, May–June, 1939, p. 39; *Religious Freedom, The Right to Practise Shechitah*, ed. Isaac Levin, Michal L. Munk, and Jeremiah J. Berman, New York, 1946, p. 46, 85.
6. H. Rabinowicz, *The Legacy of Polish Jewry*, New York, 1965, p. 61.

Chapter 21

1. A. I. Bromberg, *Rabbi Moses Teitelbaum*, Jerusalem, 1954, p. 25.
2. Ibid., p. 84.
3. Ibid., p. 83.
4. Andrew Handler, *Rabbi Eizik*, Associated University Press, 1978, p. 24.
5. Ibid., p. 87.
6. Aryeh Sole, "Subcarpathian Ruthenia 1918–1938, in *The Jews of Czechoslovakia*, vol. 1, The Jewish Publication Society of America, Philadelphia, 1968, pp. 148–149.
7. Leopold Greenberg, *Tausant Yahr yidish leben in Ungaren*, New York, 1945, p. 97.
8. Aryeh Tartakover, "The Jewish Migratory Movements in Austria in Recent Generations," in *The Jews of Austria*, ed. Josef Fraenkel, London, Vallentine Mitchell, 1967, pp. 285–311.
9. Jacob Heshel, "The History of Hasidism in Austria," in *The Jews of Austria*, pp. 347–361.

Chapter 22

1. Ed. A. I. Katsch, London, 1965, pp. 194–195.
2. Hillel Zeidman, *Tagbuch fur Varshawer Ghetto*, Buenos Aires, 1947, p. 147.
3. Emanuel Ringelblum, *Notisn fur Varshawer Ghetto*, Warsaw, 1952, pp. 297–298.
4. Zeidman, op. cit., p. 64.
5. Israel Elfenbein, "Menahem Ziemba of Praga," in *Guardians of our Heritage*, ed. Leo Jung, New York, 1958, p. 612; *Ele Ezkero* ("These will I remember"), Research Institute of Religious Jewry Inc., New York, 1957, vol. II, p. 61; Moses Prager, "Tenuat HaHasidut," in *Sepher HaBesht*, ed Maimon, pp. 265–274; Menashe Ungar, "Zaddikim Shenesfu Bashavah," in *Sepher HaBesht*, pp. 274–282.

Chapter 23

1. Maimon, *Autobiography,* p. 170.
2. Shalom Spiegel, *Hebrew Reborn,* New York, 1962, p. 124.
3. *History of the Jews,* Philadelphia, 1941, vol. V, pp. 375–396, p. 381.
4. *Mein Leben,* p. 11; Pinson, op. cit., p. 6.
5. Also, preface to the German edition, vol. 1, p. 15. The Yiddish edition, originally published in Vilna in 1931, was recently reprinted in Argentina.
6. Salo W. Baron, *History and Jewish Historians,* compiled by Arthur Herzberg and Leon A. Feldman, Philadelphia, 1964, p. 285.
7. *Al Proshat Drakhim,* Berlin, 1913, vol. II, p. 29.
8. *Berakhot,* 5:1.
9. *Sotah,* 21b.
10. L. Jacobs, "The Concept of Hasid in Biblical and Rabbinic Literature," *The Journal of Jewish Studies,* London, 1957; vol. VIII, pp. 143–154; A. Buchler, *Types of Jewish-Palestinian Piety from 70 B.C.E. to 70 C.E.,* London, 1922.
11. Bavli, *Moed Katan,* 16b.
12. Buber, op. cit., vol. 1.
13. *Or Torah,* Lvov, 1863, p. 13.
14. Samuel H. Dresner, *The Zaddik,* p. 135.
15. Yeru, *Shabbath,* 5.9.
16. Bavli, *Rosh Hashanah,* 16b.
17. Aaron Wertheim, *Halakhot Vehalikhot BeHasidut,* Jerusalem, 1960, p. 159.
18. Bavli, *Sanhedrin,* 92a, *Orah Hayim,* 170:3.
19. Bavli, *Mo'ed Katan,* 11.3.
20. Bavli, *Shabbat,* 33b.
21. *Maggid Devarav LeYaakov,* p. 44; H. J. Zimmels, *Ashkenazim and Sephardim,* London, 1958, p. 326.

Chapter 24

1. Bavli, *Sukkah,* 51b.
2. Judah b. Samuel HaHasid, *Sefer Hasidim,* ed. Wistinetzki, Berlin, 1924, p. 207, 817.
3. *Zohar, Beshalah, Vayehi,* 249b.
4. Aaron ben Tzvi of Opatow, *Keter Shem Tov,* Zolkiew, 1794–1795, p. 39.
5. Horodezky, *HaHasidut,* p. 296.
6. Dresner, *Tzofnat Pane'ah, Toledot,* op. cit., p. 82.
7. *Or Torah, Beshalah.*

8. H. Zeitlin, "Lehasidim Mizmor," ed. M. S. Geshuri, Jerusalem, 1936, p. 52.
9. Teitelbaum, op. cit., p. 283; *Kuntress Hapaalut*, Warsaw, 1876, p. 5; A. Z. Idelsohn, *Jewish Music*, p. 416; Newman, op. cit., p. 283.
10. S. A. Horodezky, *Leaders of Hasidism,* London, 1928, p. 82.
11. L. Jacobs, *Tract of Ecstasy*, p. 77.

Chapter 25

1. Solomon Ashkenazi, *Haisha Be'Ispeklerit Hayehudit*, Tel Aviv, 1953.
2. Horodezky, op. cit., p. 69.
3. Dan Ben Amos, Jerome R. Mintz, *In Praise of the Baal Shem Tov* (Shivhei HaBesht), Bloomington, 1970, p. 120.
4. See *I Samuel*, 14:49–50, and Bavli, *Erubin*, 96a.
5. *The Life of Gluckel of Hameln*, ed. Beth Zion Abrahams, East and West Library, London, 1962, p. 9.
6. Grunfeld-Rosenbaum, "Sara Schenirer," in *Jewish Leaders,* ed. L. Jung, New York, 1953, pp. 410–411; S. Yarchi, *Sara Schenirer* (Sifriat Netzach); Moshe Prager, *Sara Schenirer Em BeYisrael*, Jerusalem, Merkaz Beit Yaakov; Z. E. Kurzweil, *Modern Trends in Jewish Education*, New York, 1964, pp. 266–275.
7. S. Yarchi, *Sara Schenirer*, Sifriat Metzach, p. 10; Moshe Prager, *Sarah Schenirer Em BeYisrael*, Merkaz Beit Yaakov, Jerusalem; Z. E. Kurzweil, *Modern Trends in Jewish Education*, New York, 1964, pp. 266–275.
8. S. Yarchi, *Sarah Schenirer*, Sifriat Netzach, p. 10.

Chapter 26

1. *Zohar,* Ahrei Mot, 72.
2. *Shivhei HaBesht*, 29.
3. J. Eibeschütz, op. cit., p. 57.
4. A. J. Heschel, "Rabbi Gershon Kutover," in *Hebrew Union College Annual,* vol. xxiii, part 2, Cincinnati, 1950, pp. 20–21.
5. Printed at the end of *Ben Porat Yosef,* Korets, 1781; Simon Federbush, *HaHasidut Vetzion*, Jerusalem, 1963, p. 11.
6. *Shivhei HaBesht*, 21.
7. *Ben Porat Josef,* Emor.
8. *Midrash Phinehas*, Bilgoray, 1929, p. 16.
9. Horodezky, "Menahem Mendel of Vitebsk," op. cit., vol. IV, p. 60.
10. *Likkutei Tefillot*, Jerusalem, 1953, p. 84; Israel Halpern, *Baaliyot Harishonim shel Hasidim Le'Eretz Yisrael,* Jerusalem, 1946, p. 20; Zalman

Shazar, "Kisufe Hageh'ulah *Veraayon Haaliyah BeHasidut,*" in *Sefer HaBesht*, Mosad Rav Kook, Jerusalem, 1960, pp. 93–106.

11. Printed in 1859 in the section *Shelah.*
12. Heschel, "Unknown Documents on the History of Hasidism," *Yivo Bletter,* New York, 1952, pp. 130–131.
13. *Zikhron Ot*, Lublin, 1890, on Shemot.
14. Israel Morgenstern, *Shalom Yerushalayim*, Piotrokow, 1925; Rabinowitz, *Rabbi Simha Bunem*, p. 83. Montefiore stayed in the Holy Land from October 16–25, 1827 (*Diaries of Sir Moses*, vol. 1, p. 43) when Simha Bunem was no longer alive. However, Sir Moses left London on May 1 when Simha Bunem was still alive. On Sir Moses and the *hasidim*, see M. S. Shapira, "Moses Montefiore Ugedolei Hahasidim, in *Hado'ar*, Jubilee Volume, New York, 1927.
15. Federbush, op. cit., p. 48.
16. Bomberg, *Sefat Emet,* p. 109.
17. *The Complete Diaries of Theodor Herzl.* Vol. 1., ed. Raphael Patai, New York, 1960, p. 347.
18. *Hazfirah*, 1899; *Juedische Rundschau*, 1922; Bromberg, op. cit., p. 108; Federbush, op. cit., p. 52.
19. *The Complete Diaries*. Vol. 2, p. 505.
20. Ibid., p. 495.
21. Ibid., vol. 1, pp. 640–642; Joseph Adler, "Religion and Herzl," *Herzl Year Book*. Vol. V, ed. Raphael Patai, New York, 1961, pp. 271–305.
22. *Responsa Avnei Nezer,* sections 453–457.
23. A. I. Bromberg, *Rabbi Avrohom Bornstein*, Jerusalem, 1955, p. 102.
24. Marcus, op. cit., p. 222; Federbush, op. cit., p. 178; A. I. Bromberg, *Israel of Ruzhin*, Jerusalem, 1956, p. 160.
25. Federbush, op cit., p. 179.

Chapter 27

1. *Trial and Error,* London, 1949, p. 398.
2. Alex Bein, *The Return of the Soil,* Jerusalem, 1953, p. 378.
3. *Hameilitz*, 1887.

Chapter 28

1. *Jewish Chronicle*, October 6, 1845, p. 249; July 21, 1854, p. 356; August 22, 1856, p. 698; June 3, 1859, p. 6; March 18, 1870, p. 5; October 22, 1875, p. 484; June 8, 1876, p. 48; March 29, 1878, p. 9.

2. Alexander Marx, *Essays in Jewish Bibliography*, Philadelphia, 1947, p. 324; Solomon Schechter, *Studies in Judaism*, New York, 1896.
3. *Children of the Ghetto*, Philadelphia, 1948, p. 280.
4. Maurice Wohgelernter, *Israel Zangwill*, New York, 1964, p. 108, 110, 112, 300, 301.
5. *Dreamers of the Ghetto*, Philadelphia, 1948, p. 280.
6. Copy available from Mr. Leon Gerstler, London.
7. *Minutes of the Federation of Syagogues,* London, May 17, 1892.
8. The *Shtibl* was destroyed in the Nazi blitz in 1940.
9. J. H. Hertz, *Sermons and Addresses*, London, 1938, pp. 108–115.
10. Ibid., p. 113.
11. Printed by Elijah Ze'ev Rabinowicz, 64 High Street, Whitechapel, London; British Museum, Shelf Mark, 1967, d. 32.
12. *Darkei Hen, Torat Hen.* He died in Jerusalem, 8 *Elul*, 1920.
13. *The Jewish Times,* London, August 26, 1920; *The Jewish Chronicle,* September 3, 1920, p. 18.
14. 81 Cazenove Road, N. 16. He was the author of *Milei Dehespeda*, London, 1927.
15. Ed. H. Rabinowicz, London, 1948, p. 11.
16. Ibid., p. 11.
17. Ibid., p. 10.
18. Ibid., p. 8.
19. Ibid., p. 9.

Chapter 29

1. Morton Rosenstock, *Louis Marshal, Defender of the Jewish Rights*, Wayne State, Detroit, 1965, p. 14.
2. Berish Rosenbaum, "The Novominsker Rebbe," in *Torah Personality*, Art Scroll Series, New York, 1980, pp. 182–198.
3. Solomon Poll, *The Jewish Community of Williamsburg,* The Free Press, New York, 1962.
4. Israel Rubin, *Satmar an Island in the City*, Quadrangle Books, Chicago, 1972, pp. 40–41.
5. He stressed that Jews must not violate the three vows cited in Bavli, *Kethoboth*, 11a: that the Jews should not force their way into the Holy Land.
6. Nisson Wolpin, "My Neighbor, my father, my Rebbe," in *The Jewish Observer*, New York, November 1979, p. 12.
7. "The Lubavitch Movement," *Commentary,* New York, March–April 1957; *The American Jewish Year Book*, vol. 66, p. 79.
8. Alvin Irwin, *The Jewish Day School in America*, New York, 1966, p. 66, 77, 87–89, 209.

9. Pinchos Jung, "Remembering Reb Itzikel," in *The Torah Personality*, pp. 211–217.
10. Dresner, op. cit., pp. 121–122.
11. Gershom Scholem, "Martin Buber's Hasidism," *The Commentary Reader*, ed. Norman Podhoretz, London, 1968, pp. 451–466; "Jewish Messianism and the Idea of Progess," *Commentary*, April, 1958; Isaiah Rabinowicz, *Major Trends in Modern Hebrew Fiction*, Chicago University Press, 1968, p. 2, 35, 233, 234, 238, 240; David Patterson, *The Hebrew Novel*, Edinburgh, 1964, p. 58, 62, 73, 78, 112, 166–167, 190, 207–209.

Glossary

Adar–Twelfth month of the Jewish calendar.

Additional Prayer–See *Musaf.*

Aggadah (pl. *Aggadot*)–lit. "narration." The nonlegal part of rabbinic literature. The homiletical sections of rabbinic literature.

Agudat Yisrael–Known as the *Agudah.* "Association of Israel," a right wing, ultra-religious party.

Aliyah–Immigration to Israel, often used to refer to waves of immigrants.

Amidah–lit. "standing." The name given to the chief prayer at each of the Statutory services, whether private or public, that is recited in a standing position. It originally contained eighteen benedictions and now contains nineteen.

Amora (pl. *Amora'im*)–lit. "speaker," or "interpreter." The name given to the sages quoted in the *Gemara* (q.v.) who lived between the third and fifth centuries.

Ashkenazim–Jews of Central and Eastern Europe.

Av–Fifth month of the Jewish calendar.

Baal Shem Tov–lit. "master of the name." A name given to a man who works wonders through his piety and uses the Divine Name in accordance with the concepts of *Kabbalah.*

Baal Tefillah–lit. "master of prayer." The leader of prayer in public worship. See *Hazzan* and *Sheliah Tzibbur.*

Badhan–Master of ceremonies and merrymaker at weddings and other celebrations.

Bahur (pl. *Bahurim*)–A youth. A name generally applied to a youth attending a yeshivah (q.v.).

Bat Kol–lit. "daughter of a voice." A voice descending from Heaven to offer guidance in human affairs.

Behelfer–An assistant.

Beit Din–lit. "house of law" or "house of judgment." An assembly of three or more learned men acting as a Jewish Court of Law.

Beit Hamidrash–lit. "house of study," equipped to also serve as a place of worship.

Bilu–Spearhead group of *Hovevei Tzion* ("Lovers of Zion") who were among the first of the pioneers to settle in the Holy Land.

Breaking of the Vessels–Term denoting the idea that the endless Divine light that filled all space before creation was broken by the creation of finite beings and forms.

Cheka–Russian abbreviation of the Extraordinary Commission to combat counterrevolutionary sabotage and breach of duty in the U.S.S.R. The name of the Soviet political police (1917–1922).

Codes–The systematic compilation of talmudic law and later decisions composed during subsequent eras.

C.E.–Common Era. The term used by Jews to describe the period of the current calendar (following the advent of Jesus).

Dayan–A judge.

Deveikut–Adhesion to God. (From the Hebrew *davak,* "cleave"). *Deveikut* involved the practice of Devotion (*kavanah*), wherein man removes the barriers between himself and God and establishes spiritual communion through *hitpashtut hagashmiyut* ("divesting himself of his natural being").

Dibbuk–lit. "attachment." The dismembered spirit of a dead person. This theory of metempsychosis was developed by the disciples of Rabbi Isaac Luria.

Divine Chariot–Maaseh Merkavah.–lit. "the work of the chariot." The mystic speculations of the Divine Chariot, "God's pre-existing throne," arising from the description of Ezekiel Chapter 1 and from other sources of mysticism.

Ein Sof–The endless; a designation for the hidden Godhead beyond the *Sefirot* and the ultimate source of all being.

Elijah–Prophet in the kingdom of Israel. According to legend, after his ascent to Heaven, the prophet Elijah continued to help his fellow Jews. Elijah is regarded as the precursor of the Messiah.

Elul–Sixth month of the Jewish calendar.

Eretz Yisrael–"The Land of Israel."

Etrog–A citron. One of the "four kinds of plants" used during the Festival of *Sukkot.* "The fruit of a goodly tree" (Leviticus 23:40) was traditionally interpreted as referring to the citron.

G.P.U.–Russian abbreviation of the State Political Administration. The Cheka was renamed G.P.U. in 1922. In 1934 it was renamed N.K.V.D.

Galut–Exile, dispersion. The enforced dwelling of Jews outside the Holy Land.

Gaon (pl. *Geonim*)–Title of the head of the Babylonian talmudic academies (seventh to eleventh centuries). Also a title given to outstanding talmudic scholars.

Gelilah–lit. "rolling." The ceremony of rolling up the Scroll of the Law after Reading of the Scriptural portions.

Gemara–"compilation"; the second and supplementary part of the Talmud that interprets the first part, the *Mishnah.*

Gilgul–Transmigration of Souls, or reincarnation.

Glatt Kosher–lit. "smooth kosher." It indicates that the meats or the meat products are kosher beyond a shadow of a doubt.

Habad–An acrostic of the initial letters of the Hebrew words *Hokhmah* (wisdom), *Binah* (understanding), and *Daat* (knowledge). The name of the Lubavitch hasidic movement founded by Shneur Zalman of Liady.

Haggadah–lit. "telling." The *haggadah* is the book that tells the story of the Exodus from Egypt and is read at the Seder table on the first two nights of Passover.

Hakham–lit. "wise man." The title *Hakham* is applied to rabbis of Sephardic congregations.

Hakkafot–lit. "circuits." Processions with the Torah around the Bimah on Simhat Torah (q.v.).

Halakhah (pl. *Halakhot*)–lit. "walking." The legal elements in Jewish teachings embodying the religious philosophy underlying Jewish religious life.

Halukkah–The distribution of funds, specifically for indigent Jews in the Holy Land before 1948.

Hanukkah–lit. "dedication." The Festival celebrated for eight days from the 25th of *Kislev.*

Haskalah–lit. "enlightenment." A movement originating in eighteenth-century Germany attempting to break away from the narrow limits of Jewish life and acquire the culture and customs of the outside world.

Hasid (pl. *Hasidim*)–An adherent of Hasidism.

Hazzan–The reader who leads the synagogue service.

Hevrah Kaddisha–lit. "Holy Society." Society for the performance of the last rites and the supervision of burials.

Heder (pl. *Hedarim*)–lit. a "room." A private Hebrew school, usually a room in the teacher's house.

Herem–Form of excommunication.

Heshvan–Eighth month of the Jewish calendar.

Hol Hamo'ed–The half-festive days, the intermediate days of the Festivals of Passover and *Sukkot*.

Hoshana Rabba–Seventh day of *Sukkot* (the Festival of Booths).

Illui–Talmudic genius.

Immersion–Bathing in a *mikveh* (q.v.).

Iyyar–Second month of the Jewish calendar.

Judenrat–Council of Jewish elders; a body appointed by the Nazis to administer Jewish affairs under their supervision.

Kabbalah–Jewish mysticism and its literature.

Kaddish–lit. "Sanctification." A prayer that marks the end of a unit of the service and refers to the doxology recited in the synagogue. Also a prayer recited in memory of a dead person.

Kaftan–Polish, meaning long coat.

Kapote–Yiddish, meaning the long black coat that was formerly common among Jews of Eastern Europe and that is still worn by adherents of Hasidism.

Kavanah (pl. *Kavanot*)–lit. "aiming" or "concentration." Devotion in prayer.

Kelipot–lit. "shells" or "husks." The spirits of impurity or the principles of evil. It is frequently used in Kabbalah to denote "evil" and the source of sensual desires.

Kfar–Village.

Kiddush–The benediction recited, usually over a cup of wine before a meal, to inaugurate the Sabbath and festivals.

Kislev–Ninth month of the Jewish calendar, usually coinciding with November-December.

Klaus–German, Yiddish, meaning the prayer room of a private congregation of worship, or chapel.

Kohen (pl. *Kohanim*)–Male descendants of Aaron, members of the priestly tribe of Levi who served in the Holy Temple, and who are today still subject to certain privileges and restrictions.

Kol Nidrei–"all vows." Opening words of the formula preceding the religious service on the eve of the Day of Atonement (Yom Kippur).

Kollel–Institute for higher learning.

Kvitl (pl. *kvitlekh*) –Yiddish, meaning note of request. A petition written on slips of paper containing the name of the suppliant, the name of his mother, as well as his request.

Lag B'omer–The thirty-third day of the *Omer,* corresponding to the 18th day of *Iyyar.* It is observed as a minor holiday.

Lurian Kabbalah–The mysticism that Rabbi Isaac Luria introduced into the teaching of the Kabbalah in the sixteenth century.

Maggid (pl. *Maggidim*)–Popular preachers.

Maskil (pl. *Maskilim*)–Adherent of the Haskalah movement.

Matzah–lit. "unleavened bread."

Matzah Shemurah–lit. "guarded *matzot.*" Those *matzot* that have been carefully supervised from the time of the cutting of the wheat to the final baking.

Megillah–lit. "scroll." A term commonly applied to the Book of Esther.

Menorah–Seven-branched candelabrum.

Merkavah–See Divine Chariot.

Meshullah–lit. "messenger." A person who collects donations for religious or charitable institutions.

Mezuzah–A small parchment inscribed with twenty-two lines of biblical verses that is attached to the doorpost.

Midrash (pl. *Midrashim*)–lit. "expositions." Books of talmudic and post-talmudic times that deal with the homiletical exegesis of the Scripture.

Mikveh–Ritual bath.

Minhag (pl. *Minhagim*)–Local rite or custom in the variant liturgical usages.

Mishnah–lit. "repetition." The collection of the statements of the *tanna'im* (q.v.) edited by Rabbi Judah the Prince (135–220).

Mitnaged (pl. *Mitnagdim*)–lit. "opponents." The avowed opponents of Hasidism.

Mitzvah–lit. "commandment." A religious act or a deed of piety. There are two kinds of *mitzvot,* positive commandments and negative commandments.

Musaf–lit. "addition." The additional *Amidah* recited during the morning service on Sabbath and Festivals.

Musar–Ethics and ethical literature.
Nasi–lit. "prince."
Ne'ilah–lit "closing." The closing prayers of the Day of Atonement.
Niggun–melody.
Nisan–First month of the Jewish calendar.
Nusah–Pattern, the correct text of a prayer, also the traditional melody of a prayer.
Pale of Settlement–Certain districts in Czarist Russia where the Jews were given permission to reside.
Pesah–Passover, the festival commemorating the liberation of the Jews from their bondage in Egypt. The festival is celebrated for eight days from the 15th to the 22nd of *Nisan*.
Peshat–Plain meaning.
Pidyon–lit. "redemption." The money followers give to their rebbes.
Pilpul–An analytical method used in talmudic study. A form of talmudic debate consisting in a display of dialectical skill.
Pinkas–From the Greek "Pinkas," meaning "board" or "writing tablet." Minute book or register of Jewish communities. The word occurs in the Mishnah *Avot* 3:16, "The *pinkas* is open."
Piyyut (pl. *Piyyutim*)–Poetical compositions of a liturgical character.
Pogrom–Russian, meaning "destruction." Term used to describe an organized massacre applied particularly to attacks on the Jews in Russia.
Purim–lit. "lots." The festival that is celebrated on the 14th day of *Adar* in commemoration of the deliverance of the Jews in Persia from the hands of their wicked enemy Haman.
Rabbi–lit. "teacher." A qualified rabbinic authority.
Rav–A religious leader who was appointed by religious scholars.
Rebbe–The religious leader of a Hasidic community.
Rebbetzin–The rebbe's wife.
Rejoicing of the Law–see *Simhat Torah*.
Responsa–Written replies by qualified authorities to questions on all aspects of Jewish law, dating from the time of the late *Geonim* to the present day.
Rosh Hashanah–lit. "the head of the year." The Jewish New Year on the first and second days of *Tishri*.
Rosh Hodesh–lit. "The head of the month." The New Moon, marking the beginning of the Hebrew month.
Sabbateans–Followers of Shabbetai Tzevi.
Sanhedrin–A Council of State that existed during the century or

more preceding the fall of the Second Temple in 70 C.E. It consisted of seventy-one members and was presided over by the High Priest.

Seder–lit. "order." The Order of the festive meal and home service on the first and second nights of Passover.

Selihot–Penitential Prayers, recited on certain days of the Jewish calendar.

Semikhah–Conferment of the title of rabbi.

Sephardim–Term used to denote Jews of Spain and their descendants; it was later applied to all those who adopted the rite of the *Sephardim.*

Sefer Torah–Scroll of the Law.

Se'udah–Meal.

Shadhan–Professional marriage broker.

Shalosh Se'udot–The Third Sabbath Meal, eaten after the Afternoon Service on Sabbath and accompanied by community singing and discourses.

Shammash–Beadle.

Shavuot–Pentecost or the Feast of Weeks, celebrated on the 6th and 7th days of *Sivan,* commemorating the giving of the Torah and the ingathering of the first fruits.

Sheitl–Wig worn by Orthodox Jewish women after marriage.

Skekhinah–The Divine Presence.

Sheliah Tzibbur–Emissary of the congregation. The reader at a religious service.

Shemini Atzeret–The Feast of the Eighth Day, or the Eighth Day of the Solemn Assembly, the concluding day of Sukkot, regarded as a separate festival.

Shevat–Eleventh month of the Hebrew calendar, corresponding to January-February.

Shikkun–Colony or settlement in the Holy Land.

Shirayim–lit. "remains." The remainder of the food eaten by the *rebbe.*

Shiurim–Discourses.

Shofar–A ram's horn used in the services of New Year and at the conclusion of the Day of Atonement.

Shohet–Ritual slaughterer.

Shtetl–Village.

Shtibl (pl. *shtiblekh*)–A small room used by Hasidim for prayer.

Shulhan Arukh–lit. "Set Tables." The standard Code of Jewish Law compiled by Joseph Karo in the middle of the sixteenth century and first published in 1565. It contains four parts: *Orah Hayim*, dealing with the ritual obligations of daily life and Divine worship; *Yoreh De'ah,* dealing with dietary laws and Jewish home life; *Even Ha'ezer* on personal status, marriage and divorce; and *Hoshen Mishpat*, on Jewish civil law.

Simhah – Joy.

Simhat Torah – lit. "rejoicing of the Law." Name given in the Diaspora to the second day of *Shemini Atzeret* when the reading of the Pentateuch is completed and recommenced.

Sivan – Third month of the Jewish calendar.

Siyym – lit. "completion." Celebration marking the conclusion of a course of study.

Sparks – The divine soul in man is a spark of Godliness. In performing the Divine precepts without material objective, the "Sparks" are liberated and returned to their source. The sparks of this broken light wander throughout the universe, and only when they return (after the breakdown of the evil forces in man and in the world) to their original source in Heaven will man and the universe be redeemed.

Sukkah (pl. *Sukkot*) – The booth or tabernacle in which the Children of Israel were enjoined to dwell for seven days. The festival (*Sukkot*) commences on the 15th of *Tishri* (see Leviticus 23, 33ff). The Festival commemorates the wanderings of the Children of Israel in the wilderness.

Takkanah (pl. *Takkanot*) – Communal ordinances.

Tallit – The prayer shawl used by males during prayers. It is fringed at four corners (Numbers 15:38).

Talmud – The general sense of the word is study of the law. It is commonly used in the narrow sense to mean the comments and discussions (*Gemara*) on the text of the *Mishnah* by the Palestinian and Babylonian scholars from the third to the fifth centuries C.E., constituting the Palestinian Talmud and the Babylonian Talmud. The Babylonian Talmud (*Bavli*) contains nearly 3,000 pages and was edited by Rav Ashi (352–427), whereas the Palestinian Talmud (*Yerushalmi*) was finished in the fifth century and is only one-seventh as long as the *Bavli.*

Tammuz – Fourth month of the Jewish calendar.

Tanna (pl. *Tanna'im*) – A teacher quoted in the *Mishnah.*

Tefillin – Phylacteries, small cases containing passages from the Scriptures and affixed to the forehead and arm during the recital of the morning prayers on weekdays (Deuteronomy 7:8).

Tevet–Tenth month of the Jewish calendar.

Tikkun Hatzot–Midnight service bewailing the destruction of the Temple.

Tisha B'Av–The Fast of the Ninth of *Av*, commemorating the destruction of both the First and Second Temples (586 B.C.E. and 70 C.E.).

Tishri–Seventh month of the Jewish calendar.

Torah–lit. "Teaching." The whole body of Jewish law (written and oral) legislation, practice, and tradition.

Tosafot–Critical glosses on the Talmud by French rabbis of the twelfth and thirteenth centuries.

Tzedakah–lit. "righteousness" or "charity."

Tzaddik (pl. *Tzaddikim*)–A righteous man. Used frequently to describe a hasidic leader or *rebbe*.

Tzimtzum–"Contraction." The self-limitation of the Infinite. The withdrawal of God from the primal "space."

Viddui–Confession.

Wars of Gog and Magog–The prophecies of Ezekiel, Chapter 39, are interpreted as a vision of a great war of nations preceding the coming of the Messiah.

Yahrzeit–Anniversary of a death.

Yeshivah–Academy for Jewish studies, especially of the Talmud and religious literature.

Yetzer Hara–The evil inclination.

Yetzer Hatov–The good inclination.

Yishuv–The Jewish community in the Holy Land.

Yom Kippur–The Day of Atonement. The most solemn occasion of the Jewish Calendar, falling on *Tishri* 10 (see Leviticus 23: 26–32).

Yom Tov–lit. "a good day." Name given to a festival or holiday.

Zohar–Title of the mystical work introduced into Spain by the Spanish Kabbalists at the end of the thirteenth century and attributed to Rabbi Simeon bar Yochai of the Second Century of the Common Era.

References

Abelson, A. (1913). *Jewish Mysticism*, London.

Alfasi, Yitzhak (1959). *Toledot Hahasidut*, Tel Aviv.

______ (1953). *Rabbi Nahman MiBratzlav*, Tel Aviv.

Araten, Israel (1940). *Sefer Emet Veemunah* (Sayings of Rabbi Mendel of Kotzk), Jerusalem.

Ashkoli, A. (1954). Hahasidut BePolin. In *Beit Yisrael BePoilin*. Vol. 2, ed. I. Halperin, Jerusalem.

Baron, Salo Wittmayer (1965). *A Social and Religious History of the Jews*. Vol. X, pp. 31–51, 316–324, New York.

______ (1950). Steinschneider's Contribution to Historiography. In *Alexander Marx Jubilee Volume*, New York.

Ben Yeheskel, M. Le Mahut HaHasidut. In *Hashiloah*, Vols. XVII, XX, XXII, XXV.

Ben Zion, Raphael (1945). *The Way of the Faithful*, Los Angeles.

Berger, Israel (1910). *Esser Atarot*, Piotrokow.

______ (1925). *Esser Kedushot*, Warsaw.

Bloch, Chaim (1920). *Die Gemeinde der Chassidim ihr Werden und ihre Lehre, ihr Leben und ihr Treiben*, Berlin-Vienna.

Bromberg, Abraham Isaac (1954). *Rabbi Moses Teitelbaum MeOhel*, Jerusalem.

______ (1966). *Rabbi Abraham Mordekhai Alter MeGer*, Jerusalem.

Buber, Martin (1928). *Die Chassidischen Bücher*, Hellerau.

______ (1931). *Jewish Mysticism and the Legends of the Baal Shem*, London.

______ (1947). *Tales of the Hasidim, The Early Masters*, trans. Olga

Marx. New York.

______ (1948). *Hasidism*, New York.

______ (1958). *For the Sake of Heaven*, trans. Ludwig Lewisohn, Philadelphia.

______ (1960). *The Origin and Meaning of Hasidism*, trans. M. Friedmann, New York.

______ (1961). *Tales of the Hasidim, The Later Masters*, trans. Olga Marx, New York.

______ (1957). *Or Haganuz*, Tel Aviv.

______ (1956). *The Tales of Rabbi Nachman*, trans. Maurice Friedman, New York.

______ (1956). *The Legends of the Baal Shem*, trans. M. Friedman, London.

Bunim, H. I. (1913). HaHasidut HaHabadit. In *Hashiloah*, vol. XXVIII, pp. 250–258, 348–358; vol. XXIX (1913), pp. 217–227; vol. XXI (1914–15), pp. 242–252.

______ (1936). *Mishneh Habad*, Warsaw.

Chavel, B. (1953). Shneur Zalman of Liady. In *Jewish Leaders*, ed. L. Jung, New York. pp. 25–51.

Dawidowicz, Lucy S. (1967). *The Golden Tradition.*

Dinaburg, Ben Zion (1934). Reisaht Shel HaHasidut Veyesodateha haSocialism Ve'amshshim. In *Zion*, vol. VIII, pp. 107–115, 117–134, 179–200; vol. IX, pp. 345, 89–108, 186–197; vol. X (1945), pp. 67–77, 149–96.

Dresner, Samuel (1966). *The Zaddik*, New York.

Dubnow, Simon M. (1916–20). *History of the Jews in Russia and Poland*, trans. I. Friedlaender. 3 vols. Philadelphia.

______ (1925). *Pinkas Hamedinah* (The Minutes of the Lithuanian Council of Provinces), Berlin.

______ (1904). The Council of Four Lands in Poland and its attitude towards the Communities. In *Sefer HaYovel* (Jubilee volume in honor of Nahum Sokolow), pp. 250–261, Warsaw.

______ (1930–31). *Toledot Ha-Hasidut*, Tel Aviv.

Eileh Ezkerah ("These will I remember"). Biographies of leaders of religious Jewry in Europe who perished during the years 1939–1945, published by the Research Institute of Religious Jewry, vol. I, New York, 1956; vol. 2, 1957, vol. 3, 1959, vol. 4, 1961, vol. 5, 1963, vol. 6, 1965.

Finkel, Joshua (1960). Menahem Morgenstern of Kotzk. In *Jewish Leaders*.

Fishman, Judah Loeb, ed. (1960). *Sefer HaBesht,* Jerusalem.
Frank, Jacob (1934). *LeToledot HaTenuah HaFrankit,* Tel Aviv.
Frankel, Isar (1952). *Rabbi: Meir MeLublin,* Tel Aviv.
Friedenson, Joseph (1969). A Concise History of the Agudath Israel. In *Yaakov Rosenheim Memorial Anthology,* New York: Orthodox Library.
Friedmann, Maurice, S. *Martin Buber, Mystic, Existentialist, Social Prophet, A study in the Redemption of Evil,* The University of Chicago Library, Microfilm T. 809.
______ (1955). *Martin Buber: The Life of Dialogue,* London.
Gelber, N. M., ed. (1956). *Lublin.* In *Encyclopaedia of the Jewish Diaspora* (Heb.), Tel Aviv.
Gersh, H., and Miller, S. (1959). Satmar in Brooklyn. In *Commentary,* 28, pp. 389–399.
Geshuri, Meir Shimon (1952). *Neginah VeHasidut* (Music and Hasidism in the House of Kuzmir), Jerusalem.
______ (1953). *Hanigun VeHarikud BeHasidut* (Music and Dance in Hasidism), 5 vols, Tel Aviv.
Ginsburg, Ch. D. (1865). *The Kabbalah,* London.
Glickman, Phinehas Zelig (1938). *Der Kotzker Rebbe,* Piotrokow.
Glittzenstein, Abraham Hanok (1957). *Rabbenu HaTzemah Tzedek,* New York.
Goodman, Walter (1957). The Hasidim come to Williamsburg. In *Commentary.* 19.3.
Gourary, S. (1948). The Story of the United Lubavitcher Yeshivot. In *Jewish Education. 20:1,* New York.
Green, Arthur (1979). *Tormented Master: A Life of Rabbi Naham of Bratslav,* The University of Alabama Press.
Greenberg, Louis (1955). *The Jews in Russia: The Struggle of Emancipation.* Vol. 1, Yale University Press.
Gruenbaum, Itzhak, ed. (1953, 1958). *Warsaw,* vols. I & II. In *Encyclopaedia of the Jewish Diaspora* (Heb.), Tel Aviv.
Guttmann, Mattathiah Ezekiel (1952). *Belz, MiGibborei HaHasidut,* Tel Aviv.
______ (1952). *Rabbi Dov Milieowe,* Tel Aviv.
Hager, Barukh (1955). *Malkhut HaHasidut,* Buernos Aires.
Heschel, A. J. (1952). Rabbi Phinehas of Korzec (Heb.) pp. 213–244. In *Alei Ayin, S. Z. Schocken Jubilee Volume,* Jerusalem.
______(1985). *The Circle of the Baal Shem Tov: Studies in hasidism,* ed. Samuel H. Dresner, University of Chicago Press.

Heilman, Hayim Meir (1903). *Beit Rabbi*, Berdichev.
Hillman, D. Z. (1953). *Igrot Baal HaTanya*, Jerusalem: Hamesorah.
Horodetzky, Samuel Abba (1923). *HaHasidut VehaHasidim*, vols. I–IV, Berlin (DVIR) 1922; Tel Aviv, 1951.
______ (1922). *Shivhei HaBesht*, Berlin.
______ (1928). *Leaders of Hasidism*, trans. Maria Horodetsky Magasanik, London.
______ (1947). *Torat HaKabbalah shel R. Yitzhak Luria,* Tel Aviv.
Idelsohn, Abraham Tzvi (1948). *Jewish Music*, New York.
Jacobs, Louis (1956). *Seeker of Unity–The Life and Works of Aaron of Starosselye,* London.
Kahana, Abraham (1922). *Sefer HaHasidut*, Warsaw: Lewin-Epstein.
______ (1924). *Emunat Tzaddikim*, Warsaw.
Kamelhaer, Y. A. (1933). *Dor Deah,* Bilgoray: Kamelha; New York, 1952.
Kanzler, George (1961). *Williamsburg, A Jewish Community in Transition*, New York: Philip Feldheim.
Kleiman, J. A. (1911) *Niflaot Beit Levi*, Piotrokow.
______ (1911). *Niflaot HaMaggid MeKozienice*, Piotrokow.
______ (1916). *Niflaot Elimelekh*, Piotrokow.
______ (1925). *Niflaot HaYehudi*, Warsaw.
______ (1926). *Niflaot Rabbi Bunem*, Warsaw.
Kraushar, Alexander (1895). *Frank i Frankisci Polscy*. Vol. 2, Krakow.
______ Landau, Bezaelel, (1965). *HaGaon HaHasid NeVilna*, Jerusalem.
______ Levin, Meyer (1932). *The Golden Mountain*, New York.
Liberman, Chaim (1947). Reb Nahman Bratslaver un di Umaner Maskilim. In *Yivo Bletter*. Vol. XXIX, pp. 201–209, New York.
Lipschitz, Max A. (1967). *The Faith of a Hasid,* New York.
Mahler, Raphael (1942). *Der Kampf zwischen Haskalah un Hasidism in Galicia* (The Struggle between Haskalah and Hasidism in Galicia in the first half of the nineteenth century), New York.
______ (1939). The Austrian Government and the Hasidim during the Period of Reaction 1818–1848. In *Jewish Social Studies.* Vol. I, pp. 195–240.
Maimon, J. L., ed. (1960). *Sefer HaBesht*, Jerusalem: Mosad harav Kook.
Maimon, Solomon (1911). *Lebensgeschichte*. Dr. Jakob Fromer Munch, 1911. English trans. J. Clark Murray, 1888; new edition, London, 1954.

Miller, Ernest (1946). *History of Jewish Mysticism*, London.
Mindel, Nissan (1962). *Likkutei Amarim (Tanya)*, New York.
Minkin, Jacob S. (1955). *The Romance of Hasidism*, New York.
Mintz, Jerome R. (1968). *Legends of the Hasidim*, University of Chicago Press.
______ (1970). *In Praise of the Baal Shem Tov.*
Newman, Louis L. (1944). *The Hasidic Anthology*, New York.
______ (1962). *Maggidim and Hasidim: Their Wisdom*, New York.
Rabinovitz, Tzvi Meir. *Hamaggid MiKozienice*, Tel Aviv.
______ Rabbi Simha Bunem M'Pzizhi. In *Sinai*, vol. VII, pp. 153–157, pp. 280–295, Vol. VIII, pp. 86–88, pp. 159–163; Vol. IX, pp. 231–237, pp. 311–317, pp. 347–353; Vol. X, pp. 50–60, pp. 327–331, Vol. XI, pp. 50–53.
Rabinowicz, Harry M. (1960). *A Guide to Hasidism*, London.
______ (1960). The Slave Who Saved the City, New York.
______ (1965). *The Legacy of Polish Jewry*, New York.
Rabinowitsch, Zeev Wolf (1935). *Der Karliner Chassidismus seine Geschichte und Lehre*, Tel Aviv.
______ (1950). *Yivo Annual Jewish Social Sciences*, pp. 123–151.
______ (1970). *Lithuanian Hasidism*, London.
Raddock, Charles (1954). The Sage of Sattmur, Hasidism and Israel Politics. *The Jewish Forum*, May.
Raphael, Yizhak. Hahasidut VeEretz Yisrael. In *Sinai*, Vol. 1, pp. 74–82; vol. 2, pp. 163–172.
______ (1955). *Sefer HaHasidut*, Tel Aviv.
Rodkinson, M. L. (1876). *Toledot Amudei Habad*, Königsberg.
Schacter, Zalman (1960). How to Become a Modern Hasid. In *Jewish Heritage*, Vol. 2, pp. 33–40.
Schatz, Rivka (1968). *Hahasidut KeiMistiqah*, Jerusalem.
Schechter, Solomon (1910). *Some Aspects of Rabbinic Theology*, reprinted, New York, 1936.
Schipper, Iqwacy (1929). The Composition of the Council of Four Lands (Yiddish). In *Yivo Studies in History*. Vol. I, pp. 73–82.
Scholem, Gershom G. (1958). Baal Shem. In *HaEntsiklopediyah HaIvrit* Encyclopaedia Hebraica. Vol. 9, pp. 263–264, Jerusalem and Tel Aviv.
______ (1950). Devekuth, Communion with God in Early Hasidic Doctrine. In *The Review of Religion*, 15, pp. 115–139.
______ (1955). *Major Trends in Jewish Mysticism*, London.
______ (1961). Martin Buber's Hasidism. In *Commentary*, 32,

pp. 218–225.
______ (1956–1957). *Shabtai Tzvi*, 2 vols, Tel Aviv.
Steinmann, Eliezer (1961). *The Garden of Hasidism*, trans. Haim Shachter, Jerusalem: World Zionist Organization.
______ (n.d.), *Be'er HaHasidut, Sefer al Admorei Poilin,* Tel Aviv.
______ (1956). *Kitvei Rabbi Nahman*, Tel Aviv.
______ (1957). *Sefer Mishnat Habad*, 2 vols, Tel Aviv.
______ (1957). *Shaar HaHasidut*, Tel Aviv.
______ (1958). *Be'er HaHasidut*, Tel Aviv.
Teitelbaum, M. (1910, 1913). *Harav Miladi Umiflegget Habad.* Part I, Warsaw. Part II, Warsaw.
Tishby, I. (1945). Bein Shabta'ut LeHasidut (Between Sabbatianism and Hasidism). In Knesset, 9, pp. 268–338.
Tishby, I., and Dann, J. (1965). *Hasidut in HaEntsiklopediyah HaIvrit*, 17, pp. 756–821, Jerusalem and Tel Aviv.
Uffenheimer, Rivka Schatz (1968). *Hasidut Kamistika,* Jerusalem.
Unger, Menashe (1955). *Die Hasidische Velt* (The Hasidic World), New York.
______ (1946). *Hasidus un Lebn* (Hasidism and Life), New York.
______ (1967). *Sefer Kedoshim* (Book of Martyrs), New York.
Weinryb, Bernard D. (1973). *A Social and Economic History of the Jewish Community in Poland from 1100 to 1800*, Philadelphia: Jewish Publication Society.
Weiner, Herbert (1957). The Lubavitcher Movement I. In *Commentary,* 23, pp. 231–241.
______ (1957). The Lubavitcher Movement II. In *Commentary*, 23, pp. 316–327.
______ (1969) Mystics – The Kabbalah Today, New York.
______ (1964). Bratslav in Brooklyn. In *Judaism*. New York.
______ (1957). The Lubavitch Movement. In *Commentary,* vol. 23, pp. 231–241, 316–327.
Weiss, J. G. (1957). A Circle of Pre-Hasidic Pneumatics. In *The Journal of Jewish Studies*, 8, pp. 199–213.
______ (1953). Contemplative Mysticism and "Faith" in Hasidic Piety. In *The Journal of Jewish Studies*, 4, pp. 19–29.
Weiss, J. G. (1960). The Great Maggid's Theory of Contemplative Magic. In *Hebrew Union College Annual*, 31, 137–148.
______ (1958). The Kavanoth Prayer in Early Hasidism. In *The Journal of Jewish Studies,* pp. 163–192.
______ (1985). *Studies in Eastern European Jewish Mysticism*, ed. D. Goldstein, Oxford.

Werfel, Isaac (1940). *Hasidut VeEretz Yisrael*, Jerusalem.
______ (1947). *Sefer HaHasidut*, Tel Aviv.
Wertheim, Aaron (1960). *Halakhot Vehalikhot BaHasidut* (The Rites and Ceremonies), Jerusalem: Mosad Harav Kook.
Wilensky, Mordekhai (1970). *Hasidim Umitnagdim*, vols. 1 & 2, Jerusalem.
Ysander, Torsten (1933). *Studien zum Bestchen'schen Hasidismus*, Uppsala.
Zeitlin, Hillel (1920). Mafte'ah LeSefer HaZohar. In *Hatekufah*, vol. VI, pp. 314–334; vol. VII, pp. 353–368; vol. IX; Warsaw, 1921, pp. 265–330.
______ (1965). *Bhapardes HaHasidut VeHaKabbalah*, Tel Aviv.
Zevin, Solomon Joseph (1956–1957). *Sippurei Hasidim*, Tel Aviv.

Index